Principles of Law and Economics

Principles of Law and Economics

Daniel H. Cole

R. Bruce Townsend Professor of Law
Indiana University School of Law at Indianapolis

Peter Z. Grossman

Clarence Efroymson Professor of Economics
Butler University

PEARSON

Prentice
Hall

Upper Saddle River, New Jersey 07458

Library of Congress Cataloging-in-Publication Data

Cole, Daniel H., [date]
  Principles of law and economics / Daniel H. Cole, Peter Z. Grossman.
    p. cm.
  Includes bibliographical references and index.
  ISBN 0-13-093261-2 (alk. paper)
  1. Law-United States. 2. Law and economics. I. Title: Principles of law and economics.
II. Grossman, Peter Z., [date] III. Title.

KF385.C59 2004
349.73—dc22

                                                                          2004050280

Executive Editor: David Alexander
Editor-in-Chief: Jeff Shelstad
Project Manager: Marie McHale
Editorial Assistant: Katy Rank
Media Project Manager: Peter Snell
Executive Marketing Manager: Sharon Koch
Marketing Assistant: Melissa Owens
Managing Editor: John Roberts
Permissions Supervisor: Charles Morris
Manufacturing Buyer: Michelle Klein
Production Manager: Arnold Vila
Cover Design: Bruce Kenselaar
Cover Photo: Michael McQueen/Photographers Choice/Getty Images, Inc.
Composition: Integra Software Services
Full-Service Project Management: BookMasters, Inc.
Printer/Binder: Phoenix

Credits and acknowledgments borrowed from other sources and reproduced, with permission, in this textbook appear on appropriate page within the text.

Pearson Prentice Hall™ is a trademark of Pearson Education, Inc.
Pearson® is a registered trademark of Pearson plc
Prentice Hall® is a registered trademark of Pearson Education, Inc.

Pearson Education LTD.
Pearson Education Singapore, Pte. Ltd
Pearson Education, Canada, Ltd
Pearson Education–Japan

Pearson Education Australia PTY, Limited
Pearson Education North Asia Ltd
Pearson Educación de Mexico, S.A. de C.V.
Pearson Education Malaysia, Pte. Ltd

10 9 8 7 6 5 4 3 2 1
ISBN 0-13-093261-2

BRIEF CONTENTS

CONTENTS

PREFACE

To understand the law, and how the legal system works, students must have a basic understanding of economic principles. At the same time, the structure and performance of the economic system depend enormously on legal rules. Law and economics are, thus, closely interrelated. This book's purpose is to describe and explain those interrelations.

For the past several years, we have been teaching Law and Economics together, to law students at the Indiana University School of Law at Indianapolis and to undergraduate economics students at Butler University. One of us is an economist; the other is a law professor. For years, we have been searching for a textbook that is neither too sophisticated, too sketchy, nor too simplistic for our students. We wanted a book basic enough to teach undergraduates *and* law students possessing limited (and in some cases nonexistent) backgrounds in economics, but sophisticated enough to be of use to graduate-level scholars. Finally, we gave up waiting and wrote one ourselves.

Although law and economics analysis has attained a high level of sophistication over the years, one does not need to be a graduate-level economist to understand its basic principles and applications. This book is designed for use by undergraduates, including those who have not yet taken an introductory economics course, as well as law students with little or no previous economics training. With that target audience in mind, we kept the mathematics to a minimum, presenting the analysis in language as clear and jargon-free as possible. The economic analysis is not simplistic, but it is presented with sufficient explanations of concepts, principles, and arguments to enable novices to follow along without great difficulty.

Consistent with our commitment to relative novices in law and economics, the book begins with four chapters designed to ensure that all readers possess a basic understanding of: fundamental economic principles (Chapter 1), the structure of the U.S. legal system (Chapter 2), and the importance of combining legal and economic analyses (Chapters 3 and 4). Readers with substantial knowledge of economics may choose to skip Chapter 1. Likewise, readers with substantial experience in legal studies may choose to skip Chapter 2. Readers with substantial backgrounds in both law and economics may choose to begin with Chapter 3.

After the four introductory chapters, the book delves into traditional economic analyses of specific areas of law, including Property (Chapters 5–7), Contracts (Chapters 8–9), Torts (Chapters 10–12), and Crime (Chapter 13). Those common law topics, dominated by judge-made law, are the centerpiece of most law and economics courses. It would be a mistake, however, to suppose that the law is nothing more than what common law courts decide. The modern state is a regulatory state where laws made by legislatures and administrative bodies are at least as significant as court decisions. In recognition of the importance of regulatory law, this book also includes two chapters on the economic regulation of business. One concerns antitrust and regulated industries (Chapter 14); the other, environmental protection (Chapter 15).

Various approaches are utilized throughout the book, including conventional economic analysis (with and without descriptive figures), excerpts from fundamental works in the law and economics literature, statistical analyses, actual judicial decisions (as in law school "casebooks"), a bit of game theory, and even some history. We hope that this methodological variety, along with the question sets at the end of each chapter, enhances the reader's utility and enjoyment.

ACKNOWLEDGMENTS

This book has been four years in the making. In that time, we benefited enormously from comments, criticisms, and suggestions provided by numerous readers, many of whom remain anonymous. Among those known to us are Kenny Crews, Robin Craig, Nicholas Georgakopoulos, Michael Heise, Shi-Ling Hsu, and Andy Klein. We are grateful to them, to the dozen or so anonymous reviewers, and to five classes of law and economics students—three at the Indiana University School of Law at Indianapolis and two at Butler University—who tested the book for us in various prepublication editions. Faith Long Knotts provided able administrative assistance. Last but not least, this book never would have seen the light of day without the support of our respective families.

DHC
PZG

Indianapolis
October 2003

Chapter 1

Economic Concepts and Institutions

*T*his chapter provides a basic introduction to economic concepts and institutions. Readers already possessing substantial knowledge of economics may choose to skip this chapter, or treat it as a review.

Economics today is a highly formalized discipline; much of its literature is indecipherable to students and scholars in other fields. A basic understanding of economic theory and concepts, however, requires little mathematical ability.

WHAT ECONOMISTS STUDY

No consensus currently exists about the definition of economics or what economists study. In 1932, the English economist Lionel Robbins offered one widely accepted definition: "Economics is the science which studies human behavior as a relationship between ends and scarce means which have alternative uses."[1]

RESOURCE SCARCITY

According to Robbins's definition, the *economic problem* is the necessity of choice under scarcity. Because resources are scarce, choices must be made. Were all resources perfectly abundant, choices or trade-offs would be unnecessary. We would not need market institutions or any other mechanisms for allocating entitlements to resources because everyone could simply and costlessly have as much of anything as desired. Choice only becomes an issue when resources are scarce.

Consider the quintessential commodity resource: gold. Gold has been economically valued by diverse societies for thousands of years, regardless of differences in culture, systems of value, and political-economic structures. Yet it is easy to conceive a (mythical) world in which gold would have *zero* economic value and, so, zero price: It is the world in which gold is perfectly abundant. In this world gold is everywhere, lying at everyone's feet. Anyone possessing less than enough gold can simply bend down and scoop up more. With gold perfectly plentiful, it holds no economic value, meaning no market would exist for it. No one would pay anyone else for gold, when it is there for the taking at virtually no cost. The role of scarcity in creating economic value is the first premise of modern economic theory.

When economists use the term *scarcity*, however, they mean something slightly different from its ordinary meaning. They are concerned not with *physical scarcity* but with *economic* or *relative scarcity*. Physical scarcity concerns the amount of some resource in the world or universe. All resources are physically scarce. However, not all resources are economically or relatively scarce. Economic or relative scarcity compares the available supply of some resource with the human demand for it. Air is a physically scarce resource—only so much of it is available above, on, and below the earth's surface. Before the onset of the Industrial Revolution, however, air was not economically scarce; more than enough was available to fill all the demand at a zero price. In more recent times, thanks to the growing demand for air, both to breathe and as a repository for pollution, air has become economically more scarce. Consequently, markets for air are emerging.[2]

Like air, E. coli bacteria, which causes potentially fatal food poisoning, is physically scarce—only so much of it exists in the world—but unlike air, it is not economically scarce. The reason is simple. People do not want E. coli. The quantity of E. coli in the world greatly exceeds the quantity demanded at any price. What gives gold and air, by contrast, their economic scarcity is not just the available supply, but the relation between supply (how much gold and air are available) and demand (how much gold and air people want).

COST AND PRICE

A second premise of economic theory is that choice is costly because trade-offs are necessary. This second premise stems from the initial premise of scarcity. If all resources (including time) were perfectly abundant, making any choice would not involve any cost; making one choice would not foreclose other opportunities. In the real world of scarcity, however, making one choice often means forgoing alternative opportunities. Thus, when economists speak of the "cost" of some action or choice, they mean not only the money price, but also, and more crucially, the *opportunity cost*: what other opportunities are given up in taking the action, spending the time, or making the choice.

To understand the concept of opportunity cost, consider the following example: When you order dinner at a restaurant, the price you pay will reflect the cost to the restaurant of supplying it to you. If you order lobster rather than chicken, you will pay more because the cost of supplying the lobster is higher than the cost of supplying chicken. But the price you pay for eating at the restaurant, and the relatively higher price you pay for lobster instead of chicken, are not all the costs of your dinner. By eating at that restaurant, you have incurred *opportunity costs*, defined by what else you might have done with your money rather than spend it at *that* restaurant for *that* meal.[3] In ordering the lobster rather than the chicken, you not only pay a higher price for dinner (an *explicit* cost), but you also give up the opportunity to eat chicken instead (an *implicit* cost). By going to the restaurant to begin with, you also give up the opportunity to do something else during that time. Instead of eating, you might have worked, slept, watched television, read, or engaged in any number of other activities. Each choice, then, entails costs. As economists like to say: There is no such thing as a free lunch.

Recognizing the existence, indeed the ubiquity, of opportunity costs is one thing; evaluating them is another. Any such evaluation is bound to be subjective and contingent. A person who particularly likes lobster and hates chicken places a low value on the alternative, and so, all other things being equal, the choice of lobster entails a fairly low opportunity cost. Another person, however, who values lobster and chicken equally will incur a relatively higher opportunity cost in choosing one or the other. Note that these choices, and the implicit calculation of the expected costs and benefits, are made prior to consumption. If the lobster turns out to be puny and tough, the person may regret the decision to order it instead of the chicken, and conclude that the meal was not "worth" the cost—the cost was too high given the outcome. But such judgments can be made only in hindsight.

One corollary of opportunity costs is the notion that *economic valuations are inherently subjective*. What constitutes a cost or a benefit and the extent of costs and benefits are subjective determinations of the individual because different individuals have different preferences. To some extent, these preferences are *endogenous*, or shaped by existing social institutions.[4] Still, they remain *exogenous* (matters of choice independent of institutional structures) in important respects. For example, if Jim (a type B personality) goes bowling, he may not ordinarily consider as an opportunity cost of that decision the lost chance to skydive instead. On the other hand, if Bob (a type A personality) decides to bowl with his friend Jim on some Saturday instead of his usual skydiving, he certainly would consider the lost chance to skydive as an opportunity cost of his decision to bowl. That cost must be outweighed by the benefits of spending time with, or competing against, his friend at the bowling alley; otherwise, presumably, he would not voluntarily give up skydiving to do it.

An individual's relative valuations of goods and services are determined in part by *budget constraints* or *endowments*, which are the limit of income and wealth at that person's disposal. People order and weight their preferences in light of that limit. The less wealthy they are, the fewer goods and services they will be able to afford in the market. All people, rich and poor, have budget constraints;[5] and they are presumed in economic theory to maximize their well-being given those budget constraints.

ECONOMIC DECISIONS ARE MADE AT THE MARGINS

How do people make decisions about consumption and production? According to economic theory, they do not look at the total costs and benefits of their present and past consumption and production decisions, but rather they look at the costs and benefits of the next ones. People think at the margin; that is, how much benefit they will receive for one more unit of consumption versus the cost. How much marginal benefit does the next unit of consumption provide relative to its costs?

Suppose, for example, Jill is very thirsty and pays $1.00 for a soft drink. Given her thirst, the drink is certainly "worth" a dollar to her. But how about a second soft drink right after the first? Well, because the first quenched much of her thirst, the benefit derived from a second drink is likely to be less. Stated in more explicit economic terms, the marginal benefit Jill derives from consuming the next drink will be less than the marginal benefit she derived from the first. Assume the marginal cost of the next drink is the same as the first, $1.00. She must determine, therefore, whether the benefits she receives from that next drink are actually worth the price she pays. Jill does not need to decide that the two drinks together are worth a total of $2.00. She only needs to decide whether the marginal gain from a second drink is worth the marginal cost—the next $1.00—to her.

This behavioral postulate applies to producers as well as to consumers. Suppose a chocolate shop makes a batch of candy at a cost of $10, and sells it for $11. It earns a tidy $1 (or 10 percent) profit. Should it now go ahead and make a second batch of candy? Only if the gains from doing so are greater than the costs. If the costs of making the second batch of candy would exceed the income from sales by 50 cents, the chocolate shop will *not* produce the second batch. It is irrelevant that the total gains from the first plus the second batches would be greater than the total costs of both batches together. If making the second batch loses money, all else being equal, no rational producer will produce it.

As we will see in this book, an economic analysis of the law makes considerable use of marginal thinking and an explicit analysis of marginal benefit versus marginal cost calculations.

ALLOCATING ENTITLEMENTS TO RESOURCES

Economic textbooks routinely refer to the allocation of scarce resources. Markets, governments, firms, and individuals are all said to own and allocate resources. More accurately, what they own are not the physical resources themselves but *rights* or *entitlements* to those resources. Ronald Coase, a Noble Prize-winning economist, wrote, "What are traded on the market are not, as is often supposed by economists, physical entities but the rights to perform certain actions." Likewise, judges do not allocate physical resources but "the rights to perform certain actions . . . [as] established by the legal system."[6] Because this distinction is crucial in understanding the implications of the economic analysis of the law, this book focuses on allocations of *entitlements*, not the physical entities themselves.

DEMAND, SUPPLY, AND THE MARKET

The Law of Demand

The next premise of economic theory is that the prices and quantities of scarce goods and services in open markets will be determined by supply and demand. The *law of demand*, as illustrated in Figure 1-1, posits that the amount of the good or service demanded (q) will increase if its price ($) falls, and decrease if its price rises.[7]

Here is an illustration. Susan enjoys going to the movies once each week. She is not wealthy—her *endowment* is limited—but she manages to afford this weekly entertainment by economizing during the rest of the week; she stays at home and watches television or reads library books. Suppose that, one week, the price of going to the movies doubles. Suddenly, Susan's carefully balanced budget is threatened. Whether she can afford to continue going to the movies once a week at the new, higher price depends on the strength of her *preference* for movies compared to other, cheaper forms of entertainment, *and* on the strength of her preference for entertainment generally, as compared to other needs and desires, such as driving her car (buying gasoline), having a place to live (paying rent), and so on.[8] Susan faces several options: (1) continue her weekly tradition of going to the movies, and economize even more on other expenses; (2) go to second-run theaters where the movies are older but cheaper; (3) stop going to movies altogether, in favor of some other, cheaper form of entertainment, such as reading more library books; or (4) forgo entertainment altogether in favor of other preferences. All options other than option 1 constitute *substitute goods*. People typically substitute other goods and services if the

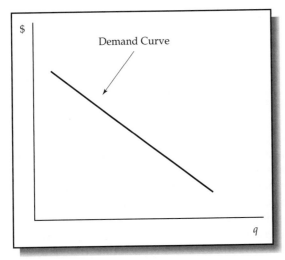

Figure 1-1
Demand Curve

cost of fulfilling the initial choice grows too high relative to their budget constraints and other preferences.

It is not the *absolute price* of attending the movies that is important in our illustration, but the *relative price*. It is the price of going to the movies *relative* to Susan's income and *relative* to the prices of fulfilling potential substitute preferences. If the price of going to the movies remained the same but Susan's income dropped, she would be faced with the same predicament. A similar issue would arise if the price of movies remained the same, her income remained the same, but her preference orderings, or her tastes, changed so that she no longer enjoyed watching movies as much, compared to other activities.

A crucial assumption of the illustration is that Susan (who, for purposes of this illustration, represents all consumers) makes decisions on the available information in such a way as to maximize her utility, wealth, or happiness. This point reflects two standard assumptions of economic theory: (1) individuals look after their self-interest; and (2) they rationally respond to price signals and other incentives in the marketplace to garner as much utility, wealth, or happiness as possible. These assumptions often engender confusion, so it is important to be clear about what they mean and do not mean. Some critics of economic theory abhor the supposition that people are invariably selfish and greedy. But this interpretation is *not* what these assumptions maintain. They merely posit that people attempt to satisfy, to the maximum extent possible under the circumstances, whatever desires or preferences they have in life. To assume that Mother Theresa maximized her preference to improve the lot of those less fortunate in life is emphatically *not* to assert that she was a greedy and egocentric individual; yet her behavior was entirely consistent with economic theory.

Another crucial assumption of the illustration is that demand for viewing movies at the theater is *elastic*. Demand is elastic when it responds strongly to relative price changes. If prices go up, the quantity demanded in the market for that good or service falls by a greater percentage than the percentage change in price. This elasticity is the case for many goods and services. For some goods, however, such as cigarettes, the percentage change in the quantity demanded resulting from price increases tends to be less than the percentage change in price. That is, if the price rises by 10 percent, the quantity demanded will fall by less, say 5 percent. Such a good is said to have relatively price *in*elastic demand. A few goods have almost *completely* inelastic demand: the quantity demanded responds hardly at all to a change in price. Consider, for example, the market for AZT, a drug prescribed to treat people infected with HIV, the virus that causes AIDS. People who are HIV-positive require AZT to continue living—a superior preference for most people. The cost of not using AZT—increased sickness and early death—is close to infinite (at least for most people). If the price of AZT goes up, assuming no effective substitutes are available, HIV-infected persons simply must continue to buy it.[9] Such complete inelasticity of demand is, then, a function of strict need and the lack of substitute goods to fill that need. When some pharmaceutical company develops an effective substitute for AZT, then demand for AZT will immediately become more elastic.

Note, finally, that the law of demand operates in two directions. Just as the quantity demanded drops in response to rising prices, so it increases in response to falling prices. If the price of going to the movies falls back to its previous level, Susan may resume her weekly movie attendance. If the price falls below previous levels, she may even go to the movies more often. All other things being equal, her consumption of movies will increase in response to the drop in prices.

The Law of Supply

The *law of supply,* described in Figure 1-2, is the flip side of the law of demand: The amount of a good supplied to the market will rise when prices rise, and fall when prices fall. Suppliers are also presumed to maximize their well-being, in this case defined as profits: sales revenue over costs.[10] When prices for a certain good or service are high, sellers will supply more of it to the market because that action will maximize their profits at higher levels of output. If the price drops, they will supply less. Indeed, if the market price drops below their costs of supplying the good or service, they won't supply it at all. A firm's supply curve is, thus, determined by its costs; and the quantity actually supplied is determined by both cost and price—the cost of producing and supplying the good relative to the price it can command in the market. This relationship holds true for all goods. Supply, like demand, may be more or less elastic, or responsive to changes in price. If it is costly to supply additional output in the short run, then even if the price rises substantially the quantity supplied may rise very little. In other words, supply is inelastic. It is generally the case, however, that in the long run supplies of all goods and services will be relatively elastic because new production facilities can be built to expand output.

To illustrate the dynamic of the law of supply, consider the market for lobsters. To catch lobsters, those engaged in lobstering need to expend time and resources: their own labor plus fuel, lobster pots, bait, and possibly assistants. If the market price of lobsters is very low, the incentive to engage in lobstering is reduced. Indeed, if the price is low enough some lobsterers may be better off seeking employment in some other sector, thereby reducing production in the lobstering industry. At a lower price, the quantity of lobsters supplied to the market will fall. By contrast, when prices rise, both existing and potential lobsterers are motivated to expend more effort

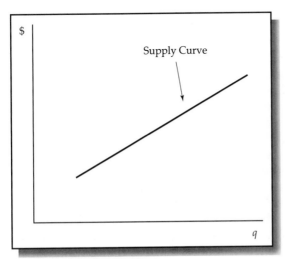

Figure 1-2
Supply Curve

on lobstering. Producers will buy more pots, expend more of their own labor, and hire additional labor to take advantage of the higher prices.[11] As a consequence, the quantity of lobsters supplied to the market will increase.

The Market: Where Buyers and Sellers Meet

The market is the locus of exchange, where suppliers/sellers meet demanders/buyers. Market demand represents that aggregation of the demand of all individual buyers (like "Susan"), and the market supply is that aggregation of supply of all individual sellers. Physical markets are not strictly necessary for exchange, but markets exist because they tend to maximize the gains from trade for both buyers and sellers. They maximize these gains, in part, by minimizing the costs of transactions. They also provide a convenient forum where buyers and sellers can meet to exchange information relatively inexpensively.

The first modern markets were established in medieval times. They were, quite literally, places, established by entrepreneurs under royal charters or franchises,[12] where sellers set up stalls or booths. Buyers came to the marketplace to purchase whatever they needed, within their budget limitations. The establishment of regular marketplaces reduced the *search costs* of both buyers and sellers; each knew where to find the other. Such markets still exist today, from the weekly farmers market set up during the summer months on some vacant lot in town to the New York Stock Exchange. Today these actual marketplaces exist alongside the virtual markets of the Internet, which provides an even lower-cost method of transacting: Buyers and sellers no longer need to leave their respective homes to find one another.

Market Equilibrium: Where Supply Meets Demand

Notice that the supply and demand curves move at cross-purposes with consumers demanding more when prices fall and suppliers supplying more when prices rise. Therefore, we necessarily reach a point at which the quantity demanded and the quantity supplied meet. This point establishes the *equilibrium price* or the *market-clearing price*, defined as that price at which the quantity of some good demanded precisely matches the quantity supplied, leaving no unsatisfied demand and no residual supply. Figure 1-3 describes how supply and demand curves cross to produce an equilibrium point.

Suppose, to continue the lobster illustration, that an equilibrium price for lobster is $7.00 per unit. At that price, everyone willing to pay that price for lobster will do so, and suppliers will provide exactly that amount to the market. At $7.00, no lobsters go unsold. In other words, the market experiences neither excess supply nor excess demand. This equilibrium point maximizes the total economic value of the lobster market. If $7.00 is the equilibrium price, then at any other price the lobster market would provide fewer social benefits. If the lobster market would provide greater social benefits at some other price, then $7.00 simply would *not* be the equilibrium price. The equilibrium price must, by definition, provide the greatest benefits for society. At any price other than the equilibrium price, social resources are not being used optimally.

The equilibrium price is changeable and achieved only fleetingly. The quantities supplied and demanded tend to shift almost continually. For example, increased labor

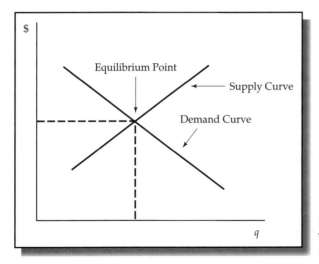

Figure 1-3
Where Supply and
Demand Meet

or fuel costs for producers will mean that at any given price fewer lobsters will be supplied to the market. Other factors will change demand.[13] For example, if the price of another popular entree, such as shrimp, rises, some people who purchased shrimp at its previous, lower price may decide to eat lobster instead. Thus, lobsters are a substitute for shrimp, and demand for lobsters increases from the increase in the price of shrimp. Given this increase in demand for lobsters, excess demand would occur at $7.00 per lobster, causing a shortage of lobster. Suppliers will attempt to exploit this additional profit opportunity by supplying more lobsters to the enlarged lobster market. However, it will cost them more to do so assuming, realistically, that it costs more to produce more lobsters. In technical terms, the marginal costs of production are rising. So the price of lobster will rise above $7.00, and the market will achieve a new equilibrium or market-clearing price somewhere above $7.00.

The key point about markets for the study of law and economics is that, in theory and often in practice, markets allocate entitlements to resources to maximize society's welfare. At a market equilibrium, the utility of buyers and the profits of producers are both maximized, a result economists define as "efficient." In the real world, however, equilibrium is not always achieved, for a variety of reasons. Indeed, in some cases market exchange is not possible.

EFFICIENCY

Efficiency is a concept used throughout this book. We need to note, however, some important limitations to this concept and its place in economic analysis. First, economics cannot tell us in advance what mix of goods and services an economy *should* produce. No one can know, before actual market transactions occur, what each market participant's preferences are, and how they rank or value those preferences. Second, economics cannot effectively aggregate the preferences of individual market participants to discern what serves society's overall welfare, except as those individuals' preferences are aggregated in actual market transactions. Economics can tell us, however, the total costs and benefits derived from various allocations of entitlements to scarce resources, given the expressed preferences of individuals in the market. They can explain the relative *efficiency* or *inefficiency* of a given allocation. Efficiency, thus, becomes the economists' proxy for social welfare; the more efficient is a given allocation, the greater the welfare benefits for society.

Productive, Allocative, and Adaptive Efficiency

Efficiency comes in various forms. *Productive efficiency* concerns the utilization of resources to achieve the highest possible level of production of a desired mix of goods and services. *Allocative efficiency* relates to the distribution of goods and services in an economy to maximize social welfare. *Adaptive efficiency* indicates the ability of, and cost to, social institutions and organizations to absorb shocks and react to changing technological and environmental circumstances over time. When economists discuss efficiency, they most often mean either productive or allocative efficiency. Though some recent literature argues that adaptive efficiency is the most important[14] measure of long-term success for any economic system,[14] the primary concern of law and economics scholars remains allocative efficiency, as will be evident throughout this book.

Measuring Allocative Efficiency: The Pareto and Kaldor-Hicks Criteria

Various *measures* of allocative efficiency are used, although two are most common: the Pareto criterion and the Kaldor-Hicks (or "potential Pareto") criterion. Of these, the Pareto criterion is more often used in theoretical models, and the Kaldor-Hicks criterion is more useful in the real world, where it serves at the basis for cost-benefit analysis.

The Pareto efficiency criterion is named for the Italian sociologist Vilfredo Pareto (1848–1923). A given allocation of entitlements to resources in society is said to be *Pareto optimal* when any possible reallocation would reduce the welfare of at least one person. Consider a market with only two goods—say, umbrellas and hats—and two consumers called Bill and Hillary. Let's assume (arbitrarily) that Bill has 50 umbrellas and 50 hats, Hillary 50 umbrellas and 40 hats. If both parties are satisfied with the allocation and cannot be made better off with more hats or umbrellas, then this allocation is considered *Pareto optimal*.

But consider a case where Bill loves hats but feels he only needs a few umbrellas, while Hillary likes both, but she has more than enough hats and could use a few more umbrellas. In that case, the two could trade and both benefit. Let's say Bill traded 20 umbrellas for 10 more hats. The new allocation gives Bill 60 hats and 30 umbrellas, which makes him happier, and gives Hillary 70 umbrellas and 30 hats, which makes her happier too. The trade makes them both better off, and so is said to be *Pareto superior* to, or a *Pareto improvement* on, the preexisting situation. If no further trades are possible without making one of them worse off, then the new allocation is *Pareto optimal*.

Note that if Bill started with 85 hats and 90 umbrellas (and Hillary 5 and 10), and he deigned to trade one of his umbrellas for one of her 5 hats, that too would be Pareto optimal if both parties were better off (or at least no worse off) after the trade. Thus, the Pareto criterion is oblivious to distributional issues. It takes initial or current distributions as it finds them, and merely evaluates whether subsequent transactions are Pareto efficient. This perspective does not say that distributional issues are, or should be, irrelevant in judging allocations of goods and services in society. But the Pareto criterion, and much of conventional economic analysis, is concerned with allocating entitlements to resources in order to *maximize* the welfare of society as a whole; it is not concerned with who gets the entitlements. In other words, economics is concerned with the size of the economic pie, not with how the pie is sliced and distributed.

Although the Pareto efficiency criterion is useful for economic modeling, it is not particularly useful for assessing many transactions in the real world for a variety of reasons. One of those reasons is that the Pareto criterion imposes strict conditions that must be met in order for any allocation of entitlements to qualify as Pareto efficient. First, the Pareto criterion requires voluntary market transactions. The absence of voluntary consent of all parties affected by a change in entitlements offers no way to ensure that none of the parties is made worse off. Second, the Pareto efficiency criterion requires actual compensation of anyone who would otherwise be made worse off by some reallocation. Consequently, the Pareto efficiency criterion is *only* useful in judging the efficiency of contract-based transactions with no negative externalities, a tiny subset of all transactions that take place in the world on a daily basis.

The Pareto principle cannot assess the value of nonmarket allocations. This point is important because, in the real world, many allocations are made through mechanisms other than the market. For instance, courts and legislatures both allocate (and reallocate) entitlements. These allocations are never made with the voluntary consent of all affected parties, and often come without compensation for potential "losers" from the allocation, to ensure that no one is left worse off. For any government action to be justified according to the Pareto efficiency criterion, every market participant would have to be persuaded to agree to it, by virtue either of gains from the allocation or compensation to offset losses stemming from it. In essence, the Pareto efficiency requires a rule of unanimity for policy making. This requirement is clearly unworkable, and probably not even desirable because it would allow any single person to forestall even obvious social improvements by refusing his or her consent. The situation assumes, of course, that nonunanimous decisions, including some that impose uncompensated-for losses on some members of the polity (or market), might be efficiency-enhancing on the whole, yielding *net* social benefits. Such an assumption can hardly be doubted, yet the Pareto efficiency criterion does not even recognize the possibility that a change in entitlements can bring about net social improvements in the absence of unanimous consent.

The limited real-world utility of the Pareto efficiency criterion led economists to experiment with other potentially more practical measures of efficiency. Two economists, Nicholas Kaldor and Sir John Hicks, both working at the London School of Economics, came up with complementary theories, which when taken individually were significantly flawed, but when put together proved useful and robust. Moreover, they published their theories in the same year, 1939, and in the same journal.[15] Their combined efficiency criterion has come to be known as Kaldor-Hicks efficiency.

The Kaldor-Hicks efficiency criterion maintains that an allocation or reallocation of entitlements to resources is efficiency enhancing if (1) it makes at least one person better off, and that person (together with other "winners") could afford *in theory* to fully compensate everyone made worse off by the allocation and still be left with a net increase in their welfare (Kaldor efficiency); *and* (2) those made worse off by the allocation or reallocation could not afford to bribe those who gain into forgoing the allocation or reallocation without suffering an even greater loss in welfare (Hicks efficiency).[16]

The Kaldor-Hicks efficiency criterion is sometimes referred to as "potential Pareto" because a Kaldor-Hicks efficient change would in theory be Pareto improving. Two critical distinctions separate the Kaldor-Hicks and Pareto criteria: Kaldor-Hicks does not (1) assume that all changes in entitlements are voluntarily market transactions or (2) require actual compensation for any change in existing allocations. These apparently minor adjustments make the Kaldor-Hicks criterion far more useful for assessing, if only imperfectly, allocations in the real world. It assumes, correctly, that net social welfare *can* be enhanced by changes in entitlements, even if some individuals suffer losses as a result. And in contrast to the Pareto efficiency criterion, Kaldor-Hicks provides a system for measuring, however imperfectly, the economic effects of such changes because it requires neither unanimous voluntary consent for a change nor actual compensation.

These same features that provide the Kaldor-Hicks efficiency criterion with its practical utility also constitute its greatest weakness: In the absence of voluntary transactions in the market, where the preferences of all participants and their subjective valuations of their preferences are exhibited and supported by willingness to pay, economic valuations cannot be unambiguously derived and compared. In other words, because Kaldor-Hicks does not require those who benefit from some allocation or reallocation to compensate those who lose, it does not provide a market-determined price by which to evaluate the winners' utility and losers' disutility. The uncertainty of valuation, in the absence of demonstrated willingness to pay, disqualifies the Kaldor-Hicks efficiency criterion in the minds of some economists.

Because it creates opportunities for mistake and manipulation, the Kaldor-Hicks criterion can never specify the efficiency of outcomes with perfect certainty.[17] However, critics of the Kaldor-Hicks criterion have nothing to offer in its place except the Pareto criterion. As we have seen, the Pareto criterion cannot be applied to transactions that occur without the voluntary consent of all affected parties, including those affected by negative externalities stemming from the transactions of others. Therefore, despite its defects, the Kaldor-Hicks criterion remains vital and will be used throughout this book in discussing the efficiency of many legal—judicial as well as regulatory—decisions that affect resource allocations.

Cost-Benefit Analysis

In the policy arena, *cost-benefit analysis* (CBA) is the embodiment of the Kaldor-Hicks efficiency criterion. CBA is used to assess whether a certain social policy choice will, in net, enhance or degrade social welfare. In a world governed by the Pareto efficiency criterion, CBA is not needed for policy analysis because all changes in entitlements will be welfare improving; otherwise, they simply would not occur. The Paretian requirements of unanimous, voluntary consent and actual compensation ensure efficient outcomes. Anyone who would suffer a loss in welfare because of some proposed change in entitlements could veto the proposed change. CBA, like the Kaldor-Hicks efficiency criterion upon which it is based, becomes useful only when the constraints of complete compensation and unanimous consent are lifted, so that someone could force changes that would reduce the welfare of others. At that point, it becomes necessary to develop some mechanism, such as CBA, to ensure (although never unambiguously) that proposed changes in existing entitlements would create a net gain for social welfare.[18]

MARKET FAILURE

Neoclassical Assumptions Versus the Real World

According to standard neoclassical economic theory (and as we discussed earlier), properly functioning markets always should maximize productive and allocative efficiency. In the real world, however, markets do not always function properly. Consequently, markets do not always attain efficient equilibria.

Neoclassical economics starts with a world in which firms and consumers operate in perfectly competitive markets. These markets are assumed to possess the following properties:

1. Markets include many buyers and sellers, all of whom have complete information about product qualities, quantities, and prices.
2. No buyer or seller has sufficient market power to control the price.
3. Market participants respond rationally to changing market conditions.
4. Firms may enter and exit the market costlessly.
5. All resources or amenities within the economy are owned and priced within the market, and all prices are determined by supply and demand.
6. All costs and benefits fall within the market, creating no *externalities*.
7. Transactions within the market are costless.

The assumptions of neoclassical theory do not reflect the reality of markets and market transacting. The assumption of zero transaction costs never reflects reality, and the other assumptions do so only rarely and incompletely. Still, many economists cling to them because they simplify real-world complexities in ways that permit economists to analyze situations and develop models that, themselves, have substantial explanatory and predictive power.[19] At least some of the standard economic assumptions reflect the actual state of affairs in the world often and sufficiently enough that it could well reduce the explanatory power of the model *not* to assume them. Few, if any, economists believe, for example, that the rational utility maximizer of economic theory accurately describes all human beings; but most people do, generally speaking, respond rationally to incentives most of the time. As Coase notes, when "faced with a choice between $100 and $10, very few people will choose $10."[20] The fact remains, however, that markets *never* function perfectly; they are always characterized by some degree of *market failure* (or *market imperfection*), defined by the extent to which they fail to achieve and maintain optimal allocative efficiency.

Imperfect Competition

Markets in the real world are characterized by *imperfect competition*. In a perfectly functioning market, the laws of supply and demand operate flawlessly to move goods and services to their highest-valued uses, thereby maximizing the gains to social welfare from trade. But where markets suffer from imperfect competition, the laws of supply or demand may not function properly; they may not establish optimally efficient equilibrium prices. This inefficiency is the case, for example, when a seller has a *monopoly* on some good for which demand is relatively inelastic (perhaps because substitute goods are unavailable).[21] In this circumstance, the seller can charge a higher price and make greater profits than a competitive market would permit. The seller's supercompetitive profits result in allocative inefficiency by consuming resources that buyers might have devoted to fulfilling other preferences. Even where monopoly is not a problem, however, markets remain more or less imperfectly competitive.

Imperfect or Asymmetric Information

Closely related to the problem of imperfect competition is that of *imperfect information*. The lack of complete information can render competition imperfect. The two forms of imperfect information are *uncertainty* and *asymmetric information*. This unequal information between sellers and buyers gives one side an advantage over the other in bargaining that allows it to gain *rents* (prices exceeding the minimum required to keep the seller from switching to some other investment opportunity). In most circumstances, the parties to a market transaction will not be able to identify every possible contingency that might arise to affect their relations. Such uncertainty will likely prevent them from maximizing the gains from trading with one another, or prevent trade at all.

Externalities

Market transactions often create *externalities* or spillover effects; that is, some of the costs or benefits associated with the transactions are not borne by those participating in the transaction but are externalized to others. Most often, economists and policy analysts are concerned with negative externalities, such as pollution. When pollution costs are externalized and borne by someone other than the producer,[22] the price of the producer's product—let's say they're widgets[23]—will not reflect those costs of production. The price of widgets will be lower than it would have been had the pollution costs been *internalized*. Because of the lower price, the market quantity of widgets (i.e., the quantity supplied and demanded) will be greater than would be socially desirable. The production of widgets is thus inefficient. Put another way,

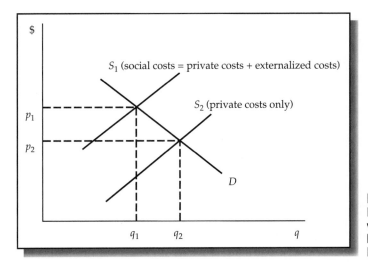

Figure 1-4 The Market for Widgets with Pollution Costs Externalized and Internalized

because the real cost of making widgets is not reflected fully in the price of the widget, too many widgets will be made and sold at too low a price. It is important to recognize that someone will bear the external cost imposed by widget making. In effect, whoever bears the pollution costs of widget production subsidizes producers and consumers of widgets. This kind of negative externality impedes allocative efficiency by sending inaccurate price signals, and the market overproduces both widgets and pollution.[24]

To illustrate, consider Figure 1-4 which, like Figure 1-3, shows supply and demand curves, only now we deal with two supply curves: S_1 and S_2. As you will recall from our earlier discussion, a firm's supply curve is determined by its costs. If a firm can externalize some of its costs—in this case, force others to pay the costs of the air pollution it produces as a by-product of widget production—it will be able to produce profitably more widgets than if it had to bear those costs. S_2 shows supply for the firm when it can ignore some of the costs it creates. An equilibrium occurs at p_2q_2, but in fact supply and demand at this point are not allocatively efficient for the economy as a whole because the costs of production are not all incorporated in S_2. The socially efficient equilibrium point is where D intersects S_1, which does incorporate the widget producer's externalized costs. As long as the widget factory produces at q_2 rather than q_1, it will produce too many widgets (and too much pollution) and sell them for too low a price.

Not all externalities are negative, however; *positive externalities* can also result. A positive externality is a benefit from some activity that the transactor cannot completely internalize for his or her own benefit; others are able to "profit" from the transactor's investment in some way. For example, if your neighbor cultivates a beautiful garden, which you can enjoy from your yard without payment, the neighbor's time and effort create external benefits for you. Arguably, many of the benefits that educators confer on society—better-educated individuals tend to be more productive and law-abiding—are externalized. Those benefits are not, however, reflected in the prices paid (as wages) to educators.

Public Goods

Some goods are never produced in socially optimal quantities if production is left to the market. This particular problem is especially prevalent for so-called *public (or collective) goods*. A "public" good is one the market will underproduce because the benefits of producing it are so costly to internalize that private investors would not be able to recover their investment costs. Public goods have two properties that prevent markets from working smoothly: joint supply and nonexcludability. The former means that one person's consumption does not prevent or reduce another person's consumption of the same good or service. Nonexcludability means that it is too costly to prevent someone from consuming the good or service without paying for it.

The lighthouse is a frequently invoked example of a public good. Obviously, lighthouses possess positive social utility; they provide a good. What makes this good a *public* good are two characteristics: (1) one person's consumption of light from the lighthouse has no effect on anyone else's ability to consume light from the lighthouse;[25] and (2) the lighthouse owner/operator cannot, as a practical matter, exclude nonpaying ships from utilizing and benefiting from the light provided by the lighthouse. Ships' captains have no incentive to pay their fair share for the lighthouse because they cannot be excluded from using the light, regardless of whether they pay. Who, then, would pay? Because of this problem, the market will provide too few (if any) lighthouses, certainly fewer than the number of lighthouses that *should* be built, given their positive utility (compared to what other goods and services are provided instead). For this reason, throughout history, lighthouses have been built primarily at public expense.[26]

We cannot, however, find any such thing as a *pure* public good. Something that is deemed a public good today (such as the atmosphere) may become efficiently privatizable at some time in the future, when the problems of nonexcludability and joint supply are resolved, e.g., by technological innovations. Economists have explained, for example, that the innovation of barbed wire in the 1870s greatly reduced the cost of enclosing land, thereby facilitating settlement and privatization of public lands in the western United States.[27] So, what counts as a public good can change.

Transaction Costs

Finally, *transaction costs* are always positive and often quite significant. It is costly to obtain information about the qualities and quantities of various goods and services. It is costly to bargain with potential sellers (or buyers) to some agreement about exchanging some goods and services for others, as well as to foresee and cover various future contingencies that might affect the agreement. Having bargained successfully, it is costly for the parties to formalize the agreement, putting it in the form of an enforceable contract. Once the contract is formalized and signed, the agreement must then be monitored or policed, which is costly. If the contract is violated by one party or another, it is costly to enforce (although some enforcement mechanisms may be less expensive than others). Such costs are ubiquitous features of real-world transactions. In other cases the costs of transacting may exceed the gains from trade, in which case trading will not occur. Transaction costs are central to the economic analysis of law.

Strategic Behavior: Free Riders and Holdouts

One common type of transaction cost is called *strategic behavior*, and two types of strategic behavior are commonly confronted in the law and economics literature: *free riders* and *holdouts*. We already discussed an example of the free rider problem: ships that use the lighthouse without paying for the privilege. Whether the lighthouse is provided by some private investor or the public treasury, ships that do not pay to use the lighthouse receive the benefits of the light (which keeps them off the rocky shoals) without sharing in the cost of providing that light. Their use of the light is price-free but not cost-free.

Free riders can greatly increase transaction costs, particularly in cases where agreement is required among a number of parties to consummate the transaction. Here's an example. A fishery comprised of 100 individual fishers is located on a bay. They are not a corporation but a loose confederation of independent contractors, who must cooperate to manage the fishery. Each of the 100 individual fishers earns $100,000 per year from the fishery, so the value of the fishery as a whole is $10 million per year. One day, the state authorities approve the siting of a new factory on the same bay. The factory will diversify the local economy and bring new jobs to the community, but will also produce harmful water pollution to the detriment of the fishery. The factory will earn annual profits of approximately $500,000. Because it has specific authorization from the state, the factory is entitled to pollute the bay; the fishers cannot shut it down through any legal action. The only way for the fishers to stop the factory and save the fishery is to purchase the entitlement from the factory in a voluntary, market transaction. This approach would be an efficient (Pareto-improving) transaction because the fishery is worth a lot more than the factory, providing greater social benefits. But the high transaction costs involved in coordinating the effort among 100 individual fishers may impede that outcome. The fishers are going to have to offer the factory something more than $500,000 to make it worth the factory's while to give up its entitlement. Let's say the factory is willing to sell for $2.5 million. Each of the 100 individual fishers would have to contribute $25,000, or one-quarter of their annual income. In a perfectly functioning market with zero transaction costs, they would certainly select this option. In the real world, though, it will not be easy. Some of the fishers can be expected to *free ride* on the efforts of the others. One fisher may demur, "I'd like to help, but I'm short on cash this year; we've got a new baby, and my wife's been ill. I hope you'll be able to save the fishery. You have my moral support." However many fishers attempt to free ride, the others will be forced to make up for the shortfall. If too many attempt to free ride, the others might not be able to make up the shortfall, and the efficient transaction would not be consummated. In this way, free riding can impede efficient transacting.

The holdout problem is another form of strategic behavior that, like the free rider problem, can greatly increase transaction costs, particularly when agreement is required among a large number of parties to complete the transaction. Here's an illustration of the holdout problem. A movie company is making a period film in a Paris neighborhood. The film is set in the 1920s, and in order to make the film appear as realistic as possible, the producers need to have satellite dishes removed from all the houses on the block for the one-week period of filming. Twenty such houses have satellite dishes on their roofs, and the film company must obtain the voluntary consent of each homeowner to accomplish its purpose. Before the company begins negotiating with each homeowner, the producers estimate a certain budget to cover what they expect to pay to have all the satellite dishes removed from all the houses for one week. The total budget amounts to $2,000, or $100 per house. The producers knock on the door of the first house and offer the owner $100 to remove her satellite dish for one week. The owner feels this is a fair offer; she doesn't watch very much television anyway. So, she readily accepts. The producers move on to the next house. Quickly, word spreads throughout the block that the filmmakers are negotiating the temporary removal of all satellite dishes on the block. As word spreads, the homeowners begin to engage in strategic behavior. The price for removing the dishes quickly rises. Even at houses where television is watched only rarely, the price demanded is higher than the producers anticipated. The price continues to grow as the producers move up the street, because the homeowners know that, when the producers reach their house, none of the previous deals matter at all, if the producers cannot obtain their acquiescence. Indeed, the film would look no less anachronistic with just two or three satellite dishes sitting on the roofs within the camera shot. It's not enough for the producers to get the agreement of a few or even most of the residents; in order to achieve its purpose, the company must obtain the agreement of every last homeowner on the block. This circumstance gives the last few homeowners tremendous leverage, which they will exercise to obtain rents. That is, they will hold out for a better deal than an efficiently functioning market, with large numbers of buyers and sellers (and substitute goods), would provide.

Like the free rider problem, the holdout problem can render inefficient some transaction that would have been efficient if only the costs of transacting were lower.

RESPONSES TO MARKET FAILURE: FIRMS AND GOVERNMENTS (AND THEIR FAILURES)

When markets fail to approach the standard assumptions of neoclassical economic theory, they cannot, by definition, achieve optimal levels of efficiency. Indeed, once the assumptions are relaxed, the market may in some circumstances be relatively inefficient compared to other possible allocation mechanisms. The economics literature addresses two alternatives to the market for organizing economic activities: firms and governments.

Firms

If the assumptions of neoclassical economic theory actually reflected the real world, the existence of firms would be unnecessary. The *firm* is an alternative to the market for organizing economic activity. It is based on contractual relations between individuals who comprise the firm. A world of costless transacting and perfectly functioning markets provides no reason for individuals to constitute a firm because they could maximize their individual well-being through independent market transacting. As Ronald Coase noted in his 1937 landmark article, "The Nature of the Firm," it is only when market transacting becomes more costly than organizing in firms that firms can become a more efficient mechanism than the market for transacting.[28] The very existence of firms indicates that markets do not always maximize allocative efficiency. Of course, the continuing existence and predominance of markets likewise indicates that markets often allocate goods and services more efficiently than firms, which are costly to establish and maintain. Put differently, firms sometimes fail, too. When they do, the market or the government may be preferable mechanisms for organizing economic activities.

Government Intervention to Correct Market and Firm Failures

As with firms, governments would not be needed as alternative resource allocation mechanisms if the assumptions of neoclassical economic theory always obtained. The purpose of government then, according to the theory of *welfare economics* associated with the English economist Arthur Pigou (1877–1959), is to correct market failures. This corrective function served as a warrant for most government regulation of economic activity in the United States during the twentieth century. Everything from minimum wage laws, price controls, and worker safety regulations, to highway speed limits, automobile air bag requirements, and pollution emissions limitations have been justified on the basis of "market failure."

The government can correct market failures in various ways. It can prevent monopolies and other inefficient forms of imperfect competition, for example, by imposing rules that permit competitive entry into an industry or prohibit the concentration of ownership within an industry. It can solve externality problems by taxing those who impose negative externalities on others, and by subsidizing those who create positive externalities. Taxes could force polluters and others to internalize the full social cost of production and so lead to the socially optimal price and quantity of production. The government could alternatively impose price controls or ration quantities for this purpose. Laws and legal systems may reduce transactions costs by providing clarity to the rules of exchange and the distribution of entitlements. Government may also provide goods directly, especially public goods, so that a socially efficient output of the goods will be produced. Thus, lighthouses often have been provided by government agencies rather than by private entrepreneurs.

Government Failure

The standard welfare economics view of government rests on dubious assumptions about how and why governments act. First and foremost, it assumes that governments are market surrogates, acting in the *public interest* to maximize social welfare by correcting market failures. It is plain, however, that governments do not only act to correct market failures; they act to achieve other goals besides economic efficiency, including moral and ethical goals. Whether governments should act solely in the interest of economic efficiency is another question. And whether government actions are always, or ever, in the "public interest" is debatable. Some economists even doubt whether any such thing as the public interest exists.[29] It is clear, in any case, that governments fail, too; that is, they do not always allocate entitlements in such a way as to maximize social welfare. When governments fail, markets or firms may be preferable mechanisms for allocating entitlements to resources.

THE SECOND-BEST (*REAL* COASEAN) WORLD

The Nobel laureate Ronald Coase has observed that we inhabit a world in which all mechanisms for organizing economic activities are "more or less failures." Markets fail, firms fail, and governments fail. We have, therefore, no universal, unequivocal, first-best institutional or organizational structure for allocating entitlements to resources. The lesson, for Coase, is to rely on those institutions and organizations that, in the circumstances, are least likely to fail *or* are likely to fail the least. For Coase, the best institution for allocating resources—the institution least likely to fail—is the one that minimizes transaction costs.

This goal is consistent with recent studies suggesting that transaction costs may comprise the largest sector of the U.S. economy, comprising more than one-half of gross national product (GNP) in 1970.[30] It also subtly changes the goal of organizing economic activity. Instead of *maximizing* social utility, wealth, or happiness, the goal has become to *minimize* certain ubiquitous costs that impede efforts to maximize social utility, wealth, or happiness. This shift from utility (or profit) maximization to cost minimization as the focus of analysis reflects the shift away from the mythical world of first-best (optimal) solutions, toward the more realistic world of the "second best." Implicit in this theory of the second best is the notion that perfection is impossible. We are constrained to choose among various imperfect alternative mechanisms for structuring economic activities. We can only make the best of an imperfect situation.

CHAPTER SUMMARY

This chapter reviewed basic principles of neoclassical economic theory, including scarcity, supply and demand, cost, and efficiency. It also explained how the real world often deviates from the assumptions of neoclassical theory, resulting in problems of market failure. Government regulation cannot be an automatic reaction to market failure because government fails, too. Finally, the chapter addressed implications of the "theory of the second best," according to which optimal solutions are infeasible.

QUESTIONS AND PROBLEMS

1. Under which circumstances in the real world is the Pareto efficiency criterion useful for determining the efficiency of transactions?
2. Under what circumstances, if any, would we conclude that a market participant has acted irrationally?
3. What do economists mean when they say, "There's no such thing as a free lunch"?
4. Many people may desire to own a sportscar, but they don't actually demand one in the market. Why not?
5. Why do externalities cause a shift in the producer's supply curve? Why do those externalities lead to inefficient allocative outcomes?

6. Are lighthouses "public goods"? Why or why not?
7. Can true public goods ever become private goods? If so, how?
8. How does the concept of Kaldor-Hicks efficiency differ from the concept of Pareto efficiency?
9. How does allocative efficiency differ from productive efficiency?
10. In a market, if supply equals demand, is the outcome necessarily efficient? If so, in what sense is it efficient?
11. Why is the demand for a life-saving drug likely to be inelastic?
12. What do economists mean by "market failure"?
13. What did Ronald Coase mean when he said that all of society's methods of organizing production and exchange are "more or less failures"?
14. What strategic problem would make it difficult to have voluntary payments for national defense?

NOTES

1. Lionel Robbins, *The Nature and Significance of Economic Science* (New York: New York University Press, 1932), p. 15. Ronald Coase noted, however, that Robbins's definition is over-broad in that economists do not (yet) purport to explain *all* human choices. Ronald H. Coase, *Essays on Economics and Economists* (Chicago: University of Chicago Press, 1994), p. 41.

2. The emergence of markets for air is exemplified by the development of tradable permitting for air pollution, whereby the government allocates pollution "allowances," which can be freely traded in the market. A less obvious example is the recent establishment of so-called "oxygen bars" in California, where customers pay to breathe pure oxygen from tanks. However, the ability of markets for air to develop is limited by technological constraints on the ability to draw and enforce boundaries in the air. For more on tradeable pollution allowances, see Chapter 15.

3. More precisely, the opportunity cost is the value of the next best (but forgone) alternative.

4. To take a simple example, many people in the United States indicate a strong preference for watching television. This preference would not likely be the case, however, in a small country with only one television channel that is controlled by a dictatorial government.

5. Generally speaking, the budget constraints of a poor person are going to limit that person's economic opportunities far more than the budget constraints of a rich person. Such a point

is, however, independent of the subjective economic valuation issue.

6. Quotes are from Ronald H. Coase, "The Institutional Structure of Production: The 1991 Alfred Nobel Memorial Prize Lecture in Economics," in R. H. Coase, *Essays on Economics and Economists* (Chicago: University of Chicago Press, 1994).

7. As Richard Posner points out, the law of demand applies not only to goods and services with explicit prices but also to goods and services with nonpecuniary benefits or "shadow prices." For example, all else being equal, students will generally select teachers with reputations for being easy graders over teachers with reputations for being tough graders. Richard A. Posner, *Economic Analysis of Law*, 5th ed. (New York: Aspen Publishers, 1998), p. 5.

8. Economists traditionally take individual preferences as they find them; they have not tried to explain how preferences are formed and ranked in the first place. However, recent studies by behavioral economics scholars examined these issues. Behavioral law and economics is discussed in the "perspectives" section of Chapter 3.

9. At some price, some individuals infected with HIV may attempt to steal rather than buy AZT. The incentives to engage or not to engage in criminal behavior are addressed in Chapter 13.

10. Note that a producer's costs also include opportunity cost, because producers, too, face alternatives. For example, instead of producing

the good, the producer could put his or her resources in the bank and earn interest—interest that is foregone in the event that production does take place.

11. This activity may, in turn, cause depletion of the lobster stock, in which case it will cost more, over time, to supply a constant amount of lobsters to the market. All other things being equal, this depletion will cause a "shift" in the supply curve for lobsters, upward and to the left, so that at every price fewer lobsters will be supplied.

12. Markets did not simply emerge out of thin air. They were instituted deliberately by entrepreneurs and governments to facilitate trade. We return to this topic of the legal-institutional structure of economic activity in Chapter 3.

13. In general, demand itself changes (as opposed to the quantity demanded, which changes with prices) when changes occur in consumer preferences, in the prices of substitute goods, in expectations about future prices, in consumer income, and in the size of the market. Supply changes result from changes in input prices, technology, expectations, and the number of producers.

14. *See* Douglass C. North, *Institutions, Institutional Change and Economic Performance* (Cambridge: Cambridge University Press, 1990), pp. 80–81.

15. Nicholas Kaldor, "Welfare Propositions in Economics," 49 ECONOMICS JOURNAL 549 (1939); J. R. Hicks, "The Foundations of Welfare Economics," 49 ECONOMICS JOURNAL 696 (1939).

16. The Kaldor and Hicks efficiency criteria are combined because each, individually, is seriously flawed. The Kaldor criterion can, in some circumstances, yield paradoxical outcomes: a change from a *status quo* may be a Kaldor improvement and, then, after the change is made, returning to the *status quo ante* may be a Kaldor improvement. Nicholas Mercuro and Steven G. Medema, *Economics and the Law: From Posner to Post-Modernism* (Princeton, NJ: Princeton University Press, 1997), p. 49. In addition, the Kaldor and Hicks tests can give contradictory results. One can show that a change would yield an improvement, while the other shows that the same change would yield a net loss to social welfare. It is only when a change satisfies both tests that the outcome can really be judged an improvement. *Ibid.* at p. 50.

17. *See*, for example, J. Gregory Sidak and Daniel F. Spulber, *Deregulatory Takings and the Regulatory Contract* (Cambridge: Cambridge University Press, 1998), pp. 219–22; Oliver E. Williamson, "Response: Regulatory Takings and the Breach of the Regulatory Contract: Some Precautions," 71 NEW YORK UNIVERSITY LAW REVIEW 1007, 1009 (1998).

18. The utility and limitations of cost-benefit analysis for environmental policy are explored in Chapter 15.

19. *See* Richard A. Posner, *Economic Analysis of Law*, 5th ed. (New York: Aspen Publishers, 1992), p. 18.

20. Ronald H. Coase, "How Should Economists Choose?" reprinted in R. H. Coase, *Essays on Economics and Economists* (Chicago: University of Chicago Press, 1994), p. 25.

21. Issues of monopoly and monopoly markets are addressed in Chapter 5's discussion of intellectual property and, in more detail, in Chapter 14, which concerns antitrust and regulated industries.

22. A cost must be borne by some person in order to be considered a cost in the first place. Thus, as Harold Demsetz has written, "[n]o harmful or beneficial effect is external to the world." Harold Demsetz, "Toward a Theory of Property Rights," reprinted in Harold Demsetz, *Ownership, Control, and the Firm* (Oxford: Basil Blackwell 1988), pp. 104, 105.

23. Economists frequently invoke the lowly widget, as an imaginary product, to exemplify economic principles. Widgets are not just imaginary; they really exist. Beer manufacturers use widgets—small, light, plastic balls, something like fishing bobbers—to control the flow of beer from cans.

24. This discussion of pollution externalities and their effects on allocative efficiency is repeated, in greater detail, in Chapter 15. It should be noted, however, that externalities do not only arise from market transactions. They can also arise from the unilateral actions of individuals or the collective actions of governments and other hierarchical organizations.

25. In economic terms, the light from the lighthouse is nonrivalrous in use.

26. Ronald Coase argued that the lighthouse example is historically inaccurate because private entrepreneurs did build lighthouses. Ronald H. Coase, "The Lighthouse in

Economics," 17 JOURNAL OF LAW & ECONOMICS 357 (1974). However, David E. van Zandt, in response to Coase, notes that those entrepreneurs were invariably subsidized by governments. David E. van Zandt, "The Lessons of the Lighthouse: "Government" or "Private" Provision of Goods," 22 JOURNAL OF LEGAL STUDIES 47 (1993).

27. Terry L. Anderson and Peter J. Hill, "The Evolution of Property Rights: A Study of the American West," 18 JOURNAL OF LAW & ECONOMICS 163 (1975).

28. Ronald H. Coase, "The Nature of the Firm" [1937], reprinted in R. H. Coase, *The Firm, The Market and the Law* (Chicago: University of Chicago Press, 1988), p. 33.

29. *See* the section in Chapter 3 on public choice theory.

30. *See* John Joseph Wallis and Douglass C. North, "Measuring the Transaction Sector in the American Economy, 1870–1970," in S. L. Engerman and R. E. Gallman (eds.), *Long-Term Factors in American Economic Growth* (Chicago: University of Chicago Press, 1986), pp. 95, 120.

Chapter 2

An Introduction to the American Legal System

A complete introduction to the law and legal institutions is beyond the scope of this book; as always, scarcity (of space) requires trade-offs. Our more limited goal is to provide a sufficient introduction to law for readers to comprehend the legal materials in subsequent chapters of this book. Law students and others with a substantial background in legal studies may skip this chapter or treat it as a review.

WHY LAW?

Scarcity Again

As with economics, the law and legal institutions are largely concerned with scarcity. If all goods were perfectly abundant, laws and legal institutions establishing rules of possession and transfer would be no more necessary than markets for exchange. Suppose gold were not scarce. What reason would there be to have laws establishing and protecting possessory rights in gold? Anyone who wanted gold (or more gold) could simply reach down and grab plenty. For that reason, no one would bother to take another's gold. And if someone *did* take another's gold, the "victim" would not complain because an unlimited amount of gold would remain available at virtually zero cost.

Unlike economics, however, scarcity is not the foundation of *all* law. Law is about much more than allocating entitlements to scarce resources among competing uses and users. As with economics, the law is concerned with efficiency, but not exclusively. The law's broader purview also includes ethics: encouraging "right" behavior and discouraging "wrong" behavior. It may well be "efficient," for example, that the law prohibits murder; but it would be a mistake to assume that the law prohibits murder for that reason or for that reason alone. The law prohibits murder because killing is "wrong," unless undertaken in self-defense, pursuant to the rules of war, or for some other exculpatory reason. The criminal law traditionally distinguishes between offenses that are *malum per se* (always and everywhere bad) and those that are *malum prohibitum* (bad because the law defines them as bad). This distinction reflects a deeper distinction between crimes against morality and crimes that are merely against society's interest.

The Purposes of Law

Legal rules serve to organize individual behavior and structure social interactions. In theory, the law punishes "bad" behavior and encourages "good" behavior. Reality is more complicated, of course. For one thing, what constitutes "good" and "bad" behavior may be in the eye of the beholder. Moreover, the legal rules often are outcomes of complex games or contests between various interest groups with stakes in the outcome. For those groups, the "purpose" of law may be to gain political and economic power. From an economic perspective, one fundamental purpose of law is to facilitate exchange because the gains from trade increase social welfare.

LEGAL INSTITUTIONS: THE RULES OF THE GAME

Legal Rules

Throughout history, *law* has been defined in many ways. According to one common definition, laws are simply commands backed by the coercive power of the state.[1] Oliver Wendell Holmes famously defined *law* as nothing but a prediction of what a court would rule in a subsequent case.[2] Another view, associated with the economist Douglass North,[3] defines laws as *institutions* comprising the *formal* "rules of the game," governing social (including economic) relations.[4] None of these definitions seems sufficient on its own, but they are not mutually exclusive. It is possible to combine them so as to define law as a prediction of what some judge will decide, with the understanding that the judicial decision will be backed by the coercive power of the state (including its judges), becoming an institution—a formal "rule of the game"—governing future behavior.

Behind the rules of the game are *metarules* of the game, which are rules about rules.[5] These second-order rules govern the process of legal rule making. The U.S. Constitution, for example, provides metarules governing the legislative process: in order for legislation to become law, both houses of Congress must approve it by majority votes, and the president must sign it. If the president fails to sign it, it can still become law if Congress overrides the president's veto by a two-thirds vote. The process of judicial rule making is similarly governed by metarules of law that, among other things, allocate burdens of proof and establish evidentiary standards.

The institutional definition of law implicitly and usefully casts doubt on a common misunderstanding about relations between markets and legal systems. The idea of a legally regulated market commonly carries a negative connotation of limited freedom or liberty to transact. By viewing laws simply as "rules of the game," however, it becomes clear that some amount of legal regulation of markets is both inevitable and beneficial, at least in a large heterogeneous society. Without legal "rules of the game," market transacting would be chaotic at best, impossible at worst, and in any case very costly. Some extent of formal legal regulation can positively enhance freedom and liberty.

Consider the legal rule requiring that automobiles be driven on the right side of the road. In one sense, it is a liberty-restricting rule; it prevents people who might want to drive on the left side of the road from doing as they please. But overall, the rule enhances freedom by creating a clear "rule of the road," which reduces the coordination costs of all drivers. The rule greatly reduces transaction costs by obviating the need for millions of individual drivers to contract with one another about which side of the road to drive on, so as to avoid accidents. To the extent that such formally institutionalized "rules of the game" are essential to market transacting, the conventional dichotomy of *markets versus government* is plainly false. The real question is: What is the appropriate legal structure for organizing individual behavior and social relations? Note how this question mirrors the question raised for economics by the *theory of the second best*. Also note that the answer to the question is likely to change over time, as circumstances change. Thus, law is not a static institution. It evolves and adapts to changing social conditions and pressures, as well as changing technologies.

The Rule of Law

Studies of law often begin with the concept of the *rule of law*, which at its simplest means precisely what it says: the law rules. In the absence of the rule of law, law is nothing more than the arbitrary, momentary whim of the ruler. It is easier, however, to define the absence of the rule of law than to define the rule of law and what it entails. As many versions of the rule of law exist as authors writing about it.

At a minimum, the rule of law requires merely that the legal rules, whatever their source, form, and contents, must apply equally to the rulers and the ruled. The rules themselves may be just or unjust, adopted according to democratic or antidemocratic processes; but as long as the law actually constrains state power, then the state may be said to comport with the rule of law. On this definition, the rule of law provides nothing more than the legal restraint of arbitrary power, so that we can distinguish, for example, between the absolutist rule of Egyptian pharaohs and the rule of King Solomon, who was constrained to some extent by theological laws. Using this minimalist conception, the rule of law is a necessary but insufficient condition for a just society. It also constitutes an aspirational goal, more than an existing institution, in that every state inevitably falls short of meeting the requirement of equal application of the laws. Countries are said to adhere to the rule of law not because they actually attain it but because they strive to do so.

The minimalist conception of the rule of law is distinguished from other, more elaborate versions, which entail additional conditions. Many versions of the rule of law require not only equal application of the laws but certain legal processes to ensure that legal rules are promulgated and known prior to their application.[6] Some versions assert that an independent judiciary is "essential for the preservation of the rule of law."[7]

On a more pragmatic level, companies that measure investment risks abroad use a rule of law index. The International Country Risk Guide's (ICRG) "Rule of Law index" measures, among other things, the extent to which a given country has "a tradition of depending on physical force or illegal means to settle claims." The ICRG implicitly defines the rule of law more broadly than the minimalist conception, but more narrowly than many other versions. In fact, the old name for the ICRG's Rule of Law index—"Law and Order Tradition"—may have been more appropriate to the panoply of institutional considerations it reflects. It is nonetheless interesting to see how the business community seized on the rule of law concept as a practical and measurable factor indicating a state's commitment to certain relations between law, politics, and power.

Criminal and Civil Law

A great diversity of legal systems exists in the world. Most highly developed legal systems, however, share certain common traits. Among them is the differentiation among areas of law. One basic differentiation is between *criminal* and *civil* law. Criminal law is concerned with deterring and punishing wrongs committed by some individual(s) against society or the state. Civil law is concerned with deterring and correcting wrongs committed by some individual(s) against others,[8] but not against society as a whole. Distinctions between criminal and civil wrongs are not always obvious,[9] but one distinction is clear: In the United States and most other countries, imprisonment is reserved as a punishment for violations of the criminal law.

Criminal and civil laws codes usually contain further divisions and subdivisions. In the United States, the civil law is subdivided into tort law, contract law, property law, and civil procedure. These subdivisions are largely artificial; they overlap in many ways. They also reflect some important differences. For example, the available remedies for a breach of contract are not the same as the remedies available for a tort (a civil wrong). The criminal law, too, differentiates *felonies* from *misdemeanors*. Once again, the main difference reflected by the distinction concerns penalties: those who commit felonies are subject to lengthy imprisonment, while those who commit misdemeanors are subject only to fines and imprisonment of up to a year at most.

Rights and Duties

The concept of a legal "right" is familiar to almost everyone, but is widely misunderstood. People *assert* "rights" all the time without considering the necessary legal implications of that assertion. In legal parlance, to assert a "right" to something— whether a property right, a human right, a civil right, or some other kind of right—is to declare that someone or everyone else has a *duty* not to interfere with your exercise of your right. Put simply, every legal right entails some identifiable, corresponding duty. This relationship remains true whether the asserted right is *positive* (created by some sovereign) or *natural*. It is the existence of the correlative duty that distinguishes a legal right from a mere privilege, liberty, license, or use.

Consider the following example: Ron purchases a piece of land in the State of Industria, upon which he constructs and operates a factory that produces rubber balls. This activity is perfectly legal at the time and location. No one else lives or works anywhere near Ron's rubber ball factory. However, as a by-product of rubber ball production, Ron's factory produces smox, an air pollutant. The smox from Ron's factory floats up into the atmosphere and floats away to who knows where. Does Ron have a "right" to emit the smox? If we answer yes, we must also be prepared to answer three further questions: (1) What is the source of Ron's right? (2) What is the extent of Ron's right? And (3), most importantly, what is the source and extent of everyone else's duty not to interfere with Ron's smox pollution? In the absence of answers to these questions, assertions of legal rights are dubious and contestable.

Liability and Remedy

Another crucial distinction in legal analysis is between the finding of *liability*—the question of whether a crime has been committed, a civil duty has been violated, or a contract has been breached—and the *remedy*. The liability question is whether someone should be held legally responsible for a certain action. The remedy question is what penalty should attach to that person's liability. As we discuss later in this book, the important distinction between liability rules and remedies is sometimes neglected by courts and commentators.

SOURCES AND AREAS OF LAW

Legal rules come from myriad sources, ranging from the arbitrary decisions of an absolute monarch or totalitarian party, to local customs and traditions, ancient writings, judicial dispute resolution (e.g., the common law), and legislation enacted according to legally recognized procedures. The legal systems of most countries in the world today are *constitutional*, in that they are founded on some written or unwritten basic law(s) that structures the rest of the legal system. Most contemporary legal systems evolved from a basis in either the (Roman) *civil law* tradition of legislation (not to be confused with the *civil part* of the legal system, which deals with noncriminal matters) or the (English) *common law* tradition of adjudication. In the civil law tradition, laws are enacted by a legislative body and applied by the courts. A smaller number of countries, including the United States, have legal systems based on the English *common law*, a body of law slowly accumulated over the centuries through the adjudication of individual lawsuits.[10] By the second half of the twentieth century, however, the common law could no longer be considered predominant in the United States. An explosion of codification and legislation clearly established the civil law tradition in this country, with the result that, today, the two primary sources of law coexist, if somewhat uneasily.

Constitutional Law

We live in an age of *constitutionalism*, in which virtually all countries construct their legal systems around a fundamental law, written or unwritten, which is the highest law of the land. It is useful to recall that not so long ago, the world knew little constitutional law. Now it is ubiquitous. Even totalitarian regimes, operating outside of the rule of law, proudly display written constitutions that express beautiful but empty sentiments about democracy and civil rights. The point is not to express cynicism about constitutionalism in general but merely to highlight the tremendous influence of constitutionalism throughout the world. Even antidemocratic and antilegal regimes feel compelled to cloak their despotism in the mantle of *faux* constitutionalism.

Constitutional law is perhaps the most successful export of the American legal system, which is not to say that it is an entirely American innovation. Ancient Greece followed a relatively democratic constitution, though it had no written document called a "constitution" England is one of the world's oldest constitutional monarchies, but it too has never had a written constitution. In England, the Constitution is said to consist in the institutions of the realm: the Crown, Parliament, and the courts. Elsewhere, constitutions are comprised of several *fundamental laws*, rather than a single constitution. On the other hand, the former Soviet Union had a written constitution, but not a constitutional system. So, it cannot be the fact of any particular document or set of documents that renders a country "constitutional."

In order to distinguish between constitutional and nonconstitutional systems, the definition of "constitutional." requires a certain mix of institutions recognized as comprising a constitutional system. Those institutions include the rule of law, which at its simplest requires that the law governs the rulers, and that the constitution governs the law. Otherwise, the constitution serves no *legal* purpose. The constitution, in fact, supplies many of the legal system's metarules: the rules for making legal rules.

The Common Law and Its Courts

After the police, the courts are the most visible part of the U.S. legal system. From televised trials and courtroom dramas most Americans are familiar with the main players—judges, prosecutors, defense attorneys, witnesses, defendants, and the jury—and the various roles they each play in the judicial process. Most people even understand important procedural aspects of trials: evidence, testimony, cross-examination, objections, closing arguments. Moreover, each year thousands of ordinary citizens serve on juries, gaining personal perspectives on the U.S. system of justice. Yet, the size, complexity, and often complicated rules of judicial procedure place the legal system beyond the comprehension of most laypersons.

According to American legal mythology (inherited from England), judges do not "make" the common law: it simply exists and they "discover" it as needed, applying it to resolve specific, concrete, individualized disputes. In reality, the common law is an evolving body of local or state law *made* by judges, who decide individual cases. In the process, these judges establish public policy on the basis of policy preferences, principles, precedents, and yes, political ideology. Policies are an *instrumental* or *purposive* influence on the common law; judges choose between alternative legal rules to fulfill preferred sociolegal goals. Principles are a *formal* influence on the common law; judges select from among alternative rules based on *reasons* and logical argument. And precedents are a *procedural* influence on the common law; judges decide cases as similar cases have been decided in the past, to ensure continuity and predictability. The influence of precedents, under the rule of *stare decisis* (literally: abide by that which was decided), enables individuals to organize their behavior in accordance with the law. Finally, it is clear that judges are sometimes influenced by personal political beliefs, however much they might try to withhold their personal preferences. Often enough the various forces of common law adjudication—policies, principles, precedents, and politics—push in the same direction; but when they diverge, the common law evolves in new directions.

It would be a mistake, however, to think of the common law as a single, unified body of law. Each sovereign state determines its own common law. Indeed, the common law can differ significantly from one state to another.

Many of the legal rules that govern socioeconomic activities in the United States have their roots in the common law. The common law subjects we will be most concerned with in this book—property, contracts, and torts—will be introduced in Chapters 5 through 12.

Statutory Law

The common law is a realm of *private* law, governing relations between individuals and resolving their disputes judicially. Private law contrasts with the realm of *public law*, which encompasses criminal and regulatory laws instituted by government (through legislative or administrative means) to organize societal relations.

The U.S. Constitution is, in a sense, the preeminent public law, a kind of *super statute* enacted by a specially appointed legislative body and approved by other specially appointed legislative bodies. The purpose of a constitution is not to resolve specific, individualized disputes between private parties, but to structure social relations. In addition to the federal constitution, each state has its own constitution, drafted by a constitutional commission and approved by the citizens in a referendum.

Aside from state and federal constitutions, public law is comprised of statutes enacted by federal or state legislatures and regulations promulgated under legislative authorization by administrative agencies. This type of lawmaking has roots in the civil law tradition, which is an older and more widespread tradition than the common law. It certainly is no less legitimate a source of law than the common law, although the first year of the law school curriculum focuses almost exclusively on common law subjects.

Today, one cannot adequately comprehend the common law without understanding legislative processes because so much of the common law has been subject to codification (legislative adaptation of common law rules) or legislative modification. No area of common law remains purely judicially determined. We inhabit an *administrative state*, where legal rules and institutions are predominantly determined by legislatures and their agencies, rather than by judges. To speak of the United States as a common law country is accurate as a matter of history and tradition, but at the dawn of the twenty-first century the common law is the smaller part of U.S. law.

In the middle of the nineteenth century, all the statutes of a state such as Indiana could fit within a single volume. "Today," according to the preeminent American legal historian Lawrence Friedman, "the collected statues of any state, even a small state, will be ten or twenty times that size."[11] The reasons for the explosion in legislation since the onset of the Industrial Revolution are varied, but one factor seems predominant: Society has become both more crowded and more complex. Consider just one technological change that altered the predominant mode of transportation in the late nineteenth and early twentieth centuries: the innovation of the internal combustion engine. The world of the automobile obviously requires not just *different* rules but *more* rules—of roads and road construction, and licensing requirements for various types of vehicles—than the world of the horse.

The Industrial Revolution also exacerbated existing social problems and out-stripped the ability of traditional common law remedies to cope, which led to legislative and regulatory responses. For example, the massive growth in industrial production in the nineteenth and twentieth centuries increased the number of pollution sources, the types and the total amounts of pollution. These changes made traditional common law remedies ineffectual in many cases, as plaintiffs found it increasingly difficult to prove that a particular defendant's pollution emissions caused a certain injury. Moreover, the transaction costs of effecting common law remedies increased dramatically, as pollution disputes involved more and more parties. First state and municipal governments, and later the federal government, responded with legislative schemes to regulate pollution emissions before the fact of harm.[12]

More recently, the innovation of e-commerce and other commercial and noncom-mercial uses of the Internet introduced an entirely new level of complexity to social interactions. In response, a whole new area of law called cyber law is in the process of development.

Not all of the growth in statutory and regulatory law is attributable to the increas-ing size and complexity of society, however. In many areas, legislatures simply substi-tuted their policy preferences for the common law determinations of judges. The entire area of criminal law, which used to be predominantly comprised of common law rules, is today thoroughly statutory. Worker's compensation statutes displaced the myriad of common law rules concerning industrial accidents that developed dur-ing the nineteenth century. Whether this shift in lawmaking from courts to legisla-tures is both legitimate and preferable is addressed in subsequent chapters.

To some extent, increases in legislative activity also develop as a self-perpetuating phenomenon of representative democracy. We elect representatives to state assemblies and the federal Congress and, as the eighteenth-century French mathematician Condorcet remarked, it is difficult to convince them of the benefits of doing nothing. All that they can do, as legislators, is enact, amend, or repeal laws. A legislator who did nothing while in office, supporting no new legislative proposals, would likely find it difficult to justify reelection to constituents. This motivation to legislate may contribute to problems of "government failure," as discussed in Chapter 1.

Administrative Law

According to the federal and state constitutions, only Congress and state legislatures can enact laws of general application. Legislatures, however, often enact statutes that are vague; and they never implement or administer statutes themselves. Such tasks are left for courts and, more frequently since the twentieth century, administrative agencies. Technically, administrative agencies are only supposed to implement and administer the laws enacted by the legislature. This implementation and administra-tion comes through promulgating "rules" that define terms, fill in statutory gaps, assign standards, establish deadlines, and so on. These rules carry the force of law (as long as they are promulgated under duly delegated legislative authority). In a real sense, then, administrative agencies *make* law.

The "laws" administrative agencies make are known as *regulations*. To carry legal force, every administrative regulation must be promulgated pursuant to an appropriately designed statutory authorization. An administrative agency cannot usurp the powers of Congress or a state legislative assembly. Once the legislature has delegated authority to it, however, the agency becomes, in effect, a mini-legislature. At the federal and state level, agency regulations comprise the most important body of legislatively created law. Even a long and complicated statute, such as the Clean Air Act, pales in size and complexity to the tens of thousands of pages of legally enforceable regulations that the Environmental Protection Agency has promulgated to implement the statute. Lawyers who practice in the field generally known as environmental law are concerned primarily with statutory provisions and administrative regulations; judicial decisions, for the most part, assume only secondary importance. The judicial role in the administrative process is primarily to ensure that administrative agencies are acting within the scope of their legislative authority. The courts also determine the legally binding interpretation of statutory language, but they typically defer to reasonable agency interpretations of their own enabling statutes.

Just as the Constitution is a *super statute* that rules over inconsistent statutes, so do statutes rule over regulations. Although regulations carry the "force of law," they are lesser laws, not on a par with duly enacted statutes. The legislature can, at its discretion, restrict, condition, or overrule a regulation, but an administrative agency may not alter the substance of statutes.

A Note on Local Custom: How Neighbors Settle Disputes

As already discussed, law is a *formal* set of institutions governing individual behavior and social interactions. It is supplemented, and sometimes overridden, by other *informal* institutions that may comprise alternative "rules of the game." Individuals and groups sometimes abjure the formal law in favor of informal mechanisms for resolving disputes, whether to avoid the expense of utilizing formal legal mechanisms or simply because they are accustomed to settling disputes in their own ways. Professor Robert Ellickson demonstrated this behavior in his 1991 study of how ranchers settle disputes in Shasta County, California.[13] He found that changes in the formal legal rules of cattle trespass (the invasion of one farmer's fields by another farmer's cattle) had virtually no effect on the way neighbors resolved actual disputes.

Even if neighbors sometimes reject formal legal mechanisms in favor of different community standards for resolving disputes, it does not mean the formal laws are without influence. Often they provide alternative approaches to dispute resolution and operate within "the shadow of the law." The formal law at least *influences* the ways in which neighbors settle disputes.

A few scholars contend, as a normative matter, that informal institutions can effectively substitute for formal legal mechanisms. In their view, formal laws may "crowd out" social norms that are at least equally effective, less expensive to enforce, and maybe more democratically legitimate.[14] Many others, however, doubt the ability of social norms to govern behavior in complex, heterogeneous societies.[15] Still others focus on complementarities and other interrelations between informal social norms and formal legal institutions.[16] We address some of the interactions between formal and informal institutions in subsequent chapters.

THE ORGANIZATION OF AMERICAN
LEGAL DECISION MAKING

The U.S. system of government is based on the concepts of federalism and dual sovereignty, which provide the foundation of the organizational structures of judicial and statutory lawmaking.

The State Court Systems

Trial Courts, Appellate Courts, and Special Courts

The American Bar Association (ABA) estimates that 98 percent of all litigation occurs in state courts.[17] No two states are quite the same, and their uniqueness is reflected in the structure of judicial administration, which differs from state to state. Figure 2-1 contains a diagram of the general structure of most states' court systems. In two-thirds of the states—typically more populous states—the court system has three levels, with a supreme court at the top, an intermediate appellate court beneath, and, at the bottom, a trial court. Specialized courts deal with certain common kinds of disputes, including probate of estates, traffic offenses, domestic relations, and juvenile crimes. The significance of these specialized courts should not be underestimated. Small claims courts, for example, process hundreds of thousands of legal claims each year. They are, in Lawrence Friedman's words, "the bargain basement of justice,"[18] providing inexpensive dispute resolution. It is noteworthy that these courts, which handle more legal disputes than any other, typically do not permit parties to be represented by attorneys.

The courts of general jurisdiction also process hundreds of thousands of cases each year, only a small percentage of which go to trial. Most cases either settle out of court or are disposed of on pretrial motions. In Virginia, fewer than 29 percent of the more than 254,000 cases filed in fiscal year 1999 were contested; and only 2 percent (fewer than 5,000) went to a jury trial. This figure includes both criminal cases brought by the state and privately filed civil lawsuits, which typically are processed in different divisions of the state court system. The high percentage of out-of-court settlements is undoubtedly due, in large measure, to the high costs of litigation. Most parties, both plaintiffs and defendants, would prefer to settle, or compromise, rather than bear the expense of litigating to an all-or-nothing conclusion.

State court judges may be popularly elected or appointed. Many states appoint a special nominating commission to select judges based on merit. In a few states, the governor or legislature exercises exclusive authority over judicial appointments. In a plurality of 21 states, however, judges are elected in either partisan or nonpartisan contests.

Pretrial and Trial Procedures

Civil Procedure. The process by which the state courts decide cases varies from the simple to the complex. The simplest judicial processes are usually found in small claims courts, where parties must represent themselves. Small claims courts have few procedural requirements prior to trial. Typically, the plaintiff must fill out some forms to file the suit, and also file a notarized affidavit swearing that they demanded compensation from the defendant prior to filing the suit. The plaintiff then must serve the defendant with the complaint and the summons. The defendant has a certain amount

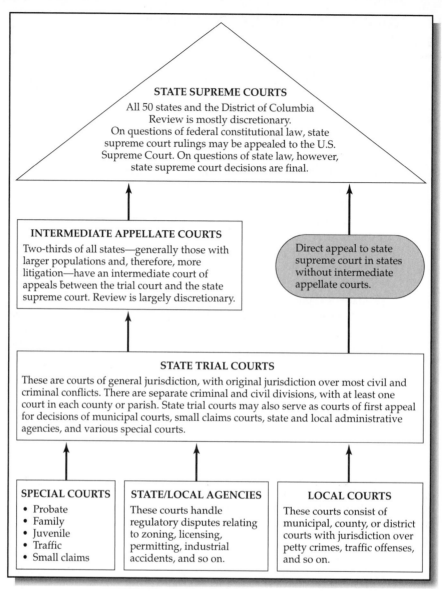

Figure 2-1 The State Court System

of time to respond by filing her answer with the court. Once the complaint and answer have been filed, a trial date is set. In many states, just prior to the actual trial the parties are required to meet in a conference room in the court to attempt to settle the dispute. If they cannot, then the judge will hear the case. No jury hears the cases in small claims court. Each party has 15 to 20 minutes to present his or her case. Sometimes the judge will take the case under advisement and issue a ruling within 30 days after the hearing. In other cases, the judge may issue a ruling from the bench immediately following the arguments. The judge's ruling ends most disputes brought in small claims courts, but aggrieved parties may appeal to the state trial courts for *de novo* review, that is, a brand new trial.

In contrast to small claims courts, the procedures in courts of general jurisdiction are complex. It is unclear whether this difference is a cause or effect of the involvement of lawyers. In any case, obtaining justice through the state courts of general jurisdiction tends to be far more expensive and time-consuming than litigating in small claims courts. Most states follow the Federal Rules of Civil Procedure, which means that trial and pretrial procedures are pretty much the same in the state court system as in the federal court system. Those procedures are discussed in the following subsection on the federal courts.

Criminal Procedure. Criminal cases follow different procedures from civil cases. In the first place, the state is almost always the named plaintiff in a criminal case, and public resources are dedicated to securing the defendant's conviction. Criminal cases begin, of course, with the arrest of the defendant. Once arrested, the defendant has a constitutional right to an attorney present for all police interrogations and at all phases of judicial proceedings from pretrial hearings to postconviction sentencing. Following the defendant's arrest, police and prosecutors gather evidence to present to the court at trial, although their scope for gathering evidence is constrained by the U.S. Constitution, which provides criminal defendants with a privilege against self-incrimination and prohibits unwarranted searches and seizures. The prosecutor will present the evidence to a *magistrate,* usually a judge, who determines whether the evidence is sufficient to send the case to trial. If not, the accused must be set free.

At trial, the prosecution bears the burden of proving to the satisfaction of the trier-of-fact—usually a jury in cases of serious offenses, but sometimes just the trial court judge—that the defendant committed the crime "beyond a reasonable doubt." The jury is responsible for determining the facts and applying the law as provided by the judge in "jury instructions" to those facts. Traditionally, the jury was comprised of 12 individuals, who had to reach their verdict unanimously to convict. Those requirements no longer obtain in most states. Some states allow conviction based on a super majority vote of, say, 9 out of 12 jurors. In other states, unanimity is required, but the jury may be composed of only 6 individuals. Constitutional guarantees of due process limit permissible combinations of jury size and voting requirements. It should be noted, however, that most criminal cases never make it to the jury. Most defendants plead guilty before or during the course of the trial, often in connection with "plea bargain" agreements entered into with the prosecutors.

Once a defendant pleads guilty or is convicted, the trial enters its sentencing phase. Criminal sentences, which may include fines, incarceration, or both, are determined by the judge in accordance with state criminal sentencing statutes. A defendant acquitted by the jury may not be retried again for the same offense. If convicted, the accused may make a motion for a new trial or file an appeal. Typical grounds for overturning a conviction on appeal include mistakes in admitting or excluding evidence and improper jury instructions.

Appellate Procedure
A small fraction of cases decided by municipal courts, specialized courts, and state district courts are appealed to higher-level courts. Most appeals are filed by "losers" at

trial, although "winners" (in civil conflicts) sometimes appeal if they are dissatisfied with the remedy granted by the trial court. The *appellant* (the party filing the appeal) alleges specific legal error(s) committed by the trial court judge, and the appellate court decides whether to review the case based on those allegations. Most states have an intermediate level of appeals courts between the trial court and the state supreme court. In some smaller states, the supreme court is the only appellate court.

The process on appeal differs substantially from the trial court process. It does not include witnesses; no new facts are presented; no jury is involved. An appellate court judge or, more typically, a panel of judges, reviews the record of the case to determine whether the trial court judge made the specific error(s) alleged by the appellant. If so, the panel may either *reverse* the trial court's decision, if the error is clearly determinative of the outcome, or *remand* (i.e., return) the case to the trial court for further proceedings consistent with the appellate court's decision. If the appeals court finds that the trial court did not make a legal error, it will *affirm* the trial court's decision.

In states with intermediate courts of appeals, the losing party in the appellate court may appeal again to the state's supreme court. However, the state supreme court may choose not to hear the case; the system does not provide for appeal by right. Partly for this reason, few state court decisions actually reach the state supreme court. In 1999, the Virginia Supreme Court granted just 223 of the 2,075 petitions for appeal from decisions of its intermediate appellate courts.

After a decision by the state's supreme court, just one further possible appeal remains, to the U.S. Supreme Court. Only state law cases with important federal constitutional implications can be appealed, or "petitioned," to the U.S. Supreme Court, and the Court's review is discretionary, unless the state law at issue holds unconstitutional some federal law.

The Federal Courts of the United States

Trial Courts, Appellate Courts, and the Supreme Court

The structure of federal court system, diagrammed in Figure 2-2, largely replicates the three-tier system of the larger states. At the bottom of the federal court pyramid is the "district" court. Every state has at least one federal district court; larger states have more than one. In total, the 94 federal district courts of the United States have original jurisdiction over most cases arising under federal law (the U.S. Constitution, statutes enacted by Congress, and subsidiary regulations), as well as cases under state law between citizens of different states when substantial sums are at stake. Currently, the amount in controversy necessary to assert this "diversity jurisdiction" is $75,000. Diversity jurisdiction gives plaintiffs a choice between using the federal courts and the courts of the defendant's home state. The purpose is to avert the possibility that the defendant's state court might be biased in favor of its own resident against a "foreign" plaintiff.

The 94 federal district courts are organized geographically into 12 circuits,[19] each of which is presided over by a U.S. Circuit Court of Appeals. Parties aggrieved by federal district court rulings have a right to appeal to the circuit court, though appeals are relatively rare. In 2000, federal appeals courts disposed of nearly 55,000 cases, compared to the almost 260,000 civil and criminal cases arising in the federal district courts.

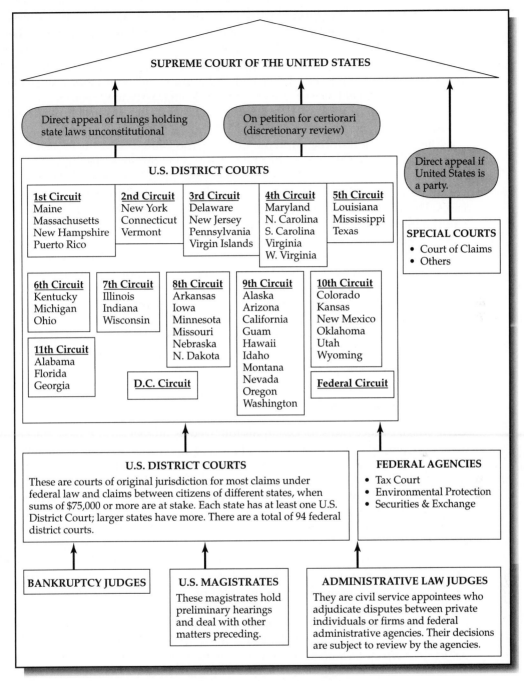

Figure 2-2 The Federal Courts of the United States

The federal circuit courts of appeals, like state intermediate appellate courts, do not review cases *de novo*; they do not replay the entire trial. Appellants raise specific issues on appeal—alleged mistakes committed by the trial court judge. A panel of three appellate court judges bases its decision to affirm, reverse, or remand the district court's ruling on written briefs and oral arguments about those precise allegations. After the panel has issued its ruling, the losing party may seek *en banc* review before all of that circuit's appeals court judges. Parties do not have to seek *en banc* review, however, before appealing to the U.S. Supreme Court.

The jurisdiction of the Supreme Court of the United States is more extensive under federal than state law. With a few important exceptions, the Supreme Court's jurisdiction is discretionary. Technically speaking, most cases are not "appealed" to the Supreme Court; instead, aggrieved parties "petition" the Court to hear their cases. The Court accepts only about 1 percent of these petitions. In its 1999 term, the Court agreed to hear just 83 out of more than 7,300 cases filed. The U.S. Supreme Court does not have complete discretion over its docket, however. Article III, Section 2(2) of the U.S. Constitution gives the Court "original" jurisdiction in cases "affecting Ambassadors, other public Ministers and Consuls, and those in which a State shall be a Party." When one state or Indian tribe sues another state on issues concerning the reach of its sovereignty or jurisdiction, the U.S. Supreme Court operates like a trial court.

In contrast to most state court judges, *all* judges of the federal courts of the United States are appointed for life, upon nomination by the president and confirmation by the Senate.

Federal Trial Procedures

Civil Trials.   Procedures for civil trials followed by all federal and most state courts are set out in the Federal Rules of Civil Procedure. A civil suit begins when the plaintiff files a complaint (the filing fee in federal court is $150) and "serves" notice on the defendant. The defendant then has a certain amount of time to file an "answer," which usually disputes the plaintiff's claim.[20] If the court agrees, it will issue a *judgment on the pleadings* in favor of the defendant.

Before the trial gets underway, the litigants engage in discovery, requesting documents and other information from each other and determining the identity of witnesses, in preparation of the case for trial. One common discovery device is the *deposition* in which witnesses are required to answer questions under oath and in the presence of a court reporter. Parties may also file pretrial motions, for instance seeking judicial rulings concerning the propriety of certain discovery requests. They may even make a pretrial motion for *summary judgment*, or a determination by the court that the defendant is, or is not, liable. On the other hand, the parties may agree to a settlement, which terminates the contest before it gets to trial. If the parties do not settle and summary judgment is either not requested or deemed unwarranted, the court will schedule a trial.

Most of us have a pretty fair idea of how trials progress from watching television courtroom dramas. The trier-of-fact, whether the jury or the judge, takes evidence from the witnesses presented by each side, who are examined and cross-examined by the respective attorneys.

When all the evidence has been presented, the attorneys for each party present their closing arguments, summing up the evidence in the light most favorable to their client. After that, the judge instructs the jury about the relevant law to apply, and charges the jury with the questions it must answer. Generally speaking, the judge will ask the jury to determine whether the defendant is more likely than not (by a preponderance of the evidence) responsible for harming the plaintiff and, if so, what the remedy should be. In trials without a jury, the judge makes all these determinations.

Criminal Trials.   The criminal trial process in the federal courts is, in most respects, similar to the process in the state courts (recounted on page 35), but with a few important exceptions. First and foremost, many federal cases arise not from arrest but from indictment by a *grand jury*.[21] Interpretation of the Fifth Amendment to the U.S. Constitution requires a grand jury indictment for virtually all felonies under federal law. A grand jury—the name signifies the number of jurors, which ranges between 16 and 23 members (in contrast to the *petit* or regular trial jury, which numbers between 6 and 12)—proceeding is not a trial, but may appear quite similar. The U.S. attorney presents evidence to the grand jury, which decides whether enough evidence exists to warrant a trial. Grand jury procedures are quite different from actual trials, and parties subpoenaed to appear before the grand jury are not afforded all the same protections that they possess in a trial court. For example, the federal rules of evidence do not apply in grand jury hearings. The prosecutor, who is, in essence, in charge of the proceedings, has far greater latitude in seeking an indictment from the grand jury than in seeking a conviction in court.

Another difference between federal and state criminal proceedings concerns the right of appeal. Several states enshrine a right to appeal criminal convictions in their state constitutions. Section 22 of the State of Washington's constitution, for example, provides convicted persons with "the right to appeal in all cases." No similar right appears in the U.S. Constitution. However, federal legislation ensures those convicted under federal law one appeal to the U.S. Court of Appeals. Neither state nor criminal convictions may be appealed as of right to the U.S. Supreme Court.

State and Federal Legislative and Regulatory Bodies and Processes

According to an old aphorism, no one who likes laws or sausages should ever watch either being made. The legislative process can be messy, cumbersome, and unappetizing; the final product often bears little resemblance to what was initially intended. That said, the lawmaking process itself is regular enough, differing only in minor respects from one state to another. The federal system for enacting laws and regulations resembles state systems in most particulars. In both cases, laws are enacted by a designated legislative body and signed into law by the executive. This process is complicated by the complex structure of committees and subcommittees. The U.S. Congress has some 250 committees and subcommittees, although the number of committees with regular legislative jurisdiction is smaller. In 2001, the Senate had 16 standing committees and 69 subcommittees with regular legislative oversight responsibilities. The State of Arizona's House of Representatives, by comparison, has 17 standing committees. Figure 2-3 shows the State of Ohio's legislative process.

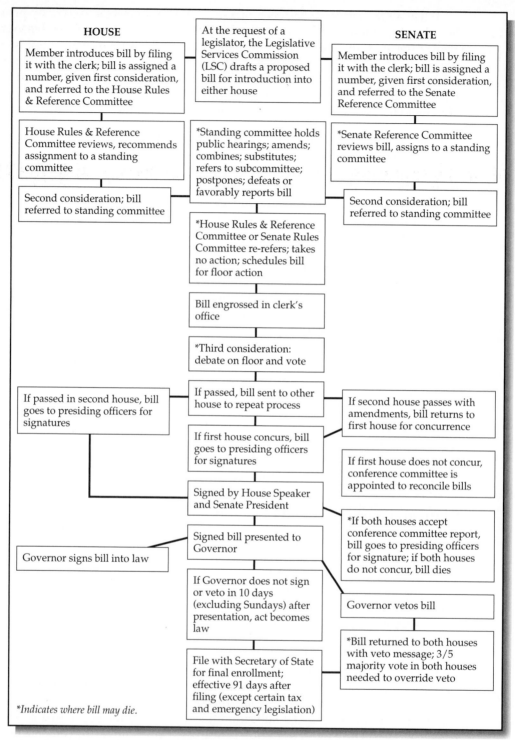

Figure 2-3 How a Bill Becomes Law in Ohio

The process by which a bill becomes law is similar at federal and state levels. In Congress, when a bill is first introduced into the House or the Senate, the clerk assigns it a title and a number. This introduction constitutes the *first reading* of the bill, which is then referred by the leadership of the majority party to the appropriate committee. The committee may *table* the bill, immediately killing it, or assign it to one of its subcommittees for public hearings. After those hearings, members of the subcommittee will debate the bill and possible amendments, and then vote on whether to recommend committee approval. When the bill comes back from the subcommittee, the full committee will debate it and any proposed amendments, and vote to either kill the bill or send it to the floor of the house for a final vote. If they send it to the floor, the clerk will read the bill as amended a second time. All members of the house then have an opportunity to debate the legislation and propose amendments. In the House of Representatives, the time period for deliberation is limited by the *cloture rule*. The Senate does not use a cloture rule; 60 votes are required to terminate deliberation and call the vote. After deliberations are closed, and legislators are ready to vote, the clerk will give the bill (as amended) its *third reading* (this time, just the title). The bill is put to a final vote. If the bill is approved, it then moves to the other house of Congress for consideration, where a similar process ensues.

It is relatively rare for both houses to approve a bill in precisely the same form; often, some amendments are made in one house that were not made in the other. So, after approval, the two (substantially similar but not identical) bills must reconciled. Both houses appoint members to a joint *conference committee* for the reconciliation process. Once the bills are reconciled, each house of Congress must approve the final product. This time, no amendments are allowed; it is a straight up or down vote. If the final version of the bill is approved by both the House and Senate, it will be sent to the president. If the president signs it, it becomes law. The president does not have to sign the bill, however, for it to become law. If the president does nothing, the bill will automatically become law after 10 days (not including Sundays). Should Congress adjourn during that 10-day period, however, the bill dies. This method is known as a *pocket veto*. The president may also affirmatively veto the bill by refusing to sign it and returning it, along with reasons for the veto, to the originating house of Congress. A presidential veto may or may not kill the bill, depending on the strength of support for the legislation in Congress. If two-thirds of senators and representatives vote to approve the measure, they *override* the president's veto, and the bill will become law.

The legislative process is regulated by the committee structure of federal and state assemblies. More than 90 percent of legislative proposals introduced in Congress never make it out of committee for a floor vote. Still, the 435 members of the House of Representatives and 100 senators in Congress produce an astounding amount of legislation each term. In 2000, of 4,247 bills introduced into the 2d Session of the 106th Congress, 410 new public laws were enacted. State legislative assemblies are hardly less productive. In its 1998 legislative session, the Virginia General Assembly approved 908 of the 2,945 bills it considered.

Congress and state legislatures are the most recognizable lawmaking bodies in society, but the statutes they produce are just the tip of the legislative and regulatory iceberg. Federal and state administrative agencies promulgate thousands of rules and regulations each year, which carry the force of law (pursuant to statutory authorization). Closer to home, local government bodies, including city councils, boards of supervisors, zoning boards, county councils, school districts, and park districts, contribute their share to society's body of law. In the 1990s, the State of California was home to nearly 5,000 local bodies with substantial law- or rule-making authority. In 1999, the Chicago City Council, which has 50 members and 19 standing committees (down from 27 in the year 1900), processed exactly 300 municipal ordinances.

In sum, the legal system involves far more than the criminal and common law courts. We inhabit a regulatory state. Our lives are affected on a daily basis by innumerable laws and the agencies that administer them. Most significantly for purposes of this book, these laws and regulations impose costs and benefits on society, creating, altering, and sometimes distorting the incentives of economic actors.

CHAPTER SUMMARY

This chapter provided a basic introduction to the legal system, including the principle of the rule of law; the distinction between criminal and civil law; the distinction between common (judge-made) law and civil (statutory) law; the nature of legal rights and duties; institutional and organizational sources of law; and the structure of legal decision making and enforcement in the United States.

QUESTIONS AND PROBLEMS

1. Is law necessary for economic exchange? If so, how?
2. What does Douglass North mean when he talks about law as "the rules of the game"?
3. How do formal laws relate to informal social norms?
4. Why is the law-making process, as described in the flowchart in Figure 2-3, so complicated?
5. How does law help to overcome the socioeconomic problem of scarcity?
6. What distinguishes the common law from legislation?
7. Define the "rule of law".
8. What constitutes the legal system?

NOTES

1. Werner Z. Hirsch, *Law and Economics: An Introductory Analysis*, 3rd ed. (New York: Academic Press, 1999), p. 2.
2. Oliver Wendell Holmes, "The Theory of Torts," 7 AMERICAN LAW REVIEW 652 (1873).
3. Douglass C. North, *Institutions, Institutional Change and Economic Performance* (Cambridge: Cambridge University Press, 1990), pp. 3–6.

4. The formal law does not comprise all of the rules of the game, however. Also included, and addressed in this chapter, are customs and informal social norms.
5. *See* Lawrence M. Friedman, *American Law: An Introduction*, rev. ed. (New York: Random House, 1998).
6. *See, e.g.,* John Locke (C. B. Macpherson, ed.), *Second Treatise of Government* (Indianapolis, IN:

Hackett Publishing Company, 1980), p. 68; Aleksandr Zinoviev, *The Yawning Heights* (New York: Random House, 1979), pp. 574–75. Rawls more generally requires "some form of due process" for the rule of law. John Rawls, *A Theory of Justice* (Boston: Harvard University Press, 1971), p. 399.

7. Joseph Raz, "The Rule of Law and Its Virtue," 93 Law Quarterly Review 195, 201 (1977).

8. This distinction between criminal and civil laws should not be confused with the distinction between the civil law tradition and the common law tradition. That later distinction goes to the source of law, rather than the type of law.

9. For example, the public nuisance lawsuit is a civil action, but it seeks to correct for general harm to society.

10. One state, Louisiana, is not a common law jurisdiction. Because of its historical ties to France, Louisiana is a civil law jurisdiction.

11. Lawrence M. Friedman, *American Law: An Introduction*, rev. ed. (New York: Random House, 1998), p. 111.

12. For more on the evolution from common law to statutory remedies for pollution problems, see Chapter 15.

13. Robert Ellickson, *Order Without Law: How Neighbors Settle Disputes* (Boston: Harvard University Press, 1994).

14. *See, for example*, Larry E. Ribstein, "Law v. Trust," 81 Boston University Law Review 553 (2001).

15. *See, for example*, David Charny, "Illusions of a Spontaneous Order: 'Norms' in Contractual Relations," 144 University of Pennsylvania Law Review 1841 (1996); Eric Posner, *Law and Social Norms* (Boston: Harvard University Press, 2000).

16. *See, for example*, Lawrence Lessig, "The Regulation of Social Meaning," 62 University of Chicago Law Review 943 (1995); Cass Sunstein, "Social Norms and Social Roles," 96 Columbia Law Review 903 (1996); Richard A. Posner, *Frontiers of Legal Theory* (Boston: Harvard University Press, 2001), pp. 302–06.

17. American Bar Association, Division for Media Relations and Public Affairs, *Facts About The American Judicial System* 1 (1999).

18. Lawrence M. Friedman, *American Law: An Introduction*, rev. ed. (New York: Random House, 1998), p. 76.

19. A thirteenth "circuit" court of appeals—the "federal circuit"—has nationwide jurisdiction over appeals of patent cases, and decisions of the courts of Federal Claims (which has jurisdiction in cases with claims of money damages against the U.S. government) and International Trade (which has jurisdiction over trade and customs cases).

20. In some cases a defendant may acknowledge the harm suffered by the plaintiff but claim no legal liability. The defendant is said to "demur" to the plaintiff's complaint.

21. All states provide a grand jury mechanism, but only a few states make regular use of it.

Chapter 3

Putting Law and Economics Together: Frameworks, History, and Perspectives

ECONOMIC AND LEGAL FRAMEWORKS

Economics and the law share the ultimate concern of organizing human behavior with respect to scarce resources. Economic markets and legal institutions are often thought of as alternative mechanisms for allocating entitlements to scarce resources among competing uses and users. They are not *just* alternatives, however, they are also closely intertwined. Legal rules are often (though not always) designed to facilitate commerce. Meanwhile, economic markets are shaped by formal (and informal) legal institutions, including property rights and freedom of contract, along with legal organizations, such as courts, to protect and enforce contracts and property rights.

The combined field of law and economics studies how legal institutions, and changes in those institutions, affect economic behavior. At the same time, of course, market relations can and do influence legal institutions and policies. History demonstates that legal systems change in response to pressures from market participants. Thus, law and economics also studies the role of economics in constructing (and reconstructing) the legal system. But law and economics is not just a *positive* discipline that describes how the economy and legal institutions interrelate. A good deal of scholarship in this area is *normative*. Normative law and economics argues for certain legal and economic institutions to maximize some function, be it utility, wealth, liberty, community, or some other desired end. It is a fundamental premise of normative law and economics that some institutions and policies are better (i.e., more efficient) than others. In studying law and economics, therefore, we must attend to both positive accounts and normative assertions concerning legal institutions affecting the economy and economic constraints on law.

In sum, this textbook is about the various ways law and economics can and do interact—sometimes symbiotically, sometimes competitively—to allocate scarce resources in society.

What Economic Analysis Offers to Legislators, Judges, and Legal Scholars

The easiest way to illustrate the importance of economic analysis to legal policy making, enforcement, and analysis is by examining what happens when legal policy makers ignore economic principles. The result can be misguided legal policies, with consequences that deviate dramatically from policy makers' intentions. Consider the following two examples of credit rate ceilings and rent control ordinances.

Credit Rate Ceilings

State governments sometimes intervene in credit markets, imposing ceilings on interest rates, in order to protect consumers from unfair and discriminatory lending practices. Almost always, these credit ceilings are motivated by real concern for the interests of consumers. Just as often, however, they have consequences that harm those very consumers.

In many cases, states set ceilings on interest rates in response to studies showing that residents of low-income neighborhoods pay more for credit in the form of higher interest rates than residents of wealthier neighborhoods. If and when these disparities reflect monopoly profits or discrimination against insular minorities, they are reprehensible and should be curtailed by government action. Sometimes, however, lenders have legitimate business reasons for charging differential interest rates for consumer credit, which have nothing to do with unlawful discriminatory motives or an ability to earn excess profits. Scant evidence exists to support claims that lenders in low-income communities earn excessive profits. To the contrary, a Federal Trade Commission (FTC) study found that "'low-income retailers earn *substantially less* on invested capital than general market retailers."[1] This finding suggests something of a paradox: creditors in low-income areas charge higher interest rates but earn lower profits. How can that be?

To economists, the answer is simple: the costs of lending in low-income areas are higher because lenders face higher default rates. It's not that poor individuals are inherently less reliable than others, but they are more susceptible to unexpected fiscal "shocks" that might prevent them from repaying loans or keeping up with payments for merchandise purchased on credit. As an empirical matter, rates of default tend to be higher in poor communities. Lenders respond to this higher risk in three possible ways: (1) refuse to lend to individuals in low-income communities; (2) charge those individuals higher interest rates; or (3) "pool" risks by charging *all* customers marginally higher interest rates so that low-risk borrowers subsidize higher-risk borrowers. The third option is unrealistic, however, because a lender that pooled risks would likely lose low-risk customers to other lenders that charged those customers lower interest rates. Competitive pressures, in essence, force lenders to differentiate rates between high-risk and low-risk loans. This practice is emphatically *not* a sign of market failure, however. It is a rational response to the higher risks of lending in low-income communities with higher rates of default.

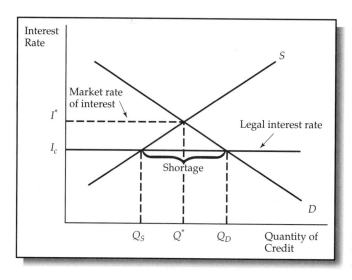

Figure 3-1
Credit-Rate Ceilings
Create Credit
Shortages

When the state introduces a law that sets a ceiling on the interest rates lenders can charge, purportedly to protect consumers, that law may result in certain unintended and undesirable consequences. If the credit rate ceiling is set below the rate of interest that reflects the actual risk of default, reputable lenders will simply withdraw from the market. Loans previously available at a relatively high interest rate will no longer be available. This scenario is reflected in Figure 3-1, which illustrates how credit rate ceilings lead to shortages in credit availability.

As legitimate lenders exit the market, "loan sharks" and other "black market" operators may take their place. Because these replacement lenders operate outside the law, they will not be constrained by the legislated interest rate ceiling. The rates of interest they charge will be even higher than preceiling interest rates, reflecting the higher risks they face, not so much from default as from law enforcement. In the end, the state-imposed credit ceiling will not accomplish its intended purpose. Instead of protecting low-income borrowers from high rates of interest, it will reduce the availability of credit, and replace reputable creditors with loan sharks who end up charging borrowers even higher interest rates.

A skeptic might note that the predictions of economic theory don't always come true—things happen differently in the real world; but not in this case. Empirical studies of credit rate ceilings—specifically, the "6 percent usury laws" that were widely legislated in the United States during the first part of the twentieth century—bear out the predictions of economic theory. Legitimate creditors, who could not afford to lend at rates below the ceiling because of the costs of lending exited the market and were replaced by loan sharks, until states repealed the usury laws. Had lawmakers paid attention to economic theory prior to enacting the usury laws, they may have avoided harming the consumers they were trying to help.

The moral of this story is *not* that government can only make matters worse. Under some circumstances, consumer protection legislation, regulation, or common law remedies are useful, even necessary, to protect consumers from fraud, racial discrimination, and other pernicious practices. The government may even play a limited role in reducing interest rates for consumers in low-income areas. It might, for example, initiate a public information campaign to reduce the default rate, which in turn would reduce interest rates. Government might even subsidize the credit market in low-income communities by providing direct low-interest loans, just as it subsidizes other economic sectors and social groups. The real moral of the story is that economic analysis can usefully inform legal policy making and avoid making bad situations worse.

Rent Control

The economic arguments against credit rate ceilings also apply to rent control ordinances, which were prevalent throughout the United States between World War II and the 1980s. Rent control came in many shapes and sizes: some ordinances simply restricted the rate of return landlords could earn from rents on their investments; others contained complicated regulations. One Chicago rent control ordinance required landlords to pay interest on tenants' security deposits; forbade landlords to charge a late fee of more than $10; authorized tenants to deduct the cost of repairs from their rent payments; and created a presumption that any attempted eviction of a tenant was in retaliation for the tenant's legitimate assertion of rights. In 1987, the U.S. Court of Appeals for the Seventh Circuit (in Chicago) upheld the constitutionality of this ordinance. The immediately interesting aspect of that case, however, is Judge Richard Posner's concurring opinion, which explains that even if the ordinance was constitutional, it was bad policy.

Chicago Board of Realtors, Inc. v. Chicago
819 F. 2d 732 (7th Cir. 1987)

Posner, C.J. (concurrence):

The stated purpose of the ordinance is to promote public health, safety, and welfare and the quality of housing in Chicago. It is . . . not the likely effect. Forbidding landlords to charge interest at market rates on late payment of rent could hardly be thought calculated to improve the health, safety, and welfare of Chicagoans or to improve the quality of the housing stock. But it may have the opposite effect. The initial consequence of the rule will be to reduce the resources that landlords devote to improving the quality of housing, by making the provision of rental housing more costly. Landlords will try to offset the higher cost (in time value of money, less predictable cash flow, and, probably, higher rate of default) by raising rents. To the extent they succeed, tenants will be worse off, or at least no better off. Landlords will also screen applicants more carefully, because the cost of renting to a deadbeat will now be higher; so marginal tenants will find it harder to persuade landlords to rent to them. Those who do find apartments but then are slow to pay will be subsidized by responsible tenants (some of them marginal too), who will be paying higher rents, assuming the landlord cannot determine in advance who is likely to pay rent on time. Insofar as these efforts to offset the ordinance fail, the cost of rental housing will be higher to landlords and therefore less will be supplied—more of the existing stock than would otherwise be the case will be converted to condominia and cooperatives and less rental housing will be built.

***

The ordinance is not in the interest of poor people. As is frequently the case with legislation ostensibly designed to promote the welfare of the poor, the principal beneficiaries will be middle-class people. They will be people who buy rather than rent housing (the conversion of rental to owner housing will reduce the price of the latter by increasing its supply); people willing to pay a higher rental for better-quality housing; and (a largely overlapping group) more affluent tenants, who will become more attractive to landlords because such tenants are less likely to be late with the rent or to abuse the right of withholding rent—a right that is more attractive, the poorer the tenant. The losers from the ordinance will be some landlords . . . the poorest class of tenants, and future tenants.

***

A growing body of empirical literature deals with the effects of governmental regulation of the market for rental housing. The regulations that have been studied, such as rent control in New York City and Los Angeles, are not identical to the new Chicago ordinance, though some—regulations which require that rental housing be "habitable"—are close. The significance of this literature is not in proving that the Chicago ordinance is unsound, but in showing that the market for rental housing behaves as economic theory predicts: if price is artificially depressed, or the costs of landlords artificially increased, supply falls and many tenants, usually the poorer and the newer tenants, are hurt. [Citations omitted.] The single proposition in economics from which there is the least dissent among American economists is that "a ceiling on rents reduces the quantity and quality of housing available." [Citation omitted.] ■

***

Note that the court, in *Chicago Board of Realtors,* did not invalidate the city's rent control ordinance. A court cannot invalidate a statute simply because it is a bad economic policy. Judges can only invalidate duly enacted statutes if they are contrary to state or federal constitutions. In this case, the court found no constitutional grounds for invalidating the rent control ordinance. Nevertheless, Judge Posner's concurrence emphasizes why it is important for lawmakers to understand basic economic principles.

Judges Need to Know Economics Too

Unlike Judge Posner, many judges seem as blissfully unaware of basic economic principles and human behavior as the legislators who enact usury and rent control laws. However, judges, too, make policy in resolving common law disputes. Consider the role of economics in the following case, and how a better understanding of economic principles on the part of the judge might have led to a different result.

In *Baker v. Weedon,*[2] the plaintiff, Anna Weedon, an elderly life tenant,[3] living on a farm left to her by her late husband John, asked the court to allow her to sell the farmland so that she might live off the proceeds. The reason she had to ask the court's permission was that, as a life tenant, she did not own the farmland outright; her ownership interest was limited. She had the right to possess it, use it, exclude others from it, and derive income from it for the rest of her life. Upon her death, the farmland would be owned by the *remaindermen*—her late husband's three grandchildren from a previous marriage. She could do nothing to the farmland that might prejudice their future (but not yet possessory) interest without their permission or a court order. And they didn't want her to sell any of the farmland. So, she sought a court order that would allow her to sell the land over their objections, which explains how the dispute came to court.

The reason Anna Weedon wanted to sell the land, and the grandchildren didn't, was largely economic, as the court explains in its decision:

Baker v. Weedon
262 So. 2d 641 (Miss. 1972)

Patterson, J.

***

Anna ceased to operate the farm in 1955 due to her age and it has been rented since that time. Anna's only income is $1000 annually from the farm rental, $300 per year from sign rental and $50 per month by way of social security payments. Without contradiction Anna's income is presently insufficient and places a severe burden upon her ability to live comfortably in view of her age and the infirmities therefrom.

In 1964 the growth of the City of Corinth was approaching Oakland Farm. A right-of-way through the property was sought by the Mississippi State Highway Department for the construction of U.S. Highway 45 bypass. The highway department located Florence Baker's three children, the contingent remaindermen by the will of John Weedon, to negotiate with them for the purchase of the right-of-way. . . .

Until the notice afforded by the highway department the grandchildren were unaware of their possible inheritance. Henry Baker [one of the grandchildren] . . . journeyed to Mississippi to supervise their interests. He appears, as was true of the other grandchildren to have been totally sympathetic to the conditions surrounding Anna's existence as a life tenant. A settlement of $20,000 was completed for the right-of-way bypass of which Anna received $7500 with which to construct a new home. It is significant that all legal and administrative fees were deducted from the shares of the three grandchildren and not taxed to the life tenant. A contract was executed in 1970 for the sale of soil from the property for $2500. Anna received $1000 of this sum which went toward completion of payments for the home.

There was substantial evidence introduced to indicate the value of the property is appreciating significantly with the nearing completion of U.S. Highway 45 bypass plus the growth of the city of Corinth. While the commercial value of the property is appreciating, it is notable that the rental value for agricultural purposes is not. It is apparent that the land can bring no more for agricultural rental purposes than the $1000 per year now received.

The value of the property for commercial purposes at the time of trial was $168,500. Its estimated value within the ensuing four years is placed at $336,000, reflecting the great influence of the interstate construction upon the land. Mr. Baker, for himself and other remaindermen, appears to have made numerous honest and sincere efforts to sell the property at a favorable price. However, his endeavors have been hindered by the slowness of the construction of the bypass.

Anna, the life tenant and appellee here, is 73 years of age and although now living in a new home, has brought this suit due to her economic distress. She prays that the property, less the house site, be sold by a commissioner and that the proceeds be invested to provide her with an adequate income resulting from the interest on the trust investment. . . .

[The chancellor below had ruled in favor of Anna. The Supreme Court, while recognizing its equitable authority to do as Anna wishes, reverses and remands the case to the chancellor, with the instruction that he allow Anna to sell only so much of the land as necessary to provide for her "reasonable needs."]

Our decision to reverse the chancellor and remand the case for his further consideration is couched in our belief that the best interest of all the parties would not be served by a judicial sale of the entirety of the property at this time. While true that such a sale would provide immediate relief to the life tenant who is worthy of this aid in equity, admitted by the remaindermen, it would nevertheless under the circumstances before us cause great financial loss to the remaindermen. ■

***

The court's conclusion—that the remaindermen would suffer a "great financial loss" if the entire farm were sold immediately—is questionable. In his opinion, Judge Patterson expresses great confidence in present- and future-value estimates of the farm, but with little justification. Economic theory suggests that any reasonably expected increase in the value of land should be revealed in present market prices.[4] Not only will the seller demand a higher price to reflect the expected value increase, but potential buyers will pay more for the land than they otherwise would. According to theory, Mr. Baker should have been able to sell the land for a price that fairly reflected the expected increase in value from completion of the highway.

Evidently, Judge Patterson did not understand how markets determine land values. He concluded that, despite "numerous and sincere efforts," Mr. Baker was unable "to sell the property at a favorable price." But "favorable" to whom? The market price of land must be "favorable" to both the seller and some potential buyer. The fact that no buyer was willing to pay Mr. Baker's price may have had nothing to do with the speed of highway construction, as the judge surmises. Judge Patterson never considers the possibility that Mr. Baker's asking price was excessive, highway or no highway; it certainly was higher than any potential buyer was willing to pay. Mr. Baker's expected valuation of the land *after* highway completion may have exceeded the expected valuations of all potential buyers.

Perhaps Mr. Baker's valuation was accurate (real estate markets *are* sometimes illiquid), but that could only be known after highway completion. Anyway, it was his subjective valuation of the farm, and isn't that what counts? The problem is, he and the other remaindermen were not the sole owners of the land. Anna Weedon was also an owner, and her subjective valuation of the land differed from Mr. Baker's. The court ruling subjugated her subjective valuation to that of the remaindermen.

Mr. Baker was perfectly willing to wait four years to validate his own subjective valuation. After all, he had little to lose by delaying the sale of the land. Apparently, he had no immediate need for the money; and even if his valuation turned out to be overly optimistic, he would still obtain the actual market value of the land, which he did not expect to decline in the meantime. His share of the proceeds from the later sale might even be higher, if, in the interim, his elderly step-grandmother passed away. It was an easy gamble for Mr. Baker to take, given that Anna Weedon bore the lion's share of the risk from delaying the sale.

The crux of the matter is whether the court should have gone along with Mr. Baker's gamble, to the manifest disadvantage of the poor life tenant, Anna Weedon, who was, after all, the primary object of her late husband's concern and beneficence. Had Judge Patterson understood economic theory and, in particular, how present market prices capture expected future benefits, he might have issued a different, more just ruling.

The court ameliorated the injustice of its ruling by authorizing the sale of as much land as necessary to provide for Anna's "reasonable needs." But this raises questions about what constitutes her "reasonable needs," and who decides. Are Anna's "reasonable needs" now to be determined by a court? And what if her needs change? Will the court order more land sold later? In light of the dubious economics of the remaindermen's valuation of the land, the court's equitable solution hardly seems preferable to an immediate, outright sale of all the land, with the proceeds invested for the present benefit of Anna and the future benefit of the remaindermen.

Limitations of the Economic Approach to Law

It is one thing to assert that lawyers, legal scholars, and legal policy makers ought to understand and pay attention to economic principles. It would be another to assert that economics completely explains, or should govern, legal decision making. Economics alone cannot explain or determine law because the purview of law is broader than that of economics. It is true that economics and law have the same ultimate goal—to maximize social welfare—but disagreement immediately arises with the effort to define and measure "social welfare."

Although economists explain the maximization of social welfare through the concept of utility, in practice they typically use the notion of efficient production, the largest possible output with the fewest inputs, and measure the value of this output to determine whether "social welfare" is increasing. This efficiency proxy, which Coase refers to as "the measure of money," gives economists the advantage over other social sciences of precision in analyzing human behavior.[5] No other social science has a comparable "objective" basis for assessing individuals' subjective values and analyzing their behavior in the world. Most economists, however, realize that efficiency remains only an imperfect proxy for social welfare.

For law, efficiency never acts as the sole determinant of social welfare. Equitable and moral considerations hold equal, or greater, importance. The goal of law traditionally lay not in the efficient society, but the just society. Even though efficiency and justice are not mutually exclusive, neither are they always hand-in-glove.

That "justice" is not reducible to "efficiency" is uncontroversial, even among proponents of the economic approach to law, as the following excerpt from Judge Richard A. Posner makes clear:

Richard A. Posner, Economic Analysis of Law

5th Ed. (New York: Aspen Publishers 1998), pp. 30–31

The economic approach to law is criticized for ignoring "justice." One must distinguish between the different meanings of this word. Sometimes it means distributive justice, the proper degree of economic equality. Although economists cannot tell society what that degree is, they have much to say that is relevant—about the actual amounts of inequality in different societies and in different periods, about the difference between real economic inequality and inequalities in pecuniary income that merely offset cost differences or reflect different positions in the life cycle, and about the costs of achieving great equality. . . .

A second meaning of justice, perhaps the most common, is—efficiency. We shall see, among other examples, that when people describe as unjust convicting a person without a trial, taking property without just compensation, or failing to make a negligent automobile driver answer in damages to the victim of his negligence, this means nothing more pretentious than that the conduct wastes resources. Even the principle of unjust enrichment can be derived from the concept of efficiency. And with a little reflection, it will come as no surprise that in a world of scarce resources waste should be regarded as immoral.

But there is more to notions of justice than a concern with efficiency. It is not obviously inefficient to allow suicide pacts; to allow private discrimination on racial, religious, or sexual grounds; to permit killing and eating of the weakest passenger of the lifeboat in circumstances of genuine desperation; to force people to give self-incriminating testimony; to flog prisoners; to allow babies to be sold for adoption; to allow the use of deadly force in defense of a pure property interest; to legalize blackmail; or to give convicted felons a choice between imprisonment and participation in dangerous medical experiments. Yet all those things offend the sense of justice of modern Americans, and all are to greater or lesser (usually greater) extent illegal. . . . [T]here is more to justice than economics. ■

Judge Posner points out that were efficiency the sole goal of law, some activities that currently are illegal, such as prostitution and cocaine trafficking, would likely be legal. Yet they remain illegal because the law, in contrast to economic theory, does not take efficiency as the lone proxy for social welfare. A complete explanation of why those activities are illegal must address moral as well as economic reasons.

This discussion is not to say, however, that the efficiency goal of economic theory is itself without moral basis. Arguably, in a world characterized by many social problems and limited resources for resolving them, it is immoral to *waste* resources. Imagine a federal regulation designed to protect public health from cancer that would cost $5 *trillion* dollars per premature death avoided. Arguably, such a regulation would constitute a great waste of social resources, which could instead be utilized to save many more lives from other risks such as homelessness, finding a cure for cancer, or making airplanes safer. This question is one of both efficiency and morality.

The Legal Structure of Economic Activity

Today, the significance of economics for understanding law is recognized almost universally. Meanwhile, economists, at least since Coase, increasingly appreciate the significance of law for understanding how economic exchange is organized.[6] Markets and supporting institutions arise together through deliberate and evolutionary legal and social policy making. All legal scholars and many economists have long understood that legal rules and processes condition economic activities. Consider the following excerpt from Karl Llewellyn's 1924 address to the American Economics Association.

Karl N. Llewellyn, "The Effect of Legal Institutions Upon Economics"

5 American Economics Review 664–682 (1924)

Among the major trends of the social sciences today is the urge toward integration of their various branches. Lawyers, in particular, have been turning to economics for light on the nature and function of law. They need to. Economists are turning to law for light on the facts and theory of economics.

***

When . . . an economist . . . spends half a life-time wrestling with the law, it comes as a shock to find law not only an obstruction, but a tool; not only a brake, but a lubricant; not only conditioned by, but itself conditioning economic life. The spheres of mutual influence seem not wholly the same. Basic economic changes shift the general character of legal rules and institutions; the property system depends on the stages of the food quest. The effects of law on economics, though powerful and pervasive, are doubtless less fundamental. The facts are time-worn.

***

Granted . . . some bearing of legal institutions upon economic life and change, what may law have to contributed to economic theory? . . . .

In the first place, legal institutions fix and guarantee the presuppositions on which the economic order rests: that physical violence will be penalized and in large part prevented; that gains by fraud will be penalized, restored, prevented where possible; that anything a man can gain without violence or fraud is rightfully his, for all time; and that changes in these presuppositions will be, in general, slow and long heralded. The presuppositions themselves are for the orthodox economist axiomatic. . . .

In the second place, law affords more of the machinery for the working out of competition than can be appreciated without some pondering. Obviously, the accumulation and flow of capital is dependent on transferable contract and divisible transferable ownership. But so is any national market, any extension of selling territory, any use of large business units, dependent on letting one man speak for and obligate another—the legal institution we call agency. Lease, sale, consignment, option—there is no end to the examples. And clearly the effectiveness of competition between sellers of the same class of goods, but especially of indirect competition among differing types of capital employment, depends on the adjustment or maladjustment of these legal institutions.

In the third place, "free" competition is rarely, if ever, free in fact, and law is one major instrument of restriction—for a variety of ends. Discriminatory price practices are penalized; discriminatory transportation rates often are maintained. In each case the aim is to equalize the approach of unequally situated sellers to a given sales territory. Or willful destruction of produce after reaching a given market is penalized. Narcotics are forbidden sale except as medicine. . . . Patents create monopolies. Other monopolies are shackled by rate regulation. Such restrictions are friction factors which in their every detail are vital to an understanding of what "competition" means in life. . . .

In the fourth place, the legal institutions of taxation and public welfare legislation have obviously far-reaching effects not only on distribution but on production, as has any government ownership or operation. This needs no argument. But it is worth stress, when one considers the tremendous shaping effect of persistent use of a given taxation type, such as the tariff, or of a given rate-making policy, such as the second-class mail rates, or of the continued absence of a given taxation type, such as that on unearned increment or on inheritance. . . . Such conditions, when continued, not only build themselves into the price level and the institutional structure of production, merchandising, and investment, not only redistribute population and wealth, but enter into expectations almost as vested as rights. . . .

In the fifth place . . . bargaining between two persons is limited not only by the desirability of the commodity, the availability of another buyer or seller, and the ability of each bargainer to go without, but also by the working rules which govern the bargaining. The displacement of caveat emptor by a rule of reasonable warranty, making a seller answer for the quality of his goods, must be regarded as affecting prices; under the new rule the seller incurs new risks and the buyer procures some insurance with his commodity. The law's machinery is increasingly put to revealing unheeded costs of production, and thereby shifting the whole basis of bargaining. . . . ■

***

It is not surprising that Dean Llewellyn, a legal scholar, would focus on the ways in which legal rules condition economic transacting. Much of modern law and economics theory, by contrast, focuses on economic explanations and prescriptions for legal policy. However, law and economics scholars today are returning increasingly to Dean Llewellyn's pursuit of studying the ways in which legal institutions and policies affect the economy.

The effects of legal rules on market competition have been obvious to legal scholars for centuries. The legal framework is critical for establishing and supporting market institutions. As Coase noted, "Economic policy involves a choice among alternative social institutions, and these are created by the law or are dependent on it."[7]

Consider the following excerpt from a 1707 English case in which the plaintiff sued the defendant for maliciously firing his gun to scare ducks away from the plaintiff's decoy pond:

Keeble v. Hickeringill
11 East 574, 103 Eng. Rep. 1127 (1707)

Holt, J.

***

[E]very man that hath a property may employ it for his pleasure and profit, as for alluring and procuring decoy ducks to come to his pond. To learn the trade of seducing other ducks to come there in order to be taken is not prohibited either by the law of the land or the moral law; but it is as lawful to use art to seduce them, to catch them, and destroy them for the use of mankind, as to kill and destroy wildfowl or tame cattle. Then when a man useth his art or his skill to take them, to sell and dispose of for his profit; this is his trade; and he that hinders another in his trade or livelihood is liable to an action for so hindering him. . . .

[W]here a violent or malicious act is done to a man's occupation, profession, or way of getting a livelihood, there an action lies in all cases. But if a man doth him damage by using the same employment; as if Mr. Hickeringill had set up another decoy on his own ground near the plaintiff's, and that had spoiled the custom of the plaintiff, no action would lie, because he had as much liberty to make and use a decoy as the plaintiff. This is like the case of 11 H. 4, 47.[8] One schoolmaster sets up a new school to the damage of an antient school, and thereby the scholars are allured from the old school to come to his new. (The action was held there not to lie.) But suppose Mr. Hickeringill should lie in the way with his guns, and fright the boys from going to school, and their parents would not let them go thither; sure that schoolmaster might have an action for the loss of his scholars. 29 E. 3, 18. A man hath a market, to which he hath toll for horses sold: a man is bringing his horse to market to sell: a stranger hinders and obstructs him from going thither to the market: an action lies, because it imports damage . . . . And when we do know that of long time in the kingdom these artificial contrivances of decoy ponds and decoy ducks have been used for enticing into these ponds wildfowl, in order to be taken for the profit of the owner of the pond, who is at the expense of servants, engines, and other management, whereby the markets of the nation may be furnished; there is great reason to give encouragement thereunto; that the people who are so instrumental by their skill and industry so to furnish the markets should reap the benefit and have their action. ■

***

This early eighteenth-century judicial decision directly affected the market for ducks. By establishing rules of the duck-hunting "game"—specifically, by outlawing acts likely to reduce the supply of ducks for the market—the court facilitated the efforts of suppliers and reduced prices for buyers. However, Justice Holt's ruling cannot be characterized as purely *legal*; it is not a simple application of existing law to the facts of the particular case. It is at least equally a policy determination of what constitutes fair, as opposed to unfair, competition. It is, in sum, a legal policy decision that is informed by, and conditions, economic activity. Justice Holt's ruling draws a boundary between fair (lawful) and unfair (unlawful) competition that allows market participants to organize their behavior accordingly. And it draws the boundary in such a way as to maximize gains from trade (at least in the short run), ensuring that more ducks will be provided to the market than would likely have been the case if the court had ruled in favor of Hickeringill.

A HISTORY OF LAW AND ECONOMICS

Law and economics today is a major area of scholarship and study in both law schools and economics departments. Its roots extend back hundreds of years to the works of Adam Smith, Karl Marx, and the German Historical School. In the eighteenth century, it was commonly thought that "law and economics are ever and everywhere complementary and mutually determinative, like form and content."[9] A nineteenth-century English economist, T. E. C. Leslie, "suggested that law, in its bearings on the operation of the economic function in society, is a subject demanding the economist's investigation."[10]

Progressive Era Law and Economics

The "first great law and economics movement" arose on both sides of the Atlantic just prior to the progressive era, beginning in the late nineteenth century.[11] Oliver Wendell Holmes wrote in 1897 that "for the rational study of law the blackletter man may be the man of the present, but the man of the future is the man of statistics and the master of economics."[12] Holmes perhaps exaggerated the demise of the blackletter lawyer, but showed prescience about the future role of economic analysis in legal studies. In the first decades of the twentieth century, legal scholars—particularly those in the Legal Realist movement[13]—used economic methods to compare alternative legal rules and policies. We already introduced one of their number, Karl Llewellyn, a professor at the Columbia University Law School, who in 1924 addressed the American Economics Association on the legal foundations of economic activity.

Most progressive era law and economics research did not come from legal scholars, however, but from economists.[14] In 1904, Thorsten Veblen published "the first comprehensive neoclassical analysis of the nature of the business firm."[15] In *The Theory of the Business Enterprise*, Veblen noted how the law, which focused on individual rights and discrete contracts, was ill-prepared to deal with business enterprises, which were hierarchical and anti-individualistic by nature. Ten years later, Richard T. Ely published *Property and Contract in their Relations to the Distribution of Wealth*, which advanced a traditional institutionalist thesis: that the distribution of wealth in society is a function of the existing legal order, rather than some natural economic order. Ten years after that (in 1924), John R. Commons, who had been a student of both Veblen and Ely, published *Legal Foundations of Capitalism*, which explored the ways in which court decisions and statutes defined and described the economic system. Commons analyzed cases, statutes, and administrative rules "to probe their impact on the development of modern capitalism and thereby to illuminate the interrelations between legal and economic processes."[16] Not content merely to study the interactions of law and economics from the ivory tower, Commons personally drafted most of Wisconsin's social welfare legislation, which served as a progressive model for the rest of the country.

Some progressive era economists interested in law actually joined law faculties, prefiguring a practice that became common in later decades of the twentieth century. Henry Simons held joint appointments in economics and law at the University of Chicago. Robert Hale, who was both a lawyer and an economist, was Karl Llewellyn's colleague at Columbia Law School. Later in his career, Hale published *Freedom Through Law: Public Control of Private Governing Power* (1952). As Steven Medema has written, "Hale saw legal and economic processes as inseparable and described the economy as a structure of coercive power arrangements and relationships, which necessitated an understanding of the formation and structure of the underlying distribution of economic power." Most significantly, Hale "felt that the judicial application of economic principles was necessary to ascertain the economic consequences—allocative and distributive—of the legislation" subject to constitutional challenge.[17]

Between 1900 and 1937, the economists, legal scholars, and political scientists who comprised the "first great law and economics movement" published several influential books and more than six dozen articles "bearing upon law and economics."[18] But the incipient, interdisciplinary field they created languished inexplicably during and after World War II, until it was resurrected in the late 1950s by scholars with a different agenda at the University of Chicago.

The Coasean Revolution

One contribution to the progressive law and economics movement went unnoticed by virtually everyone. In London in 1937, a young economist named Ronald Coase published an article entitled "The Nature of the Firm," which explained the existence of the hierarchical business firm on the basis of "transaction costs."[19] Coase's argument started from the premise that the existence of the firm could not be explained under the assumptions of neoclassical economic theory simply because the firm itself was costly to establish. If it cost nothing to use the market's price mechanism, as neoclassical theory assumed, no one would bear the trouble and expense of organizing transactions through firms; all transacting would be carried out through discrete contracts in the market. But, of course, firms *do* exist. For Coase, this fact alone proved that the free market's price system *is* costly to utilize—sometimes so costly that it becomes cheaper for contractors to establish organizational hierarchies, or firms, to replace certain market transactions.

Coase's theory of the firm, particularly his observation that markets were costly to utilize and that sometimes it was cheaper to transact in hierarchies, seemed to fit well within the progressive era law and economics agenda. If firms could sometimes be more efficient than markets, then arguably states could as well. Coase himself noted some years later that "government is, in a sense, a super-firm but of a very special kind."[20] But Coase's goal was not to justify increased state intervention in markets.

Coase's later works belie any progressivist or statist interpretation of his transaction-cost theory of the firm. In a 1959 article, "The Federal Communications Commission,"[21] Coase argued that market mechanisms, such as auctions, are preferable to bureaucratic mechanisms for allocating segments of the radio frequency spectrum. Coase presented the same general arguments more systematically a year later in "The Problem of Social Cost."[22] In that article, which is the focus of Chapter 4 of this textbook, Coase argued against a fundamental tenet of welfare economics: that the government should always intervene to internalize externalities and, more generally, to correct market failures. Coase pointed out the obvious: that governments can and do fail too. Coase offers no reason to suppose that government regulations always or usually entail fewer or lesser inefficiencies than the market failures they are presumably designed to correct.

It was not a call for a return to *laissez-faire*, however. Coase maintained that, in theory at least, government could sometimes allocate entitlements to resources more efficiently than markets—specifically, when the costs of transacting in markets or firms were relatively high compared to the costs of transacting through the state.[23] Still, his assertions about government failure constituted a direct rebuke to progressive era law and economics, which presumed that government intervention was always called for in the event of market failure.

Coase's development of transaction-cost economics between 1937 and 1960 was reflected, coincidentally, in a sharp political realignment that occurred among law and economics scholars between the end of the progressive era and the 1960s. During that time, progressive era law and economics scholars looked favorably upon government intervention to correct market failures and reduce the social failings of large business enterprises. By contrast, the scholars who developed modern law and economics at the University of Chicago in the 1960s and 1970s strongly favored free markets and the common law against government and its regulations. Coase, himself, transcended this political swing, however, as he consistently maintained the need for comparative institutional analyses, using the metric of transaction costs, to determine the best (or least bad) allocation mechanisms for specific circumstances.

Modern Law and Economics

Modern law and economics emerged with the founding of the *Journal of Law and Economics* at the University of Chicago Law School in 1958. Through that journal and the astonishing productivity of its leading scholars, including Richard Posner, Gary Becker, Ronald Coase, and Harold Demsetz,[24] the University of Chicago jump-started and, from the 1960s to the 1980s, dominated the field of law and economics.

Modern law and economics differed substantially from progressive era law and economics not only in its ideology but also in its research agenda. Whereas the progressive institutionalists of the 1920s and 1930s sought to explain the legal basis of economic outcomes, the scholars associated with modern law and economics in the 1960s and 1970s used economic analysis to explain legal outcomes. They applied neoclassical economic theory to the law, judging legal rules according to their efficiency or inefficiency. Modern law and economics scholars, sometimes using formal mathematical techniques, rigorously tested rules of property, contracts, torts, and criminal law to ascertain whether those rules were efficient. By 1972, Richard Posner was able to conclude that common law rules were generally efficient, and therefore not in need of substantial revision by legislative or other means. This conclusion followed from the apparent fact that common law judges, explicitly or implicitly, rendered efficient decisions.[25] As Richard Epstein recently explained, "Posner's *Economic Analysis of Law* . . . sounded most explicitly the modern theme of economic imperialism: You name the legal field, and I will show you how a few fundamental principles of price theory dictate its implicit economic structure."[26]

The Posnerian research agenda of modern law and economics—focusing on the efficiency characteristics of legal rules—held sway into the 1970s. By the middle of that decade, however, scholars both inside and outside the field were raising serious questions about the value of neoclassical economic theory, and its efficiency goal, for understanding law. Some critics pointed out that an efficiency-based analysis of legal rules, especially those rules respecting the allocation of property rights, is necessarily circular because innumerable efficient allocations are possible for any distribution of resources. Others wondered why society would consciously choose to abandon evidently efficient common law rules in favor of presumptively less-efficient regulatory rules. Still others complained about the Posnerians' use of price theory to explain the nonprice phenomenon of legal rules. Because legal rules are not determined in voluntary, free-market exchanges, economists have no objective basis for making the interpersonal utility comparisons needed to determine the ultimate impact of legal rules on social welfare.[27] Some legal scholars also noted that legislation and regulations often are designed for expressly redistributional or equitable purposes; so to judge them on efficiency grounds is to miss the point.

These criticisms did not destroy modern law and economics. To the contrary, they arguably strengthened the field by forcing it to expand beyond the narrow confines of neoclassical economic theory. This expansion did not mean a return to the methods and agenda of "the first great law and economics movement," though some movement occurred in that direction. The current research agenda, methodology, *and* ideology of law and economics scholars are far broader at the turn of the twenty-first century than in the 1920s or the 1970s, as the next section explains.

PERSPECTIVES ON LAW AND ECONOMICS

Ronald Coase has suggested that most of economic theory over the last 200 years amounts to little more than a series of footnotes to the work of Adam Smith.[28] By the same token, the entire body of modern law and economics scholarship can be described as a series of footnotes to Coase,[29] whose groundbreaking work cleared several fertile paths of inquiry.

Contrary to the conventional wisdom of scholars outside the discipline, law and economics today is neither a homogeneous "movement" nor a monolithic ideology, but a collection of varied and sometimes conflicting perspectives and approaches. This variety, rather than some common, rigid ideological vision, makes law and economics an exciting and widely influential field of study and scholarship.

The so-called Chicago school of neoclassical law and economics remains a market leader. This section briefly introduces the main schools of law and economics, beginning with the Chicago school. Because brevity necessarily requires sacrifice of detail, readers should be forewarned that the following introductions do not capture many of the existing variations and differentiations within each school of law and economics.[30] However, the differences among schools of thought in law and economics receive further elaboration in subsequent chapters, as they relate to specific topics and issues.

The Chicago School: Neoclassical Law and Economics

The Chicago (or Posnerian) school of law and economics analyzes and explains legal rules according to the basic microeconomic precepts of neoclassical economic theory. The Chicago school treats individuals as rational preference-maximizers, who respond to legal rules and decisions just as they do to market prices: to maximize their own net benefits. When, for example, Marie decides whether to drive her car faster than the posted speed limit, she implicitly or explicitly calculates the benefits of driving faster versus the costs, which include the likelihood of being caught times the magnitude of the fine for speeding, plus the increased likelihood times the magnitude of any accident that might result from a marginal increase in speed. If and only if the total expected benefits exceed the total expected costs, will she drive faster than the posted speed limit. Importantly, *if* she decides to exceed the speed limit, her action is *unreasonable* as a matter of law but *rational* as a matter of economic theory.

Implicit in the premise that individuals respond rationally to legal rules and decisions is that they also respond rationally to *changes* in legal rules and decisions. Thus, according to Chicago school theorists, legal rules constitute nonmarket "prices," which establish costs for violating rules. Individuals rationally adjust their law-abiding or -breaking behavior in response to changes in legal rules that either raise or lower the expected costs of violations. The tougher the legal rules and penalties associated with murder, for example, the less likely any individual will be to commit that crime, all other things being equal.

Another premise of Chicago school law and economics is that legal rules can and should be judged according to their nominal or relative economic efficiency. In selecting from among alternative legal rules, policy makers should choose the alternative that would achieve their goal at the lowest total cost to society. This proposition is, of course, a normative one. Much of the normative economic analysis of Chicago school scholars supports the view that common law rules are efficient, even though most common law judges do not purport to decide cases according to efficiency criteria, and do not support their decisions with explicit cost-benefit analyses.

Because it relies heavily on the standard assumptions of neoclassical economic theory, Chicago school law and economics is subject to many of the same criticisms that apply to that theory. Critics point out that the Chicago school's assumptions about how individuals behave are unrealistic; their viewpoint neglects the important role served by social and legal institutions in structuring both preferences and incentives. This viewpoint also has a pronounced ideological bias in favor of markets/common law over legislation/regulation and other alternative institutions and organizations.[31]

Public Choice

Public choice theory consists of two basic components: a theory of how political processes work and a theory of how individuals cooperate to achieve political and economic ends.

As a theory of how political processes work, public choice applies economic theory to politics, treating politicians and bureaucrats as rational maximizers of their own self-interests, rather than as servants of some mythic public interest. Outcomes of the political process, including legislation and regulation, do not reflect deliberative efforts to enhance some objective social welfare function but reflect instead the preferences of individual decision makers, given the incentive structures created by political institutions, including voting rules, jurisdictional rules, decision-making procedures, and committee structures. Although political markets operate like economic markets, according to public choice theory, the preferences of politicians and bureaucrats differ markedly from those of ordinary market participants. Whereas ordinary market participants generally seek to maximize their material well-being, politicians and bureaucrats seek to maximize their power, jurisdiction, administrative turf, budgets, and, most importantly, prospects for reelection.

Politicians and bureaucrats are not, of course, the only individuals who participate in, and seek to benefit from, political markets. Interest groups made up of any aggregation of individuals send their lobbyists to manipulate legislative, regulatory, and other political processes to their advantage. Public choice writers explain the behavior of these groups in political markets with the *theory of collective action*. That theory, in essence, explains how smaller groups coalesced around a distinct issue are likely to assert greater influence over policies concerning that issue than broader, more diffuse coalitions, even if those broader coalitions represent the majority sentiment. Thus, legislative outcomes may reflect minority, rather than majority, preferences.

Associated with this theory of collective action, and with public choice theory generally, is the concept of "rent seeking," which describes the diversion of resources from productive economic activities to efforts to obtain unearned benefits in the political arena. When, for example, a would-be monopolist invests large sums of money lobbying legislators to gain a monopoly entitlement, the investment constitutes rent-seeking behavior.

As a normative matter, public choice theory prescribes institutional solutions to collective action and rent-seeking problems. If the goal is to prevent small groups from asserting undue influence over political processes, and thereby to reduce "wasteful" rent seeking, legal rules must minimize opportunities for influencing political processes and obtaining rents. The easiest way to curb this behavior is by generally limiting the government's overall influence over the economy. The absence of legislative and regulatory institutions governing economic activities means less opportunity to obtain rents, and resources that might otherwise be wasted on rent seeking will be devoted instead to productive activities.

Criticism of public choice theory includes its failure to account for the wealth of factors that motivate human behavior beyond calculated self-interest. This failure reduces the theory's power to explain political behavior and predict outcomes. For example, public choice theory cannot explain why people vote in elections. The chances that any individual vote will decide an election are infinitesimal, and the costs of gathering information about candidates and casting votes surely outweighs the benefits from voting. Of course, people do vote.

A Note on Arrow's Theorem and Public Choice Theory

Central to public choice theory is Kenneth Arrow's impossibility theorem,[32] according to which it is impossible to discern social preferences through voting when voters have a multiplicity of choices. The theorem is best explained by example. Imagine a referendum in a small town with only 30 voters. The referendum concerns the menu for the annual town picnic. The city has identified three possible main courses, each of which is listed on the ballot: (1) hamburgers; (2) barbequed chicken; and (3) roast pork. Ten of the voters (Group I) prefer hamburgers to chicken, and chicken to pork. Ten other voters (Group II) prefer chicken to pork, and pork to hamburgers. And the final group (Group III) of 10 voters prefers pork to hamburgers, and hamburgers to chicken. So what main course do the voters prefer? It's impossible to say. The balloting will come out a tie: 10 to 10 to 10.

A conventional way of averting this result is to hold a series of votes, with each vote involving only two choices. So, for example, the first ballot might ask voters which they prefer as between only hamburger and chicken. Then, the second ballot would ask them their preference as between the winner from the first ballot and pork. This serial voting will avoid the tie, but still not reveal voter preferences; it fails to reflect the voters' actual preferences between hamburgers, chicken, and pork but only the order in which the votes were taken. It is the so-called "cycling" problem.

If, on the first ballot, voters are offered the choice of hamburger and chicken, hamburger will prevail because 20 out of the 30 voters prefer it to chicken. Then, on the second ballot, pork will prevail because 20 out of 30 voters prefer it to hamburger. But change the ordering of votes and see what happens. Suppose the first ballot offers the choice of pork or chicken. Chicken will prevail because 20 out of 30 voters prefer it to pork. Pork, which was the ultimate "preference" from the previous balloting, has lost on the first ballot this time around. Now, in the second round of balloting, hamburger will prevail because 20 out of 30 voters prefer it to chicken. In another iteration of balloting, chicken would come out on top. The ultimate selection, in each case, depends entirely on the order in which the options were considered.

A critical implication of Arrow's impossibility theorem is that the political process (and other nonmarket processes involving a multiplicity of choices) yields results that have an indeterminate affect on social welfare because the choices do not unambiguously reflect social preferences. This implication raises serious questions about the "public interest" model of political and administrative institutions, and warrants the attention paid by public choice theory to the political processes and institutions that mold incentive structures and influence policy outcomes.

Institutional Law and Economics

Institutional law and economics has its roots in the first great law and economics movement of the early twentieth century. Compared to Chicago school law and economics and public choice theory, institutional law and economics is premised on a far broader understanding of the factors that motivate human actions, including formal legal and political institutions and informal social norms, habits, and customs. Economic markets are part and parcel of these formal and informal institutions.

These factors have important implications for the concept of economic efficiency. According to standard neoclassical economic theory and the Chicago school of law and economics, a single efficient solution exists to every legal problem, irrespective of the preexisting assignment of legal entitlements. Institutional law and economics repudiates this claim, arguing that an efficient solution under one set of entitlements and institutional circumstances may not be an efficient solution under another. To focus exclusively on attaining efficient outcomes, while neglecting the underlying legal rules and social norms that largely determine what constitutes "efficiency," is to beg a crucial question of combined economic, legal, and social policy. Nicholas Mercuro and Steven G. Medema explain:

> Because efficiency is a function of rights, and not the other way around, it is circular to maintain that efficiency alone can determine rights. Since costs, prices, outputs, wealth, and so on are derivative of a particular rights structure, so too are cost minimization, value-of-output maximization, and wealth maximization. Different specifications of rights will lead to different (and economically noncomparable) minimizing or maximizing valuations. The result is that an outcome that is claimed to be efficient is efficient only with regard to the assumed initial structure of rights.[33]

This perspective raises serious questions about the Chicago school's preference for the common law because of its efficiency. Compared to what? Institutionalists concede that common law rules tend to be efficient, but that outcome explains nothing if efficiency is itself a function of the choice of a particular set of common law rules. Any rule choice, which entails a set of rights or entitlements, yields an efficient outcome.

For essentially the same reasons, institutionalists reject the public choice theory of rent seeking. That theory rests on a strong distinction between government and market allocations of entitlements that institutionalists abjure. The government is ubiquitous, including in market transacting. Without government-created and government-enforced institutions, such as freedom of contract and property rights, markets could scarcely exist. To the extent that the market is itself a government institution, what basis is there for characterizing market activities as productive or efficiency-enhancing, but government allocations, generally, as wasteful responses to rent seeking?

So far, institutional law and economics appears to be a largely deconstructive enterprise, obliterating the distinction between government and market and denying any special normative status to the concept of "efficiency." In place of standard efficiency analysis, however, this approach offers an alternative basis for evaluating various allocations and means of allocating entitlements: comparative institutional analysis.

Instead of either ignoring the institutional basis of economic activity (as neoclassical theory tends to do), the institutionalists merely suggest that law and economics scholars pay attention not just to theoretical efficiency arguments but compare the outcomes of economic activities under different allocations and alternative institutional arrangements. The goal is not normative but descriptive—to provide a more accurate explanation of economic and legal interrelations.

Institutional law and economics nevertheless is criticized for its failure to provide a more rigorous analytical framework in place of the neoclassical framework it discards. Although it recognizes that institutions and institutional choices affect determinations of efficiency, it fails to offer a theory that would provide a legitimate basis—aside from mere personal or political preference—for choosing among alternative institutional arrangements and allocations of entitlements to resources.[34]

A Note on Evolutionary Economics

Institutional economics posits that the economic system evolves in response to changes in the legal system. As legal rules and institutions change, so too does the structure of the economy, including the determination of productive and allocative efficiency. Some economists, building on this insight of institutional economics, have developed a distinct but related theory of evolutionary economics.

The theory of evolutionary economics differs from institutional economics mainly in its focus on how market participants respond to changing circumstances. Institutionalists are, generally speaking, content to assume that market participants act to maximize their welfare or wealth, under existing institutional arrangements and given preexisting allocations of entitlements. Evolutionary economists, by contrast, offer a more nuanced account of how those participants react and respond to institutional changes. Relying on theories of evolutionary biology, evolutionary economists focus on how firms and other market actors absorb and react to institutional *shocks*—those changes in market structures that result from legal and other social changes.

New Institutional Economics

The *new* institutional economics builds on "old" institutionalist arguments about the embeddedness of economic activity in social and legal institutions, using Ronald Coase's fundamental insight about the critical role that *transaction costs* play in determining economic structures and performance. The ubiquity of transaction costs necessarily influences the structure of institutions including legal institutions and the choices individuals make.

As we discuss in Chapter 4, Coase was uninterested in the dream world of neoclassical theory, which requires no explanation because it is based on a tautology: whatever is *is* efficient under assumptions of perfect information, rationality, and competition. He was singularly interested in the *real* world of economic transacting under circumstances of positive and often quite high transaction costs. Coase wanted to discover why, and when, economic activities are sometimes organized through mechanisms other than markets, specifically firms and governments.

This insight led Coase and other scholars back to the kind of comparative institutional analysis advocated by the old institutionalists but with a useful new metric: *transaction costs*. The costs of transacting not only (positively) *explain* why different institutional arrangements result in differing levels of economic performance but can also (normatively) *prescribe* certain institutional or organizational solutions as more efficient than others. This prescription, then, requires a certain understanding of what institutions (and organizations) are.

Although no single, universally accepted set of definitions has been developed, most scholars working in law and economics follow Douglass North's definition of *institutions* as the "rules of the game," consisting in both the formal *legal* rules and the informal social norms that govern individual behavior and structure social interactions including economic transacting. *Organizations*, by contrast, are the structural mechanisms, such as courts, agencies, firms, and clubs, which utilize, alter, and enforce institutions.

The research agenda of the new institutional economics is broad and ecumenical, including contributions from virtually every discipline that touches on institutions and institutional change. German New Institutionalists Eirik Furubotn and Rudolf Richter provided the following concise summary of the various research arms of the new institutional economics:

Eirik G. Furubotn and Rudolf Richter, Institutions and Economic Theory: The Contribution of the New Institutional Economics

New York: UMP, 1998, pp. 31–32

1. *Transaction-cost economics:* Transaction costs arise in connection with the exchange process and their magnitude affects the ways in which economic activity is organized and carried out. Included within the general category of transaction costs are search and information costs, bargaining and decision costs, and policing and enforcement costs. Transaction-cost economics is concerned particularly with the effect such costs have on the formation of contracts. . . .

2. *Property-rights analysis:* The system of property rights in an economic system defines the positions of individuals with respect to the utilization of scarce resources. Since the allocation of property rights influences the incentives and human behavior in ways that are generally predictable, a basis exists for studying the impact of property-rights arrangements on economic outcomes. . . .

3. *Economic theory of contracts:* As a "relative" of both transaction-cost economics and property-rights analysis, contract theory deals with incentive and asymmetric information problems. The latter fall into two distinct categories. There can be asymmetric information between the parties to a contract and asymmetric information between the contractual parties on one side and a third party (e.g., the court) on the other. Accordingly, we may distinguish between two variant types of contract theories.

   a. *Agency theory* deals with problems of asymmetric information between contractual parties. The asymmetric information in question can exist either before or after a transaction has taken place. . . .

   b. *Relational and incomplete contract theory* focuses on informational asymmetries that can arise between the parties to a (usually longer-term) contract on one side and a third party on the other. An important objective of such contracts is to overcome the postcontractual opportunism that may result from the difficulties courts or other third parties face in verifying the execution of contractual obligations. Credible commitments and self-enforcing commitments are important topics in this field. . . .

4. **The new institutional approach to economic history:** The work of economic historians following this methodological line is concerned with the application and extension of concepts such as transaction costs, property rights, and contractual relationships to historical experience. One important objective is to establish a theory of the institutional structure of society as a whole. As would be expected, writers in this field are especially concerned with making institutions endogenous variables within a general economic model. . . .

5. **The new institutional approach to political economics:** In recent years, the new institutional economics movement has given impetus to the development of the so-called New Economics of Organization (NEO). This approach, pioneered by [Oliver] Williamson and drawing on ideas developed independently by [Douglass] North, has been applied in various fields of political science. The areas affected include the theory of the state, government organization, public administration, international organization, and the emergence and change of (political) institutional arrangements, among others.

   In general, it can be said that the close relationship between the political and the economic sides of social systems, which has been the basic object of study for political economy, is now viewed from the perspective of transaction costs and their effects on property rights and contractual arrangements. ■

Behavioral Law and Economics

Neoclassical economic theory and the Chicago school of law and economics rely on a conception of rationality that often fails to describe how individuals actually make economic decisions in the world. People are not constantly processing every single bit of information they receive and deliberately calculating the costs and benefits of the thousands upon thousands of discrete decisions they make every day. According to behavioral law and economics scholars, they could not possibly do so even if they tried.

Behavioral law and economics describes the work of diverse economists, legal scholars, sociologists, political scientists, and anthropologists who are concerned with developing more accurate models of human socioeconomic behavior. Their starting point is Nobel laureate Herbert Simon's (1916–2001) observation that we all suffer from cognitive limitations of varying degrees. These limitations constrain our abilities to act rationally, as economists historically have understood that term. Simon, thus, sought to replace the neoclassical conception of unbounded rationality with a more realistic notion of *bounded rationality*.[35]

Boundedly rational human beings, Simon showed, are unable to perform the kinds of on-the-fly calculations of costs and benefits that neoclassical theorists assumed. Instead, they take cognitive shortcuts, utilizing "rules of thumb" and other heuristic devices to economize on decision-making costs. For instance, when deciding on a house to buy, consumers rarely calculate to the penny what they can afford, given their existing assets plus the discounted present value of an income stream over a certain number of years. Instead, they use a standard formula, such as one-quarter or one-third of current annual income. They sacrifice some accuracy in calculation for the sake of saving time and decision-making effort.

Simon's findings are consistent with the transaction-cost approach of the new institutional economics. Indeed, the concept of bounded rationality is central to the new institutionalist account of why contracts in the real world deviate from the neoclassical conception of perfect (or perfectible) contracts.[36] Moreover, rules of thumb and other heuristic devices may be viewed, through a new institutional lens, as mechanisms for economizing on transaction costs, given cognitive limitations. In other words, it may sometimes be both rational and efficient to rely on rules of thumb, even if those rules may sometimes lead to erroneous decisions (i.e., decisions that fail to maximize utility). Bounded rationality is only the starting point for behavioral law and economics scholars who raise doubts even about the new institutionalists' relatively weak (compared to the neoclassical model) conception of rationality.

According to more recent behavioral law and economics research, cognitive limitations are even more severe than Herbert Simon supposed. Recent research on *framing effects*, for example, shows that the *way* choices are presented may influence the decisions people make. Consider, for example, a doctor who is trying to inform a patient about the odds of surviving some surgical procedure. The doctor might say that "90 percent of patients in your condition survive this surgery"; or the doctor might say that "10 percent of patients in your condition do not survive this surgery." The rationality assumption of conventional economic theories makes no distinction between these two statements; they say exactly the same thing. Behavioral studies show, however, that it *does* make a difference in patient decision making. Patients who are told that 90 percent survive surgery are far more likely to agree to undergo the procedure than those who are told that 10 percent do not survive.[37] Is this behavior rational, based on economists' understanding of that term?

Behavioral studies also challenge conventional economic wisdom about the nature of individuals' preferences and preference-orderings. The *sine qua non* of rationality for the economist is *transitivity*. If, for example, Sam (this morning) prefers eggs to pancakes, and pancakes to waffles, then Sam will not choose waffles when presented with a choice of eggs or waffles. So far, nothing in the behavioral law and economics literature challenges this transitivity assumption. However, economists also generally assume preferences to be context-independent, so that if Sam learns that oatmeal is yet another option for breakfast, then he will not choose pancakes or waffles over eggs. In reality, however, preferences often prove to be context sensitive, so that the preferences an individual reveals in one context might differ substantially from, or even conflict with, preferences that same individual would reveal in another, only slightly different context.

These and other lessons from behavioral law and economics carry important implications not only for the way economic analysis is done but for the structure of legal rules, which after all seek to influence human behavior. Consider, for example, the "endowment effect," another behavioral phenomenon that challenges conventional economic assumptions.[38] Neoclassical theory posits that a single individual should place the same value on a good whether they are a potential buyer or seller of that good. Thus, if Bob values a clock at precisely $100, he should be indifferent between having $100 in hand or having the clock, whether he is a potential buyer or seller of the clock. If the clock is priced at $99, and he does not yet own it, he should buy it. If he already owns the clock, and some buyer offers him $101 for it, he should sell it (assuming transaction costs are insignificant). In theory, Bob's valuation of the clock should not rise or fall depending on whether he already owns it. In reality, however, Bob's valuation may well depend on whether he owns the clock because of the *endowment effect*. His offer price for the clock is likely to be significantly lower than his ask price.

This discrepancy has important implications for theories of market exchange and for the legal structure of property rights. If sellers systematically value goods more than buyers do because of the endowment effect, then we would expect to find a *status quo bias* favoring the existing distribution of entitlements to goods, and disfavoring exchange. And because individual valuations of goods are likely to turn on the allocation of property rights—whether they own something—the law's allocation of property rights can obviously and significantly affect, if not determine, ultimate economic outcomes, *even in the absence of transaction costs.*[39]

One should be cautious, however, not to read too much into the findings of behavioral law and economics studies. For one thing, conventional notions of economic rationality still work quite well; they adequately explain and predict a great deal of market behavior. As Ronald Coase pointed out (and as previously quoted in Chapter 1), when "faced with a choice between $100 and $10, very few people will choose $10."[40] Partly for this reason, even behavioral law and economics scholars caution against throwing the baby out with the bath water:

> [I]t is unproductive to see a *general* struggle between economic analysis of law and behavioral law and economics. The question is what kinds of assumptions produce good predictions about the effects of law, and this will vary with context. Sometimes the simple assumptions of conventional analysis work entirely well; sometimes it is necessary to introduce complications by, for example, saying a bit more about what is counted in the utility function (such as a desire to be treated fairly, and a willingness to punish those who act unfairly), or incorporating bounded rationality.[41]

Moreover, as Richard Posner points out, behavioral law and economics does not yet constitute a theory in its own right. To date, its focus has been almost entirely on empirical work, poking holes in the assumptions of neoclassical economic theory without providing any theoretical construct with which to replace it.[42] What, after all, are the theoretical implications of the endowment effect? Do we expect owners of *all* goods *always* to value those goods more highly? If so, why do entitlements to goods *ever* change hands after the initial allocation? If not, how do we explain the difference between goods to which, or contexts in which, the endowment effect seemingly applies, and goods to which, or contexts in which, it either does not apply or applies more weakly?

Behavioral law and economics is still in its infancy. At some point, theory is likely to start catching up with the data. Already, however, the influence of behavioral law and economics research is being felt throughout legal and economic studies.[43]

It will be useful to remember that law and economics comprises a variety of distinct perspectives as you work through the materials in subsequent chapters. From time to time, those differing perspectives will be raised to make various points about specific legal-economic topics.

Chapter Summary

This chapter showed why economic analysis is important for lawyers, judges, and legal scholars, and how legal rules structure economic activity. In many respects, the economy and the law are interdependent and synergistic. This relationship is what legitimates, even necessitates, their joint treatment under the rubric of "law and economics." The history of the discipline now known as law and economics goes back hundreds of years, but the "first great law and economics movement" occurred during the first two decades of the twentieth century. "Modern" law and economics emerged in the late 1950s with the founding of the *Journal of Law and Economics* at the University of Chicago, and took off with the publication in that journal in 1960 of Ronald Coase's seminal work, "The Problem of Social Cost," which is the subject of the next chapter. Law and economics should not, however, be exclusively identified with a single thinker or a single school. It is an increasingly diverse discipline, comprised of several schools of thought, all of which add insight into the relations between the legal system and economic activity.

Questions and Problems

1. In the famous case of *Miller v. Schoene*,[44] the U.S. Supreme Court upheld a Virginia statute that required, on the order of the State entomologist, destruction of red cedar trees infected by "cedar rust" disease, in order to prevent the infestation and destruction of neighboring apple orchards. "Cedar rust" is a condition that is not harmful to cedar trees but toxic to apple trees. Apple tree orchards constitute a significant economic industry in the State of Virginia. Cedar trees, by contrast, have only limited economic value for ornamental landscaping. Explain how different schools of law and economic thought might assess the Virginia statute.[45]

2. Should lenders be allowed to charge any interest rate they want on loans?

3. Why should economists be concerned with legal rules?

4. Should everything that is efficient be legal?

5. What kind of incentives does the court's decision in *Keeble v. Hickeringill* create for economic activity?

6. If rent control is always a bad idea, what can policy makers do to ensure the availability of low- and moderate-income housing?

7. Do speed limits and other rules of the road affect economic activity? If so, do they increase or decrease economic activity?

8. How might an economically sophisticated judge have ruled in the case of *Baker v. Weedon*?

9. Karl Llewellyn notes the ways in which markets and market behavior are structured by law. But in tribal societies, people engage in exchange without formal law. Why is the law needed for modern American society, but not for tribal societies?

10. What distinguishes new institutional economics from old institutionalism?

11. How do neoclassical and behavioral schools of law and economics differ with respect to the concept of rationality?

1. *Quoted in* Ejan Mackaay, *Economics of Information and Law* (New York: Kluwer Academic Publishers, 1982), p. 6.

2. 262 So. 2d 641 (Miss. 1972).

3. It should be noted that a life tenant is not like a lessee in a landlord-tenant relationship, but is an *owner* of real estate. However, a life tenant's ownership interest is limited in duration, and limited by interests of the remaindermen, those who will become the possessors of the land after the life tenant's death. The life tenant and the remaindermen do not stand in a landlord-tenant relationship, but in a correlative ownership relationship.

4. Put in more technical terms, present prices should reflect the discounted present value of expected future increases in land values. For more on the process of discounting and the selection of a discount rate, see Chapter 15.

5. Ronald H. Coase, *Economics and Contiguous Disciplines, reprinted in* R. H. Coase, *Essays on Economics and Economics* (Chicago: University of Chicago Press, 1994), p. 44.

6. As the historian of economic theory, Mark Blaug, wrote, "Coase's writings have created an entirely new discipline of Law and Economics in teaching us that the legal system, far from being an unnecessary cancerous growth imposed on a market economy, is absolutely vital to its very foundation." Mark Blaug, *Economic Theory in Retrospect*, 5th ed. (Cambridge: Cambridge University Press, 1997), p. 585.

7. Ronald H. Coase, *The Firm, the Market, and the Law* (Chicago: University of Chicago Press, 1988), p. 28.

8. This citation is to a case decided in the eleventh year of the reign of Henry IV (1410).

9. Fritz Berolzheimer, *The World's Legal Philosophies* (1912) pp. 22–23, *quoted in* Colin A. Cooke, "The Legal Content of the Profit Concept," 46 *YALE LAW* 436, 436 (1937).

10. Colin A. Cooke, "The Legal Content of the Profit Concept," 46 *YALE LAW JOURNAL* 436, 437 (1937), *citing* T. E. C. Leslie, *Essays in Political and Moral Philosophy* (1879), p. 404.

11. *See* Herbert Hovenkamp, "The First Great Law and Economics Movement," 42 *STANFORD LAW REVIEW* 993 (1990).

12. Oliver Wendell Holmes, "The Path of the Law," 10 *HARVARD LAW REVIEW* 457, 469 (1897).

13. The "legal realists" rejected legal determinism and formalist models of legal decision making, in favor of instrumental, institutional, and social explanations, which focused on the practical motivations of judges.

14. In England in the 1930s, the Chancery lawyer D. Hughes Parry could point to only one other English lawyer who was "bold enough to venture into the borderland between law and economics." D. Hughes Parry, "Economic Theories in English Case Law," 47 *LAW QUARTERLY REVIEW* 183, 188 (1931).

15. Herbert Hovenkamp, "Law and Economics in the United States: A Brief Historical Survey," 19 *CAMBRIDGE JOURNAL OF ECONOMICS* 331, 333 (1995).

16. *Ibid.*

17. Steven G. Medema, "Wandering the Road from Pluralism to Posner: The Transformation of Law and Economics in the Twentieth Century," 30 *HISTORICAL POLITICS ECONOMICS AND* 202 (1998). For a recent, sympathetic analysis of the historical and contemporary value of Hale's work, see Barbara Fried, *The Progressive Assault on Laissez Faire: Robert Hale and the First Law and Economics Movement* (Boston: Harvard University Press, 1998).

18. Samuel Herman, "Economic Predilection and the Law," 31 *AMERICAN POLITICAL SCIENCE REVIEW* 821, 827 n. 35 (1937).

19. Ronald H. Coase, "The Nature of the Firm," *ECONOMICA* 4 (1937), *reprinted in* R. H. Coase, *The Firm, the Market, and the Law* (Chicago: University of Chicago Press, 1988), p. 33.

20. Ronald H. Coase, "The Problem of Social Cost," 3 *JOURNAL OF LAW & ECONOMICS* 1 (1960), *reprinted in* R. H. Coase, *The Firm, the Market, and the Law* (Chicago: University of Chicago Press, 1988), pp. 95, 117.

21. Ronald H. Coase, "The Federal Communications Commission," 2 *JOURNAL OF LAW & ECONOMICS* 1 (1959).

22. Ronald H. Coase, "The Problem of Social Cost," 3 *JOURNAL OF LAW & ECONOMICS* 1 (1960), *reprinted in* R. H. Coase, *The Firm, the Market,*

and the Law (Chicago: University of Chicago Press, 1988), p. 95.

23. *Ibid.*, p. 118. Also see Chapter 4 of this book.

24. Only one of these men—Richard Posner—is a legal scholar; the others are all economists. More generally, Ejan Mackaay noted that few of the contributors during the early days of the modern law and economics movement were lawyers. Guido Calabresi (at Yale Law School) and Henry Manne (at the Universities of Rochester and Miami) were, like Posner, exceptional. *See* Ejan Mackaay, "History of Law and Economics," I ENCYCLOPEDIA LAW OF AND ECONOMICS 65, 75 (2000).

25. *See ibid.*, p. 76.

26. Richard Epstein, "Law and Economics: Its Glorious Past and Cloudy Future," 64 UNIVERSITY OF CHICAGO LAW REVIEW 1167, 1168 (1997).

27. This amounts to a critique of the Kaldor-Hicks efficiency criteria, which we introduced in Chapter 1.

28. Ronald H. Coase, "The Institutional Structure of Production," *in* R. H. Coase, *Essays on Economics and Economists* (Chicago: University of Chicago Press, 1994), pp. 3–4.

29. This is almost literally true; it is not easy to find an article in the literature that does not cite to Coase's "The Problem of Social Costs."

30. For a more thorough introduction to the various schools of law and economics thought, see Nicholas Mercuro and Steven G. Medema, *Economics and the Law* (Princeton, NJ: Princeton University Press, 1997).

31. The Chicago school of law and economics does not include every scholar who taught at the University of Chicago. Ronald Coase, for example, does not identify himself as a member of the Chicago school. He is a founder of the new institutional economics (NIE), a school of thought that differs significantly from the Chicago school, and a founding member of that school's chief organization, the International Society for New Institutional Economics.

32. *See* Kenneth Arrow, *Social Choice and Individual Values* (New Haven, CT: Yale University Press, 1951).

33. Nicholas Mercuro and Steven G. Medema, *Economics and the Law* (Princeton, NJ: Princeton University Press, 1997), p. 118.

34. According to Ronald Coase, institutional law and economics is a school in search of a theory:

"The American institutionalists were not theoretical but anti-theoretical, particularly where classical economic theory was concerned. Without a theory they had nothing to pass on except a mass of descriptive material waiting for a theory, or a fire." Ronald Coase, "The New Institutional Economics," 140 J. INSTITUTIONAL AND THEORETICAL ECONOMICS 229, 230 (1984). For a defense of institutionalism's contributions to economic theory, *see* Geoffrey M. Hodgson, "The Approach of Institutional Economics," 36 JOURNAL OF ECONOMIC LITERATURE 166 (1998).

35. *See, for example*, Herbert Simon, "Rationality as Process and a Product of Thought," 68 AMERICAN ECONOMIC REVIEW 1 (1978); Herbert Simon, "Rational Decision Making in Business Organizations," 69 AMERICAN ECONOMIC REVIEW 493 (1979).

36. *See* Chapter 8.

37. Donald A. Redelmeier, Paul Rozin, and Daniel Kahneman, "Understanding Patients' Decisions," 270 JOURNAL AMERICAN OF THE MEDICAL ASSOCIATION 72 (1993).

38. *See, for example*, Daniel Kahneman, Jack L. Knetsch, and Richard H. Thaler, "The Endowment Effect, Loss Aversion, and Status Quo Bias," 5 JOURNAL OF ECONOMIC PERSPECTIVES 193 (1991); Daniel Kahneman, Jack L. Knetsch, and Richard H. Thaler, "Experimental Tests of the Endowment Effect and the Coase Theorem," 98 JOURNAL OF POLITICAL ECONOMY 1325 (1990).

39. On the implications of the endowment effect for the so-called "Coase theorem," *see* Chapter 4.

40. Ronald H. Coase, "How Should Economists Choose?" *reprinted in* R. H. Coase, *Essays on Economics and Economists* (Chicago: University of Chicago Press, 1994), p. 25.

41. Cass R. Sunstein, "Behavioral Law and Economics: A Progress Report," 1 AMERICAN LAW & ECONOMICS REVIEW 115, 147 (1999). *See also* Gregory Mitchell, "Why Law and Economics' Perfect Rationality Should Not Be Traded for Behavioral Law and Economics' Equal Incompetence," 91 GEORGETOWN LAW JOURNAL 67 (2002); Matthew Rabin, "Psychology and Economics," 36 JOURNAL OF ECONOMIC LITERATURE 11, 12–13 (1998).

42. *See* Richard A. Posner, "Rational Choice, Behavioral Economics, and the Law," 50 STANFORD LAW REVIEW 1551 (1998). Compare

Posner's assessment of behavioral law and economics with Coase's similar assessment of "old" institutional economics, *supra* note 33.

43. For a more comprehensive introduction to behavioral law and economics, *see* Cass R. Sunstein, ed., *Behavioral Law & Economics* (Cambridge: Cambridge University Press, 2000); Daniel Kahneman, "Maps of Bounded Rationality: Psychology for Behavioral Economics," 93 AMERICAN ECONOMICS REVIEW 1449 (2003).

44. 276 U.S. 272 (1928).

45. For a comparison of "old" institutional and public choice theories, *see* Warren J. Samuels, "Interrelations Between Legal and Economic Processes," 14 JOURNAL OF LAW & ECONOMICS 435 (1971); James M. Buchanan, "Politics, Property, and the Law: An Alternative Interpretation of *Miller et al. v. Schoene*," 15 JOURNAL OF LAW & ECONOMICS 439 (1972); Warren J. Samuels, "In Defense of a Positive Approach to Government as an Economic Variable," 15 JOURNAL OF LAW & ECONOMICS 453 (1972).

Chapter 4

"The Problem of Social Cost" and Modern Law and Economics

*M*ost scholars of law and economics today, whatever their "school" (see Chapter 3), agree that their discipline owes a great deal to a single work: Ronald Coase's 1960 essay, "The Problem of Social Cost."[1] More than four decades after its publication, the article still provokes intense scholarly debate and interest. Few other modern works in all of economics have been so influential or so often cited. It was a main reason why its author was awarded the Nobel Prize in economics in 1991. Ironically, few works have been so consistently misunderstood and misrepresented as "The Problem of Social Cost." It seems to be cited more often than it is read.

This chapter explores Coase's important work and explains how and why it changed the nature of the debate in law and economics, and why its concerns are still relevant today for an understanding of the role of law in economic life. It remains of fundamental importance in all subfields of law and economics.

THE NATURE OF SOCIAL COST PROBLEMS: COASE VERSUS PIGOU

Coase did not set out, in "The Problem of Social Cost," to revolutionize the study of law and economics. His main purpose in writing the paper was to critique the prevailing welfare economics view of externalities (as defined in Chapter 1). That view, developed by the economist Arthur Pigou,[2] provided a seemingly obvious solution to pollution problems and similar externalities: the one who creates the externality should pay for its amelioration either through taxes or through penalties such as fines. Thus, externalities would be internalized by the polluter. To put the proposition more succinctly, the Pigovian prescription was: the polluter should pay.

This approach was endorsed throughout the economics profession. It became virtually an article of faith that a polluter should pay not only as a matter of equity but also as a matter of efficiency because externalities lead to market failures. If, for example, some production costs—say, air pollution—associated with producing widgets are externalized, the price of widgets in the market will not fully reflect the costs associated with their production. Widget prices will be lower with externalities than they would be with no externalization of production costs. All other things being equal, those lower prices lead to more sales of widgets. Consumers buy more widgets at a price of $8 (with pollution costs externalized) than they would at a price of $10 each (with pollution costs internalized). The extra money they expend on widgets will not be available for other purposes, reflecting the ubiquity of opportunity costs (as discussed in Chapter 1). Sales of other goods and services may decline because of the inaccurate price signals sent to consumers in the widget market. Meanwhile, neither the widget consumer nor the widget producer is bearing the pollution costs associated with widget production. Someone else must be.[3] They are, in effect, subsidizing the widget market by bearing costs associated with that market without being market participants. The result is allocative inefficiency in the market. Too many widgets are purchased, relative to other goods and services.

Pigou's solution to the problem of externality was simply to force the producer to internalize the cost, for instance through a tax, where the marginal tax rate would equal the unit value of the externality. Once the cost was imposed on the producer, the market failure would resolve. The price of widgets in the market would accurately reflect *all* the costs of production.

For decades, economists accepted at face value Pigou's explanation of the problem and his policy prescription for resolving externalities. If a widget factory was emitting smoke and someone downwind suffered harm as a result, Pigou and subsequent economists would conclude that the factory should pay a tax equal to the amount they saved from externalities. Those tax burdens would find their way into the prices of widgets, which would rise (all other things being equal). Assuming the tax rate is set correctly, the posttax price of widgets should lead to an efficient allocation of resources to widget making. This formulation seemed both logical and "fair," but it begged some important questions that Ronald Coase posed for the first time in "The Problem of Social Cost."

In the first place, Coase noted, the costs in the foregoing example are not created by just one party: the polluter. They are bilateral problems created by both the polluter and the downwind neighbor. In Coase's view, it takes at least two to create an external cost: someone to produce it and someone else to bear it. If the neighbor were not there, no externality would occur just as surely as if no pollution ever went up the factory's smokestack. The neighbor's contribution to the joint or social cost problem is easiest to comprehend where the polluter is there first, and the neighbor moves in later. In such a case, would we still conclude that the polluter alone caused or created the harm?[4]

The externality is bilateral in another sense. Not only do the polluter and the downwind neighbor combine to produce the harm, one of them is bound to suffer harm as a result of their conflicting preferences. If the factory is entitled to pollute, it thereby harms the neighbor. But if the factory is prevented from polluting, then the factory clearly suffers harm. This dilemma raises the inherent problem of joint or social cost situations: Who gets to impose harm on whom? From an economic point of view, Coase argues that the goal should be to minimize the total harm because that way the social product is maximized. But the situation provides no reason to presume, as Pigou does, that it is always less costly for the polluter, rather than the neighbor, to avoid or abate the harm.

Suppose the neighbor could avoid all the pollution harm simply by closing the windows on his house one day each month at an implicit, subjectively valued cost of $100 per year; but it would cost the factory 1,000 times that amount to avoid creating the harmful pollution in the first place. Further suppose no other neighbors who might be harmed by the pollution from the factory live in the vicinity. In this case, the evidence suggests that the neighbor is the *least cost avoider*—the party capable of avoiding or abating the harm at the lowest cost—so that the factory should be entitled to pollute.

The total social cost, or the sum of private costs to all parties, is affected by the allocation of the legal right or entitlement to either the polluter or the neighbor. If the factory possesses the entitlement, it will pollute and the neighbor will bear the costs. But if the neighbor holds the entitlement, the factory pays the costs associated with the pollution or may be enjoined from polluting at all. Those costs may or may not be the same regardless of who possesses the entitlement. If not, then the distribution of legal entitlements will not only affect the distribution of private and social costs, but may affect their magnitude as well. Therefore, the operation of the legal system, in allocating entitlements to pollute or be free of pollution, could affect economic outcomes. It might even play a determining role in the efficiency of production and exchange.

Coase's reconceptualization of externalities as bilateral or multilateral problems of social cost startled economists, most of whom had been schooled in the Pigovian tradition. Even neoclassical economists, who did not associate themselves with Pigovian welfare economics, found Coase's approach to social cost isues difficult to accept at first. When Coase first presented his ideas to a seminar at the University of Chicago, the participants reportedly were quite skeptical at first, and only gradually came around to Coase's way of thinking. Unfortunately, as we shall see, the lessons many have taken from Coase's "The Problem of Social Cost" were not the ones Coase intended.

THE COASE THEOREM

No Problems of Social Cost Would Arise in a World of Perfect Competition, Complete Information, and Costless Transacting

The structure of Coase's argument in "The Problem of Social Cost" figures nearly as prominently in the history of economic ideas as the substance of that argument. Coase began by asking the reader to envision a mythical world in which property rights are completely specified and "the operation of the pricing system is without cost." In this world, information is essentially complete and transacting is costless. It is, in effect, a world in which all the assumptions of neoclassical economic theory obtain.

This world of neoclassical perfect competition also demonstrated a theoretical problem of Pigou's analysis. Pigou assumed competitive markets. But Coase showed that if the world conforms to the neoclassical model of competition, Pigou's solution to externality problems is not wrong but unnecessary because all externality problems would be solved efficiently by the market.

The assumption of zero transaction costs also carries crucial implications for law. Simply put, in a world of zero transaction costs, law is irrelevant. Whatever the initial allocation of property rights (or entitlements), and whatever the legal rules governing resource use, parties will costlessly contract to the most efficient allocation of entitlements to resources. Coase illustrated this point with a hypothetical land-use conflict between a crop farmer and neighboring cattle rancher. Without a fence separating their lands, the rancher's cattle sometimes wander onto the farmer's land, damaging the farmer's crops. Any increase in the size of the rancher's herd would increase the damage. This problem has several possible outcomes: One party or the other can pay to put up fencing; the cattle can stray and damage the crop, with one or the other party bearing the cost of that damage; the farmer can stop farming; or the cattle rancher can cease raising cattle. The issue from the standpoint of social costs and benefits is which outcome yields the greatest net benefits, defined as the highest value of production of cattle and/or crops.

Coase sets up a simple arithmetic example to demonstrate how the best outcome would necessarily be attained, no matter who holds the initial entitlement, if transacting is costless. First, assume that the farmer has the entitlement to be free from crop damage. In that case, the rancher will adopt the strategy that permits the highest level of cattle production at the lowest cost, including the possibility of paying the farmer not to plant on acres adjacent to the rancher's land. The farmer will accept payment over planting if as a result the farmer's net benefit is greater.

Table 4.1 describes a situation in which the damage to the farmer from the rancher's cattle amounts to $90; it would cost the rancher $110 for fencing; it would cost the farmer $100 in forgone net profits not to plant crops in the first place; and it would cost the rancher $200 not to raise cattle. In this instance, the lowest cost approach would be for the rancher to allow the cattle to roam and pay the farmer $90 in damages. If transacting is costless, the parties would reach that outcome.

Table 4.1 If Transaction Costs Are Zero, Farmer and Rancher Will Attain Lowest Cost Solution Regardless of the Initial Allocation of the Entitlement

		COST
If Farmer Has Entitlement, Rancher Will Allow Cattle to Roam and Pay Farmer $90 in Damages.	a. Allow cattle to roam and pay damages.	90
	b. Put up fence.	110
	c. Pay farmer not to plant crops.	100
	d. Don't raise cattle.	200
If Rancher Has Entitlement, Farmer Will Allow Cattle to Roam and Suffer Damage of $90.	a. Allow cattle to roam and suffer damage.	90
	b. Put up fence.	110
	c. Don't plant crops.	100
	d. Pay rancher not to raise cattle.	200

If, however, the rancher has the entitlement to run cattle on the farmer's land without any liability for the damage, the farmer must consider the cost of fencing, absorbing the crop damage costs, or leaving the field unplanted. The costs are exactly as previously stated, and so is the outcome. The farmer's lowest cost solution is to plant and suffer the $90 in crop damages from the rancher's cattle. The only difference is that, instead of receiving compensation from the rancher for the damage, the farmer absorbs the damage cost.

So, the outcomes differ based on changes in entitlements, but in the world of zero transaction costs, the difference is entirely distributional. In both cases, the herd size will be the same and the fields will be planted. As Coase explained, "The ultimate result (which maximizes the value of production) is independent of the legal position [of the parties] if the pricing system is assumed to work without cost."[5] Put differently, in a world of zero transaction costs, the outcome is invariant to the arrangement of entitlements, and that outcome is always efficient; therefore, a Pigovian (government) solution is not needed.

It might seem unfair to require the farmer to bear the costs as the victim of the cattle rancher's herd. Neither party, though, can assume *ex ante* that society as a whole benefits from less ranching and more farming. Indeed, no social costs would arise if the farmer were not there to begin with. The problem exists because it is a joint cost situation: one party or another will possess an entitlement and the other will bear the cost. But the total costs and benefits will not vary in a world of costless transacting.

Again, Coase used the basic assumptions of neoclassical economics to reach a startling conclusion. If the world really did conform to the perfect competition paradigm, then law would matter only as it affected distribution; it could not affect the total social product. Moreover, no "problem" would ever exist between rancher and farmer. They would not experience a conflict because they would arrive at the lowest cost solution necessarily without Pigovian taxes. Nor would the liable party contest that issue in court because such a contest would be pointless. Indeed, courts could not possibly exist in a world of zero transaction costs. Simply put, courts *are* transaction costs. Even if they could exist in a world of costless transacting, they would have no role to play. Entitlements would be known and completely defined, which must be true given the assumption of costless information. Both parties would completely understand their respective rights and duties from the first moment they acquired their land. Those rights and duties, and their implications, would be fully accounted for in their original land purchase prices. They might be transferred, as in the case where for a payment the farmer agrees not to plant. But the respective rights and obligations of all parties would be completely specified to cover all contingencies, and all parties would understand them. Always.

The world of zero transaction costs not only eliminates the need to resolve disputes over property entitlements; it would eliminate disputes over contracts as well, and would eliminate the need for a tort system of any kind. All contracts would be "perfect," covering all contingencies, and specifying completely the remedies. Torts would be unknown because torts result from the absence of contracts or contract imperfections. In this world, where transacting is costless, all liability issues are pre-resolved under contract.[6] Whereas in the real world it is impossible for the driver of a car to contract with all potential victims of an accident, in the world of zero transaction costs it would be not only possible but certain and costless.

Obviously, this zero-transaction-cost world is fanciful, but Coase posited it to make an important analytical point. If institutions such as the law, and organizations such as the police and courts, exist, then we cannot possibly be in a world of costless transacting or, for that matter, in a world that corresponds to the assumptions of a neoclassical model of perfect competition. In fact, transacting is never costless, and when one looks at the law and related organizations, it is clear that the costs may well be higher or lower depending on how entitlements are distributed, how contracts are written, and how enforcement is carried out. In other words, in the real world of costly transacting, the outcome is not invariant with the allocation of the entitlement.

Coase made a similar point, many years earlier, in his 1937 paper, "The Nature of the Firm."[7] In a world of complete information and costless transacting, Coase argued, the business firm—a hierarchical organization comprised of owners/managers and employees—would serve no efficiency-enhancing purpose. All parts of production, from raw materials to finished retail products, could be efficiently accomplished by independent contractors in the free market. By virtue of the assumption of zero transaction costs, it would cost nothing to contract, to measure performance, and to enforce contract terms (all parts of the transaction process). Consequently, all specialization, division of labor, and coordination of productive activities could be as, or more, efficiently accomplished by independent contracting in markets as by hierarchical firms. Business firms would have no reason to exist.

Of course, business firms *do* exist. They exist because, in the real world, transacting in the market is costly. It costs something to use the price mechanism. Moreover, information is incomplete and costly to obtain. Sometimes, it is less expensive to organize economic activities in firms, rather than through discrete market transactions among independent contractors. At different times, the reverse is true: it is less expensive to use the market than to organize activities in firms.

In "The Nature of the Firm," Coase showed that firms mattered because they could improve productive efficiency. More than 20 years later, in "The Problem of Social Cost," he similarly showed that the law and government matter to the extent, as well as the distribution, of social costs. If transacting is costly, then conflicts may arise between neighbors, such as the crop farmer and the cattle rancher in Coase's example. Moreover, the distribution of legal entitlements and other legal rules governing resource use may influence the extent and severity of such conflicts. It will always cost something to resolve the conflicts that arise. Because transacting is costly, we cannot expect the parties to resolve their disputes amicably through the market's price mechanism. The government may have a legitimate role to play in resolving conflicts and correcting market failures that can and do arise in a world of incomplete information, imperfect competition, and costly transacting.

We can illustrate how transaction costs can affect outcomes by returning to Coase's rancher and farmer story. The various costs remain the same as in Table 4.1, except, as illustrated in Table 4.2, transaction costs are now added. We assume that

Table 4.2 If Transaction Costs Are Positive, the Allocation of the Entitlement Might Determine Whether or Not the Least-Cost Solution Is Attained

		COST	+ TRANSACTION COSTS	= TOTAL COSTS
If Farmer Has Entitlement, Rancher Will Put Up a Fence at Cost of $110.	a. Allow cattle to roam and pay damages.	90	25	115
	b. Put up fence.	110	0*	110
	c. Pay farmer not to plant crops.	100	25	125
	d. Don't raise cattle.	200	0*	200
If Rancher Has Entitlement, Farmer Will Allow Cattle to Roam and Suffer Damage of $90.	a. Allow cattle to roam and suffer damage.	90	0*	90
	b. Put up fence.	110	0*	110
	c. Don't plant crops.	100	0*	100
	d. Pay rancher not to raise cattle.	200	25	225

* Transaction costs arise whenever there is interaction between the two parties; unilaterally adopted solutions entail no transaction costs.

whenever one party seeks to persuade the other to change a behavior, one of them must bear $25 in transaction costs. So, if the rancher wants the farmer to install a fence, one or the other of them must bear not only the cost of the fencing but also the $25 transaction cost. Similarly, if the farmer has the entitlement but the rancher is willing to pay damages, transaction costs will apply. No transaction costs will arise, however, in any solution that does not require any cooperation between the two parties. So, for example, if the rancher holds the entitlement, and the farmer decides to put up a fence, no transaction costs apply because the farmer can put up a fence without the permission or cooperation of the rancher.

Now, consider the impact of these transaction costs on the potential outcomes of the conflict. If the rancher holds the entitlement, the outcome is the same as before because the farmer's lowest cost solution is simply to suffer the damages. On the other hand, if the farmer holds the entitlement, the rancher must either pay damages of $90, plus $25 in transaction costs; build a fence for $110 (with no transaction costs); arrange with the farmer not to plant crops, at a cost of $100 plus $25 in transaction costs; or stop raising cattle at a cost of $200. Here, the rancher's lowest-cost option is to build the fence for $110, which is $20 more expensive than the farmer's best option, if the rancher had held the initial entitlement. Thus, in the presence of positive transaction costs, the allocation of entitlements clearly matters for economic efficiency.

Although Coase was explicit about the ultimate point of his article—transacting is always costly and, therefore, the law matters—that was not universally the message that scholars took from it. Instead, Coase's colleague and fellow Nobel laureate, George Stigler, took the basic argument about the invariant efficiency of a zero-transaction-cost world and described it as the "Coase theorem." This label was misleading, although not completely inaccurate. "The Problem of Social Cost" did include a lengthy argument about the invariance of efficient outcomes in a zero-transaction-cost world. The problem was that Stigler took the argument to be the signal contribution of "The Problem of Social Cost." Many other scholars followed him in doing so. The lesson of the paper for many of these readers was that the Coase theorem (and Coase's essay overall) shows that if we can reduce transaction costs nearly to zero in legal disputes we will always get efficient outcomes. That reading is far from Coase's intention, which was to emphasize the critical importance of positive transaction costs in the *real* world.

Critiques of the Coase Theorem

Coase, himself, was quite clear about the world of the Coase theorem. He felt that "it would not seem worthwhile to spend much time investigating the properties" of such a mythical world,[8] which he had employed merely as an analytical device to illustrate the ultimate importance of law for real-world economic systems. However, to his chagrin, much has been written precisely about this fanciful, perfect neoclassical world. Some even attacked Coase, ironically and erroneously, for the unrealistic assumptions of the Coase theorem. In response to his critics, Coase noted that nearly every critique of his essay has been "invalid, unimportant, or irrelevant."[9]

Briefly, criticisms of the Coase theorem can be grouped as follows:

1. Coase is too ideological in asserting that the market can solve all externality problems.
2. The Coase theorem is not verified empirically by events and transactions in the real world.
3. Coase doesn't take into account the effects of initial wealth and how they might alter the impacts of any distribution of entitlements.

Only the third criticism is of any interest because, with some assumptions and qualifications, exchange in the world of the Coase theorem might be said to raise prices of some goods and services and thus make some people worse off. The first criticism is basically a misreading of the article; and the second is irrelevant, as Coase suggests, because it is impossible to empirically verify something that cannot exist. As for the third, as Coase points out, those making the argument do not appreciate the meaning of a world without transaction costs. In such a world, property when purchased is fully valued to account for the possession, or lack of possession, of an entitlement to that property. Consequently, distributional effects are fully accounted for in the price. In addition, rights and duties would be completely specified accounting for all future contingencies from the time the property is first acquired. The fact that this situation cannot possibly exist only serves to emphasize that the extensive literature criticizing the Coase theorem often simply misses the overriding point of the article, which concerns the real world of positive, ubiquitous transaction costs.

"The Problem of Social Cost" uses actual cases that illustrate the way a zero-transaction-cost world might resolve or, more accurately, avoid a potential conflict over entitlements. These cases serve two other important functions. First, they show how the real world functions where costs are positive for all transactions, where the outcome is determined by fallible judges operating with limited and incomplete information, and where the entitlement is clearly in dispute. Second, they show what in some ways was the most important point for Coase: that responsibility for costs is by definition unclear because externality problems are intrinsically bilateral or multilateral, joint or social cost questions, not unilateral problems with a clear perpetrator, who "causes" the problem, and a victim, as Pigou described them.

Sturges v. Bridgman
1 Ch. D. 852 (1879)

Thesiger, L. J.

The Defendant in this case is the occupier, for the purpose of his business as a confectioner, of a house in Wigmore Street. In the rear of the house is a kitchen, and in that kitchen there are now, and have been for over twenty years, two large mortars in which the meat and other materials of the confectionery are pounded. The Plaintiff, who is a physician, is the occupier of a house on Wimpole Street, which until recently had a garden at the rear, the wall of which garden was a party-wall between the Plaintiff's and the Defendant's premises, and formed the back wall of the Defendant's kitchen. The Plaintiff has, however, recently built upon the site of the garden a consulting room, one of the side walls of which is the wall just described. It has been proved that in the case of the mortars, before and at the time of the action brought, a noise was caused which seriously inconveniences the Plaintiff in the use of his consulting room, and which, unless the Defendant had acquired the right to impose the inconvenience, would constitute an actionable nuisance. The Defendant contends that he had acquired the right . . . by uninterrupted use for more than twenty years.

***

[L]aws governing the acquisition of [entitlement because of use] stands thus: Consent or acquiescence of the owner of the [disputed land] lies at the root of prescription. . . . [A person] cannot, as a general rule, be said to consent or to acquiesce in the acquisition by his neighbor of an easement through an enjoyment of which he has no knowledge, actual or constructive, or which he contests and endeavors to interrupt, or which he temporarily licenses.

***

It is said that if this principle is applied in cases like the present, and were carried out to its logical consequences, it would result in the most serious practical inconveniences for a man might go say into the midst of the tanneries of Bermondsey, or into any other locality devoted to a particular trade or manufacture of a noisy or unsavory character, and, by building a private residence upon a vacant piece of land, put a stop to such trade or manufacture altogether. The case also is put of a blacksmith's forge built away from all habitations, but to which, in the course of time, habitations approach. We do not think that either of these hypothetical cases presents any real difficulty. As regards the first, it may be answered that whether anything is a nuisance or not is a question to be determined, not merely by an abstract consideration of the thing itself, but in references to the circumstances; what would be a nuisance in Belgrave Square would not necessarily be so in Bermondsey; and where a locality is devoted to a particular trade or manufacture carried on by the traders or manufacturers in a particular and established manner not constituting a public nuisance, Judges and juries would be justified in finding and may be trusted to find, that the trade or manufacture so carried out in that locality is not a private or actionable wrong. As regards the blacksmith's forge, that is really an item per item case with the present. It would be on the one hand in a very high degree unreasonable and undesirable that there should be a right of action for acts which are not in the present condition of the adjoining land, and possibly never will be any annoyance or inconvenience to either its owner or occupier; and it would be on the other hand in an equally degree unjust, and from a public point of view, inexpedient that the use and value of the adjoining land should, for all time and under all circumstances, be restricted and diminished by reason of the continuance of acts incapable of physical interruption, and which the law gives no power to prevent. The smith in the case supposed might protect himself by taking a sufficient curtilage to ensure what he does from being any time an annoyance to his neighbor, but the neighbor himself would be powerless in the matter. Individual cases of hardship may occur in the strict carrying out of the principle upon which we found our judgment, but the negation of the principle would lead even more to individual hardship, and would at the same time produce a prejudicial effect upon the development of land for residential purposes. The Master of the Rolls of Court granted the relief which the Plaintiff prayed for, and we are of opinion that his order is right and should be affirmed. ∎

***

In analyzing *Sturges v. Bridgman*, Coase argued that the dispute between doctor and neighboring confectioner was "exactly the same" as his hypothetical rancher-farmer example. And given an arbitrary distribution of entitlements and costless transacting, it was clear that the "decision of the courts concerning liability for damages would be without effect on the allocation of resources"[10] Even without the court's intervention (indeed in the world of the Coase theorem this issue would never come before a court), regardless of whether the doctor held the entitlement to be free from noise or the confectioner held the entitlement to use his mortars, the entitlement would have gone to the one with the highest valued use, and only the distribution of these costs would have been affected. If, say, the doctor held the entitlement but the confectioner's business created a higher social product, the two sides would bargain so that effectively the doctor would sell his entitlement for more than he would have obtained if he used it himself.

Of course *Sturges v. Bridgman* did go to court, which illustrates a second point: that the entitlement was not clearly defined to begin with and the process of determining it was anything but costless. Indeed, the confectioner was quite certain that he had or should have had the entitlement because he had for so long acted as though he did and was not told to stop. Students at first reading of this case tend to sympathize with the confectioner's point of view, and believe the decision was unjust. However, simply being first to use a resource, and having had the liberty to use it, did not give Bridgman, the confectioner, a legal entitlement.

The *Sturges* case is usefully compared to another: *Hadachek v. Sebastian*.[11] In that case, Hadachek had been making bricks at a plant on the outskirts of Los Angeles for years. No one complained that it produced smoke, noise, or other nuisances until the plant was no longer on the outskirts, but rather in the middle of an increasingly populated area of the city. A city ordinance prohibited brick making operations within city limits. Hadacheck claimed this constituted an unlawful taking of his property, which he argued was useful only for brickmaking. The court, however, upheld the ordinance as a legitimate police-power regulation. No entitlement had been given or implied by virtue of the fact that Hadachek had previously been allowed to make bricks unhindered. When the entitlement was to be decided in court, no reason dictated why it could not be granted to the residents instead of Hadachek.[12]

The *Sturges* case illustrates another point. The ruling of Judge Thesiger and his fellow judges on the appeals court (as well as the lower court judge's verdict they affirmed) did, in fact, make an economic judgment. The decision was specifically intended to determine how the land was to be used; the judges expressly hoped that it would aid "the development of the land for residential purposes." Was residential use more highly valued? Apparently it was more highly valued by the judges. But no evidence was adduced to show that it was more highly valued by the market. The value of the social product was not obviously maximized by this decision. Indeed Coase notes that from the standpoint of maximizing output the court's decision, awarding the entitlement to the doctor, would have been justified "only if the value of the additional residential facilities obtained was greater than the value of cakes lost. But of this the judges seem to have been unaware."[13]

Finally, *Sturges v. Bridgman* illustrates the joint cost aspect of all externality problems. Clearly, the confectioner did impose a cost on the surgeon, even if the surgeon could be said to have brought it on himself by moving his office to a wall adjacent to the noise. But once the office was constructed, a resolution to the conflict required the imposition of costs on one or both of the parties. Given the indeterminacy of entitlement allocation at the outset of the case, it is impossible to identify who was the transgressor and who was the victim. Both parties created the problem, the conflict, and the cost. The same is true in the next case.

Bryant v. Lefever
4. C.P.D. 172 (1879)

[In this case, plaintiff and defendants had lived for about forty years in neighboring houses of approximately the same height. The plaintiff was able, in that time, to light any fireplace in his house without chimney smoke blowing back into his house. In 1876, however, the defendants chose to rebuild their house so that an adjacent wall was now higher than the plaintiff's house. Moreover, the former stacked lumber on the roof making the height of their house that much greater. The result was that now when the plaintiff lit his fireplaces smoke blew back into his house. He sued and was initially awarded damages. Then the case was heard by the court of appeals.]

Bramwell, L.J.

***

[I]t is said, and the jury have found, that the defendants have done that which has caused a nuisance to the plaintiff's house. We think there is no evidence of this. No doubt there is a nuisance, but it is not of the defendants' causing. Their house and their timber are harmless enough. It is the plaintiff who causes the nuisance by lighting a coal fire in a place the chimney of which is placed so near the defendants' wall that the smoke does not escape but comes into the house. Let the plaintiff cease to light his fire; let him move his chimney; let him carry it higher, and there would be no nuisance. Who, then, causes it? It would be very clear that the plaintiff did, if he had built the house or chimney after the defendants had put the timber on their roof; and it is really the same though he did so before the timber was there. But (what is in truth the same answer) if the defendants cause the nuisance, they have a right to do so. If the plaintiff has not the right to the passage of air, except subject to the defendants' right to build or put timber on their house, then his right is subject to their right, and though a nuisance follows from the exercise of their right, they are not liable.

***

Cotton, L.J.

***

Here it is found that the erection of the defendants' wall has sensibly and materially interfered with the comfort of human existence in the plaintiff's house, and it is said this is a nuisance for which the defendants are liable. Ordinarily this is so, but the defendants have done so not by sending onto the plaintiff's property any smoke or noxious vapour but by interrupting the egress of smoke from the plaintiff's house in a way to which the plaintiff has no legal right. The plaintiff creates the smoke, which interferes with his comfort. Unless he has a right to get rid of this in a particular way which has been interfered with by the defendants, he cannot sue the defendants, because the smoke made by himself, for which he has not provided any effectual means of escape, causes him annoyance. ∎

***

The judges in *Bryant v. Lefever* agree that Bryant is liable for the nuisance because he lights his fires. Coase argues, however, that the judges oversimplify the problem:

> Who caused the smoke nuisance? The answer seems fairly clear. The smoke nuisance was caused both by the man who built the wall and by the man who lit the fires. Given the fires, there would have been no smoke nuisance without the wall; given the wall, there would have been no smoke nuisance without the fires. Eliminate the wall or the fires and the smoke nuisance would disappear. On the marginal principle, it is clear that both were responsible and both should be forced to include the loss of amenity due to the smoke as a cost in deciding whether to continue the activity which gives rise to the smoke.[14]

In the world of the Coase theorem, Coase goes on to say, we would expect precisely that result, and given the benefits and the costs to both, the entitlement to light fires or build the wall would be allocated to that user who valued the entitlement most highly. If that result required a rearrangement of entitlements, a costless transaction would occur.

Again, we don't live in the world of the Coase theorem and so a neat and inevitably efficient rearrangement may not take place. In the real world, says Coase:

> [O]nce the cost of carrying out market transactions [positive transaction costs] are taken into account, it is clear that such a rearrangement of rights will only be undertaken when the increase in the value of production consequent to the rearrangement is greater than the costs which would be involved in bringing it about. When it is less, the granting of an injunction (or the knowledge that it would be granted) or the liability to pay damages may result in an activity being discontinued (or may prevent its being started) which would be undertaken if market transactions were costless. In these conditions, the initial delimitation of rights does have an effect on the

efficiency with which the economic system operates. One arrangement of rights may bring about a greater value of production than any other. But unless this is the arrangement of rights established by the legal system, the costs of reaching the same result by altering and combining rights through the market may be so great that this optimal arrangement of rights, and the greater value of production which it would bring, may never be achieved.[15]

Here is the reason why Coase wanted to start his argument with a zero transaction assumption and the world of the Coase theorem: law matters because it affects transaction costs, and transaction costs affect the incentives of economic actors. Government regulation that assigns cost on what Coase believes to be a mistaken premise could well lead to greater cost than the alternative of doing "nothing about the problem at all."[16] That is, the social costs may well be higher (to return to the argument of Pigou) from a polluter-pays premise than from some alternative. However, Coase stressed that any solution "has costs, and there is no reason to suppose that government regulation is called for simply because the problem is not well handled by the market or the firm."[17] In the end, the set of institutions and organizations that should be chosen by society to affect solutions should "come from a detailed investigation of the actual results of handling the problem in different ways."[18] And even though the institutional mechanism for deciding such questions must be decided on a case-by-case basis, the goal presumably will be clear enough: to find the mechanisms and the distribution of entitlements that will maximize production and lower social cost.

THE COURTS AND THE DELIMITATION OF ENTITLEMENTS

The courts clearly play a major role in the functioning of an economic system when they allocate and delimit entitlements, which effect social costs. As Coase notes,

> [W]hen market transactions are so costly as to make it difficult to change the arrangement of rights established by law, the courts directly influence economic activity. It would therefore seem desirable that the courts should understand the economic consequences of their decisions and should, insofar as this is possible without creating too much uncertainty about the legal position itself, take these consequences into account when making their decisions. Even when it is possible to change the delimitation of rights through market transactions, it is obviously desirable to reduce the need for such transactions and thus reduce the employment of resources in carrying them out.[19]

Coase also argues that in many cases the courts, more than economists (such as Pigou and his followers), do at least implicitly recognize the joint or social cost nature of externalities. Moreover, courts are prepared to settle entitlements, where they are in dispute, on the party they believe will increase net social benefits. As noted, in the *Sturges* case the judges explicitly engage in economic policy making, deciding which activities should be given precedence in the Wimpole-Wigmore neighborhood. In another instance, the case of *Adams v. Ursell*,[20] the court argued that a fish-and-chips store was a nuisance in its current location but would not have been elsewhere in the same neighborhood or even elsewhere on the same street. Such cases, Coase argues, provide anecdotal evidence that the courts, more often than legislatures (and more often than economists) understand the reality of the joint cost problem and look to settle the matter by a ruling that would lead to a maximization of the social product.

> [T]he courts are, in effect, making a decision on the economic problem and determining how resources are to be employed. It was argued that the courts are conscious of this and they often make, although not always in a very explicit fashion, a comparison between what would be gained and what would be lost by preventing actions which have harmful effects.[21]

Some scholars would question the claim that courts tend to be cognizant of joint costs and the economic impacts of their rulings. Not surprisingly, in some cases (some of which are excerpted in this book) judges grossly misapply economic arguments. Court decisions in some cases also give reason to doubt whether courts have the institutional capacity to make social or economic policy. Coase's basic point, however, remains valid. In the cases he describes, judges are tacitly, if not quite directly, weighing the economic outcomes that will emerge from an arrangement or rearrangement of entitlements. In that sense, they do recognize the basic economic problem, which is the need to find, through the arrangement of entitlements, a satisfactory allocation of resources under ubiquitous conditions of scarcity.

"THE PROBLEM OF SOCIAL COST" AND MODERN LAW AND ECONOMICS

In the last sections of the article, Coase returns to the work of Pigou and uses a Pigovian example to show how a unidirectional, perpetrator-victim approach to externalities can lead to outcomes that increase social cost and lower social product. Coase's critique of Pigou was not only the principal motivating factor of the article. The critique also carries important implications for public policies related to pollution and other externalities. Ultimately, Coase's essay had even greater impacts. It became the seminal work in modern law and economics.

Here are four of the broader, general contributions of this essay:

1. In a world of positive transaction costs, law matters.
In the world of the Coase theorem, formal law is not necessary. Coase argued in this paper that clear entitlements need to be allocated albeit randomly. Then resources would inevitably go to those who valued them most highly, and the result would necessarily maximize social product. Or, as other scholars would say, the result would be *allocatively efficient*. The economist Steven Cheung argued, and Coase concurred, that in the world of the Coase theorem, no initial allocation of entitlements is even necessary for an efficient outcome;[22] market participants will costlessly define and allocate entitlements, as needed, by discrete contracting. The Coase theorem provides no basis for choosing between rival methods of social

organization. The assumptions of zero transaction costs, efficient resource allocation, and complete information are as consistent with socialist central planning as they are with free markets.

In a positive transaction cost world, the allocation of entitlements is often unclear, and when that is the case exchange may become prohibitively costly. Consider the farmer and the rancher: if both believe they hold the entitlement and know no clear rule to establish and enforce agreements, then the parties should see no reason to agree on the distribution of costs. Possibly neither is able to produce, or arrangements are made that are self-enforcing but may be very costly to both parties. Legislatures and courts establish rights and duties of economic actors in order that exchange may be facilitated, but these rights and duties are never perfectly delineated. In some cases, the allocation of rights and duties may be so imperfect or incomplete that exchange becomes too costly to undertake.

Transaction costs are a useful metric for determining the degree to which law is likely to increase (or decrease) economic exchange. Coase argued in "The Nature of the Firm" (1937) that transaction costs are the reason why firms exist and are necessary for efficient economic performance, so he argued in "The Problem of Social Cost" (1960) that transaction costs explain the existence of law and its necessity for efficient economic performance.

2. Law creates and alters economic incentives.

Economic concerns will affect how the law is (or should be) structured and how entitlements are allocated. At the same time, the law structures, and changes in the law alter, economic calculations and outcomes. Coase focused specifically on whether a legal rule, administrative practice, or court-determined rearrangement of entitlements raised or lowered output in society. In other words, did a legal rule advance or retard economic performance? In a world of zero transaction costs, he shows, this question would not even be raised. In a world of positive transaction costs, however, it is crucial.

In a ruling such as *Sturges*, for example, the decision of the judges will increase investment in residential and professional space and decrease commercial space in the neighborhood in question. Is this direction beneficial? The answer is not immediately obvious, but at least the clarification of entitlement reduces the cost of investment for some even as it raises it for others. In many instances, Coase argues, we can measure whether the outcome of allocation of entitlements serves to increase social product relative to alternatives. This argument is no doubt correct, although measurement itself may be so costly as to make a comprehensive study in many cases impossible. Still, the comparative analysis of different arrangements of entitlements or even legal regimes is the only way for society to choose those institutions that reduce social cost and increase social product.

3. Policy decisions should be made on the basis of comparative institutional analyses.

Coase's arguments about the centrality of law suggest a methodology for the study of the economic impact of laws and legal rulings: scholars should utilize a comparative institutional analysis, examining the costs and benefits of alternative allocations of entitlements, and measuring the net social benefit of each alternative. Many scholars have utilized this approach to examine the impact of court rulings and legislative changes. Does a law seem likely to raise or lower social product? What would be the likely result of an alternative? To get the highest level of social product, liability for harm should go to the one who can avoid it at lowest cost.

This goal begs an important question: How exactly do we get solutions to conflicts over resources that will get us the largest increases in social product? It should be noted at the outset that in a world of incomplete information and positive transaction costs (the real Coasean world), true social welfare maximization or optimization is as much a chimera as zero transaction costs. At best, we get a second-best result. Indeed, Coase remarked that all forms of economic organization—government, markets, and firms—are, to a greater or lesser extent, failures.[23] None give you an optimal result.

The key, according to Coase, is to allocate the entitlements in such a way as to create the least cost for society as a whole. To achieve allocative efficiency, we must move beyond simplistic, unidirectional (e.g., Pigovian) conceptions of externalities.

4. Entitlements (property rights) should be allocated so as to minimize joint or social costs.

Coase's analysis of social cost problems leads him to a normative prescription: courts (and other organizations that allocate property rights) should allocate property rights and duties so as to minimize joint or social costs. They can accomplish this goal by imposing the burden (or duty) of cost avoidance or abatement on the party that can do so at the lowest cost. Thus, the entitlement or property right should be allocated to the party with the higher costs of avoidance or abatement. By allocating rights and duties in this way, social costs would be minimized, even if transaction costs impede any further reallocation of those rights and duties.

Coase's normative solution to joint or social cost problems conflates two distinct questions:

1. What is the least-cost solution?
2. Which party should bear that cost?

Just because the farmer (from Coase's farmer and rancher hypothetical) might be the least-cost avoider does not mean necessarily that the farmer should bear the burden of implementing the least-cost solution. It may seem inequitable to impose the burden on the farmer, even as the least-cost avoider, when the rancher is profiting from the trespass of cattle onto the farmer's land. It should be possible to combine a Coasean least-cost solution with a more equitable remedy. For example, the court might hold the rancher liable, but limit the remedy to the lesser of the farmer's actual damages and reasonable avoidance costs.

CHAPTER SUMMARY

This chapter reviewed Ronald Coase's seminal theory of transaction costs, starting with the inaptly named Coase theorem, according to which the law (specifically, legal allocations of property rights and duties) does not affect the ultimate allocation of entitlements in a world of costless transacting: if transaction costs are zero (which they never really are), entitlements to resources will inevitably be allocated for optimal efficiency. The mythical world of the Coase theorem was not, however, the world Coase set out to explain. Rather, his primary concern was to explain the importance of law (specifically, the allocation of property rights and duties) in the real world of ubiquitous, always positive, and often quite high transaction costs. In this world, where transaction costs can and do impede efficient economic exchange, it becomes especially important that property rights and duties are allocated (by courts, legislatures, and other allocation organizations) so as to maximize the social product; that is, by minimizing social costs.

QUESTIONS AND PROBLEMS

1. According to Coase, who caused the harm in *Sturges v. Bridgman*?
2. Explain how Coase's approach to externalities differs from Pigou's.
3. What are the limits of Coase's joint cost theory of harm? Is it appropriate to say that laws prohibiting murder "harm" those who would like to commit murders? Under what circumstance might the social costs of prohibiting murder exceed the social costs of not prohibiting murder?
4. Coase recognizes that courts play an important role in the economy. They must resolve disputes so as to minimize transaction costs and maximize the social product. But are courts institutionally well-suited to engage in the kind of economic analysis that would lead them to make decisions that minimize transaction costs? Even if they are, what evidence is there that they deliberately do so? Is there any reason to believe, for example, that Lord Judge Thesinger, in *Sturges v. Bridgman*, was concerned to reach a decision that either minimized transaction costs or maximized social efficiency?
5. Given that Coase posited the world of zero transaction costs as a counterfactual, designed to illustrate the importance of transaction costs in the real world, why have economists and some legal scholars spent so much time and energy arguing about the so-called Coase theorem?
6. Was it unfair for the City of Los Angeles to prohibit Mr. Hadachek from continuing to make bricks within the city's limits? If so, what do you mean by "unfair"?
7. How might a judge have applied comparative institutional analysis in the *Sturges* case?
8. Discuss the following: In *Bryant v. Lefevre*, Lefevre was the best cost avoider, and so Bryant should have received the entitlement.
9. Empirical studies suggest that litigants rarely bargain around the court's allocation of the entitlement (property right). What might explain that finding?

NOTES

1. Ronald H. Coase, "The Problem of Social Cost," 3 JOURNAL OF LAW & ECONOMICS 1 (1960), reprinted in R. H. Coase, *The Firm, The Market, and the Law* (Chicago: University of Chicago Press, 1988), p. 95.
2. *See* Arthur Pigou, *The Economics of Welfare* (New York: AMS Press, 1978 [1924]).
3. A cost, whether internal or external, must be borne by someone, otherwise it is not a cost. If the cost is not borne by the producer of the cost or someone who contracts with that producer, then it is an external cost, or externality.
4. For an illustration of this issue, see the case of *Del Webb v. Spur*, excerpted in Chapter 6.
5. Ronald H. Coase, "The Problem of Social Cost," 104 JOURNAL OF LAW & ECONOMICS 1 (1960).
6. Even if some disputes were not preresolved by contract, they would be resolved as soon as they arose, by further costless contracting, per the assumption of zero transaction costs.

7. Ronald H. Coase, "The Nature of the Firm," 4 *ECONOMICA* (November 1937), *reprinted in* R. H. Coase, *The Firm, the Market, and the Law* (Chicago: University of Chicago Press, 1988), p. 33.

8. R. H. Coase, *The Firm, the Market, and the Law* (Chicago: University of Chicago Press, 1988), p. 15.

9. R. H. Coase, *The Firm, the Market, and the Law* (Chicago: University of Chicago Press, 1988), p. 159.

10. Ronald H. Coase, "The Problem of Social Cost," 106 *JOURNAL OF LAW & ECONOMICS* 1 (1960).

11. 239 U.S. 394 (1915).

12. Being the first to use a resource may in some cases stand as a good argument for awarding an entitlement, as we note in the next chapter.

13. Ronald H. Coase, "The Problem of Social Cost," 107 *JOURNAL OF LAW & ECONOMICS* 1 (1960).

14. Ronald H. Coase, "The Problem of Social Cost," 111 *JOURNAL OF LAW & ECONOMICS* 1 (1960).

15. Ronald H. Coase, "The Problem of Social Cost," 115 *JOURNAL OF LAW & ECONOMICS* 1 (1960).

16. Ronald H. Coase, "The Problem of Social Cost," 118 *JOURNAL OF LAW & ECONOMICS* 1 (1960).

17. Ronald H. Coase, "The Problem of Social Cost," 118 *JOURNAL OF LAW & ECONOMICS* 1 (1960).

18. Ronald H. Coase, "The Problem of Social Cost," 119 *JOURNAL OF LAW & ECONOMICS* 1 (1960).

19. Ronald H. Coase, "The Problem of Social Cost," 119 *JOURNAL OF LAW & ECONOMICS* 1 (1960).

20. 1 Ch. 269 (1913).

21. Ronald H. Coase, "The Problem of Social Cost," 131–132 *JOURNAL OF LAW & ECONOMICS* 1 (1960).

22. Steven N. S. Cheung, "Will China Go Capitalist?" Hobart Paper 94, (1986), p. 37; R. H. Coase, *The Firm, The Market, and the Law* (Chicago: University of Chicago Press, 1988), p. 15.

23. Ronald H. Coase, "Discussion: The Regulated Industries," 54 *AMERICAN ECONOMICS REVIEW* 194, 195 (1964).

Chapter 5

Property I: Acquisition

*T*he concept of property is central to both law and economics. From a legal point of view, the allocation of property rights determines who controls—and, just as importantly, who does not control—access to and use of resources. From an economic perspective, as we learned in the preceding chapter on "The Problem of Social Cost," the allocation of property rights structures economic activity and affects efficiency in the real world of positive transaction costs. This chapter explores the meaning, sources, and economic consequences of property.

WHAT IS PROPERTY?

Rights and Duties Respecting Things

There is no such thing as property. Property is a sociolegal relationship between people respecting things. Property must be relational because the very notion of property *rights* entails the idea of property *duties*. To say that one person has a property right in something is necessarily to say that at least one other person—perhaps all other people—have a corresponding obligation not to interfere with that rightholder's control (to the extent of their title) of the thing. At its most basic, then, property is about the concomitant rights and duties of owners and nonowners with respect to the control of resources.

Not One Right, But a Bundle of Rights

Property is not just one right but a bundle of several rights, including (among others) the right to possess, the right to use, the right to alienate, and the right to exclude. In some circumstances, the nominal owner will possess all the attendant rights of property, but it is not at all uncommon for specific rights to be limited or missing altogether. For example, the owner of stock in a corporation has property in the corporation, but no right to possess specific corporate assets. Even the right to exclude, which is generally thought to be the *sine qua non* of property,[1] may be limited. In the case of *State v. Shack*,[2] the New Jersey Supreme Court ruled that the owner of a farm could not exclude publicly funded health and legal advisers from entering his land in order to provide advice and assistance to the seasonal migrant workers the farm owner employed. In some circumstances, the right to exclude may be missing entirely. In England, for example, National Parks are mostly superimposed on privately owned lands. After it receives National Park designation, a land parcel remains in nominal private ownership, but the private owner holds no legal right to exclude members of the public from accessing the park.

What Makes a Right "Property"?

The phrase *property rights* implies something distinctive. What makes a property right different from, say, a human right or some other kind of right? In contrast to some legal scholars,[3] many law and economics scholars treat property rights (and duties) just like other kinds of rights. What makes a right a "property right," for them, is merely the fact that it is a right that relates to some thing or resource. Some rights may be treated or enforced differently from others, which is, as we shall see, a function of the circumstantial costs of transacting, rather than any essential difference between kinds of rights.

Ownership and Relativity of Title

Common (nonlegal) understandings of property tend to be based on a "mine and thine" conception of property, according to which one either owns something or does not. From this perspective, property rights are clear and absolute. The legal reality of property, however, has always been far more complicated, to a point where the notion of ownership becomes ambiguous.

As noted previously, property rights constitute entitlements to access and use resources. Pursuant to the "bundle of rights" notion of property, it is not only possible but quite common for more than one person to hold property rights with respect to a single object at the same time. If you purchase a new car on credit, you "own" the car, but the creditor holds a security interest in it. If you do not pay off the loan, the creditor may be able to repossess the car from you. Even after you pay off the auto loan, you may not be the only person with property rights in the car. If you drive it to a fancy restaurant, and leave it with the parking attendant, you enter a legal relationship known as a *bailment*. Pursuant to that relationship, the parking attendant gains substantial, though limited, property rights in your car. The attendant has the right to possess your car against the claims of anyone other than you. The same is true of a friend who simply borrows your car: your friend has the right to possess it, and can enforce that right against everyone except you, the true owner. These examples illustrate the concept of relativity of title, according to which several different persons may have property interests, or entitlements, in a single object at the same time. This concept is not the same thing as "co-ownership," in which two or more persons share coextensive interests. Relativity of title, as the name suggests, denotes different quanta of property rights. The bailee (the parking attendant) is not a co-owner with the bailor, possessing equal rights. The bailee's title is inferior to the true owner's, but superior to all others' claims.

Most of the time, the person we call the "owner" has paramount title or the strongest claim to the thing, but not always. Under some circumstances, however rare, the law prefers the claims of subsequent possessors to prior owners.

Suppose that Bob owns a fine watch, which he loses one day during a walk in the park. No identifying marks on the watch indicate who is the owner or disclose where to find him. A few days later, Jim is wandering about the park with his handy metal detector, and he discovers the watch. Jim immediately takes the watch to the best jewelry store in town for evaluation. The jewelry store owner tells Jim that the watch is worth approximately $10,000, and offers to sell it for him on consignment. Jim agrees. A week later, the watch is sold for $10,000 to Steve, who knows nothing about the prior history of the watch. All he knows is that it is a nice looking watch, and he wants to buy it. The jewelry store owner pays Jim $7,500, keeping a 25 percent sales commission for selling the watch. Approximately one month after purchasing the watch, Steve is at a dinner party, where Bob also happens to be present. Bob recognizes his old watch at once, and asks Steve how and where he acquired it. A few days later, after a bit of investigation, including a visit to the jewelry store from which Steve purchased the watch, Bob claims that the watch is his, and demands that Steve return it to him. Steve refuses, claiming that he owns the watch. So who should own the watch, the original owner (Bob) or the recent purchaser (Steve)? Consider that question in light of the following case.

Paschal v. Hamilton

363 So. 2d. 1360 (Miss. 1978)

Patterson, J:

Paschal filed suit in the Circuit Court of Oktibbeha County for replevin of an automobile. The trial court directed a verdict for defendants Billy and Geneva Hamilton.

The sole issue presented, one of first impression, in this Court is: May a bona fide purchaser of an automobile for value take good title from one who procured the automobile by fraudulent purchase?

Paschal was the owner of an automobile and advertised it for sale. A prospective buyer made an offer which was accepted. The following day the buyer appeared at Paschal's home and gave a check to Paschal's wife in exchange for the car and title. Subsequently the check was dishonored as a forgery.

After the car had been resold several times, it was purchased by the Hamiltons from a used car dealer in Starkville, Mississippi. Paschal later located the car through law enforcement officials and brought this action for replevin.

The Mississippi Uniform Commercial Code . . . provides:

§§ 75–2–403. Power to transfer; good faith purchaser of goods; "entrusting."

(1) A purchaser of goods acquires all title which his transferor had or had power to transfer except that a purchaser of a limited interest acquires rights only to the extent of the interest purchased. A person with voidable title has power to transfer a good title to a good faith purchaser for value. When goods have been delivered under a transaction of purchase the purchaser has such power even though (a) the transferor was deceived as to the identity of the purchaser, or (b) the delivery was in exchange for a check which is later

dishonored, or (c) it was agreed that the transaction was to be a "cash sale," or (d) the delivery was procured through fraud punishable as larcenous under the criminal law.

(2) Any entrusting of possession of goods to a merchant who deals in goods of that kind gives him power to transfer all rights of the entruster to a buyer in ordinary course of business.

(3) "Entrusting" includes any delivery and any acquiescence in retention of possession regardless of any condition expressed between the parties to the delivery or acquiescence and regardless of whether the procurement of the entrusting or the possessor's disposition of the goods have been such as to be larcenous under the criminal law.

(4) The rights of other purchasers of goods and of lien creditors are governed by the chapters on Secured Transactions (Chapter 9), Bulk Transfers (Chapter 6) and Documents of Title (Chapter 7). (Emphasis added).

It is clear on the facts that the original sale involved "goods [which] have been delivered under a transaction of purchase. . . . " Therefore, 1(d) is controlling and good faith purchasers (here the Hamiltons) take a good title. While the Commercial Code rule may seem harsh, it is in line with the purposes of the Code, to promote commerce and business by simplifying and making uniform the law dealing with commercial transactions. . . .

We also note that this rule is not inconsistent with prior cases holding that the purchaser of a stolen vehicle does not obtain good title, since there the transferor did not obtain the vehicle by "delivery under a transaction of purchase.". . .

The judgment of the trial court is affirmed. ∎

Because the car was not stolen but obtained by fraud, the bona fide purchaser (BFP) has title superior to that of the prior, rightful owner.

Economic arguments can be made both for and against the outcome in *Paschal v. Hamilton*. On the pro side, the goal of the Uniform Commercial Code (UCC), as the Mississippi Supreme Court notes, is to promote commerce. To that end, it is crucial that buyers be able to trust the title they receive from reputable sellers, when they purchase goods in the ordinary course of business. Moreover, the prior, rightful owner was arguably the lower-cost avoider in this case because he was in a better position than the BFP to guard against the fraud that occurred. He, not the BFP, had contact with the defrauder; so he, not the BFP, was in the best position to adjudge the defrauder's trustworthiness (or lack thereof). This line of reasoning might also be true in cases of simple theft, though in those cases the prior, rightful owner prevails over the BFP. In the case of theft, at least, the prior, rightful owner does not give up possession willingly. The rightful owner does not choose to transact with the thief, and so has less control than in situations where possession is transferred through fraud or deceit.

On the con side, the result in *Paschal v. Hamilton* appears to reward crooks, as long as they defraud owners rather than engage in simple theft. Even though the BFP prevails over the prior, rightful owner, the later is not without recourse. The BFP has title superior to the prior, rightful owner, but the prior, rightful owner still has title superior to both the car dealer and the defrauder, each of whom profited wrongfully from his property. The prior, rightful owner may well be able to recover damages from the car dealer who purchased the vehicle from the defrauder—it is unlikely that the dealer would be considered a BFP under the UCC.[4] The defrauder too would be liable to the prior, rightful owner in a tort action and could be subject to criminal prosecution by the state.

Most law and economics scholars, when they write about property, focus exclusively on private property, as if all property were private, which is not the case. Ancient Roman lawyers distinguished four types of property regimes: private (*res privatae*), public (*res publicae*), common (*res communes*), and nonproperty or open access (*res nullius*).

Res Privatae

When people talk about property and property rights, they usually are presumed to refer to private property. Private property is defined as property rights held either by a single private individual or a small group of co-owners. A majority of land in the United States is held in private ownership.

Res Publicae

When property is nominally "owned" by the public at large or owned by the state on behalf of the public, this type of ownership is referred to as public or state ownership. Some economists and legal scholars in the public choice tradition doubt the existence of any such thing as public property. In their view, property owned by everyone is either owned by no one (*res nullius*) or de facto controlled by, and in the interests of, politicians and bureaucrats. They also argue that so-called "public resources" should be privatized in order to maximize economic value. The fact remains, however, that 42 percent of land in the United States is owned publicly and controlled by the federal, state, or local governments. Even if "public" ownership is inefficient (or simply a myth), popular support for the privatization of Yellowstone National Park, for example, is virtually nonexistent.

Res Communes

Common property is a hybrid form, combining features of both private and public property; and it is often mistakenly conflated with nonproperty. At its most basic, common property is simply private property owned by more than one individual. When law and economics scholars write about common property, however, they tend to mean property owned by a group comprised of more than just a few individuals. Examples of common property include fisheries, where the fishers, as a self-governing organization, establish rules governing fishing locations, take-limits, and so on. This type of common property situation is conventionally distinguished from private property by the collective nature of decision making concerning resource allocation and use. It is also distinguished from public property based on the fact that the decision makers are the local resource users themselves, rather than politicians or bureaucrats located far from the resource. Often, common property regimes are portrayed in the law and economics literature as inefficient compared to stylized private property regimes. It is worth noting, however, that many common property regimes have functioned well over long periods of time in different parts of the world, and persist to this day.

Res Nullius

Common property is often conflated with nonproperty/open-access, but it is easy to see that they are distinct institutions. Common property involves at least two groups: (1) the resource users/decision makers, and (2) other, non-co-owners of the common property, who have no access or use rights. With nonproperty/open-access by contrast, the resource is free for access and use by all. In reality, nonproperty/open-access does not constitute a property regime at all, but denotes the absence of any other property institution. One apparent reason for the conflation of common property and open access is the use of the term *commons* to describe any area not owned by private individuals or the public/state. It remains crucially important, however, to distinguish between commons, which are collectively owned by some nonstate group to the exclusion of others, and commons, which are completely open-access so that no one has the right to exclude anyone else.

Mixed Property Regimes

In addition to these Roman law categories of property systems, many hybrid forms developed over time, which combined elements of two or more ownership regimes For example, commonfield agriculture, which combines elements of individual private ownership and common property, persisted throughout Northern Europe for more than 1,000 years, and still persists in mountainous regions of South America and Japan. Where this form of agriculture is practiced, land parcels are privately owned for purposes of crop cultivation, but commonly owned for purposes of pasturage. While under cultivation, the private landowner has the right to exclude neighbors from grazing their sheep or cattle on the arable land. But when the land lies fallow, the neighbors possess common rights of pasturage. The land cycles between private and common property with respect to its distinct amenity-values of crop production and pasturage.

Property Regime Choice

The fact that various property systems coexist in the world raises the question of property regime choice: Which system—private, public, common, or open access—works best when? This question is much easier to ask than answer. The complexities of the real world seem to defy simple (or simplistic) solutions, such as "private property is always best" or "public property is always best." Even the father of capitalism, Adam Smith (1723–1790), recognized the value of limited public ownership of land:

> Lands, for the purposes of pleasure and magnificence, parks, gardens,
> public walks, &c., possessions which are every where considered as causes
> of expence, not as sources of revenue, seem to be the only lands which, in
> a great and civilized monarchy, ought to belong to the crown.[5]

In addition, private property rights are costly to define, allocate, and enforce. It is reasonable to expect that, in some cases, the costs of instituting a private property regime might exceed the benefits. In those cases, resources are likely to be held in common or public ownership, if they are subject to any property regime at all.

On the other side of the coin, not even the communist Karl Marx (1818–1883) sought to abolish all private property, only property in the "means of production" (which modern economists would call "factors of production"). Nothing Marx wrote would support public or communal ownership of inherently personal items such as toothbrushes or underwear.

ECONOMIC FUNCTIONS OF PROPERTY

Questions of property regime choice presume some social goal(s) or purpose(s), which property is instituted to accomplish. Theorists have discussed a wide variety of property purposes, both ethical—cultivating individual moral development—and economic. Among economic purposes of property, four predominate: Property serves as the basis of exchange, resource conservation, and capitalization and investment.

Economic Exchange

Open any introductory economics textbook, and you will read that property is fundamental to economic exchange;[6] that is, in the absence of well-defined property rights, markets do not function well because the costs of transacting are high. Buyers are far more likely to enter into transactions when they have confidence that sellers actually own and can convey good title to the resources they are selling.

Resource Conservation

Property does not only serve the purpose of facilitating contracting and exchange. It also promotes resource conservation.

Garrett Hardin, "The Tragedy of the Commons"
121 Science 1243 (1968)

***

Picture a pasture open to all. It is to be expected that each herdsman will try to keep as many cattle as possible on the commons. Such an arrangement may work reasonably satisfactorily for centuries because tribal wars, poaching, and disease keep the numbers of both man and beast well below the carrying capacity of the land. Finally, however, comes the day of reckoning, that is, the day when the long-desired goal of social stability becomes a reality. At this point, the inherent logic of the commons remorselessly generates tragedy.

As a rational being, each herdsman seeks to maximize his gain. Explicitly or implicitly more or less consciously, he asks: "What is the utility to me of adding one more animal to my herd?" This utility has one negative and one positive component.

1. The positive component is a function of the increment of one animal. Since the herdsman receives all the proceeds from the sale of the additional animal, the positive utility is nearly +1.
2. The negative component is a function of the additional overgrazing, created by one more animal. Since, however, the effects of overgrazing are shared by all the herdsmen, the negative utility for any particular decision making herdsman is only a fraction of −1.

Adding together the component partial utilities, the rational herdsman concludes that the only sensible course for him to pursue is to add another animal to his herd. And another; and another. . . . But this is the conclusion reached by each and every rational herdsman sharing a commons. Therein is the tragedy. Each man is locked into a system that compels him to increase his herd without limit—in a world that is limited. Ruin is the destination toward which all men rush, each pursuing his own best interest in a society that believes in the freedom of the commons. Freedom in a commons brings ruin to all. . . .

What shall we do? We have several options. We might sell [the commons] off as private property. We might keep them as public property, but allocate the right to enter them. The allocation might be on the basis of wealth, by the use of an auction system. It might be on the basis of merit, as defined by some agreed-upon standards. It might be by lottery. Or it might be on a first-come, first-served basis, administered to long queues. These, I think, are all the reasonable possibilities. They are all objectionable. But we must choose—or acquiesce in the destruction of the commons. . . . ■

Hardin demonstrates with elegant simplicity that scarce natural resources, in the absence of property rights or government regulation, will tend to be overused and degraded. The purpose of property, in this account, is to control access to and use of scarce resources. By assigning someone or some group the right to exclude others, property law promotes resource conservation. It internalizes to the owner(s) more of the costs of resource use decisions as well as the benefits of conservation. Just as important, privatization makes their conservation decisions enforceable (via the right to exclude) against other potential users. Thus, if the owner of a certain patch of pasture decides not to graze one more head of cattle on it, no one else has the right to exploit that forgone opportunity (unless they buy the right from the current owner).

A brief digression on Hardin's "Tragedy of the Commons" as a Prisoners' Dilemma Game.

One way to explore problems such as that raised by Hardin is to utilize the theory of games. Game theory allows us to examine the consequences of various kinds of strategic interactions and how economic actors might not reach a socially or even personally beneficial outcome, even as they rationally pursue their goals.

The dilemma posed by Hardin can be illustrated by a common game model known as the Prisoner's Dilemma. In this game, two captured thieves (Thief 1 and Thief 2) are taken to separate interrogation rooms. Each is promised a light sentence in return for testimony against the other. This dilemma offers four possible outcomes: (1) If Thief 1 testifies against Thief 2, and Thief 2 does not testify against

Thief 1, Thief 2 will receive a harsh sentence and Thief 1 will receive probation. (2) If Thief 2 testifies against Thief 1, but Thief 1 does not testify against Thief 2, Thief 1 will receive a harsh sentence, and Thief 2 will receive only probation. (3) If they both refuse to testify, neither can be convicted of the major charge; they are only convicted of minor charges carrying very short prison sentences or fines. And (4), if they both testify, both will receive substantial sentences. The "best" strategy for each prisoner individually is to testify against the other; but the "best" strategy for the two of them collectively is to cooperate and not testify against one another.

The same is true in Hardin's story of the tragedy of the commons—sometimes called the "herder model." If the herders agree to cooperate by restraining the size of their herds in order to conserve the common pasture, they will be best off in the aggregate. If one adds to a herd but another does not, the former gains at the latter's expense. If both add to their herds, the tragedy of the commons ensues, and both wind up with nothing.

The payoff matrix shown below describes the possible outcomes of a game between two herders grazing cattle on an open-access pasture. Suppose the maximum sustainable carrying capacity of the pasture—the level at which the pasture will not be overexploited, leading to "tragedy"—produces total output for society equal to 10 units of profit, which is divided in half, 5 and 5. If the two herders cooperate, they will each realize 5 units of profit. Their combined profit of 10 units is the best outcome for society as a whole. If one of them "defects" (i.e., does not cooperate) and grazes extra cattle, while the other maintains the original herd size, the defector will obtain a higher profit of 7 (the added profit minus the portion of costs the herder must bear), and the cooperating herder will suffer a net loss of -1 (bearing greater and greater costs). Note that total (social) profit falls to 6. But the dominant strategy (i.e., the individually rational maximizing strategy) is for both herders to defect, which will ruin the commons and result in decreasing private (individual) and social gains (which are zero in the bottom, right-hand quadrant of the payoff matrix) or even social losses (substitute a negative number for the zeros in the bottom, right-hand quadrant). Thus, individually rational strategies can lead to socially inefficient outcomes.

When Hardin refers to "the tragedy of the commons," it is not completely clear whether he means common property resources, as defined earlier in this chapter,

		Herder 2	
		Cooperate	Noncooperate
Herder 1	Cooperate	5, 5	$-1, 7$
	Noncooperate	7, -1	0, 0

or nonproperty/open-access resources. His title suggests common property resources, and yet he postulates "a pasture open to all," which signifies not common property but nonproperty/open-access. In the following excerpt, however, economist Harold Demsetz clearly asserts that the creation of individual, private property resolved resource conservation problems that historically arose not just in open-access commons but also in common property regimes.

Harold Demsetz, "Toward a Theory of Property Rights"

57 American Economics Review 347–357 (1967)

In the world of Robinson Crusoe property rights play no role. Property rights are an instrument of society and derive their significance from the fact that they help a man form those expectations which he can reasonably hold in his dealings with others. These expectations find expression in the laws, customs, and mores of a society. An owner of property rights possesses the consent of fellow men to allow him to act in particular ways. An owner expects the community to prevent others from interfering with his actions, provided that those actions are not prohibited in the specifications of his rights.

It is important to note that property rights convey the right to benefit or harm oneself or others. Harming a competitor by producing superior products may be permitted, while shooting him may not. A man may be permitted to benefit himself by shooting an intruder but be prohibited from selling below a price floor. It is clear, then, that property rights specify how persons may be benefitted and harmed, and, therefore, who must pay whom to modify the actions taken by persons. The recognition of this leads easily to the close relationship between property rights and externalities.

Externality is an ambiguous concept. For the purposes of this paper, the concept includes external costs, external benefits, and pecuniary as well as nonpecuniary externalities. No harmful or beneficial effect is external to the world. Some person or persons always suffer or enjoy these effects. What converts a harmful or beneficial effect into an externality is that the cost of bringing the effect to bear on the decisions of one or more of the interacting persons is too high to make it worthwhile, and this is what the term shall mean here. "Internalizing" such effects refers to a process, usually a change in property rights, that enables these effects to bear (in greater degree) on all interacting persons.

A primary function of property rights is that of guiding incentives to achieve a greater internalization of externalities. Every cost and benefit associated with social interdependencies is a potential externality. One condition is necessary to make costs and benefits externalities. The cost of a transaction in the rights between the parties (internalization) must exceed the gains from internalization. In general, transacting costs can be large relative to gains because of "natural" difficulties in trading or they can be large because of legal reasons. In a lawful society the prohibition of voluntary negotiations makes the cost of transacting infinite. Some costs and benefits are not taken into account by users of resources whenever externalities exist, but allowing transactions increases the degree to which internalization takes place.

THE EMERGENCE OF PROPERTY RIGHTS

If the main allocative function of property rights is the internalization of beneficial and harmful effects, then the emergence of property rights can be understood best by their association with the emergence of new or different beneficial and harmful effects.

Changes in knowledge result in changes in production functions, market values, and aspirations. New techniques, new ways of doing the same things, and doing new things—all invoke harmful and beneficial effects to which society has not been accustomed. It is my thesis in this part of the paper that the emergence of new property rights takes place in response to the desires of the interacting persons for adjustment to new benefit-cost possibilities.

The thesis can be restated in a slightly different fashion: property rights develop to internalize externalities when the gains from internalization become larger than the cost of internalization. Increased internalization, in the main, results from changes in economic values, changes which stem from the development of new technology and the opening of new markets, changes to which old property rights are poorly attuned. A property interpretation of this assertion requires that account be taken of a community's preferences for private ownership. Some communities will have less-developed private ownership systems and more highly developed state ownership systems. But, given a community's tastes in this regard, the emergence of new private or state-owned property rights will be in response to changes in technology and relative prices.

I do not mean to assert or deny that the adjustments in property rights which take place need be the result of a conscious endeavor to cope with new externality problems. These adjustments have arisen in Western societies largely as a result of gradual changes in social mores and in common law precedents. At each step of this adjustment process, it is unlikely that externalities per se were consciously related to the issue being resolved. These legal and moral experiments may be hit-and-miss procedures to some extent but in a society that weights the achievement of efficiency heavily, their viability in the long run will depend on how well they modify behavior to accommodate to the externalities associated with important changes in technology or market values.

***

The partial concentration of benefits and costs that accompany private ownership is only part of the advantage this system offers. The other part, and perhaps the most important, has escaped our notice. The cost of negotiating over the remaining externalities will be reduced greatly. Communal property rights allow anyone to use the land. Under this system it becomes necessary for all to reach an agreement on land use. But the externalities that accompany private ownership of property do not affect all owners, and, generally speaking, it will be necessary for only a few to reach an agreement that takes these effects into account. The cost of negotiating an internalization of these effects is thereby reduced considerably. The point is important enough to elucidate.

Suppose an owner of a communal land right, in the process of plowing a parcel of land, observes a second communal owner constructing a dam on adjacent land. The farmer prefers to have the stream as it is, and so he asks the engineer to stop his construction. The engineer says, "Pay me to stop." The farmer replies, "I will be happy to pay you, but what can you guarantee in return?" The engineer answers, "I can guarantee you that I will not continue constructing the dam, but I cannot guarantee that another engineer will not take up the task because this is communal property; I have no right to exclude him." What would be a simple negotiation between two persons under a private property arrangement turns out to be a rather complex negotiation between the farmer and everyone else. This is the basic explanation, I believe, for the preponderance of single rather than multiple owners of property. Indeed, an increase in the number of owners is an increase in the communality of property and leads, generally, to an increase in the cost of internalizing.

The reduction in negotiating cost that accompanies the private right to exclude others allows most externalities to be internalized at rather low cost. ∎

***

Demsetz elaborates on several of the same arguments that Hardin made (a year later) in "The Tragedy of the Commons." Where Hardin proffered two solutions to the "tragedy," privatization and regulation, Demsetz sets out to show why the privatization solution in particular is likely to successfully conserve scarce natural resources. He argues that property both internalizes externalities and reduces the costs of transacting.

Demsetz's arguments about how property rights reduce externalities is basically the same as Hardin's. When a rancher adds one more head of cattle to common grazing lands, many of the costs associated with that decision are externalized to other ranchers (each of whose cattle will find marginally less forage, and consequently will weigh less when taken to market). Conversely, if one rancher decides not to add one more head of cattle to the herd on the commons, many of the benefits of that decision are externalized to the other ranchers, any of whom can internalize those benefits by adding more of their own cattle to the commons. When, however, a private owner of grazing lands decides to add or not add one more head of cattle to the herd, he bears virtually all of the costs and benefits from that decision.

What Demsetz really adds to Hardin's analysis is the argument that privatization of the commons also reduces the costs of transacting. It does so by reducing the universe of people who need to cooperate in order to conserve any particular scarce resource. Conservation of a commons, as a commons, requires multiple contracts between each user and every other user. As Demsetz notes, this requirement can lead to high negotiating costs, even if parties do not engage in strategic behavior (both holdout and free-rider problems, as described in Chapter 1). Conservation of privately owned resources, by contrast, requires only a decision by the private owner(s), which will be enforced against others (nonowners) pursuant to the right to exclude.

Capitalization and Investment

In addition to making possible the conservation of scarce resources, the institution of property facilitates economic development and growth. Economists since Adam Smith have recognized land as an important source of production both for the output of the land itself and for its use as collateral for other forms of production. Land is economically valuable. That value can be transformed into money, which in turn can be utilized for investment in other kinds of productive assets. But not always, and not everywhere. The fact that land is economically valuable is a necessary but not sufficient condition for obtaining a loan that would convert its economic value into cash. In addition, banks and other creditors will demand proof that the borrower actually owns (i.e., possesses legal title) to the land. In the absence of such proof, banks and other creditors typically will not make the loan because of the risk that someone else might show up later with a better claim over the land than the borrower.

Suppose the Building and Loan Bank loans Bailey $1 million based on her claim of ownership of Blackacre, a piece of land worth an estimated $10 million. Subsequently, Potter turns up, claiming that he, not Bailey, owns Blackacre. If the courts uphold Potter's claim, then suddenly the bank loses the collateral that secured its loan to Bailey. If Bailey subsequently defaults on her loan payments, the Building and Loan cannot take over Blackacre because Potter owns Blackacre, and Potter was not a party to the transaction between Bailey and the bank. Of course, banks know about this risk, and so they try to minimize it at the time they make the loan by obtaining guarantees that the borrower actually possesses the best legal title. Prior to granting the loan or mortgage, they will search the legal records for competing claims; and, just in case a competing claim does arise in the future, they will require the borrower to purchase title insurance. A title insurance company, in turn, will issue the policy only if it is fairly certain that no other claimant has better legal title.

So, it is not the physical existence of land or other assets that provides the basis for full economic utilization but the combination of economically valuable assets and the sociolegal fact of functional and secure property systems to govern those assets.

As the Peruvian economist, Hernando de Soto, has written:[7]

> Formal property systems can be easily used as collateral for a loan; as equity exchanged for investment; as an address for collecting debts, rates, and taxes; as a locus point for the identification of individuals for commercial, judicial, or civic purposes; and as a liable terminal for receiving public utility services, such as energy, water, sewage, telephone, or cable services. While houses in advanced nations are acting as shelters or workplaces, their [legal] representations are leading a parallel life, carrying out a variety of additional functions to secure the interests of other parties.

De Soto refers to the legal system of property as a "staircase" by which countries move "from the universe of assets in their natural state to the conceptual universe of capital where assets can be viewed in their full productive potential."[8] By facilitating the easy conversion of economically valuable assets such as land into more liquid forms, property rights allow economic resources to be more quickly and easily moved to their highest and best (i.e., most profitable) uses, which in turn allows for higher levels of economic growth.

Anticompetitive Effects of Monopoly Property Rights: Incentives to Innovate Versus Market Competition in Intellectual Property Law

As just discussed, the institution of property rights creates incentives to invest by ensuring third-party (state) enforcement of property rights. The importance of this point can hardly be overstated. No farmer, except one who could afford a private police force, would invest the time, effort, and money required to raise crops, unless assured of later possession of the crops.

Beyond the real property (land) context, the state creates incentives for investment in socially useful innovations though the system of intellectual property. By granting inventors monopoly property rights in their creations, the law encourages their creative activities. As the U.S. District Court for the Northern District of California recently explained in *U.S. v. Elcom, Ltd.*[9]

> The purpose of the [Constitution's] Intellectual Property Clause [Art. I, § 8, cl. 8] is to promote the useful arts and sciences. Thus, the government is empowered to grant exclusive rights to inventors and authors in their respective inventions and original works of authorship, for limited times. This allows the inventor/author a reasonable time in which to reap the economic fruits of his or her inventive or creative labor. As a result of this economic incentive, people are encouraged to engage in inventive and originally expressive endeavors, thereby promoting the arts and sciences. In addition, because the grant of property rights is to be of limited duration,

the public will generally benefit, once the exclusive rights expire and the invention or expression becomes dedicated to the public.

Despite the court's suggestion of a win-win situation for creators and consumers, an inherent tension exists between two important economic values: (1) the desirability of exclusive property rights in socially useful ideas to create incentives for innovation, and (2) the benefits of competition in the marketplace.

During the term of a patent or copyright, the creator holds a monopoly on the market for goods created. As in all cases where free market competition is stifled, the result is likely to be market failure to maximize social welfare. Not only is the monopoly producer enabled to recoup actual innovation expenditures, but sometimes supernormal profits by maintaining prices high above the marginal cost of production, without fear of lower-priced competition.[10] Circumstances change, of course, after the intellectual property rights expire. Under current law, patent rights expire after 20 years, and copyrights expire 70 years after the author or composer dies. Competitors are then free to enter the field, and prices will tend to fall toward the marginal costs of production.

The inherent tension between the social desire to promote scientific and artistic innovation through the creation of intellectual property rights and the equally strong social desire for competitive and efficiently functioning markets requires some trade-off or balance between the two social goals. The U.S. Constitution strikes a balance, as the court indicated in *Elcom*, by requiring time limits on intellectual property rights to ensure that any market distortions resulting from monopoly pricing are only temporary. The common law courts (prior to the enactment of the 1976 Copyright Act[11]) fashioned a somewhat different balance, which tended to favor market competition over property rights in ideas. For example, under the common law, the author of a book received an automatic copyright that lasted only until general publication. Once the book was published, the author lost all rights so that everyone else became free to copy the book, unless the author expressly reserved rights under the Copyright Act.

The following case both illustrates and explains the common law's preference for competitive markets and consumers over the property claims of creators and innovators, at least when it comes to utilitarian goods.

Cheney Brothers v. Doris Silk Corp.

35 F. 2d 279 (2d Cir. 1929), cert. denied, 281 U.S. 728 (1930)

L. Hand, Circuit Judge.

The plaintiff, a corporation, is a manufacturer of silks, which puts out each season many new patterns, designed to attract purchasers by their novelty and beauty. Most of these fail in that purpose, so that not much more than a fifth catch the public fancy. Moreover, they have only a short life, for the most part no more than a single season of eight or nine months. It is in practice impossible, and it would be very onerous if it were not, to secure design patents upon all of these; it would also be impossible to know in advance which would sell well, and patent only those. Besides, it is probable that for the most part they have no such originality as would support a design patent. Again, it is impossible to copyright them under the Copyright Act (17 USCA §§ 1 et seq.), or at least so the authorities of the Copyright Office hold. So it is easy for anyone to copy such as prove successful, and the plaintiff, which is put to much ingenuity and expense in fabricating them, finds itself without protection of any sort for its pains.

Taking advantage of this situation, the defendant copied one of the popular designs in the season beginning in October, 1928, and undercut the plaintiff's price. This is the injury of which it complains. The defendant, though it duplicated the design in question, denies that it knew it to be the plaintiff's, and there thus arises an issue which might be an answer to the motion. However, the parties wish a decision upon the equity of the bill, and, since it is within our power to dismiss it, we shall accept its allegation, and charge the defendant with knowledge.

The plaintiff asks for protection only during the season, and needs no more, for the designs are all ephemeral. It seeks in this way to disguise the extent of the proposed innovation, and to persuade us that, if we interfere only a little, the solecism, if there be one, may be pardonable. But the reasoning which would justify any interposition at all demands that it cover the whole extent of the injury. A man whose

designs come to harvest in two years, or in five, has prima facie as good right to protection as one who deals only in annuals. Nor could we consistently stop at designs; processes, machines, and secrets have an equal claim. The upshot must be that, whenever any one has contrived any of these, others may be forbidden to copy it. That is not the law. In the absence of some recognized right at common law, or under the statutes—and the plaintiff claims neither the statutes—a man's property is limited to the chattels which embody his invention. Others may imitate these at their pleasure. . . .

True, it would seem as though the plaintiff had suffered a grievance for which there should be a remedy, perhaps by an amendment of the Copyright Law, assuming that this does not already cover the case, which is not urged here. It seems a lame answer in such a case to turn the injured party out of court, but there are larger issues at stake than his redress. Judges have only a limited power to amend the law; when the subject has been confided to a Legislature, they must stand aside, even though there be an hiatus in completed justice. . . . Congress might see its way to create some sort of temporary right, or it might not. Its decision would certainly be preceded by some examination of the result upon the other interests affected. Whether these would prove paramount we have no means of saying; it is not for us to decide. Our vision is inevitably contracted, and the whole horizon may contain much which will compose a very different picture.

The order is affirmed. ■

As Judge Learned Hand notes in *Doris Silk*, intellectual property is mostly a creature of federal constitutional and statutory law. In the United States, Congress has chosen which kinds of innovations, in which fields of endeavor, deserve the protection that property rights afford. New pharmaceuticals and new songs are protected by statutorily created patents and copyrights, respectively. But dress designs receive no such protection. Likewise, anyone can copy or improve the formula for Chanel No. 5 perfume, for example, and attempt to compete head-to-head with the original in the market. In deciding that very issue, the 9th Circuit U.S. Court of Appeals recognized that:

> [D]isapproval of the copyist's opportunism may be an understandable first reaction, "[b]ut this initial response to the problem has been curbed in deference to the greater public good." . . . By taking his "free ride," the copyist, albeit unintentionally, serves an important public interest by

offering comparable goods at lower prices. On the other hand, the trademark owner, perhaps equally without design, sacrifices public to personal interests by seeking immunity from the rigors of competition.[12]

It is noteworthy that Chanel and the fashion industry as a whole have survived, even flourished, without the protection of monopoly property rights for the goods they create and market. But perfume is one thing; a potentially life-preserving pharmaceutical is another. The relatively great social interest in medical innovations may partly explain why they, but not dress designs, are protected with intellectual property rights. In addition, the research and development costs of creating a new pharmaceutical may be several orders of magnitude higher than the costs of designing and marketing a new dress. If so, property rights protections might be needed to create sufficient incentives to innovate. Beyond patents, Congress's decision to protect literary and musical creations, but not fashion creations, with copyright seems a much closer case. Here any discrepancy in average investment must be relatively small. Regardless, society—at any rate, its duly elected representatives—has concluded that literary or musical creators warrant greater incentives than fashion designers.

SOURCES OF PROPERTY

Intellectual property rights are created by the sovereign. In the United States, the Constitution expressly provides that Congress may, at its discretion, promote the useful arts and sciences by establishing intellectual property rights for limited durations. Pursuant to this authorization, Congress has enacted patent, copyright, and trademark laws.

Not all property rights stem from the legislature, of course. The common law courts both create and protect property rights; but the judiciary, like the legislature, is a branch of the state. Whether other, nonstate sources of property rights exist has been a topic of debate among philosophers, legal scholars, and economists for centuries.

Bottom-Up Theories of Property: Prepolitical or Natural Property Rights

According to the seventeenth-century philosopher John Locke, property rights arise naturally, regardless of state authorization, recognition, and enforcement, from human labor. When individuals mix their labor with some thing, they gain rights in that thing. To borrow Locke's own example, if, while walking down a tree-lined lane, you stoop to pick up an acorn, you gain property rights in that acorn.

The obvious question for Locke's labor theory of property is: How much labor gets you how much property? The modern American philosopher Robert Nozick puts the question this way: "If I own a can of tomato juice and spill it in the sea so that its molecules (made radioactive, so I can check this) mingle evenly throughout the sea, do I thereby come to own the sea, or have I foolishly dissipated my tomato juice?"[13]

One, often overlooked, aspect of Locke's labor theory of property acquisition is his proviso that mixing labor with something gives rise to private property rights only "at least where there is enough, as good is left in common for others."[14] This notion is tantamount to saying that people can acquire exclusive private property rights only in goods that are not scarce. For all important purposes, such an exception would appear to swallow the rule of acquisition through labor. Some economists argue, however, that the institution of private property rights can make some resources less scarce by creating appropriate incentives for individuals to produce more of them. So, for example, if farmers had no property rights in the wheat they grew, wheat (and wheat-based products) would be far more scarce.

Locke's is not the only natural or prepolitical theory of property. Another is implied in Austrian economist Friedrich von Hayek's theory of "spontaneous organization." According to this theory, social institutions, including property regimes, contracts, and markets arise spontaneously in the absence of state intrusions. Individuals, in a state of liberty, naturally derive cooperative institutions to enhance their well-being.

> With respect to some objects, the notion of individual property must have appeared very early, and the first hand-crafted tools are perhaps an appropriate example. The attachment of a unique and highly useful tool or weapon to its maker might, however, be so strong that transfer became so psychologically difficult that the instrument must accompany him even into the grave—as in the *tholos* or beehive tombs of the Mycenaean period. Here the fusion of inventor with "rightful owner" appears, and with it numerous elaborations of the basic idea, sometimes accompanied also by legend, as in the later story of Arthur and his sword Excalibur—a story in which the transfer of the sword came about not by human law but by a "higher" law of magic or "the powers."[15]

Recent research into "social norms" and practices provides empirical support to Hayek's idea that the state is not necessary to create, allocate, or enforce property. Economic historians have observed that California's property systems for hard-rock minerals and water did not originate with the state or its courts. In fact, they originated before there was a State of California. They were invented by the miners themselves to avoid and resolve disputes during the Gold Rush of the late 1840s. Those rules later received official recognition by the courts of the subsequently created state, and eventually by California's legislature.[16] Elinor Ostrom has written about local, self-generated common property regimes governing fisheries.[17] And the legal scholar Robert Ellickson observes that social rules respecting boundaries among ranchers in Shasta County, California, trump *de jure* property rights. The ranchers follow social norms of responsibility for maintaining boundary fences and compensating for damage caused by roaming livestock, regardless of formal legal rules that create substantially different rights and duties.[18]

Top-Down: Political Definition and Allocation of Property

Other scholars remain unconvinced by natural rights, or bottom-up, theories of property. The late eighteenth-century English political philosopher Jeremy Bentham famously derided natural law-based theories of property as "nonsense upon stilts."[19] In his theory of legislation, Bentham offered an alternative, positivist theory of property:

> Property is nothing but a basis of expectation; the expectation of deriving certain advantages from a thing which we are said to possess, in consequence of the relation in which we stand towards it.
>
> There is no image, no painting, no visible trait, which can express the relation that constitutes property. It is not material, it is metaphysical; it is a mere conception of the mind. . . . The idea of property consists in an established expectation; in the persuasion of being able to draw such or such an advantage from the thing possessed, according to the nature of the case. Now this expectation, this persuasion, can only be the work of law. I cannot count upon the enjoyment of that which I regard as mine, except through the promise of the law which guarantees it to me. It is law alone which permits me to forget my natural weakness. It is only through the protection of law that I am able to inclose a field, and to give myself up to its cultivation with the sure though distant hope of harvest. . . .
>
> Property and law are born together, and die together. Before laws were made there was no property; take away laws, and property ceases.

U.S. Supreme Court Justice Oliver Wendell Holmes expressed a similar notion of rights. In his 1897 article, "The Path of the Law," Holmes argued that a claim of "right" (or "duty") ultimately amounts to nothing more than a prediction of what a court will rule when faced with a choice between competing claims.[20]

In recent years, public choice scholars have weighed in with their own positive explanations of property rights, which depend on the state every bit as much as Bentham's utilitarian theory. Itai Sened, for example, notes that "property rights in land, as they exist today in England. . . did not result from any general consent of land owners to create a government that would protect their natural rights. Property rights in land developed in the eleventh and twelfth centuries when the Norman kings started protecting such rights in order to facilitate the collection of taxes." Sened propounds a positive theory of property according to which "[g]overnment officials commit themselves to protect private property rights in order to induce productivity. Like the kings and queens of England, they realize that in the absence of well-defined property rights, economic growth and prosperity are likely to be compromised." If that happens, the ruler is likely to lose the support of her citizens, and increase her risk of being deposed. "Let there be no mistake about it," Sened concludes, "there is nothing natural, or particularly ethical, about property rights, as such. Property rights emerge because they serve some tangible interests of particular individuals. Such rights cannot emerge or persist unless they serve, directly or indirectly, the interests of the central authorities that pay a remarkable cost to protect and enforce them."[21]

Finally, no consensus exists about where property rights come from. In reality, it is more likely than not that property stems from numerous and diverse sources. One would be naive, however, to suppose that property rights long persist in the absence of formal, social recognition and enforcement.

ALLOCATING PROPERTY RIGHTS

From an ecumenical point of view, it is easy to identify several bottom-up and top-down sources of property rights in society. These sources include both the organizations that allocate rights, such as courts and legislatures, and institutions, or the "rules of the game" according to which property rights are defined and allocated.

Allocation Organizations

We previously encountered the two most prominent state organizations that define and allocate property rights: the courts and the legislature. Less obvious, but not necessarily less important, sources of property rights include administrative agencies, contracts, and social norms.

Courts

In the *Paschal v. Hamilton* case, excerpted on pages 92–93 of this chapter, the court allocated property rights to a car in a dispute between the car's original owner, who had been defrauded, and a bona fide purchaser for value without notice. The bona fide purchaser prevailed and was deemed to be the owner. Similarly, when courts resolve nuisance and trespass cases, as we saw in the case excerpts in Chapter 4 and will see again in the next chapter, they necessarily allocate property rights between claimants. For example, in enjoining the confectioner from creating noise that interfered with the neighboring doctor's medical practice, the court in *Sturges v. Bridgman* (pages 80–81 of Chapter 4) allocated property rights to the doctor and imposed property duties on the confectioner.

Legislatures

In the Patent Act,[22] the Congress of the United States established the ground rules for obtaining and protecting personal property rights in scientific inventions and technical innovations. Under § 101 of the Act, "[w]hoever invents or discovers any new and useful process, machine, manufacture, or composition of matter, or any new and useful improvement thereof, may obtain a patent." And § 261 confirms that patents "have the attributes of . . . property."

Administrative Agencies

Pursuant to duly enacted statutory authorizations, administrative agencies make decisions to allocate property rights. The Patent Act, for example, does not allocate any specific property rights to anyone. Congress could do so, of course. It has in the past, for instance in granting public lands to private companies to facilitate construction of the transcontinental railways. Such specific congressional grants are increasingly rare. For the most part, Congress merely provides the statutory basis in accordance with which some administrative agency, such as the U.S. Patent Office, actually allocates property rights. On March 7, 1876, the Patent Office issued Patent No. 174,465 to Alexander Graham Bell for his invention of the telephone.

Contracts

In 1848, James Wilson Marshall, a carpenter working for John A. Sutter, discovered gold while building a sawmill on the south fork of the American (now the Coloma) River. Thus began the California "Gold Rush." Within a year, as many as 10,000 "forty-niners" were digging and panning for gold in Northern California. At the time, no federal laws governed property rights in mining claims, and California was not yet a state. So it was up to the miners themselves to devise a system that would govern rights to mining claims. The economic historian John Umbeck discovered that the miners "contracted" with one another to establish secure and stable property rights.

The miners at Jackass Gulch had a typical "contract" which provided:

1. That each person can hold "one claim by virtue of occupation," but it "must not exceed one hundred feet square."
2. That a claim or claims if held by purchase "must be under a bill of sale, and certified by two disinterested persons as to genuineness of signature and of the consideration."
3. That a "jury of five persons shall decide any question arising under the previous articles."
4. That notices of claims must be posted upon the ground chosen, and must be renewed every ten days "until water to work the said claims can be had."
5. That, as soon as there is a sufficiency of water for working a claim, "five days absence from said claim, except in case of sickness, accident or reasonable excuse," shall forfeit the property.
6. "That these rules shall extend over Jackass and Soldier gulches and their tributaries."[23]

Recently, other economists have taken issue with Umbeck's thesis that the mining "contracts" provided a basis for establishing secure property rights. Instead, according to Karen Clay and Gavin Wright, "The main historical features of mining districts may best be understood by viewing them . . . as institutions for managing access to a nonrenewable resource, in what was fundamentally an open-access context."[24] No one denies, however, that the local mining codes, however effective or ineffective, were not imposed by any government outside of the mining communities themselves. The miners' rules greatly influenced subsequently enacted federal mining laws and the State of California's unique system of water law.

Social Norms

In the following excerpt, Robert Ellickson explains how property conflicts in a rural American community are resolved not by resort to formal legal rules and litigation but by social norms of cooperation.

Robert C. Ellickson, Order Without Law: How Neighbors Settle Disputes

Cambridge, MA: Harvard University Press, 1991, pp. 52–53

In rural Shasta County [California] . . . trespass conflicts are generally resolved not in "the shadow of the law" but, rather, beyond that shadow. Most rural residents are consciously committed to an overarching norm of cooperation among neighbors. In trespass situations [where the cattle of one rancher come onto the land of another], their applicable particularized norm, adhered to by all but a few deviants, is that an owner of livestock is responsible for the acts of his animals. Allegiance to this norm seems wholly independent of formal legal entitlements. Most cattlemen believe that a rancher should keep his animals from eating a neighbor's grass, regardless of whether the range is open or closed. . . .

The norm that an animal owner should control his stock is modified by another norm that holds that a rural resident should put up with ("lump") minor damage stemming from isolated trespass incidents. The neighborly response to an isolated infraction is an exchange of civilities. A trespass victim should notify the animal owner that the trespass has occurred and assist the owner in retrieving the stray stock. Virtually all residents have telephones, the standard means of communication. A telephone report is usually couched not as a complaint but rather as a service to the animal owner, who, after all, has a valuable asset on the loose. Upon receiving a telephone report, a cattlemen who is a good neighbor will quickly retrieve the animals (by truck if necessary), apologize for the occurrence, and thank the caller. ■

The fact that social norms of neighborliness prevail over legal allocations of property rights (and duties) is not particularly surprising. Most of us, presumably, prefer to settle disputes with our neighbors amicably, without recourse to the law, especially where the stakes are not particularly high. Reliance on social norms of neighborly cooperation may in many cases entail lower transaction costs than insistence upon formal legal rights. More surprising, perhaps, is Ellickson's finding (not disclosed in the preceding excerpt) that the lawyers involved in resolving boundary disputes in Shasta County mistakenly thought the prevailing social norms were the legal rules.

Allocation Institutions

So far, we have canvassed various social organizations that allocate property rights. The next question is how they make their allocation decisions. Courts and other organizations base their property allocation decisions on a wide variety of institutions, or "rules of the game." These rules include first possession, just deserts, and utility/wealth maximization.

First Possession

Nearly everyone knows the legal maxims "first in time, first in right" and "possession is 9/10ths of the law."[25] A kind of default presumption views the person in possession of something as having a lawful claim to it. This presumption is not rebuttable by another who has no right of possession, but it may be reputed by someone with a superior claim of right, often based on prior possession.

One stark illustration of the power of first possession is the story of preemption. Throughout the nineteenth century, the federal government of the United States engaged in a somewhat inconsistent policy of disposing of, or privatizing, publicly owned lands. To a considerable extent, the federal policy followed, rather than led to, settlement. In other words, settlers trespassed and squatted on public lands not yet offered for sale and waited for the federal government to retroactively recognize their claims, as it did, for example, in the 1841 General Preemption Act, § 10 of which provided:

> [E]very person being the head of a family, or widow, or single man, over the age of twenty-one years, and being a citizen of the United States . . . who since the first day of June, A.D. eighteen hundred and forty, has made or shall hereafter make a settlement in person on the public lands . . . and who shall inhabit and improve the same, and who has or shall erect a dwelling thereon, shall be, and is hereby, authorized to enter with the register of the land office for the district in which such land may lie, . . . any number of acres not exceeding one hundred and sixty, . . . to include the residence of such claimant, upon paying to the United States the minimum price of such land, ... [emphasis added].

Although the principle of first possession is powerful in law, it does not always result in the most efficient allocation of property rights. According to Coase's normative principle (explained in Chapter 4), property rights (entitlements) should be allocated so as to minimize joint or social costs that arise from land-use conflicts. Joint or social costs are minimized by allocating the property right to the party with the higher costs of abating or avoiding harm; the property duty should be imposed on the least cost avoider. It may sometimes be the case that subsequent possessors are lower cost avoiders than first possessors, but not always.

Just Deserts

At a glance, the rule of just deserts might appear coextensive with the rule of first possession. But the first possessor may not always be the most deserving property owner. Sometimes, property is allocated to accomplish certain, supposedly just, ends regardless of priority (and often regardless of efficiency). For example, among the first beneficiaries of grants of federally owned lands following the Revolutionary War were the veterans who fought in the war. It was a form of compensation for their service to their country. Under the Land Ordinance of 1785,[26] land was allotted to veterans in accordance with rank. A major general received 1,100 acres; a colonel, 500 acres; and ordinary soldiers, 100 acres.

From a public choice perspective, it is clear that Congress was motivated by more than a sense of justice and a sincere desire to compensate those who had fought to win America's independence. In the years immediately following the Revolutionary War, concern was great that impoverished and disaffected soldiers might attempt to wrest government control from the civilian authorities. From this perspective, the land grants to veterans were in the nature of bribes to secure social peace and government security.

Utility/Wealth Maximization

War veterans and settlers were not the only beneficiaries of federal land grants in the nineteenth century. So, too, were railroads. The railroad grants could not, however, be explained under justificatory theories of first possession or just deserts. They were purely utilitarian, wealth-maximizing measures.

The Pacific Railroad Act of 1862,[27] for example, was designed to "aid in the construction of a railroad and telegraph line from the Missouri River to the Pacific Ocean." To that end, the federal government granted the Union Pacific Railroad Company a right of way through public lands, encompassing 200 feet along either side of the tracks, plus up to 500 additional parcels of public lands, and including the right to use all stones, timber, and other materials useful for the construction of the rail line. In total, during the nineteenth century, Congress granted 34 million acres of public lands to the railroads. In addition, the federal government gave them low-interest construction loans. States also contributed lands for railroad construction, and frequently gave the railroads the power of eminent domain to condemn additional private lands as needed. Whether these grants were actually expected to benefit all of society by spurring economic growth or merely constituted successful rent seeking by the railroad "robber barons" is another, debatable question.

The railroad land grants, along with similar grants to canal builders and other interest groups, were no doubt influenced by public choice pressures—concentrated interests effectively lobbied Congress in pursuit of their own narrow interests, rather than any, more broadly conceived public interest. That said, the land grants also constituted privatization—the transformation of public property into private property, which is generally thought by economists to be efficiency-enhancing because private owners, unlike public land managers (politicians and bureaucrats) are likely to manage the resources they own so as to maximize their long-run economic benefits. To the extent this supposition is true—and it is, generally, true—private ownership of resources tends to lead naturally to higher levels of economic production and total social wealth.

CHAPTER SUMMARY

This chapter explored the economic purposes of property, and how property rights are defined and allocated in the first instance by several different organizations utilizing various institutional approaches. Property rights are meaningless, however, no matter how they are defined and allocated, if they are not enforced. The next chapter addresses the various ways and the extent to which property rights are protected by the legal system. As we shall see, the protection of property rights strongly influences both the definition and allocation of such rights. Chapter 7, then, explores the limits of property.

QUESTIONS AND PROBLEMS

1. What do law and economics scholars mean by *property rights*? And what do they mean by *ownership*?
2. If well-defined property rights are a prerequisite to sustained economic growth, as economists maintain, what explains the lack of well-defined property rights in much of the world?
3. Why is defection (noncooperation) the dominant strategy for players in a Prisoner's Dilemma game?
4. According to Harold Demsetz, why do property rights emerge at some point in the socioeconomic development of virtually every society?
5. Demsetz implies that property evolves unidirectionally from nonproperty or common property to individual, private property. Under what circumstances would property move from individual ownership to collective ownership?[28]
6. Is first possession always, or ever, an economically sound basis for allocating property rights?
7. What reasons would explain why informal social norms might be more efficient than legal rules? Can you think of any ostensibly inefficient social norms?
8. Should dress designers be entitled to property protection for their ideas?
9. Garrett Hardin was personally pessimistic about resource use in the world. He feared environmental destruction and resource conflicts (including wars). Is this conclusion inevitable, based on his analysis in "The Tragedy of the Commons"?
10. Should Yellowstone National Park be privatized? Why or why not?

NOTES

1. *See* Thomas W. Merrill, "Property and the Right to Exclude," 77 NEBRASKA LAW REVIEW 730, 730 (1998).
2. 58 N.J. 297 (1971).
3. *See, for example*, Thomas W. Merrill and Henry E. Smith, "What Happened to Property in Law and Economics?" 111 YALE LAW JOURNAL 357 (2001). Merrill and Smith resurrect the historical understanding of property rights as rights in rem, which means they are good against the entire world. Contract-based rights, by contrast, are in personam; they pertain only as between the contracting parties (and in some cases discernible third parties).
4. Merchants are generally held to a higher level of inquiry about the state of title than consumers. It would be a rare case in which a court would find a dealer to be a bona fide purchaser for value without notice of some defect in title.
5. Adam Smith, *The Wealth of Nations* (New York: Modern Library 1994 [1776]) 1994), p. 887.
6. *See, for example*, Timothy Tregarthen and Libby Rittenberg, *Economics* (New York: Worth Publishing, 2000), p. 133; N. Gregory Mankiw, *Principles of Microeconomics* (Belmont, CA: International Thomson Publishing, 2001), pp. 239–40; John B. Taylor, *Principles of Microeconomics* (Boston: Houghton Mifflin, 2001), p. 13.
7. Hernando de Soto, *The Mystery of Capital: Why Capitalism Triumphs in the West and Fails Everywhere Else* (New York: Basic Books, 2000), p. 51.
8. Hernando de Soto, *The Mystery of Capital: Why Capitalism Triumphs in the West and Fails Everywhere Else* (New York: Basic Books, 2000), p. 51.
9. 203 F. Supp. 2d 1111, 1140 (N.D. Cal. 2002).
10. A patent holder may not necessarily be able to charge monopoly prices, however, because the market may include effective substitutes for the patented good.

11. 17 U.S.C. §301 (2003). Today, all copyright protection is statutory and automatic; registering for a copyright for legal protection is not necessary. These statutory rights are not unlimited; others can, for example, make "fair use" of the copyright holder's work. However, these limitations are designed not to infringe on the commercial value of the copyright, for example, by introducing market competition in order to minimize prices for consumers.

12. *Smith v. Chanel*, 402 F. 2d 562, 568–9 (9th Cir. 1968), quoting *American Safety Table Co. v. Schreiber*, 269 F. 2d 255, 272 (2d Cir. 1959).

13. Robert Nozick, *Anarchy, State, and Utopia* (New York: Basic Books, 1974), p. 175.

14. John Locke, *Two Treatises of Government, Book II*, [1690] (1991), ch. V.

15. Friedrich von Hayek (W.W. Bartley III, ed.), *The Fatal Conceit* (Chicago: Univeristy of Chicago Press, 1988), p. 30.

16. See John Umbeck, *A Theory of Property Rights: With Application to the California Gold Rush* (Ames, IA: Iowa State University Press, 1981); Richard O. Zerbe and C. Leigh Anderson, "Culture and Fairness in the Development of Institutions in the California Gold Fields," 61 *Journal of Economic History* 114–143 (2001).

17. Elinor Ostrom, *Governing the Commons: The Evolution of Institutions for Collective Action* (Cambridge: Cambridge University Press, 1991).

18. Robert C. Ellickson, *Order Without Law: How Neighbors Settle Disputes* (Cambridge, MA: Harvard University Press, 1991).

19. Jeremy Bentham, *Anarchical Fallacies* (Edinburgh, 1843), art. ii.

20. Oliver Wendell Holmes, "The Path of the Law," in Oliver Wendell Holmes, *Collected Legal Papers* (New York: Harcourt, Brace, and Co., 1920 [1897]), p. 169.

21. Itai Sened, *The Political Institution of Private Property* (Cambridge: Cambridge University Press, 1997), pp. 4–7.

22. 35 U.S.C. § 1 et seq. (2001).

23. John Umbeck, *A Theory of Property Rights—With Application to the California Gold Rush* (Ames, IA: Iowa State University Press, 1981), p. 94.

24. Karen Clay and Gavin Wright, "Order Without Law? Property Rights During the California Gold Rush," Stanford University Economics Working Paper No. 03–008 (June 2003).

25. See *Corporation of Kingston-Upon Hull v. Horner*, 98 Eng. Rep. 807, 815 (1774).

26. 29 Journal of the Continental Congress 917 (March 4, 1785).

27. 12 U.S. Statutes At Large 449 (1862).

28. *See, for example*, Carol M. Rose, "Energy and Efficiency in the Realignment of Common-Law Water Rights," 19 *JOURNAL OF LEGAL STUDIES* 261 (1990); Barry Field, The Evolution of Property Rights, 42 *KYKLOS* 319 (1989).

Chapter 6

Property II: Protection

Because property rights never are specified perfectly, and because some people just do not pay attention to the property rights of others, conflicts frequently arise. One person takes another's car, or pollutes a neighbor's land, or quotes at length from an author's book without permission. These acts may be intentional; the taker knows that the act is wrong. The act causing the conflict may also be unintentional; the taker mistakenly gets in another's car, for example. Either way, a property conflict arises, which the courts (or some other social organization) must resolve.

Property rights disputes are resolved by determining which party has the superior claim or entitlement. Making this determination is not always as simple as it might seem. When property rights conflicts come to court, as they frequently do, the court uses a two-stage process to determine who has or gets the property. First, the court determines whether the defendant is liable for the harm allegedly caused to the plaintiff. A finding of no liability constitutes a determination that the defendant has not contravened or interfered with any property right belonging to the plaintiff. In some cases, a finding of no liability actually locates a property right in the defendant. Suppose, for example, that Mark is in actual possession of land that John claims as his own. John files an action in ejectment (literally, an action to eject the defendant) to "quiet" (settle) title to the land. If the court finds that Mark is *not* liable, that finding constitutes a determination that Mark's claim to the land is superior to John's. In any case, a determination that the defendant is not liable resolves the dispute. If, however, the court finds that the defendant is liable, that finding constitutes a determination that the plaintiff possesses, at least initially, some property right that the defendant has violated. This determination does not, however, end the judicial process but leads to its second stage, the remedy decision, which is addressed in the next section of this chapter.

From a Coasean economic point of view, property rights conflicts should be resolved in order to maximize the social product by minimizing the joint or social costs stemming from the conflict. To do so, courts and other organizations charged with resolving property rights conflicts should impose the burden on the least cost avoider by awarding the property rights to the other party. This outcome is not, however, an explicit goal of legal rules for resolving property disputes. In practice, courts do not seek to impose liability on least cost avoiders, and remedies designed to protect property rights often fail to minimize social costs.

DETERMINING LIABILITY

The legal system offers two primary theories for determining liability for interference with property rights: strict liability and negligence/reasonableness. Under the theory of strict liability, the defendant is liable for any harm caused to the plaintiff's property, regardless of fault or the slightness of the harm. Under the reasonableness test of negligence theory, the defendant is liable only for "unreasonable" harm. Whether harm is unreasonable may be determined by a cost-benefit test, which weighs the harm to the plaintiff against the benefits created by the defendant's activity, or by a more ambiguous test. This test looks at whether the defendant's activity exceeds the threshold of acceptable conduct in the community, and produces more harm than the plaintiff should have to accept.

Strict Liability: Trespass and Nuisance Distinguished

A *trespass* is defined as the direct, physical invasion of another's land. It is an old hybrid—partly common law, partly statutory—cause of action, with roots in English statutes from the thirteenth century. It remains to the present day a strict liability action. If someone steps foot onto land posted (with a sign) against trespass, that person is liable, even if she did not intend to trespass and her act caused no actual harm to the landowner or the property. The trespass action serves to "quiet," that is to say certify, title to land by enforcing the legitimate landowner's right to exclude. If the court finds that the plaintiff's title is superior to the defendant's, it will hold the defendant liable for trespass. If the court concludes, however, that the defendant's title is superior to that of the plaintiff, the defendant will not be liable for trespass.

Nuisance law is nearly as old as trespass, and it, too, used to be a strict liability cause of action. A common law nuisance is defined as a "nontrespassory invasion of land," one that is either indirect or "nonphysical." Distinguishing between trespass and nuisance based on the physical or nonphysical nature of the invasion precedes the invention of the microscope, when we did not know that all invasions are necessarily physical. In the middle of the nineteenth century, it made sense to say that a nuisance created by noxious odors was nonphysical because odors could not be seen or felt. Today, of course, we know that odors are embodied in molecules, which are physical—they have mass. Still, the common law's distinction between trespass as physical invasion and nuisance as nonphysical invasion persists.

Another distinction between trespass and nuisance is not obsolete: trespass and nuisance protect different rights of property. Trespass protects the legitimate landowner's right to exclude. Nuisance protects the landowner's property right in "use and enjoyment" of the land.

Despite these distinctions, nuisances used to be treated similarly to trespasses. Both were strict liability offenses. It did not matter that the defendant's act caused no actual harm, or yielded great benefits beyond the harm it caused. If the defendant violated the plaintiff's right to exclude or right to use and enjoy land, then the defendant was liable.[1]

Modern Nuisance Law

Today, trespass remains a strict liability offense, but not so nuisance. Beginning in the latter half of the nineteenth century, in the wake of the Industrial Revolution, the strict liability rule for nuisances began to be criticized for obstructing socially useful development activities. In other words, it was thought to be inefficient. Courts responded by switching from strict liability to a fault-based, reasonableness test for nuisance. As reflected today in the American Law Institute's Second Restatement of Torts, liability for nuisance is determined by a modified cost-benefit test: The defendant is liable for nuisance if the harm to the plaintiff exceeds the benefits created by the defendant's activity or if the harm to the plaintiff is either "serious" or "severe" (however those two terms might be defined). In contrast to the old strict liability regime, nuisance defendants are *not* liable if the utility of their conduct outweighs the harm to the plaintiff *and* the plaintiff's harm is deemed to be less than "serious." The following case explains the historical evolution of nuisance law.

Carpenter v. Double B Cattle Company, Inc.

105 Idaho 320, 669 P.2d 643 (Id. App. 1983)

Burnett, Judge

***

This lawsuit was filed by a group of homeowners who alleged that expansion of a nearby cattle feedlot had created a nuisance. The homeowners claimed that operation of the expanded feedlot had caused noxious odors, air and water pollution, noise and pests in the area. The homeowners sought damages and injunctive relief. The issues of damages and injunctive relief were combined in a single trial, conducted before a jury. Apparently, it was contemplated that the jury would perform a fact-finding function in determining whether a nuisance existed and whether the homeowners were entitled to damages, but would perform an advisory function on the question of injunctive relief. The district judge gave the jury a unified set of instructions embracing all these functions. The jury returned a verdict simply finding that no nuisance existed. The court entered a judgment for the feedlot proprietors, denying the homeowners any damages or injunctive relief. This appeal followed. For reasons appearing below, we vacate the judgment and remand the case for a new trial.

The homeowners contend that the jury received improper instructions on criteria for determining the existence of a nuisance. The jury was told to weigh the alleged injury to the homeowners against the "social value" of the feedlot, and to consider "the interests of the community as a whole," in determining whether the nuisance existed. . . .

The concept of nuisance originated in the law of property. At common law, a distinction was maintained between two encroachments upon property rights—interference with possession of land, and interference with the use and enjoyment of land. The first type of encroachment was subject to an "assize of novel disseisen," a remedy for trespass. The latter form of encroachment was subject to an "assize of nuisance," a remedy for a variety of invasions which diminished the owner's enjoyment of his property without dispossessing him of it. Thus, nuisance and trespass have common roots in property law, and occasionally it is difficult to distinguish between them. But where an invasion of property is merely incidental to the use of adjoining property, and does not physically interfere with possession of the property invaded, it generally has been classified as a nuisance rather than as a trespass. . . .

The early concepts of nuisance and trespass shared the common law's reverence for property rights. Invasions of property were deemed wrongful *per se*, and the parties responsible for such invasions were subject to a form of strict liability. . . .

***

The property-oriented, English concept of a nuisance had its analogue in early American law. In one illustrative case of the nineteenth century, an American court held that title to land gave the owner the right to impregnate the air with odors, dust and smoke, pollute his own water and make noises, provided that he did not substantially interfere with the comfort of others or injure the use or enjoyment of their property. . . .

However, as the English concept of nuisance was assimilated into American law, it underwent a transformation. It ceased to be solely a creature of

property law. . . . [N]uisance law came to protect life and health, as well as property. A nuisance signified not merely an infringement of property rights, but a wrong against both person and property—a tort.

***

The Second Restatement [of Torts] treats . . . an "intentional" invasion as a nuisance if it is "unreasonable." Section 826 of the Second Restatement now provides two sets of criteria for determining whether this type of nuisance exists:

> An intentional invasion of another's interest in the use and enjoyment of land is unreasonable if
> a. the gravity of the harm outweighs the utility of the actor's conduct, or
> b. the harm caused by the conduct is serious and the financial burden of compensating for this and similar harm to others would not make the continuation of the conduct not feasible.

The present version of § 826 . . . recognizes that liability for damages caused by a nuisance may exist regardless of whether the utility of the offending activity exceeds the gravity of the harm it has created. . . .

Evidence of utility does not constitute a defense against recovery of damages where the harm is serious and compensation is feasible. Were the law otherwise, a large enterprise, important to the local economy, would have a lesser duty to compensate its neighbors for invasion of their rights than would a smaller business deemed less essential to the community. In our view, this is not, and should not be, the law.

***

However, our view is not based simply upon general notions of fairness; it is also grounded in economics. The Second Restatement deals effectively with the problem of "externalities." . . . Where an enterprise externalizes some burdens upon its neighbors, without compensation, our market system does not reflect the true costs of products or services provided by that enterprise. Externalities distort the price signals essential to the proper functioning of the market.

This problem affects two fundamental objectives of the economic system. The first objective, commonly called "efficiency" in economic theory, is to promote the greatest aggregate surplus of benefits over the costs of economic activity. The second objective, usually termed "equity" or "distributive justice," is to allocate these benefits and costs in accordance with prevailing societal values. The market system best serves the goal of efficiency when prices reflect true costs; and the goal of distributive justice is best achieved when benefits are explicitly identified to the correlative costs.

Although the problem of externalities affects both goals of efficiency and distributive justice, these objectives are conceptually different and may imply different solutions to a given problem. In theory, if there were no societal goal other than efficiency, and if there were no impediments to exchanges of property or property rights, individuals pursuing their economic self-interests might reach the most efficient allocation of costs and benefits by means of exchange, without direction by the courts. See Coase, *The Problem of Social Cost*, 3 J.L. & ECON. 1 (1960). However, the real world is not free from impediments to exchanges, and our economic system operates within the constraints of a society which is also concerned with distributive justice. Thus, the courts often are the battlegrounds upon which campaigns for efficiency and distributional justice are waged. ■

***

As Judge Burnett explains in *Carpenter*, the shift in nuisance liability regimes has been marginal. Under strict liability, nuisance defendants were liable for any harm, no matter how small. Today, under the Second Restatement of Torts § 826, defendants are liable only for "unreasonable" harm. The harm is unreasonable if it exceeds the utility of the defendant's conduct or is serious.

Judge Burnett offers sound economic reasons for holding nuisance defendants liable for serious harm, even if the utility of their conduct is great. But those same reasons would support holding nuisance defendants liable for "nonserious" harms as well. The question is whether nuisance plaintiffs should bear any external costs from the activities of nuisance defendants.

At one point in his decision, Judge Burnett cites Coase's "The Problem of Social Cost" for the proposition that, "if there were no impediments to exchange" (i.e., no transaction costs), courts would not be needed to resolve nuisance disputes. Such disputes would either not arise in the first place, or they would be immediately and costlessly resolved by the parties themselves. Unfortunately, Judge Burnett neglects another passage from "The Problem of Social Cost" that is potentially even more useful for resolving nuisance disputes. Specifically, Coase suggests that the Restatement's—and Judge Burnett's—focus on the seriousness of the harm is not the most important consideration. Rather, the court should focus on which party is the best cost avoider. If the plaintiff could avoid or abate the nuisance harm at lower cost than the defendant, then the defendant should not be liable, even if the harm to the plaintiff is serious. If, however, the nuisance defendant is the better cost avoider or abater, then the defendant should be liable even if the utility of the conduct is great and the harm resulting from the nuisance is small.

THE REMEDY DECISION

Once a court has determined that the defendant is liable for harming the plaintiff or the plaintiff's property, it has several different remedy options: Compensatory damages may include compensation for future, as well as past and present, harm.

Injunctive relief amounts to an order to the defendant to leave the plaintiff's property alone. The remedy decision can have a decisive effect on the allocation of property rights, and on allocative efficiency.

Types of Remedies

Guido Calabresi and A. Douglas Melamed, "Property Rules, Liability Rules, and Inalienability: One View of the Cathedral"

5 Harvard Law Review 1089 (1972)

I. INTRODUCTION

***

The first issue which must be faced by any legal system is one we call the problem of "entitlement." Whenever a state is presented with the conflicting interests of two or more people, or two or more groups of people, it must decide which side to favor. . . . The entitlement to make noise versus the entitlement to have silence, the entitlement to pollute versus the entitlement to breathe clean air, the entitlement to have children versus the entitlement to forbid them—these are the first order of legal decisions.

***

The state not only has to decide whom to entitle, but it must also simultaneously make a series of equally difficult second-order decisions. These decisions go to the manner in which entitlements are protected and to whether an individual is allowed to sell or trade the entitlement. In any given dispute, for example, the state must decide not only which side wins but also the kind of protection to grant. . . . We shall consider three types of entitlements—entitlements protected by property rules, entitlements protected by liability rules, and inalienability entitlements.

An entitlement is protected by a property rule to the extent that someone who wishes to remove the entitlement from its holder must buy it from him in a voluntary transaction in which the value of the entitlement is agreed upon by the seller. It is the form of entitlement which gives rise to the least amount of state intervention: once the original entitlement is decided upon, the state does not try to decide its value. It lets each of the parties say how much the entitlement is worth to him and gives the seller a veto if the buyer does not offer enough. Property rules involve a collective decision as to who is to be given an initial entitlement but not as to the value of the entitlement.

***

Whenever someone may destroy the initial entitlement if he is willing to pay an objectively determined value for it, an entitlement is protected by a liability rule. This value may be what it is thought the original holder of the entitlement would have sold it for. But the holder's complaint that he would have demanded more will not avail him once the objectively determined value is set. Obviously, liability rules involve an additional stage of state intervention: not only are entitlements produced, but their transfer or destruction is allowed on the basis of a value determined by some organ of the state rather than by the parties themselves.

An entitlement is inalienable to the extent that its transfer is not permitted between a willing buyer and a willing seller. The state intervenes not only to determine who is initially entitled and to determine the compensation that must be paid if the entitlement is taken or destroyed, but also to forbid its sale under some or all circumstances. Inalienability rules are thus quite different from property and liability rules. Unlike those rules, rules of inalienability not only "protect" the entitlement, they may also be viewed as limiting or regulating the grant of the entitlement itself.

It should be clear that most entitlements to goods are mixed. Taney's house may be protected by a property rule in situations where Marshall wishes to purchase it, by a liability rule where the government decides to take it by eminent domain, and by a rule of inalienability in situations where Taney is drunk or incompetent. This article will explore two primary questions: (1) In what circumstances should we grant a particular entitlement? And (2) In what circumstances should we decide to protect that entitlement by using a property, liability, or inalienability rule?

***

III. RULES FOR PROTECTING AND REGULATING ENTITLEMENTS

Whenever society chooses an initial entitlement it must also determine whether to protect the entitlement by property rules, by liability rules, or by rules of inalienability. In our framework, much of what is generally called private property can be viewed as an entitlement which is protected by a property rule. No one can take the entitlement to private property from the holder unless the holder sells it willingly and at the price at which he subjectively values the property. Yet a nuisance [one person's unreasonable interference with another's use and enjoyment of land] with sufficient public utility to avoid injunction has, in effect, the right to take property with compensation. In such a circumstance, the entitlement to the property is protected only by what we call a liability rule: an external, objective standard of value is used to facilitate the transfer of the entitlement from the holder to the nuisance. Finally, in some instances we will not allow the sale of the property at all, that is we will occasionally make the entitlement inalienable.

***

A. Property and Liability Rules

Why cannot society simply decide . . . who should receive any given entitlement, and then let its transfer occur only through a voluntary negotiation? Why, in other words, cannot society limit itself to the property rule? To do this it would need only to protect and enforce the initial entitlements from all attacks, perhaps through criminal sanctions, and to enforce voluntary contracts for their transfer. Why do we need liability rules at all?

In terms of economic efficiency the reason is easy enough to see. Often the cost of establishing the value of an initial entitlement by negotiation is so great that even though a transfer of the entitlement would benefit all concerned, such a transfer will not occur. If a collective determination of the value were available instead, the beneficial transfer would quickly come about.

Eminent domain [the power by which government takes private property for public use] is a good example. A park where Guidacres, a tract of land owned by 1,000 owners in 1,000 parcels, now sits would, let us assume, benefit a neighboring town enough so that 100,000 citizens of the town would each be willing to pay an average of $100 to have it. The park is Pareto desirable if the owners of the tracts of land in Guidacres actually value their entitlements at less than $10,000,000 or an average of $10,000 a tract. Let us assume that in fact the parcels are all the same and all the owners value them at $8,000. On this assumption, the park is, in economic efficiency terms, desirable—in values foregone it costs $8,000,000 and is worth $10,000,000 to the buyers. And yet it may well not be established. If enough of the owners hold out for more than $10,000 in order to get a share of the $2,000,000 that they guess the buyers are willing to pay over the value which the sellers in actuality attach, the price demanded will be more than $10,000,000 and no park will result. The sellers have an incentive to hide their true valuation and the market will not succeed in establishing it.

An equally valid example could be made on the buying side. Suppose the sellers of Guidacres have agreed to a sales price of $8,000,000 (they are all relatives and at a family banquet decided that trying to hold out would leave them all losers). It does not follow that the buyers can raise that much even though each of 100,000 citizens in fact values the park at $100. Some citizens may try to free-load and say the park is only worth $50 or even nothing to them, hoping that enough others will admit to a higher desire and make up the $8,000,000 price. Again there is no reason to believe that a market, a decentralized system of valuing, will cause people to express their true valuations and hence yield results which all in fact agree are desirable.

Whenever this is the case an argument can readily be made for moving from a property rule to a liability rule. If society can remove from the market the valuation of each tract of land, decide the value collectively, and impose it, then the holdout problem is gone. Similarly, if society can value collectively each individual citizen's desire to have a park and charge him a "benefits" tax based upon it, the freeloader problem is gone. If the sum of the taxes is greater than the sum of the compensation awards, the park will result.

***

Of course, the problems with liability rules are equally real. We cannot be at all sure that landowner Taney is lying or holding out when he says that his land is worth $12,000 to him. The fact that several neighbors sold identical tracts for $10,000 does not help us very much; Taney may be sentimentally attached to his land. As a result, eminent domain may grossly undervalue what Taney would actually sell for, even if it sought to give him his true valuation of his tract. In practice, it is so hard to determine Taney's true valuation that eminent domain simply gives him what the land is worth "objectively" in the full knowledge that this may result in over or under compensation. The same is true on the buyer side. . . .

The example of eminent domain is simply one of numerous instances in which society uses liability rules. Accidents is another. If we were to give victims a property entitlement not to be accidentally injured we would have to require all who engage in activities that may injure individuals to negotiate with them before an accident, and to buy the right to knock off an arm or a leg. Such pre-accident negotiations would be extremely expensive, often prohibitively so. To require them would thus pre-clude many activities that might, in fact, be worth having. And, after an accident, the loser of the arm or leg can always very plausibly deny that he would have sold it at the price the buyer would have offered. Indeed, where negotiations after an accident do occur—for instance pretrial settlements—it is largely because the alternative is a collective valuation of the damages.

***

We should also recognize that efficiency is not the sole ground for employing liability rules rather than property rules. Just as the initial entitlement is often decided upon for distributional reasons, so too the choice of a liability rule is often made because it facilitates a combination of efficiency and distributive results which would be difficult to achieve under a property rule.

B. Inalienable Entitlements

Thus far we have focused on the questions of when society should protect an entitlement by property or liability rules. However, there may remain many entitlements which involve a still greater degree of societal intervention: the law not only decides who is to own something and what price is to be paid for it if it is taken or destroyed, but also regulates its sale—by, for example, prescribing preconditions for a valid sale or forbidding a sale altogether. Although these rules of inalienability are substantially different from the property and liability rules, their use can be analyzed in terms of the same efficiency and distributional goals that underlie the use of the other two rules.

While at first glance efficiency objectives may seem undermined by limitations on the ability to engage in transactions, closer analysis suggests that there are instances, perhaps many, in which economic efficiency is more closely approximated by such limitations. This might occur when a transaction would create significant externalities—costs to third parties.

For instance, if Taney were allowed to sell his land to Chase, a polluter, he would injure his neighbor Marshall by lowering the value of Marshall's land. Conceivably, Marshall could pay Taney not to sell his land; but, because there are many injured Marshalls, freeloader and information costs make such transactions practically impossible. The state could protect the Marshalls and yet facilitate the sale of the land by giving the Marshalls an entitlement to prevent Taney's sale to Chase but only protecting the entitlement by a liability rule. It might, for instance, charge an excise tax on all sales of land to polluters equal to its estimate of the external cost to the Marshalls of the sale. But where there are so many injured Marshalls that the price required under the liability rule is likely to be high enough so that no one would be willing to pay it, then setting up the machinery for collecting valuation will be wasteful. Barring the sale to polluters will be the most efficient result because it is clear that avoiding pollution is cheaper than paying its costs—including its costs to the Marshalls.

Another instance in which external costs may justify inalienability occurs when external costs do not lend themselves to collective measurement which is acceptably objective and nonarbitrary. This nonmonetizability is characteristic of one category of external costs which, as a practical matter, seems frequently to lead us to rules of inalienability. Such external costs are often called moralisms.

If Taney is allowed to sell himself into slavery, or to take undue risks of becoming penniless, or to sell a kidney, Marshall may be harmed, simply because Marshall is a sensitive man who is made unhappy by seeing slaves, paupers, or persons who die because they have sold a kidney. Again Marshall could pay Taney not to sell his freedom to Chase the slaveowner; but again, because Marshall is not one but many individuals, freeloader and information costs make such transactions practically impossible. Again, it might seem that the state could intervene by objectively valuing the external cost to Marshall and requiring Chase to pay that cost. But since the external cost to Marshall does not lend itself to an acceptable objective measurement, such liability rules are not appropriate.

In the case of Taney selling land to Chase, the polluter, they were inappropriate because we *knew* that the costs to Taney and the Marshalls exceeded the benefits to Chase. Here, though we are not certain of how a cost-benefit analysis would come out, liability rules are inappropriate because any

monetization is, by hypothesis, out of the question. The state must, therefore, either ignore the external costs to Marshall, or if it judges them great enough, forbid the transaction that gave rise to them by making Taney's freedom inalienable.

***

There are two other efficiency reasons for forbidding the sale of entitlements under certain circumstances: self paternalism and true paternalism. Examples of the first are Ulysses tying himself to the mast or individuals passing a bill of rights so that they will be prevented from yielding to momentary temptations which they deem harmful to themselves. This type of limitation is not in any real sense paternalism. It is fully consistent with Pareto efficiency criteria, based on the notion that over the mass of cases no one knows better than the individual what is best for him or her. It merely allows the individual to choose what is best in the long run rather than in the short run, even though that choice entails giving up some short run freedom of choice. Self paternalism may cause us to require certain conditions to exist before we allow a sale of an entitlement; and it may help explain many situations of inalienability, like the invalidity of contracts entered into when drunk, or under undue influence or coercion. But it probably does not fully explain even these.

True paternalism brings us a step further toward explaining such prohibitions and those of broader kinds—for example the prohibitions on a whole range of activities by minors. Paternalism is based on the notion that at least in some situations the Marshalls know better than Taney what will make Taney better off. Here we are not talking about the offense to Marshall from Taney's choosing to read pornography, or selling himself into slavery, but rather the judgment that Taney was not in the position to choose best for himself when he made the choice for erotica or servitude.

***

Finally, just as efficiency goals sometimes dictate the use of rules of inalienability, so, of course, do distributional goals. Whether an entitlement may be sold or not often affects directly who is richer and who is poorer. Prohibiting the sale of babies makes poorer those who can cheaply produce babies and richer those who through some nonmarket device get free an "unwanted" baby. Prohibiting exculpatory clauses in product sales makes richer those who were injured by a product defect and poorer those who were not injured and who paid more for the product because the exculpatory clause was forbidden. Favoring the specific group that has benefitted may or may not have been the reason for the prohibition on bargaining. What is important is that, regardless of the reason for barring a contract, a group did gain from the prohibition. ∎

***

Calabresi and Melamed's terminology is potentially confusing. In distinguishing between "property rules" and "liability rules," they refer only to types of *remedies* for harm to property. The phrase *liability rules* does not refer to the rule of liability, that is, strict liability versus the reasonableness standard of tort law. Rather, it refers to a specific type of remedy: money damages. Thus, Calabresi and Melamed's liability rules and property rules come into play only after legal liability is established. A defendant who is liable will be subject to either a property rule (injunctive relief) or a liability rule (money damages). A defendant who is not liable, paradoxically (because of Calabresi and Melamed's terminology) will not be subject to any liability rule.

Calabresi and Melamed also discuss how liability rules, in contrast to property rules, constitute "objective" and "collective" valuations of the harm the defendant imposes on the plaintiff's property. These terms may also be misleading. A court's determination of damages is not "objective." Judicial property valuations may be supported by expert witnesses, such as real estate appraisers, who compare the plaintiff's property with others in the area that have recently sold. However, one piece of land is not necessarily comparable with another. In fact, it is a fundamental tenet of property law that each individual parcel of land is unique. Meanwhile, it is a fundamental tenet of economic theory that there is no such thing as objective or intrinsic value. One cannot objectively determine the present economic value of something prior to the fact of its sale from a willing seller to a willing buyer at some mutually agreed upon price. The 1,000 potential buyers and sellers for one and the same piece of land may arrive at 1,000 different valuations. Were the value of property objectively determinate, we would expect them all—as well as all expert appraisers in court—to agree. In practice, however, appraisers for competing litigants never agree about the "objective" economic value of a given piece of land.

Moreover, a lone trial court judge's assessment of damages hardly qualifies as "collective." When the court requires Taney to pay Chase $1,000 for harming the latter's property with his pollution, it is not a "collective" social determination of the value of the harm to Chase's property. What could enable the judge to determine social value better than the parties themselves? The transaction costs that might prevent the parties from bargaining to the most efficient allocation of the entitlement could well be lower than the cost to the court of assessing the damages.[2] In that case, property rules might well be preferable to liability rules.

The following examples show how courts fashion remedies in practice. Notice how the rulings fit, or do not fit, within Calabresi and Melamed's framework.

Whalen v. Union Bag and Paper Co.
208 N.Y. 1 (1913)

Werner, J.

The plaintiff is a lower riparian owner upon Kayaderosseras creek in Saratoga county, and the defendant owns and operates on this stream a pulp mill a few miles above plaintiff's land. This mill represents an investment of more than a million dollars and gives employment to 400 or 500 operatives. It discharges into the waters of the creek large quantities of a liquid effluent containing sulphurous acid, lime, sulphur, and waste material consisting of pulp wood, sawdust, slivers, knots, gums, resins and fibre. The pollution thus created, together with the discharge from other industries located along the stream and its principal tributary, has greatly diminished the purity of the water.

The plaintiff is the owner of a farm of two hundred and fifty-five acres, and the trial court has found that its use and value have been injuriously affected by the pollution of the stream caused by the defendant. The defendant conducts a business in which it has invested a large sum of money and employs great numbers of the inhabitants of the locality. . . . The majority of the learned court below reduced the damages suffered by the plaintiff to $100 a year, and reversed that portion of the decree of the trial court which awarded an injunction. The setting aside of the injunction was apparently induced by a consideration of the great loss likely to be inflicted on the defendant by the granting of the injunction as compared with the small injury done to the plaintiff's land by that portion of the pollution which was regarded as attributable to the defendant. Such a balancing of injuries cannot be justified by the circumstances of this case. It is not safe to attempt to lay down any hard and fast rule for the guidance of courts of equity in determining when an injunction shall issue. As Judge Story said: "It is impossible to foresee all the exigencies of society which may require their aid and assistance to protect rights or redress wrongs.". . .

One of the troublesome phases of this kind of litigation is the difficulty of deciding when an injunction shall issue in a case where the evidence clearly establishes an unlawful invasion of a plaintiff's rights, but his actual injury from the continuance of the alleged wrong will be small as compared with the great loss which will be caused by the issuance of the injunction. This appeal has been presented as though that question were involved in the case at bar, but we take a different view. Even as reduced at the Appellate Division, the damages to the plaintiff's farm amount to $100 a year. It can hardly be said that this injury is unsubstantial, even if we should leave out of consideration the peculiarly noxious character of the pollution of which the plaintiff complains. The waste from the defendant's mill is very destructive both to vegetable and animal life and tends to deprive the waters with which it is mixed of their purifying qualities. It should be borne in mind also that there is no claim on the part of the defendant that the nuisance may become less injurious in the future. Although the damage to the plaintiff may be slight as compared with the defendant's expense of abating the condition, that is not a good reason for refusing an injunction. Neither courts of equity nor law can be guided by such a rule, for if followed to its logical conclusion it would deprive the poor litigant of his little property by giving it to those already rich. It is always to be remembered in such cases that "denying the injunction puts the hardship on the party in whose favor the legal right exists instead of on the wrongdoer.". . .

***

The judgment of the Appellate Division, in so far as it denied the injunction, should be reversed and the judgment of the Special Term in that respect reinstated, with costs to the appellant. ∎

At one time, courts automatically enjoined nuisances, as the court did in *Whalen*, no matter how slight the harm to the plaintiff and no matter how socially valuable the defendant's activity. Such automatic injunctions were inefficient in cases where the defendant's conduct produced net social benefits, that is, benefits in excess of costs, including harm to nuisance plaintiffs. Over time, courts recognized this problem, and quickly moved away from granting injunctions in favor of money damages, which allowed nuisance defendants to continue their conduct, as long as they were willing to compensate nuisance plaintiffs for resulting harms.

Liability Rules: Money Damages

Boomer v. Atlantic Cement Co.
26 N.Y. 2d 219 (1970)

Bergan, Judge

Defendant operates a large cement plant near Albany. These are actions for injunction and damages by neighboring land owners alleging injury to property from dirt, smoke and vibration emanating from the plant. A nuisance has been found after trial [that is, the defendant was found liable for the harm], temporary damages have been allowed; but an injunction has been denied.

The public concern with air pollution arising from many sources in industry and in transportation is currently accorded ever wider recognition accompanied by a growing sense of responsibility in State and Federal Governments to control it. Cement plants are obvious sources of air pollution in the neighborhoods where they operate. The ground for the denial of injunction, notwithstanding the finding both that there is a nuisance and that plaintiffs have been damaged substantially, is the large disparity in economic consequences of the nuisance and of the injunction. This theory cannot, however, be sustained without overruling a doctrine which has been consistently reaffirmed in several leading cases in this court and which has never been disavowed here, namely that where a nuisance has been found and where there has been any substantial damage shown by the party complaining an injunction will be granted.

The rule in New York has been that such a nuisance will be enjoined although marked disparity be shown in economic consequence between the effect of the injunction and the effect of the nuisance . . . .

The problem of disparity in economic consequence was sharply in focus in *Whalen v. Union Bag & Paper Co.* (208 N. Y. 1). A pulp mill entailing an investment of more than a million dollars polluted a stream in which plaintiff, who owned a farm, was "a lower riparian owner". The economic loss to plaintiff from this pollution was small. This court, reversing the Appellate Division, reinstated the injunction granted by the Special Term against the argument of the mill owner that in view of "the slight advantage to plaintiff and the great loss that will be inflicted on defendant" an injunction should not be granted (p. 2). "Such a balancing of injuries cannot be justified by the circumstances of this case", Judge Werner noted (p. 4). He continued: "Although the damage to the plaintiff may be slight as compared with the defendant's expense of abating the condition, that is not a good reason for refusing an injunction" (p. 5).

On the other hand, to grant the injunction unless defendant pays plaintiffs such permanent damages as may be fixed by the court seems to do justice between the contending parties. All of the attributions of economic loss to the properties on which plaintiffs' complaints are based will have been redressed.

The nuisance complained of by these plaintiffs may have other public or private consequences, but these particular parties are the only ones who have sought remedies and the judgment proposed will fully redress them. The limitation of relief granted is a limitation only within the four corners of these actions and does not foreclose public health or other public agencies from seeking proper relief in a proper court.

It seems reasonable to think that the risk of being required to pay permanent damages to injured property owners by cement plant owners would itself be a reasonable effective spur to research for improved techniques to minimize nuisance.

. . . [I]t seems fair to both sides to grant permanent damages to plaintiffs which will terminate this private litigation. The theory of damage is the "servitude on land" of plaintiffs imposed by defendant's nuisance.

The judgment, by allowance of permanent damages imposing a servitude on land, which is the basis of the actions, would preclude future recovery by plaintiffs or their grantees placed beyond debate by a provision of the judgment that the payment by defendant and the acceptance by plaintiffs of permanent damages found by the court shall be in compensation for a servitude on the land.

Although the Trial Term has found permanent damages as a possible basis of settlement of the litigation, on remission the court should be entirely free to re-examine this subject. It may again find the permanent damage already found; or make new findings.

The orders should be reversed, without costs, and the cases remitted to Supreme Court, Albany County to grant an injunction which shall be vacated upon payment by defendant of such amounts of permanent damage to the respective plaintiffs as shall for this purpose be determined by the court.

Jasen, J. (dissenting).

I agree with the majority that a reversal is required here, but I do not subscribe to the newly enunciated doctrine of assessment of permanent damages, in lieu of an injunction, where substantial property rights have been impaired by the creation of a nuisance . . . .

I see grave dangers in overruling our long-established rule of granting an injunction where a nuisance results in substantial continuing damage. In permitting the injunction to become inoperative upon the payment of permanent damages, the majority is, in effect, licensing a continuing wrong. It is the same as saying to the cement company, you may continue to do harm to your neighbors so long as you pay a fee for it. Furthermore, once such permanent damages are assessed and paid, the incentive to alleviate the wrong would be eliminated, thereby continuing air pollution of an area without abatement . . . .

This kind of inverse condemnation may not be invoked by a private person or corporation for private gain or advantage. Inverse condemnation should only be permitted when the public is primarily served in the taking or impairment of property. The promotion of the interests of the polluting cement company has, in my opinion, no public use or benefit. ■

The court in *Boomer* gave the defendant the choice between an injunction and paying "permanent damages." Permanent damages are not the same as actual damages. They are "actual damages" (damages suffered up to a certain date) *plus* estimated "future damages" from the continuing nuisance. Typically, courts calculate permanent damages by estimating the difference in the fair-market value of the plaintiff's land before and after the nuisance.[3]

The main reason courts sometimes award permanent damages rather than actual damages is to reduce the social costs, including their own administrative costs, of potentially recurring litigation. In cases of continuing nuisances, an actual damages award would only compensate the plaintiff up to the date of the court's judgment; any damages suffered thereafter would require the plaintiff to sue again. By awarding permanent damages the first time, the court avoids recurring litigation of the same dispute, and thereby reduces costs.

However, permanent damages also have a significant drawback, as Judge Jason notes in his dissent. Once the defendant pays the permanent damages, she no longer has an incentive to abate the nuisance; she has, in effect, purchased a perpetual servitude or easement over the plaintiff's property. Since the defendant will have no future liability to the plaintiff, she has no incentive to find ways to eliminate or reduce the harm stemming from her activities. But there are at least two caveats to this. First, there may be other potential plaintiffs who have not yet sued. They are not barred by the earlier permanent damages award, and so they give the defendant some continuing incentive to abate the nuisance. Second, the government can create inducements of its own, as it has done with pollution control legislation (as discussed in Chapter 15).

One further way to ameliorate the incentive problem created by permanent damages remedies is to make them less than permanent. The court might, for instance, award periodic damages, which would allow the plaintiff to return to court after 5, 10 or 20 years to seek another remedy.[4] This would provide the defendant with some continuing incentive to abate the nuisance. It would also permit the court to reassess the relative costs and benefits of the defendant's conduct in light of new technological developments that may have reduced the cost of abatement, for example. Of course, periodic damages would, all else being equal, raise the administrative costs for the courts over an alternative permanent damages remedy.

Whether permanent or temporary, damages remedies are not necessarily more efficient than injunctions. When the nuisance-causing activity is clearly inefficient – producing more social costs than benefits – then an injunction is likely to be as efficient as a damage remedy. Even where the nuisance-causing activity is socially efficient, a damage award can be every bit as inefficient as injunctive relief, if the court either over-estimates or under-estimates the extent of harm. Calculating damages can be a real problem for courts, as explained in Chapter 11.

Hybrid Property/Liability Rules

Spur Industries v. Del E. Webb Development Co.
108 Ariz. 178 (1972)

Cameron, Vice Chief Justice

From a judgment permanently enjoining the defendant, Spur Industries, Inc., from operating a cattle feedlot near the plaintiff Del E. Webb Development Company's Sun City, Spur appeals. Webb cross-appeals. Although numerous issues are raised, we feel that it is necessary to answer only two questions. They are:

1. Where the operation of a business, such as a cattle feedlot is lawful in the first instance, but becomes a nuisance by reason of a nearby residential area, may the feedlot operation be

enjoined in an action brought by the developer of the residential area?

2. Assuming that the nuisance may be enjoined, may the developer of a completely new town or urban area in a previously agricultural area be required to indemnify the operator of the feedlot who must move or cease operation because of the presence of the residential area created by the developer?

***

In 1956, Spur's predecessors in interest . . . developed feedlots . . . in an area between the confluence of the usually dry Agua Fria and New Rivers. The area is well suited for cattle feeding and in 1959, there were 25 cattle feeding pens or dairy operations within a 7-mile radius of the location developed by Spur's predecessors. In April and May of 1959, the Northside Hay Mill was feeding between 6,000 and 7,000 head of cattle and Welborn approximately 1,500 head on a combined area of 35 acres.

In May of 1959, Del Webb began to plan the development of an urban area to be known as Sun City. For this purpose . . . some 20,000 acres of farmland, were purchased for $ 15,000,000 or $ 750.00 per acre. This price was considerably less than the price of land located near the urban area of Phoenix, and along with the success of Youngtown was a factor influencing the decision to purchase the property in question.

***

Accompanied by an extensive advertising campaign, homes were first offered by Del Webb in January 1960 and the first unit to be completed was south of Grand Avenue and approximately 2 miles north of Spur. By 2 May 1960, there were 450 to 500 houses completed or under construction. At this time, Del Webb did not consider odors from the Spur feed pens a problem and Del Webb continued to develop in a southerly direction, until sales resistance became so great that the parcels were difficult if not impossible to sell.

***

By December 1967, Del Webb's property had extended south to Olive Avenue and Spur was within 500 feet of Olive Avenue to the north . . . . Del Webb filed its original complaint alleging that in excess of 1,300 lots in the southwest portion were unfit for development for sale as residential lots because of the operation of the Spur feedlot.

Del Webb's suit complained that the Spur feeding operation was a public nuisance because of the flies and the odor which were drifting or being blown by the prevailing south to north wind over the southern portion of Sun City. At the time of the suit, Spur was feeding between 20,000 and 30,000 head of cattle, and the facts amply support the finding of the trial court that the feed pens had become a nuisance to the people who resided in the southern part of Del Webb's development. The testimony indicated that cattle in a commercial feedlot will produce 35 to 40 pounds of wet manure per day, per head, or over a million pounds of wet manure per day for 30,000 head of cattle, and that despite the admittedly good feedlot management and good housekeeping practices by Spur, the resulting odor and flies produced an annoying if not unhealthy situation as far as the senior citizens of southern Sun City were concerned. There is no doubt that some of the citizens of Sun City were unable to enjoy the outdoor living which Del Webb had advertised and that Del Webb was faced with sales resistance from prospective purchasers as well as strong and persistent complaints from the people who had purchased homes in that area.

***

It is noted, however, that neither the citizens of Sun City nor Youngtown are represented in this lawsuit and the suit is solely between Del E. Webb Development Company and Spur Industries, Inc.

MAY SPUR BE ENJOINED?

The difference between a private nuisance and a public nuisance is generally one of degree. A private nuisance is one affecting a single individual or a definite small number of persons in the enjoyment of private rights not common to the public, while a public nuisance is one affecting the rights enjoyed by citizens as a part of the public. To constitute a public nuisance, the nuisance must affect a considerable number of people or an entire community or neighborhood.

Where the injury is slight, the remedy for minor inconveniences lies in an action for damages rather than in one for an injunction.

Thus, it would appear from the admittedly incomplete record as developed in the trial court, that, at most, residents of Youngtown would be entitled to damages rather than injunctive relief.

We have no difficulty, however, in agreeing with the conclusion of the trial court that Spur's operation was an enjoinable public nuisance as far as the people in the southern portion of Del Webb's Sun City were concerned.

***

. . . [T]he operation of Spur's feedlot was both a public and a private nuisance. They could have successfully maintained an action to abate the nuisance. Del Webb, having shown a special injury in the loss of sales, had a standing to bring suit to enjoin the nuisance. The judgment of the trial court permanently enjoining the operation of the feedlot is affirmed.

MUST DEL WEBB INDEMNIFY SPUR?

A suit to enjoin a nuisance sounds in equity and the courts have long recognized a special responsibility to the public when acting as a court of equity . . . . In addition to protecting the public interest, however, courts of equity are concerned with protecting the operator of a lawfully, albeit noxious, business from the result of a knowing and willful encroachment by others near his business.

In the so-called "coming to the nuisance" cases, the courts have held that the residential landowner may not have relief if he knowingly came into a neighborhood reserved for industrial or agricultural endeavors and has been damaged thereby:

> "Plaintiffs chose to live in an area uncontrolled by zoning laws or restrictive covenants and remote from urban development. In such an area plaintiffs cannot complain that legitimate agricultural pursuits are being carried on in the vicinity, nor can plaintiffs, having chosen to build in an agricultural area, complain that the agricultural pursuits carried on in the area depreciate the value of their homes. The area being *primarily agricultural,* any opinion reflecting the value of such property must take this factor into account . . . ."

***

Were Webb the only party injured, we would feel justified in holding that the doctrine of "coming to the nuisance" would have been a bar to the relief asked by Webb, and, on the other hand, had Spur located the feedlot near the outskirts of a city and had the city grown toward the feedlot, Spur would

have to suffer the cost of abating the nuisance as to those people locating within the growth pattern of the expanding city . . . .

***

There was no indication in the instant case at the time Spur and its predecessors located in western Maricopa County that a new city would spring up, full-blown, alongside the feeding operation and that the developer of that city would ask the court to order Spur to move because of the new city. Spur is required to move not because of any wrongdoing on the part of Spur, but because of a proper and legitimate regard of the courts for the rights and interests of the public.

Del Webb, on the other hand, is entitled to the relief prayed for (a permanent injunction), not because Webb is blameless, but because of the damage to the people who have been encouraged to purchase homes in Sun City. It does not equitably or legally follow, however, that Webb, being entitled to the injunction, is then free of any liability to Spur if Webb has in fact been the cause of the damage Spur has sustained. It does not seem harsh to require a developer, who has taken advantage of the lesser land values in a rural area as well as the availability of large tracts of land on which to build and develop a new town or city in the area, to indemnify those who are forced to leave as a result.

Having brought people to the nuisance to the foreseeable detriment of Spur, Webb must indemnify Spur for a reasonable amount of the cost of moving or shutting down. It should be noted that this relief to Spur is limited to a case wherein a developer has, with foreseeability, brought into a previously agricultural or industrial area the population which makes necessary the granting of an injunction against a lawful business and for which the business has no adequate relief.

It is therefore the decision of this court that the matter be remanded to the trial court for a hearing upon the damages sustained by the defendant Spur as a reasonable and direct result of the granting of the permanent injunction. Since the result of the appeal may appear novel and both sides have obtained a measure of relief, it is ordered that each side will bear its own costs.

Affirmed in part, reversed in part, and remanded for further proceedings consistent with this opinion. ■

The Arizona Supreme Court suggests, in *Spur*, that because Del Webb came to the nuisance (*i.e.*, the feedlot was already there when Del Webb started its development), it deserved no relief. "Coming to the nuisance" is the legal doctrine that corresponds to economic arguments of market compensation for nuisances. Arguably, the market pre-compensated Del Webb for the harm stemming from the nuisance. Del Webb bought the land for its Sun City development in a predominantly agricultural area. Why there, rather than in some urban or suburban area? No doubt, at least in part, because the price of land is lower in agricultural areas. One reason why land is less expensive in agricultural areas is that agricultural land uses entail pests and odors. Individuals who dislike livestock odors will not pay as much for land surrounded by livestock as they would pay for land free of livestock and associated odors. In a real sense, Del Webb's purchase agreement for the land implicitly included the flies and odors that were already there. If the developer wanted to avoid those odors and flies, it could have bought land elsewhere, in a nonagricultural area, such as Scottsdale. Of course, it would have had to pay more for suburban or urban land. Alternatively, it could have bought some of Spur's land, in a voluntary market transaction, to create a buffer zone between its residential land and surrounding agricultural lands.

But if Del Webb came to the nuisance, why did the court hold Spur liable? The court explains that its motive was to provide a remedy for the residents of Sun City, who bought their homes from Del Webb. This is unconvincing. If Del Webb was guilty of "coming to the nuisance," then the residents of Sun City surely were as well. Presumably, the price they paid for their lots reflected the relatively low price Del Webb paid for the land, which included flies, odors, and everything else that comes along with land in agricultural areas. Like Del Webb, they received the benefits of their bargains, and were pre-compensated by the market for the flies and odors. Nevertheless, the Arizona Supreme Court felt obliged to protect the residents, but not Del Webb, by enjoining Spur's feedlot, even though no single resident of Sun City was a party to the lawsuit.

A unique feature of the *Spur* ruling was the court's requirement that the plaintiff, Del Webb, compensate the defendant for its reasonable costs of closing or relocating arising from the injunction. The court's purpose was almost certainly equitable, rather than economic. Obviously, it felt that simply enjoining the feedlot would provide an unfair and unearned windfall to Del Webb. Because the developer was largely responsible for creating the land-use conflict in the first place, the court evidently felt it only fair that Del Webb should participate in the costs arising from the conflict.

Arguably, it would have been more fair and more efficient for the court to deny the plaintiff any remedy at all. Consider the incentive effect of the court's ruling for feedlot operators like Spur. The court enjoined Spur's feedlot as a nuisance in an agricultural area dominated by feedlots. If a feedlot is a nuisance in that location, it must be a nuisance everywhere. But feedlots are not socially undesirable. Society (with the exception of vegetarians) wants its steaks and hamburgers, which means it wants feedlots. But where? The court's ruling in *Spur* creates substantial uncertainty for those who already own feedlots and for those who might enter that business. That uncertainty increases the cost of doing business.

As a direct consequence of rulings like *Spur*, and under pressure from agricultural interests, state governments began enacting "right to farm" statutes, which (among other things) reinstated the "coming to the nuisance" doctrine as a decision rule. If the feedlot or other agricultural activity, in a predominantly agricultural area, predated residential (or other) development, then the agricultural activity could not be enjoined as a nuisance.

Provisions of Arizona's right-to-farm law, enacted in 1981 (nine years after the *Spur* decision), are fairly typical:

A. Agricultural operations conducted on farmland that are consistent with good agricultural practices and established prior to surrounding nonagricultural uses are presumed to be reasonable and do not constitute a nuisance unless the agricultural operation has a substantial adverse effect on the public health and safety.

B. Agricultural operations undertaken in conformity with federal, state and local laws and regulations are presumed to be good agricultural practice and not adversely affecting the public health and safety.[5]

Inalienability Rules

In addition to injunctive relief and damages awards, Calabresi and Melamed discussed a third remedy, known as an "inalienability rule." This rule goes beyond injunctive relief in securing the owner's entitlement. Not only are others prevented from infringing it, with or without compensation, but the holder of the entitlement cannot lawfully sell it, even if she wants to. The following case of *Andrus v. Allard* presents an application of a legislatively-imposed inalienability rule.

Andrus v. Allard

444 U.S. 51 (1979)

Brennan, Justice.

The Eagle Protection Act [16 U.S.C. § 668] and the Migratory Bird Treaty Act [16 U.S.C. § 703] are conservation statutes designed to prevent the destruction of certain species of birds. Challenged in this case is the validity of regulations promulgated by appellant Secretary of the Interior that prohibit commercial transactions in parts of birds legally killed before the birds came under the protection of the statutes. The regulations provided in pertinent part:

50 CFR § 21.2(a) (1978):
    "Migratory birds, their parts, nests, or eggs, lawfully acquired prior to the effective date of Federal protection under the Migratory Bird Treat Act . . . may be possessed or transported without a Federal permit, but may not be imported, exported, purchased, sold, bartered, or offered for purchase, sale, trade, or barter. . . . "

50 CFR § 22.2(a) (1978):
    "Bald eagles, alive or dead, or their parts, nests, or eggs lawfully acquired prior to June 8, 1940, and golden eagles, alive or dead, or their parts, nests, or eggs lawfully acquired prior to October 24, 1962, may be possessed or transported without a Federal permit, but may not be imported, exported, purchased, sold, traded, bartered, or offered for purchase, sale, trade or barter. . . . " . . . .

Appellant Secretary of the Interior contends that both the Eagle Protection and Migratory Bird Treat Acts contemplate regulatory prohibition of commerce in the parts of protected birds, without regard to when those birds were originally taken. Appellees respond that such a prohibition serves no purpose, arguing that statutory protection of wildlife is not furthered by an embargo upon traffic in avian artifacts that existed before the statutory safeguards came into effect. . . .

Our point of departure in statutory analysis is the language of the enactment . . . .

The terms of the Eagle Protection Act plainly must be read as appellant Secretary argues. The sweepingly framed prohibition in § 668(a) makes it unlawful to "take, possess, sell, purchase, barter, offer to sell, purchase or barter, transport, export or import" protected birds. Congress expressly dealt with the problem of pre-existing bird products by qualifying that general prohibition with the proviso that "nothing herein shall be construed to prohibit *possession or transportation*" of bald or golden eagle parts taken prior to the effective date of coverage under the Act. (Emphasis supplied.)

***

Further, when Congress amended the Eagle Protection Act in 1962 to cover golden eagles, it once again excepted only possession and transportation of pre-existing artifacts from the general ban. 76 Stat. 1246. And it is particularly relevant that Congress has twice renewed and amended the statute without rejecting the Department's view that it is authorized to bar the sale of pre-existing artifacts.

***

The prohibition against the sale of bird parts lawfully taken before the effective date of federal protection is fully consonant with the purposes of the Eagle Protection Act. It was reasonable for Congress to conclude that the possibility of commercial gains presents a special threat to the preservation of eagles because that prospect creates a powerful incentive both to evade statutory prohibitions against taking birds and to take a large volume of birds. The legislative draftsmen might well view evasion as a serious danger because there is no sure means by which to determine the age of bird feathers; feathers recently taken can easily be passed off as having been obtained long ago . . . .

***

[The Court then proceeds to consider the appellees' contention that the federal prohibition on sale or purchase of bird artifacts constitutes a taking of private property without just compensation, in violation of the Fifth Amendment to the U.S. Constitution.]

***

The regulations challenged here do not compel the surrender of the artifacts, and there is no physical invasion or restraint upon them. Rather, a significant restriction has been imposed on one means of disposing of the artifacts. But the denial of one traditional property right does not always amount to a taking. At least where an owner possesses a full "bundle" of property rights, the destruction of one "strand" of the bundle is not a taking, because the aggregate must be viewed in its entirety . . . . In this case, it is crucial that appellees retain the rights to possess and transport their property, and to donate or devise the protected birds.

It is, to be sure, undeniable that the regulations here prevent the most profitable use of appellee's property. Again, however, that is not dispositive. When we review regulation, a reduction in the value of property is not necessarily equated with a taking . . . . In the instant case, it is not clear that appellees will be unable to derive economic benefit from the artifacts; for example, they might exhibit the artifacts for an admissions charge. At any rate, loss to future profits— unaccompanied by any physical property restriction— provides a slender reed upon which to base a takings claim. Prediction of profitability is essentially a matter of reasoned speculation that courts are not especially competent to perform. Further, perhaps because of its very uncertainty, the interest in anticipated gains has traditionally been viewed as less compelling than other property-related interests . . . ."

***

It is true that appellees must bear the costs of these regulations. But, within limits, that is a burden borne to secure "the advantage of living and doing business in a civilized community." *Pennsylvania Coal Co. v. Mahon*, [260 U.S. 393 (1922)] at 422 (Brandeis, J., dissenting). We hold that the simple prohibition of the sale of lawfully acquired property in this case does not effect a taking in violation of the Fifth Amendment. ■

***

The court in *Allard v. Andrus* upheld a federal regulation that deprived owners of the right to sell eagle feathers. After the regulation, individuals could possess and own, but not sell, the feathers. Their ownership interest is "protected" by an inalienability rule.

The case also has something to say about the *limits* of private property. Just because someone is the nominal "owner" of something does not mean that person exercises sole authority and control over it. (Whether or not the nominal owner *should* be the sole authority and controller is another question.) The fact of the matter is that property rights are not (and never have been) absolute. They are delimited in various ways – by the rights of neighbors as we have discussed in this chapter, and by the government, (supposedly) on behalf of the public, as we discuss in the next chapter.

CHAPTER SUMMARY

This chapter has explored the various rules and reasons for protecting property rights. By and large, the legal system protects the existing allocation of property rights by imposing liability on those who interfere with those rights. However, a finding of liability does not necessarily determine who has the property right. The *remedy* for the interference also has a bearing on the allocation of property. Historically, courts protected property rights with equitable remedies, such as injunctions. Violators would be prohibited from interfering further with the plaintiffs' rights. Since the late nineteenth century, however, courts have moved away from automatic injunctions as remedies for property violations, in favor of damages remedies. This change has affected the allocation of property rights. If a plaintiff's property rights are protected only with a damages remedy, the court is, in effect, permitting the defendant who interferes with the plaintiff's property to force a sale of the plaintiff's rights, without the plaintiff's consent, to the defendant at a court ordered price. It is not only the *fact* of legal protection of property that affects economic exchange; *how* those rights are protected also affects economic activity.

QUESTIONS AND PROBLEMS

1. Was the common law's shift from strict liability to a rule of reasonableness for nuisance law, as described in the *Carpenter* case, efficiency-enhancing?
2. Under the old common law doctrine of "coming to the nuisance," plaintiffs could not complain if the defendant was already in place, conducting his activity, before the plaintiff arrived on the scene. Today, this doctrine is generally not a decision rule (it does not *automatically* bar the plaintiff's claim), but a mere factor for courts to consider in deciding nuisance cases. Does the result in *Spur* suggest that it should be reinstated as a decision rule?
3. Why are some rights protected by inalienability rules? Shouldn't all entitlements be available for efficiency-enhancing exchange?
4. Why did the court in *Boomer* give the defendant the option of suffering an injunction or paying permanent damages?

5. Under what circumstances are injunctions likely to be as efficient, or more efficient, than some alternative damages remedy?
6. Why is protection of property rights important for economic exchange?
7. If we were in the world of the "Coase theorem," why would property rules and liability rules have identical outcomes?
8. Why have states enacted "right to farm" laws? What do such laws do? Are they efficiency enhancing?

NOTES

1. *See Rylands v. Fletcher*, [LR] 3 HL 330 (1868), excerpted in Chapter 7.
2. *See* Mitchell Polinsky, "Resolving Nuisance Disputes: The Simple Economics of Injunctive and Damage Remedies," 32 STANFORD LAW REVIEW 107 (1980); James Krier and Stewart Schwab, "Property Rules and Liability Rules: The Cathedral in Another Light," 70 NEW YORK UNIVERSITY LAW REVIEW 440 (1995).
3. The problems of calculating future damages are discussed in Chapter 15.
4. This has been suggested by, for example, William F. Baxter and Lillian R. Altree, *Legal Aspects of Aircraft Noise*, 15 J.L. & ECON. 1 (1972).
5. Ariz. Rev. Stat. Ann. secs. 3–111 to 3–112 (1995).

Chapter 7

Property III: Limits

PRIVATE LAW LIMITATIONS

Nuisance Law as a Limitation on Property

The same institutions that *protect* property rights also serve to *limit* them. Nuisance law protects Smith in the use and enjoyment of his land by limiting what his neighbor, Jones, can do with her land, and vice versa. In this respect, private property rights are correlative: one landowner's rights begin where the rights of another end.

Rylands v. Fletcher
3 H L 330 (1868)

Lord Cairns

My Lords, in this case the Plaintiff (I may use the description of the parties in the action) is the occupier of a mine and works under a close of land. The Defendants are the owners of a mill in his neighbourhood, and they proposed to make a reservoir for the purpose of keeping and storing water to be used about their mill upon another close of land, which, for the purposes of this case, may be taken as being adjoining to the close of the Plaintiff, although, in point of fact, some intervening land lay between the two. Underneath the close of land of the Defendants on which they proposed to construct their reservoir there were certain old and disused mining passages and works. There were five vertical shafts, and some horizontal shafts communicating with them. The vertical shafts had been filled up with soil and rubbish, and it does not appear that any person was aware of the existence either of the vertical shafts or of the horizontal works communicating with them. In the course of the working by the Plaintiff of his mine, he had gradually worked through the seams of coal underneath the close, and had come into contact with the old and disused works underneath the close of the Defendants.

In that state of things the reservoir of the Defendants was constructed. It was constructed by them through the agency and inspection of an engineer and contractor. Personally, the Defendants appear to have taken no part in the works, or to have been aware of any want of security connected with them. As regards the engineer and the contractor, we must take it from the case that they did not exercise, as far as they were concerned, that reasonable care and caution which they might have exercised, taking notice, as they appear to have taken notice, of the vertical shafts filled up in the manner which I have mentioned. However, my Lords, when the reservoir was constructed, and filled, or partly filled, with water, the weight of the water bearing upon the disused and imperfectly filled-up vertical shafts, broke through those shafts. The water passed down them and into the horizontal workings, and from the horizontal workings under the close of the Defendants it passed on into the workings under the close of the Plaintiff, and flooded his mine, causing considerable damage, for which this action was brought.

***

We think that the true rule of law is, that the person who, for his own purposes, brings on his land and collects and keeps there anything likely to do mischief if it escapes, must keep it in at his peril; and if he does not do so, is prima facie answerable for all the damage which is the natural consequence of its escape. He can excuse himself by shewing that the escape was owing to the Plaintiff's default; or, perhaps, that the escape was the consequence of vis major, or the act of God; but as nothing of this sort exists here, it is unnecessary to inquire what excuse would be sufficient. The person whose grass or corn is eaten down by the escaping cattle of his neighbour, or whose mine is flooded by the water from his neighbour's reservoir, or whose cellar is invaded by the filth of his neighbour's privy, or whose habitation is made unhealthy by the fumes and noisome vapours of his neighbour's alkali works, is damnified without any fault of his own; and it seems but reasonable and just that the neighbour who has brought something on his own property (which was not naturally there), harmless to others so long as it is confined to his own property, but which he knows will be mischievous if it gets on his neighbour's, should be obliged to make good the damage which ensues if he does not succeed in confining it to his own property. But for his act in bringing it there no mischief could have accrued, and it seems but just that he should at his peril keep it there, so that no mischief may accrue, or answer for the natural and anticipated consequence. And upon authority this we think is established to be the law, whether the things so brought be beasts, or water, or filth, or stenches. ■

The court in *Rylands v. Fletcher* makes clear that a landowner's property *rights* are accompanied by a property *duty* not to interfere with others' use and enjoyment of their own land. Of course, as Coase showed (see Chapter 4), to the extent nuisance law prevents someone from doing as they please with their land, they themselves are harmed. Hence, nuisances are reciprocal in nature, which is especially well illustrated in the following case.

Ampitheaters, Inc. v. Portland Meadows

184 Or. 336 (1948)

Brand, J.

***

During the summer of 1945 the defendant commenced arrangements for the purchase of land and the construction thereon of a one-mile race track. On 25 August, 1945, an option for the purchase of 21 acres of the required land was secured from H. M. Seivert who is one of the promoters of the theater project and is the owner of the land on which the theater is situated. On 15 October, 1945, defendant applied for a license to operate a race meet to be held in May, 1946, and the license was issued. In October and early November, 1945, extensive newspaper publicity was given to the race track project, featuring the fact that the property would be lighted for night racing. . . .

During the fall of 1945 the land on which the plaintiff's theater was located was being prepared and equipped for night auto racing by Northwest Sports, Inc., an activity which, like that of the defendant, would have involved the use of flood lights. On 29 November, 1945, a lease agreement was executed between Northwest Sports, Inc., and the promoters of the plaintiff corporation, entitling the lessees and their assignee, Ampitheaters, Inc., to construct and operate a drive-in outdoor motion picture theater upon the property adjoining the race track of defendants. But the lease provided that the operation of the theater must not interfere with the operations of the same property for auto racing. . . . At least some of the promoters of the theater project knew that the race track was to be lighted for night racing, though they may not have known the volume or extent of the proposed lighting.

The outdoor theater was completed and commenced operating on 31 August, 1946. The race track was completed and the first races held fifteen days later. The plaintiff invested $135,000 in the construction of the outdoor theater and sums greatly in excess of that amount were expended by the defendant in the development of the race track and facilities. The lighting facilities alone involved an investment by the defendant of $100,000. . . .

In installing outdoor moving picture theaters, it is necessary to protect the premises from outside light interference. For that purpose the plaintiff constructed wing fences for a considerable distance on each side of the screen [and along the road] . . . for the purpose of excluding the light from [passing automobiles]. . . . It was also necessary to construct a shadow box extending on both sides and above the screen for the purpose of excluding light from the moon and stars. . . . The extreme delicacy of plaintiff's operation and the susceptibility of outdoor moving pictures to light in any form was conclusively established by the evidence.

In order to illuminate the defendant's race track for night horse racing, approximately 350 1500-watt lights are mounted in clusters on 80-foot poles placed at intervals of approximately 250 feet around the track. The flood lights are, in general, directed at the track, but there is substantial evidence to the effect that reflected light "spills" over onto the plaintiff's premises and has a serious effect on the quality of the pictures shown on the screen. . . . [T]here is also substantial evidence that plaintiffs have suffered financial loss as the result of the illumination of which they complain. On one occasion at least, plaintiffs felt themselves required to refund admission fees to their patrons on account of the poor quality of the picture exhibited. The evidence discloses that the light from the defendant's race track when measured at plaintiff's screen is approximately that of full moonlight.

Upon the opening of the racing season in September, 1946, the plaintiff immediately complained to the defendant concerning the detrimental effect of defendant's lights, and shortly thereafter suit was filed. In the fall of 1946 the defendant, while denying liability, nevertheless made substantial efforts to protect the plaintiff from the effect of defendant's lights. One hundred hoods were installed on the lights, and particular attention was given to those nearest to the plaintiff's property. . . . [T]hirty louvers were also installed for the purpose of further confining the light to the defendant's property. These efforts materially reduced, but did not eliminate the conditions of which plaintiff complains.

***

[After determining that the case concerned nuisance— under a reasonableness standard for liability—rather than trespass, which is a strict liability cause of action, the court proceeded to assess the plaintiff's claim.]

***

Plaintiff relies upon the general definition of a nuisance. . . . A private nuisance is defined as "anything done to the hurt, annoyance or detriment of the lands or hereditaments of another, and not amounting to a trespass." Definitions in such general terms are of no practical assistance to the court.

***

Notwithstanding the fact that the existence *vel non* of a nuisance is generally a question of fact, there have arisen several rules of law which guide and sometimes control decision. It is established law that an intentional interference with the use and enjoyment of land is not actionable unless that interference be both substantial and unreasonable. Restatement of the Law of Torts, Vol. 4, § 822, Comment g, and § 826, comment a.

***

It is highly significant that an identical principle has been applied where the uses to which a plaintiff puts his land are abnormally sensitive to the type of interference caused by the defendant.

"No action will lie for nuisance in respect of damage which, even though substantial, is due solely to the fact that the plaintiff is abnormally sensitive to deleterious influences, or uses his land for some purpose which requires exceptional freedom from any such influences. . . .

***

[T]he plaintiff's only basis for complaint is the fact that it is attempting to show upon the screen moving pictures, and that operation is such a delicate one that it has been necessary for the plaintiff to build high fences to prevent the light of automobiles upon the public highway from invading the property and to build a shadow box over the screen to protect it from the ordinary light of the moon and stars, and that it now claims damages because the lights from the defendant's property, which it has not excluded by high fences, shine with the approximate intensity of full moonlight upon the screen and interfere

thereby with the showing of the pictures. We think this is a clear case coming within the doctrine . . . that a man cannot increase the liabilities of his neighbors by applying his own property to special and delicate uses, whether for business or pleasure.

***

By way of summary, we have found no case in which it has been held that light alone constitutes a nuisance merely because it damaged one who is abnormally sensitive or whose use of land was of a peculiarly delicate and sensitive character.

It is not our intention to decide the case upon authority alone, divorced from reason or public policy. . . . Neither party can claim any greater social utility than the other. Both were in process of construction at the same time, and the case should not be decided upon the basis of the priority of occupation.

***

We do not say that the shedding of light upon another's property may never under any conditions become a nuisance, but we do say that extreme caution must be employed in applying any such legal theory. The conditions of modern city life impose upon the city dweller and his property many burdens more severe than that of light reflected upon him or it. ∎

***

Who caused the nuisance in *Ampitheaters, Inc. v. Portland Meadows*? The court suggests that it has no way to decide. Thus, the court acknowledges that the harm is reciprocal in nature. The outdoor theater was harmed by the light coming from the race track. Had the court ruled in the plaintiff's favor, the race track would have been harmed by the interference with its night racing. At the very least, the defendant would have had to invest a great deal more money to prevent the harm to the plaintiff. Even though it was not liable, the race track took reasonable precautions by installing light hoods and louvers. The theater owner, by contrast, did not take sufficient precautions, according to the court. Specifically, it could have, but did not, install high fences to block the light. However, the court does not undertake a Coasean best cost avoider analysis to determine which action would provide the least cost solution to the joint cost problem. Instead, the court simply finds the theater owner's use of the land so "abnormally sensitive" that it would be unfair to impose the burden on the owner of the neighboring race track, even if he might be the best cost avoider.

Private Land-Use Planning: Covenants

In addition to common law cause of actions, various types of private, contractual, or quasi-contractual mechanisms have been devised for limiting private property rights and uses. For example, the deeds for residential lots in subdivisions frequently include *covenants* that restrict the uses to which the owner can put the land. Somewhat paradoxically, by limiting the freedom of lot owners to use their lots as they please, such covenants frequently increase the value of the land. Put yourself in the position of a person who is looking to buy a lot on which to construct a 5,000 square foot single-family dwelling. You have a choice between two subdivisions, one of which has a single-family residential covenant, the other of which does not restrict land uses in any way. Assume no public zoning.[1] If you buy in the first subdivision, you cannot build anything other than a single-family home, but neither can your neighbors. The same covenant that restricts your freedom also benefits you by restricting what your neighbors can build on their land. In the other subdivision, you have more freedom to do what you like with your land, but so do your neighbors. In that subdivision, your next door neighbor can build and operate a junkyard right next to your single-family home. If your intention is to build a single-family residence, the cost to you of the single-family residential covenant is likely to be quite low, compared to the benefits stemming from the application of the same covenant to neighboring lands. Thus, subdivision developers can maximize the value of the lots they are selling by inserting into each deed a covenant restricting development to single-family homes.

Covenants are, however, also useful for uneconomic and nefarious, discriminatory purposes. For example, the famous case of *Shelly v. Kramer*[2] involved a deed with a covenant providing that the house could not be occupied "by any person not of the Caucasian race." The house was subsequently sold to an African-American family. Neighbors sued to enforce the covenant against them. The Supreme Court of Missouri upheld and enforced the covenant. The Supreme Court of the United States subsequently ruled that state court enforcement of the racial covenant constituted state-supported discrimination, in violation of the equal protection clause of the 14th Amendment to the U.S. Constitution.

Even legitimate and economically efficient covenants can become inefficient over time. Under the doctrine of changed conditions, obsolete and inefficient covenants can be removed by court order. But such a court order is not necessarily easy to obtain, as the following case illustrates.

Rick v. West

228 N.Y.S. 2d 195 (N.Y. Sup.Ct. 1962)

[In 1946, a developer named Rick subdivided 62 vacant acres of land he owned in Westchester County, New York. A declaration of covenants, which restricted each lot to single-family dwellings, was filed in court. In 1956, Rick sold a lot to West, which was subject to the covenant. Upon that lot she constructed a single-family dwelling. A year later, the land was zoned for single-family residential. Subsequently, Rick contracted to sell 45 acres of the subdivided land to an industrialist for industrial development. The sale was made contingent on rezoning the land. The town board voted to rezone the 45 acres, but West would not agree to release the covenant which benefitted her land. So, the sale to the industrialist fell through. Rick then conveyed his remaining acreage to the plaintiffs. In 1961, the plaintiffs sought to sell 15 acres of the subdivided land to Peekskill Hospital, but West again declined to release the plaintiffs from the covenant.

This time the plaintiffs sued, seeking a court order that the covenant was no longer enforceable under the doctrine of changed conditions. The court ruled in favor of the defendant, West, finding insufficient evidence of changed conditions with respect to the plaintiff's parcel of land or the neighborhood generally.]

Hoyt, J.

The parcel in question would doubtless by its topography and proximity to fast-growing suburban areas make a desirable location for the hospital. The hospital authorities would like to acquire it, and the plaintiffs would like to sell it, and it may be asked why should defendant owning a most respectable, but modest, home be permitted to prevent the sale, or in any event why should the covenants be not determined nonenforceable and the defendant relegated to pecuniary damages.

Plaintiffs' predecessor owned the tract free and clear of all restrictions. He could do with the parcel as he saw best. He elected to promote a residential development and in the furtherance of his plan, and as an inducement to purchasers he imposed the residential restrictions. The defendant relied upon them and has a right to continue to rely thereon. It is not a question of balancing equities or equating the advantages of a hospital on this site with the effect it would have on defendant's property. Nor does the fact that defendant is the only one of the few purchasers from plaintiffs' predecessor in title who has refused to release the covenants make defendant's insistence upon the enforcement of the covenants no less deserving of the court's protection and safeguarding of her rights. ■

***

The court in *Rick v. West* refused to protect the defendant's right to enforce the covenant with what Calabresi and Melamed call a liability rule (money damages), but instead enforced the right with a property rule (an injunction). This ruling does not mean, however, the plaintiffs and the hospital are left without any recourse. They can still seek a market-based solution. Specifically, they can try to purchase West's release of the covenant through a voluntary market transaction, the same mechanism by which the covenants were imposed in the first place.

PUBLIC LAW LIMITATIONS ON PRIVATE PROPERTY

Beyond private land-use limitations, various public law mechanisms restrict private land uses, including the common law public nuisance action, zoning and other forms of land-use regulation, and eminent domain.

Governments hold two inherent powers for regulating uses of private property: the police power and the eminent domain power. These powers are inherent of government in that they are enforceable even if not specifically enumerated in constitutions.

Police Power Regulation

Two forms of police power regulation are most commonly used for regulating private property: public nuisance claims and zoning.

Public Nuisance

A nuisance is a *public* nuisance if it affects the public at large. Private individuals can bring a public nuisance action if they can show "special damages"; that is, the damages they suffer must be above and beyond those suffered by the public at large. If so, they can vindicate their private rights and public rights at the same time. Most public nuisance actions, however, are brought by state or local government officials to ameliorate public harms ranging from pollution[3] to prostitution.[4] From an economic point of view, the purpose of public nuisance law is to internalize externalities that private actors impose on the public. The question remains as to whether the social benefits from internalizing the externality exceed the cost.

One significant difference between public and private nuisances is in the remedy. Injunctive relief, although not automatic in cases of public nuisance, is far more likely because of the widespread and usually greater extent of the harm.[5]

In dealing with public nuisances, governments have a choice to sue under common law public nuisance doctrine or regulate nuisance-causing activities under their police powers. Air pollution control regulations, for example, are in the nature of nuisance-control measures. They are typically based on explicit statutory authorizations, and involve administrative processes. But like common law public nuisance suits, such regulatory measures often are enforced in court.[6]

Zoning

Zoning is a process by which a local government determines how land in different areas of town is used. Zoning regulation is justified as a police power measure, designed to prevent public nuisances that might arise if incompatible land uses were allowed in the same area. It is, in a sense, the most comprehensive form of nuisance regulation. In contrast to the public nuisance action, it is inherently regulatory. The role of the courts is limited to interpreting, enforcing, and adjudicating the constitutionality of zoning measures and the administrative decisions of local zoning boards.

Village of Euclid v. Ambler Realty Co.
272 U.S. 365 (1926)

Sutherland, Justice

***

Building zone laws are of modern origin. They began in this country about twenty-five years ago. Until recent years, urban life was comparatively simple; but with the great increase and concentration of population, problems have developed, and constantly are developing, which require, and will continue to require, additional restrictions in respect of the use and occupation of private lands in urban communities. Regulations, the wisdom, necessity, and validity of which, as applied to existing conditions, are so apparent that they are now uniformly sustained, a century ago, or even half a century ago,

probably would have been rejected as arbitrary and oppressive. Such regulations are sustained, under the complex conditions of our day, for reasons analogous to those which justify traffic regulations, which, before the advent of automobiles and rapid transit street railways, would have been condemned as fatally arbitrary and unreasonable. . . .

The ordinance now under review [which set forth the various uses—residential, commercial, industrial—to which different parcels of land in Euclid could be put], and all similar laws and regulations, must find their justification in some aspect of the police power, asserted for the public welfare. The line which in this field separates the legitimate from the illegitimate assumption of power is not capable of precise delimitation. It varies with circumstances and conditions. A regulatory zoning ordinance, which would be clearly valid as applied to the great cities, might be clearly invalid as applied to rural communities. . . .

[T]he question whether the power exists to forbid the erection of a building of a particular kind or for a particular use, like the question of whether a particular thing is a nuisance, is to be determined, not by an abstract consideration of the building or the thing considered apart, but by considering it in connection with the circumstances of the locality. . . . A nuisance may be merely a right thing in the wrong place—like a pig in the parlor instead of the barnyard. If the validity of the legislative classification for zoning purposes be fairly debatable, the legislative judgment must be allowed to control. . . .

There is no serious difference of opinion in respect of the validity of laws and regulations fixing the height of buildings within reasonable limits, the character of materials and methods of construction, and the adjoining area which must be left open, in order to minimize the danger of fire or collapse, the evils of over-crowding, and the like, and excluding from residential sections offensive trades, industries and structures likely to create nuisances. . . .

***

If it be a proper exercise of the police power to relegate industrial establishments to localities separated from residential sections, it is not easy to find a sufficient reason for denying the power because the effect of its exercise is to divert an industrial flow from the course which it would follow to the injury of the residential public if left alone, to another course where such injury will be obviated. It is not meant by this, however, to exclude the possibility of cases where the general public interest would so far outweigh the interest of the municipality that the municipality would not be allowed to stand in the way.

We find no difficulty in sustaining restrictions of the kind thus far reviewed. The serious question in the case arises over the provisions of the ordinance excluding from residential districts, apartment houses, business houses, retail stores and shops, and other like establishments. This question involves the validity of what is really the crux of the more recent zoning legislation, namely, the creation and maintenance of residential districts, from which business and trade of every sort, including hotels and apartment houses, are excluded. Upon that question, this Court has not thus far spoken. The decisions of the state courts are numerous and conflicting; but those which broadly sustain the power greatly outnumber those which deny altogether or narrowly limit it; and it is very apparent that there is a constantly increasing tendency in the direction of the broader view. . . .

***

The matter of zoning has received much attention at the hands of commissions and experts, and the results of their investigations have been set forth in comprehensive reports. These reports, which bear every evidence of painstaking consideration, concur in the view that the segregation of residential, business, and industrial buildings will make it easier to provide fire apparatus suitable for the character and intensity of the development in each section; that it will increase the safety and security of home life; greatly tend to prevent street accidents, especially to children, by reducing the traffic and resulting confusion in residential sections; decrease noise and other conditions which produce or intensify nervous disorders; preserve a more favorable environment in which to rear children, etc. With particular reference to apartment houses, it is pointed out that the development of detached house sections is greatly retarded by the coming of apartment houses, which has sometimes resulted in destroying the entire section for private house purposes; that in such sections very often the apartment house is a mere parasite, constructed in order to take advantage of the open spaces and attractive surroundings created by the residential character of the district. Moreover, the coming of one apartment house is followed by others, interfering by their height and bulk with the free circulation of air and monopolizing the rays of the sun which otherwise would fall upon the smaller homes, and bringing, as their necessary accompaniments, the disturbing noises incident to increased traffic and business, and the occupation, by means of moving and parked automobiles, of larger portions of the streets, thus detracting from their safety and depriving children of the privilege of quiet and open spaces for play, enjoyed by those in more favored localities, until, finally, the residential character of the neighborhood and its desirability as a place of detached residences are utterly destroyed. Under these circumstances, apartment houses, which in a different environment would be not only entirely unobjectionable but highly desirable, come very near to being nuisances.

If these reasons, thus summarized, do not demonstrate the wisdom or sound policy in all respects of those restrictions which we have indicated as pertinent to the inquiry, at least, the reasons are sufficiently cogent to preclude us from saying, as it must be said before the ordinance can be declared unconstitutional, that such provisions are clearly arbitrary and unreasonable, having no substantial relation to the public health, safety, morals, or general welfare. . . .

***

Decree reversed. ■

Note that the Supreme Court's endorsement of comprehensive zoning in the *Ambler Realty* case is limited. After citing reasons why zoning might be good policy, the Court declines to conclude that it *is* good policy. It merely concludes that zoning is not such patently bad policy—arbitrary and unreasonable—as to warrant judicial invalidation on constitutional grounds.

The question remains as to whether zoning is good policy. From the economist's point of view, the answer to that question depends on the efficiency or inefficiency of zoning regulations. Supporters of zoning attempt to justify it economically as a method of internalizing widespread externalities arising from dissimilar and conflicting land uses. According to Robert Ellickson, zoning is a relatively efficient way to resolve coordination/externality problems across different properties in large, urban areas, mainly because of the high transaction costs associated with large numbers of landowners with diverse interests. But, he suggests, zoning is relatively inefficient—compared with private land-use restrictions such as nuisance law, covenants, and Coasean bargaining—where conflicts are likely to involve just a few close neighbors.[7] Thus, the economic case for zoning is based largely on the scale of the coordination/externality problem to be resolved.

Even if it is sometimes economically legitimate, zoning, like private covenants, may be used for socially nefarious purposes, such as excluding politically and economically disadvantaged groups. So-called "exclusionary zoning" is unconstitutional, but it is not always easy to distinguish economically and constitutionally legitimate zoning from unlawful exclusionary zoning. The question is largely one of intent: Is the government legitimately seeking to resolve or avoid land-use conflicts? Or, is it merely serving the interests of the "haves" by excluding the "have-nots"?

Eminent Domain

Aside from the ability to regulate property uses or sue under the police power, governments possess the power of eminent domain, which authorizes them to take title away from private landowners, with or without their consent. The term *eminent domain* literally means highest ownership, the implication being that all private landownership is subject to the state's assertion of superior title. So, if the government does not like what Jones is doing with her land, it always has the option, beyond suing for public nuisance or regulating under the police power, of claiming the land for public use.

In the United States, the government's power of eminent domain is subject to two conditions enshrined in the 5th Amendment to the U.S. Constitution: (1) it must take the land for "public use"; and (2) it must provide "just compensation." The public use condition is designed to ensure that government exercises of eminent domain are in the public interest, rather than the private interest of some favored person or group. However, the courts have interpreted "public use" so broadly as to permit eminent domain takings of land that have almost any public interest, however limited. In the infamous case of *Poletown Neighborhood Council v. City of Detroit*,[8] the Michigan Supreme Court upheld the City of Detroit's taking, by eminent domain, of an entire working-class neighborhood to provide land for a new General Motors Cadillac plant. The court found that the anticipated economic benefits to the City of Detroit of providing the land for General Motors's use were sufficient to satisfy the public use condition.

In *Poletown*, all of the dispossessed residents of the working-class neighborhood were compensated, as the 5th Amendment to the U.S. Constitution requires. They were paid for their land. According to the courts, "just compensation" equals fair market value. One problem, of course, is that in eminent domain takings, the price is not determined in free market negotiations. Rather, the government sets the price it is willing to pay. If the dispossessed landowner disputes that amount, he or she can sue, in which case a court ultimately assesses "just compensation." Either way, the dispossessed owner's subjective willingness to accept is irrelevant to the property valuation.

CONSTITUTIONAL LIMITATIONS ON PUBLIC REGULATION OF PRIVATE PROPERTY: REGULATORY TAKINGS LAW

The fact that the government can either regulate private property under its police power or take property away under eminent domain raises an intriguing issue of policy choice. It might be both possible and rational for government officials to avoid paying compensation for many eminent domain takings by using the police power instead. In some cases the government has no choice. If it wants to build a road, it cannot use its police power to force private landowners to allow it to be built on their lands; rather, the government *must* take title to the land and pay compensation under eminent domain. On the other hand, the government never would resort to eminent domain to shut down a house of prostitution or stop some other illegal activity. In many cases, however, the government seemingly does have a choice between police power/nuisance regulation and compulsory purchase by eminent domain.

Consider, for example, a mining company that owns a great deal of land, including the minerals underlying the surface. It has no use for the "surface estate"; it only values the minerals of the "subsurface estate." So, it sells off the surface estate to a group of private owners, expressly reserving the right to remove minerals from beneath the surface, and allocating to the owners of the surface estate the risk that their lands might subside as a consequence. But no mining occurs for a very long time. Eventually, the owners of the surface estate incorporate a town on the site, complete with schools, restaurants, and a retail shopping district. Later, the mining company announces plans to begin mining under the town. The town appeals to the state legislature to take action to prevent the mining company from exercising its rights under the original land-sale contract. The state legislature obviously has a choice to make: it can seek to prevent the mining company from causing harm to other properties in the town through police power/nuisance regulation; or it can take away the mining company's property rights in the subsurface estate and pay "just compensation."

In 1966, the State of Pennsylvania enacted a law to *regulate* land subsidence caused by mining. The law required mining companies to leave 50 percent of the coal in place to provide support for the surface estate. Miners were also made liable for subsidence, even if they had expressly reserved the right to cause subsidence when they sold the surface estate. The state claimed that the law was intended and designed to prevent public harm from mining activities that amount to nuisances. But the Keystone Bituminous Coal Association contended that the law was merely an eminent domain taking disguised as a nuisance-control measure, so that the state would not have to pay compensation. The case rose to the U.S. Supreme Court, which upheld the Pennsylvania law as a legitimate police power regulation, not requiring compensation.[9]

The state does not always get off the hook so easily, however. Especially in recent years, courts, including the U.S. Supreme Court, have grown increasingly distrustful of legislative motives. When the government purports to regulate property under the police power, but the effect of the regulation is more in the nature of an eminent domain taking, the courts will require the government to compensate, *as if* it were exercising its power of eminent domain. This regulatory takings doctrine has its origin in a famous case from 1922, the facts of which are strikingly similar to *Keystone Bituminous Coal Association*:

Pennsylvania Coal Co. v. Mahon
260 U.S. 393 (1922)

Holmes, Justice

This is a bill in equity brought by the [Mahons] to prevent the Pennsylvania Coal Company from mining under their property in such way as to remove the support and cause a subsidence of the surface and of their house. The bill sets out a deed executed by the Coal Company in 1878, under which the plaintiffs claim. The deed conveys the surface, but in express terms reserves the right to remove all the coal under the same, and the grantee takes the premises with the risk, and waives all claim for damages that may arise from mining out the coal. But the plaintiffs say that whatever may have been the Coal Company's rights, they were taken away

by an [1921] Act of Pennsylvania . . . commonly known as the Kohler Act. The Court of Common Pleas found that if not restrained the defendant would cause the damage to prevent which the bill was brought, but denied an injunction, holding that the statute if applied to this case would be unconstitutional. On appeal the Supreme Court of the State agreed that the defendant had contract and property rights protected by the Constitution of the United States, but held that the statute was a legitimate exercise of the police power and directed a decree for the plaintiffs. A writ of error was granted bringing the case to this Court.

The statute forbids the mining of anthracite coal in such way as to cause the subsidence of, among other things, any structure used as a human habitation, with certain exceptions, including among them land where the surface is owned by the owner of the underlying coal and is distant more than one hundred and fifty feet from any improved property belonging to any other person. As applied to this case the statute is admitted to destroy previously existing rights of property and contract. The question is whether the police power can be stretched so far.

Government hardly could go on if to some extent values incident to property could not be diminished without paying for every change in the general law. As long recognized, some values are enjoyed under an implied limitation and must yield to the police power. But obviously the implied limitation must have its limits, or the contract and due process clauses are gone. One fact for consideration in determining such limits is the extent of the diminution. When it reaches a certain magnitude, in most if not all cases there must be an exercise of eminent domain and compensation to sustain the act. So the question depends upon the particular facts. The greatest weight is given to the judgment of the legislature, but it always is open to interested parties to contend that the legislature has gone beyond its constitutional power.

This is the case of a single private house. No doubt there is a public interest even in this, as there is in every purchase and sale and in all that happens within the commonwealth. Some existing rights may be modified even in such a case. . . . But usually in ordinary private affairs, the public interest does not warrant much of this kind of interference. A source of damage to such a house is not a public nuisance even if similar damage is inflicted on others in different places. The damage is not common or public. . . . The extent of the public interest is shown by the statute to be limited, since the statute ordinarily does not apply to land when the surface is owned by the owner of the coal. Furthermore, it is not justified as a protection of personal safety. That could be provided for by notice. Indeed the very foundation of this bill is that the defendant gave timely notice of its intent to mine under the house. On the other hand the extent of the taking is great. It purports to abolish what is recognized in Pennsylvania as an estate in land—a very valuable estate—and what is declared by the court below to be a contract hitherto binding the plaintiffs. If we were called upon to deal with the plaintiffs' position alone, we should think it clear that the statute does not disclose a public interest sufficient to warrant so extensive a destruction of the defendant's constitutionally protected rights.

***

It is our opinion that the act cannot be sustained as an exercise of the police power, so far as it affects the mining of coal under streets or cities in places where the right to mine such coal has been reserved. . . . What makes the right to mine coal valuable is that it can be exercised with profit. To make it commercially impracticable to mine certain coal has very nearly the same effect for constitutional purposes as appropriating it or destroying it. This we think that we are warranted in assuming that this statute does.

It is true that in *Plymouth Coal Co. v. Pennsylvania*, 232 U.S. 531, it was held competent for the legislature to require a pillar of coal to be left along the line of adjoining property, that, with the pillar on the other side of the line, would be a barrier sufficient for the safety of the employees of either mine, in case the other should be abandoned and allowed to fill with water. But that was a requirement for the safety of employees invited into the mine, and secured an average reciprocity of advantage that has been recognized as a justification of various laws.

The rights of the public in a street purchased or laid out by eminent domain are those that it has paid for. If in any case its representatives have been so short sighted as to acquire only surface rights without the right of support, we see no more authority for supplying the latter without compensation than there was for taking the right of way in the first place and refusing to pay for it because the public wanted it very much. The protection of private property in the Fifth Amendment presupposes that it is wanted for public use, but provides that it shall not be taken for such use without compensation. . . . When this seemingly absolute protection is found to be qualified by the police power, the natural tendency of human nature is to extend the qualification more and more until at last private property disappears. But that cannot be accomplished in this way under the Constitution of the United States.

The general rule at least is, that while property may be regulated to a certain extent, if regulation goes too far it will be recognized as a taking. It may be doubted how far exceptional cases, like the blowing up of a house to stop a conflagration, go—and if they go beyond the general rule, whether they do not stand as much upon tradition as upon principle. In general it is not plain that a man's misfortunes or necessities will justify his shifting the damages to his neighbor's shoulders. We are in danger of forgetting that a strong public desire to improve the public condition is not enough to warrant achieving the desire by a shorter cut than the constitutional way of paying for the change. As we already have said, this is a question of degree—and therefore cannot be disposed of by general propositions. But we regard this as going beyond any of the cases decided by this Court. . . .

We assume, of course, that the statute was passed upon the conviction that an exigency existed that would warrant it, and we assume that an exigency exists that would warrant the exercise of eminent domain. But the question at bottom is upon whom the loss of the changes desired should fall. So far as private persons or communities have seen fit to take the risk of acquiring only surface rights, we cannot see that the fact that their risk has become a danger warrants the giving to them greater rights than they bought.

Decree reversed. ■

The Supreme Court's *Pennsylvania Coal* ruling had virtually no immediate effect on the extent of government regulation. For 70 years, the Court did not find any other "regulatory takings" under Justice Holmes's "diminution-in-value" test, including in cases, as we have already seen, that were factually quite similar to *Pennsylvania Coal*. Then, in 1992 the Supreme Court made clear that regulatory takings doctrine and the diminution-in-value test are here to stay.

Lucas v. South Carolina Coastal Council
505 U.S. 1003 (1992)

Scalia, Justice.

In 1986, petitioner David H. Lucas paid $ 975,000 for two residential lots on the Isle of Palms in Charleston County, South Carolina, on which he intended to build single-family homes. In 1988, however, the South Carolina Legislature enacted the Beachfront Management Act, . . . , which had the direct effect of barring petitioner from erecting any permanent habitable structures on his two parcels. . . . A state trial court found that this prohibition rendered Lucas's parcels "valueless.". . . This case requires us to decide whether the Act's dramatic effect on the economic value of Lucas's lots accomplished a taking of private property under the Fifth and Fourteenth Amendments requiring the payment of "just compensation." U.S. Const., Amdt. 5.

***

Prior to Justice Holmes's exposition in *Pennsylvania Coal Co. v. Mahon* . . . , it was generally thought that the Takings Clause reached only a "direct appropriation" of property, . . . or the functional equivalent of a "practical ouster of [the owner's] possession,". . . Justice Holmes recognized in *Mahon*, however, that if the protection against physical appropriations of private property was to be meaningfully enforced, the government's power to redefine the range of interests included in the ownership of property was necessarily constrained by constitutional limits. . . . If, instead, the uses of private property were subject to unbridled, uncompensated qualification under the police power, "the natural tendency of human nature [would be] to extend the qualification more and more until at last private property disappeared.". . . These considerations gave birth in that case to the oft-cited maxim that, "while property may be regulated to a certain extent, if regulation goes too far it will be recognized as a taking.". . .

Nevertheless, our decision in *Mahon* offered little insight into when, and under what circumstances, a given regulation would be seen as going "too far" for purposes of the Fifth Amendment. In 70-odd years of succeeding "regulatory takings" jurisprudence, we have generally eschewed any "'set formula'" for determining how far is too far, preferring to "engage in . . . essentially ad hoc, factual inquiries.". . . We have, however, described at least two discrete categories of regulatory action as compensable without case-specific inquiry into the public interest advanced in support of the restraint. The first encompasses regulations that compel the property owner to suffer a physical "invasion" of his property. In general (at least with regard to permanent invasions), no matter how minute the intrusion, and no matter how weighty the public purpose behind it, we have required compensation. . . .

The second situation in which we have found categorical treatment appropriate is where regulation denies all economically beneficial or productive use of land. . . . As we have said on numerous occasions, the Fifth Amendment is violated when land-use regulation "does not substantially advance legitimate state interests *or denies an owner economically viable use of his land.*". . .

We have never set forth the justification for this rule. Perhaps it is simply, as Justice Brennan suggested, that total deprivation of beneficial use is, from the landowner's point of view, the equivalent of a physical appropriation. . . . Surely, at least, in the extraordinary circumstance when *no* productive or economically beneficial use of land is permitted, it is less realistic to indulge our usual assumption that the legislature is simply "adjusting the benefits and burdens of economic life.". . . And the *functional* basis for permitting the government, by regulation, to affect property values without compensation—that "Government hardly could go on if to some extent values incident to property could not be diminished without paying for every such change in the general law,". . . does not apply to the relatively rare situations where the government has deprived a landowner of all economically beneficial uses.

On the other side of the balance, affirmatively supporting a compensation requirement, is the fact that regulations that leave the owner of land without economically beneficial or productive options for its use—typically, as here, by requiring land to be left substantially in its natural state—carry with them a heightened risk that private property is being pressed into some form of public service under the guise of mitigating serious public harm. . . . As Justice Brennan explained: "From the government's point of view, the benefits flowing to the public from preservation of open space through regulation may be equally great as from creating a wildlife refuge through formal condemnation or increasing electricity production through a dam project that floods private property.". . . The many statutes on the books, both state and federal, that provide for the use of eminent domain to impose servitudes on private scenic lands preventing developmental uses, or to acquire such lands altogether, suggest the practical equivalence in this setting of negative regulation and appropriation. . . .

We think, in short, that there are good reasons for our frequently expressed belief that when the owner of real property has been called upon to sacrifice *all* economically beneficial uses in the name of the common good, that is, to leave his property economically idle, he has suffered a taking. . . .

***

It is correct that many of our prior opinions have suggested that "harmful or noxious uses" of property may be proscribed by government regulation without the requirement of compensation. For a number of reasons, however, we think the South Carolina Supreme Court was too quick to conclude that principle decides the present case. . . .

***

When it is understood that "prevention of harmful use" was merely our early formulation of the police power justification necessary to sustain (without compensation) **any** regulatory diminution in value; and that the distinction between regulation that "prevents harmful use" and that which "confers benefits" is difficult, if not impossible, to discern on an objective, value-free basis; it becomes self-evident that noxious-use logic cannot serve as a touchstone to distinguish regulatory "takings"—which require compensation—from regulatory deprivations that do not require compensation. *A fortiori* the legislature's recitation of a noxious-use justification cannot be the basis for departing from our categorical rule that total regulatory takings must be compensated. If it were, departure would virtually always be allowed. . . .

Where the State seeks to sustain regulation that deprives land of all economically beneficial use, we think it may resist compensation only if the logically antecedent inquiry into the nature of the owner's estate shows that the proscribed use interests were not part of his title to begin with. . . . This accords, we think, with our "takings" jurisprudence, which has traditionally been guided by the understandings of our citizens regarding the content of, and the State's power over, the "bundle of rights" that they acquire when they obtain title to property. It seems to us that the property owner necessarily expects the uses of his property to be restricted, from time to time, by various measures newly enacted by the State in legitimate exercise of its police powers; "as long recognized, some values are enjoyed under an implied limitation and must yield to the police power.". . . And in the case of personal property, by reason of the State's traditionally high degree of control over commercial dealings, he ought to be aware of the possibility that new regulation might even render his property economically worthless (at least if the property's only economically productive use is sale or manufacture for sale). . . . In the case of land, however, we think the notion pressed by the Council that title is somehow held subject to the "implied limitation" that the State may subsequently eliminate all economically valuable use is inconsistent with the historical compact recorded in the Takings Clause that has become part of our constitutional culture.[15] ∎

***

[15]Justice Blackmun [in his dissenting opinion] is correct that early constitutional theorists did not believe the Takings Clause embraced regulations of property at all, . . . but even he does not suggest (explicitly, at least) that we renounce the Court's contrary conclusion in *Mahon*. Since the text of the Clause can be read to encompass regulatory as well as physical deprivations. . . we decline to do so as well.

Justifications for Regulatory Takings Law in the Law and Economics Literature

Public Choice

Justices Holmes and Scalia each presented what amount to "public choice" explanations for extending the Fifth Amendment's just compensation requirement to regulatory, as well as physical, takings. Justice Holmes wrote in *Pennsylvania Coal v. Mahon* that "When the seemingly absolute protection [of property] is found to be qualified by the police power, the natural tendency of human nature is to extend the qualification more and more until at last private property disappears." Justice Scalia, in the *Lucas* case, was more direct in asserting that legislatures can be expected to divert the costs of regulations, whether needful or not, from the public/voters generally to discrete individual landowners. He mentions the "heightened risk that private property is being pressed into public service in the guise of mitigating serious public harm." And in a footnote to his opinion (not reprinted), Justice Scalia adds that because virtually any government regulation can be claimed to prevent some public harm or other, it cannot be trusted to choose between police power regulation and eminent domain taking: "Since such a [police power] justification can be formulated in practically every case, this amounts to a test of whether the legislature has a stupid staff. We think the Takings Clause requires courts to do more than insist upon artful harm-preventing characterizations."[10]

Neither the *Pennsylvania Coal* Court nor the *Lucas* Court abolished the distinction between police power regulation, for which no compensation is due, and eminent domain takings, for which just compensation must be paid. Instead, the Courts shifted authority for characterizing the state's action from the legislature to the judiciary, and set limits on the scope of legitimate police power regulation. After *Lucas*, the state can avoid compensating for regulations that deprive the landowner of virtually all economic value only if the activities being regulated amount to common law private nuisances. In addition, the government need not compensate for non-nuisance-related police power regulations that do not "go too far"—that is, if the regulation reduces property values substantially but not, say, by 90 percent or more, the government does not have to compensate, even if the activity being regulated does not amount to a common law private nuisance.

In recent years, some states, including Florida and Texas, enacted laws providing for compensation of regulatory takings where property values are reduced by as little as 25 or 50 percent. Such legislative enactments raise interesting public choice issues of their own. They also raise questions about Justice Scalia's characterization of legislative motivations

Efficiency, Productivity, and Demoralization Costs

Harvard Law Professor Frank Michelman has provided an efficiency-based argument in favor of compensating private property owners for *some* regulatory takings.

Frank Michelman, "Property, Utility, and Fairness: Comments on the Ethical Foundations of 'Just Compensation' Law"

80 Harvard Law Review 1165, 1168–9, 1214–8 (1967)

***

Such questions as those of distinguishing the "police power" from the "power of eminent domain" and of calculating "just compensation" . . . seem to derive from a broader question: When a social decision to redirect economic resources entails painfully obvious opportunity costs, how shall those costs ultimately be distributed among all the members of society? Shall they be permitted to remain where they fall initially or shall the government, by paying compensation, make explicit attempts to distribute them in accordance with decisions made by whatever process fashions the tax structure, or perhaps according to some other principle? Shall the losses be left with the individuals on whom they happen first to fall, or shall they be "socialized"?

A strictly utilitarian argument leading to the specific identification of "compensable" occasions would have a quasi-mathematical structure. Let us define three quantities to be known as "efficiency gains," "demoralization costs," and "settlement costs." "Efficiency gains" we define as the excess of benefits produced by a measure over losses inflicted by it, where benefits are measured by the total number of dollars which prospective gainers would be willing to pay to secure adoption, and losses are measured by the total number of dollars which prospective losers would insist on as the price of agreeing to adoption. "Demoralization costs" are defined as the total of (1) the dollar value necessary to offset disutilities which accrue to losers and their sympathizers specifically from the realization that no compensation is offered, and (2) the present capitalized dollar value of lost future production (reflecting either impaired incentives or social unrest) caused by demoralization of uncompensated losers, their sympathizers, and other observers disturbed by the thought that they themselves may be subject to similar treatment on some other occasion. "Settlement costs" are measured by the dollar value of the time, effort, and resources which would be required in order to reach compensation settlements adequate to avoid demoralization costs. Included are the costs of settling not only particular compensation claims presented, but also those of all persons so affected by the measure in question or similar measures as to have claims not obviously distinguishable by the available settlement apparatus.

A measure attended by positive efficiency gains is, under utilitarian ethics, prima facie desirable. But felicific calculation under the definition given for efficiency gains is imperfect because it takes no account of demoralization costs caused by a capricious redistribution, or alternatively, of the settlement costs necessary to avoid such demoralization costs. When pursuit of efficiency gains entails capricious redistribution, either demoralization costs or settlement costs must be incurred. It follows that if, for any measure, both demoralization costs and settlement costs (whichever were chosen) would exceed efficiency gains, the measure is to be rejected; but that otherwise, since either demoralization costs or settlement costs must be paid, it is the lower of these two costs which should be paid. The compensation rule which then emerges is that compensation is to be paid whenever settlement costs are lower than both demoralization costs and efficiency gains. But if settlement costs, while lower than demoralization costs, exceed efficiency gains, then the measure is improper regardless of whether compensation is paid. The correct utilitarian statement, then, insofar as *the issue of compensability* is concerned, is that compensation is due whenever demoralization costs exceed settlement costs, and not otherwise.

***

[I]t seems in order to ask what criteria of compensability will emerge if the practice of compensation is taken to have the purpose of quieting people's unease about the possibility of being strategically exploited.

It seems obvious, to begin with, that this unease will be stirred by any spectacle of capricious redistribution which could easily have been avoided. Capricious redistributions will not be tolerated, even as accidental adjuncts of efficiency-dictated measures, when compensation settlements can be reached without much trouble, that is, when settlement costs are low. The clearer it is that the claimant has sustained an injury distinct from those sustained by the generality of persons in society, and the more obviously there appears to be some objectively satisfactory measure of his disproportionate or distinctive injury, the more compelling will his claim to compensation become.

Society, moreover, will have to avoid not only those capricious redistributions which a compensation payment could easily offset, but also those practically noncompensable ones which cannot plausibly be said to be necessitated by the pursuit of efficiency. Thus, measures whose efficiency is open to grave question will have to be rejected unless attended by compensation even though their arguable efficiency is enough to justify their adoption in some form. Payment of compensation in such cases may furnish a necessary assurance that the measure is not simply a disguised attempt to redistribute deliberately, by confirming the hypothesis that society deems the measure a "gainful" (efficient) one in the only ethically sure sense. Therefore, as the collective allocational measure approaches the limit of doubtful efficiency, the claim for compensation will become more compelling.

Other intertwined branches of a compensability inquiry could grow out of a utilitarian purpose to cater to the sense of security by preserving an illusion of long-run indiscriminateness in the distribution of social burdens and benefits. Thus the magnitude of the imposition would plainly be relevant: is it of quotidian variety, or is it once in a lifetime mayhem? But magnitude of individual burden, no matter how purposively conceived, reveals only a fragment, meaningless by itself, of the whole picture. We need additional information. For example, is the burden for which compensation is sought a rare and peculiar one, or do like burdens seem to have been widely, even though not uniformly, scattered about the community? Is there implicit in the measure some reciprocity of burdens coupled with benefits (as, for example, in a measure restricting a large area to residential development) or does it channel benefits and burdens to different persons? How likely does it seem that members of the class burdened by the measure were able to wield enough effective influence in the process leading to its adoption to have extracted some compensatory concession "in kind"? ∎

***

Legal Process Theory and the Economics of Just Compensation

The last question of the Michelman excerpt—about the ability of affected individuals to participate in and influence the regulatory process—became a centerpiece of William Fischel's theory of regulatory takings. In *Regulatory Takings: Law, Economics, and Politics*, Fischel concludes that "'just compensation' persists because democratic bodies continue to insist on it. They insist on it for political reasons, wanting to spread out concentrated burdens. Thus, the real issue for judges is to ask which types of regulatory bodies are apt to impose unfairly concentrated burdens. The nature of politics, rather than the law of property, is the more fruitful line of inquiry."[11] Fischel goes on to assert that courts should more closely supervise local government and politically insulated bureaucratic regulations because process-failures—the lack of voice in the political process on the part of those most likely to be negatively affected by the regulations—are more likely in those governmental arenas. Specifically, local governments, because they and the populations they represent tend to be more homogeneous than larger governmental units and the populations they represent, are more likely to enact measures that systematically impose costs on outsiders. As for the "politically isolated agency," "it usually has a single mandate, so that adverse economic effects are of little concern to it."[12] One consequence of this tendency "is a disinclination to listen when adversely affected people complain. The shared problem of the independent agencies is their inclination to discount the voices of outsiders. This does not require that all such discounting be regarded as a taking, but it does call for a more careful weighing of settlement and demoralization costs by judges."[13] In other words, judges should more closely scrutinize local governments and bureaucratic regulations for compensable takings, but give more latitude to state and federal governments, where "outsiders" are fewer and political processes more pluralistic.

Comparative Institutional Analysis of Regulatory Takings Law

Recently, Neil Komesar examined the regulatory takings issue from a Coasean, comparative institutional perspective, and his conclusion is instructive if surprising: "Even if the regulatory process is highly flawed (and it is), the severe problems in the market and the adjudicative process may mean that the corrupt, excessive, and repressive regulatory process is the best of bad alternatives. In a quintessential example of the ironies of comparative institutional analysis, it may even be the best friend the Lucases of the world have."[14] Komesar believes that the property rights of David Lucas and other developers might be protected more effectively by the political process than they possibly could be by judicial enforcement of constitutional remedies. Note Komesar's (and Coase's) general lesson: It is not good enough to criticize one institutional solution to land-use conflicts; government regulation may be every bit as untrustworthy as Komesar, Holmes, and Scalia each have suggested, but it is vitally important to consider the alternative problems that arise from either the absence of regulation (market failure) or judicial limitations on it (the inherent minoritarian bias and information deficit of unelected and politically unaccountable judges). The goal should be, as Coase has written, to choose that institutional structure of property rights that fails least.

CHAPTER SUMMARY

This chapter showed how private property rights are delimited by the private property rights of others (e.g., private nuisance), private contracting (e.g., covenants), and the public's right to be free from unreasonable harm to health and safety (e.g., public nuisance law and the regulatory state). Although private owners are free to contractually limit their own property rights in almost any way and to almost any extent, the state's ability to limit private property rights to protect public health and safety itself must be limited. If the state regulates private property too much, it will have to pay compensation for a "taking."

QUESTIONS AND PROBLEMS

1. Why might private plaintiffs prefer to sue for public, rather than private, nuisance?
2. Did the court arrive at the correct outcome in the *Portland Ampitheaters* case?
3. A beautiful and pristine valley in the State of Grace has remained untouched by economic development activities. The valley is, however, privately owned by 15 individuals, each of whom owns a 400-acre parcel. The state legislature passes a law to preserve the valley in its pristine and undeveloped state. Does this regulation confer public benefits or prevent public harms? What difference does it make? Who should decide?
4. What is the public choice explanation for government regulation? Is that explanation consistent with state laws that make it easier for landowners to obtain compensation for regulatory impositions?
5. In the *Lucas* case, if the Supreme Court had upheld the lower court's ruling against Mr. Lucas's claim, what effect might that decision have had on the incentives of private landowners? (Does the excerpt from Professor Michelman provide any guidance?)
6. Some towns and cities have no zoning regulations, but industrial facilities tend to cluster with other such facilities. Why might economists expect this phenomenon to happen?
7. Explain what is meant by the "police power" over property.
8. In the *Poletown* case, the City of Detroit took properties from individual home and business owners and gave them to one of the world's largest and wealthiest private corporations. Under what conditions would this scenario be economically efficient?

NOTES

1. For a discussion of zoning, see the next section of this chapter.
2. 334 U.S. 1 (1948).
3. *See, for example, Washington v. General Motors Corp.*, 406 U.S. 109, 114 (1972), in which the Court refers to air pollution as "one of the most notorious types of public nuisance in modern experience."
4. *See, for example, City of Miami v. Keshbro, Inc.*, 717 So. 2d 601 (Fla. Dist. Ct. App. 1998).
5. This prevalence of injunctive relief may explain why private plaintiffs prefer to sue in public nuisance, whenever possible.
6. *See, for example, State of New Jersey v. Mundet Cork Corp.*, 8 N.J. 359 (1952), which upholds and enforces a state air pollution control statute. Regulations are not only enforced by courts, however. They are sometimes enforced by fines or orders of government administrative agencies.
7. Robert Ellickson, "Alternatives to Zoning: Covenants, Nuisance Rules, and Fines as Land Use Controls," 40 *University of Chicago Law Review* 681 (1973).
8. 410 Mich. 616 (1981).
9. *Keystone Bituminous Coal Association v. DeBenedictus*, 480 U.S. 470 (1987).
10. 505 U.S. at 1025 n.12.
11. William A. Fischel, *Regulatory Takings: Law, Economics, and Politics* (Cambridge, MA: Harvard University Press, 1995), p. 4.
12. William A. Fischel, *Regulatory Takings: Law, Economics, and Politics* (Cambridge, MA: Harvard University Press, 1995), p. 331.
13. William A. Fischel, *Regulatory Takings: Law, Economics, and Politics* (Cambridge, MA: Harvard University Press, 1995), p. 331.
14. Neil Komesar, *Law's Limits: Rule of Law and the Supply and Demand of Rights* (Cambridge: Cambridge University Press, 2001), p. 106.

Chapter 8

Contracts I: Formation and Enforcement

The importance of contracting in creating and maintaining a modern economy cannot be overstated. We have contracts for employment, apartment rentals, building and construction, bank loans, car rentals, and even marriage. We have contracts between producers and consumers, producers and producers, producers and government, government and consumers. Contracts are made between parties in the same country and between citizens of different countries. Thousands upon thousands of contracts are written, performed, and enforced every day.

We take for granted a reliable system of contracting. We believe that if we sign a contract, it will be enforced not only today but also tomorrow, next week, or a decade from now, if its terms have not been fulfilled by that time. Reliable contract enforcement is not universal, however. In some countries the legal institutions underlying contract reliability do not exist. It is inevitably the case that where contracting is hampered, economic growth and development suffer.

In this chapter we will examine the law and economics of contracts: why contracts exist, why they sometimes fail—that is, why contracts are sometimes breached—and how the law, through the courts, tries to deal with contract failure. And further, whether economic principles can help us understand how remedies to contract breaches might lead to improvement in the formation of contracts and hence to greater overall economic efficiency.

THE BASICS OF CONTRACT LAW

The Nature of a Contract

At its essence, a contract is a promise—a legally enforceable promise. Thus, if the bank gives you a loan, based on your promise to pay back the loan at a certain rate over a certain period of time, the combination of the bank's loan and your promise create an enforceable contract. If you fail to live up to your promise, you will be in breach of the contract, and the bank can take you to court to enforce it.

The crucial aspect of a contract, and the reason why its economic importance is so great, is that it permits voluntary economic exchange where parties perform at different times. Thus the bank, in the preceding example, pays you the loan today in exchange for a promise of repayment with interest at sometime (or times) in the future.

The following is an excerpt from a contract between the railroad express firm of G. A. Nichols and Livingston & Co. and the Reading Rail Road Company written in 1847.[1] The railroad promised to attach to one of their trains each day a car that would be used solely by the express company for its package delivery business:

> The Reading Rail Road Company agrees to run your express car once each way daily over their Road from Pottsville and Philadelphia, laden with any articles (except gunpowder and fireworks) not exceeding 3000 lbs, and to allow one of your agents to travel in their passenger train with said car. . . . Further to execute promptly all repairs to said car when it may require them. . . .
>
> In return for which accommodation, your firm pay to the Reading Rail Road Co. in advance on the first day of every month Two Hundred and fifty = ($250) Dollars and agree to the following conditions. To be responsible for all damages whatever sustained by the goods or articles in said express car . . . whether arising from stealth, wet, fire, breakage or any other causes. To guarantee the Reading Rail Road Co. from any claims for damages for injuries sustained by your agent traveling in their train. . . .

In this simple contract, both parties are promisors and promisees. The railroad made a promise to provide a service to the express company; and the express company promised, in turn, to pay the railroad for that service. Each party's promise constituted "consideration" for the promise of the other. Each party is giving up something in return for the other's promise. This consideration is a critical component of contracts, distinguishing them from unenforceable *gratuitous promises* (a distinction we will explore in greater detail a bit later in this chapter). It does not necessarily have to be in monetary form to be binding, but promises without consideration are deemed gratuitous, and therefore are not legally enforceable.

Once the contract is made (with consideration), both parties act with the expectation of performance. They will spend money and other resources relying on the promised performance of the other party. The express firm, in the preceding example, will hire agents, acquire the capital for loading and delivery, and probably advertise to the effect that they offer service along the route of the Reading

Railroad. These expenditures made in *reliance* on the promise of the railroad mean that a definite cost will result if the contract is breached by the railroad. If the express company did not expect the contract to be enforceable, it would be unlikely to make expenditures in reliance on the contract. The greater the uncertainty of contract enforcement, the higher the risks involved in relying on the other party's promises.

Enforcement

As we have seen, exchange across time is difficult and costly without reliable contract enforcement. The time difference in performance creates the potential for "opportunistic" behavior. If the railroad company knows that the contract it entered with the express company is unenforceable, then it could just take the money from the express company but not carry the car as promised. If you know the terms of your bank loan are unenforceable, then you have no incentive (other than personal ethics) to honor your promise, and the bank would have no expectation that you would pay it back. As a result, banks would cease to make loans. More generally, no one would undertake any form of exchange that involved temporal differences in performance; no one would agree to pay for something that was not already made; no one would make anything on a promise alone.

The consequences of nonenforcement can be illustrated by Game Theory. In Chapter 5 (pages 97–98) we used a game model to demonstrate how socially inefficient outcomes can arise as economic agents act simply to protect their own interests. In this game, we again have two players who are parties to a contract. The first player agrees to buy all of the goods produced by the second, but the second will produce them only if payment is made in advance of production. If the contract is enforceable, the second player will take the money and begin production. Otherwise, the first player will not pay up front.

The payoff matrix at the top of the next page shows why nothing will be produced if contract enforcement is doubtful. Start with two parties: Player 1 and Player 2. If both perform, they will each make a profit of X. But if Player 2 takes Player 1's money and then fails to keep his end of the bargain, Player 1 earns -X and Player 2 2X (the second player's profit rises because he gets the first player's money for nothing). If Player 1 thinks that Player 2 will take off with the money, then she will not pay before Player 2 performs; but Player 2 demands payment prior to performance. In that case, they both spend nothing and earn nothing.[2]

If contracts are enforceable, the outcome of the game is changed. Assuming that a contract is properly created in the first place, then a nonperformance strategy is unviable. If Player 1 performs and Player 2 does not, a court would order Player 2 to pay Player 1 the amount of X or to perform the contract as written, which we assume would lead to the same payoff. Indeed, Player 2's payoff would be less than X, because he would incur court costs. He would be better off performing than not.

Developed economies like those of the United States or western European countries depend on reliable and affordable third-party enforcement. The institutions of enforcement are overwhelmingly through the formal law, through enforceable civil court action. In the United States, the Constitution commits the government to enforce contracts.[3]

		Player 2	
		Perform	Not Perform
Player 1	Perform	X, X	−X, 2X
	Not Perform	0, 0	0, 0

Although enforcement is necessary, it need not be administered only through the formal institutions of law. For example, "first-party" enforcement is a possibility. The party who suffers costs as the result of another's breach of promise or contract can take matters into her own hands. But this kind of "self-help" is frowned upon in most societies because it tends to lead to violence, which is socially costly. Another alternative exists in traditional societies or among members of closely connected social and ethnic groups, where enforcement can be affected through informal social sanctions.

An interesting case involves the Jewish diamond merchants of New York City.[4] Each day they make promises with one another to deliver thousands, even millions, of dollars worth of diamonds without formal contracts. Yet breach is almost unknown. Most of the merchants are observant Jews from the same community. Their cultural homogeneity facilitates trust, which reduces the need for third-party enforcement. In the event of a dispute, the parties seek the judgment of a rabbi. Though they are under no legal requirement to accept the rabbi's decision, it is always accepted. To ignore it would invite social ostracism and business ruin. The merchant's reputation would be irreparably harmed. No one would transact with a party who would not accept those particular rules of the game.

Even where no explicit social ties exist, reputation and the prospect of long-term relationships would permit contracting parties to use enforcement mechanisms outside of the court system. Insurance companies, for example, do not file malpractice claims against the attorneys who mishandle cases entrusted to them. Rather, the insurers use the implicit threat that they will sever ties with law firms that perform poorly. Because firms stand to earn millions of dollars annually serving large insurance companies, such a threat creates an incentive to perform well.

Most transactions, however, cannot be enforced this way. Most economic exchange is impersonal, and involves transactions between people without social, familial, or religious ties. Yet so important is economic exchange through time, that parties, as indeed they have done for thousands of years, will seek means of insuring enforcement even when appeals to legal authority are impossible. In post-Soviet Russia, for example, parties have used extralegal enforcers—sometimes referred to as "mafiosi"—to insure that contract terms are performed. This method can be effective but, like first-party enforcement, it tends to be very costly. The payment to the enforcers is typically quite high, which means that contract terms will reflect the added cost of the complete transaction. This premium in turn will mean that fewer contracts will be written. If the value of performance is not greater than the cost, including transaction costs, no one will enter into a contract unless the benefits are large enough to cover the high transaction costs inherent in private enforcement systems. Moreover, since the enforcement mechanism is highly unstable, fewer long-term contracts will be created. Few people would be willing to invest in a project where performance is expected ten or even two years from the time the contract is written, when enforcement depends not on the stability of law but rather on the ability to find extralegal enforcers at that future time who *might* be available but only at an indeterminately higher cost.

We can get a sense of the great economic importance of deferred exchange relations in history when we consider the lengths to which parties would go to secure a contract and provide some check against opportunism. During the Renaissance, Italian merchants would contract with Byzantine traders for spices and other goods from Asia especially desired by European consumers. The traders would promise to procure a shipment of, say, spices in exchange for a sum of money to be paid, on delivery, by the Italian merchant. This contract would require a substantial investment on the trader's part, before the merchant would have to perform. Presumably, the trader would not be willing to make the investment without some sort of security to ensure the merchant's later performance. In Renaissance Venice, it was quite common for merchants to secure their promises by sending a son or other near relative as a hostage to the trader. If, upon the trader's later performance, the merchant refused to pay, the trader could then recoup at least some of the losses by selling the hostage into slavery. Hostage sales seem to have been fairly rare occurrences, however. Merchants typically valued their relations more than their money; so the act of hostage-giving signaled that the merchants valued performance of the contract more than a breach. Though successful in most cases, it was an expensive way to insure a deal. Not only was it expensive for the hostage, but for the merchant who lost the hostage's labor for the time—months or more—it could take the trader to procure the spices and deliver them to the merchant.

Should Contracts Always Be Enforced?

As we will discuss, sometimes a contract simply *cannot* be enforced. For example, an actor contracts to perform in a theater on a given day but on the day before, the theater burns down. *Impossibility* voids the contract. At other times, a contract *should not* be performed. In general, however, contracts should be enforced as written, even when one party to the contract does less well than anticipated. The logic behind this statement may not be immediately obvious. After all, when a voluntary exchange takes place, both parties expect to be better off, otherwise they would not have entered into the agreement in the first place. Voluntary exchange—contracts—lead to Pareto improvements (we recall from Chapter 1) only when they make at least one party better off and no party worse off, and the contract externalizes no significant costs to nonparties.

Consider the following case: A customer pays a car dealer to provide him with a car containing certain options (a special paint color, seat style, etc.) that he thinks he will especially enjoy. He pays the money because he expects he will value the options more than he values the money. The dealer provides the car as requested, but the buyer discovers, upon delivery of the car, that he does not really get the enjoyment he expected from those options. In fact, he feels worse off than if he had not agreed to buy the car in the first place. The exchange turns out, after signing and upon the car dealer's performance, to be Pareto inferior for the buyer. The question, then, is whether economic efficiency is not better served by allowing the buyer to refuse delivery and keep his money.

The answer is, of course, no. Although it is true that contracts are intended to pro-mote mutually beneficial exchange for private ends, the failure to enforce any contract simply because, *ex post*, it did not meet one party's *ex ante* expectations would jeopardize the institution of contracting itself. If anyone could tear up a contract simply because he did not like the result, then contracts as a whole become unenforceable. The bank, then, could not be sure that borrowers would not tear up their mortgage agreements; the express company could not be sure that, next month, the railroad would not demand twice as much money for the same service. So, even when a particular contract does not improve one party's wealth or utility, the consequences of nonenforcement would be potentially ruinous for social welfare as a whole. From a Coasean perspective, if contracts are unenforceable—if they could be repudiated at will by either party—it would raise the social costs of exchange, and reduce the social product. Consequently, if we guess wrong and enter a contract that turns out to be disadvantageous for us, social welfare is best served if the law nevertheless enforces that contract against us. Without enforceable, and actually enforced, contracts, the functioning of any modern economy that depends so much on impersonal exchange would be greatly impaired.

Contract Failure

Some exceptions apply to the general rule that contracts should always be enforced. Sometimes failed contracts should not be enforced for reasons of both economic efficiency and equity. The remainder of this chapter considers the reasons for failure and the appropriate remedies in the event of failure. In essence, all contracts fail for the same reason: they are inevitably incomplete and imperfect. If contracting parties could foresee, and provide for, every possible contingency that might arise during the contract's lifetime, then contracts would never fail. But to specify *all* contingencies is beyond the realm of possibility. It would require complete information about every possible interaction the parties might face while the contract was in force. Information costs, and transaction costs generally, would be infinite. For this reason, no contract is ever perfect. Not every contingency is provided for because the costs of gathering the necessary information and providing for some contingencies would exceed the value of not just the extra clause but, in some cases, the entire contract. In fact, contracts are written to economize on transaction costs. Parties often resort to "model" contracts containing standard, or boilerplate, clauses. Such contracts are written to cover common circumstances, not the contingencies or exigencies that might arise in a particular case. It is those excluded contingencies or exigencies that give rise to most contract failures and breaches.[5]

Two Economic Views of Contract Failure and the Role of Courts

Different schools of economic thought (as set out in Chapter 3) will focus on different aspects of the problem of contract failure and the specific role that the courts play, or should play, in resolving it. A public choice theorist, for example, might look at how a court's behavior is influenced by how much the parties spend to win the case, as well as how judges and individual jurors benefit from certain decisions. Old institutionalists, on the other hand, would likely want to examine the political power structure that contract institutions might be serving.

In this section, we will look at two different approaches to contract failure and the role of the court: neoclassical and new institutional. Though they share some similarities in their respective analyses, these two schools of economic thought ultimately say different things about what courts can hope to accomplish when confronted with failed contracts.

The Neoclassical Model of Perfect Contracts

The neoclassical approach to contracting begins, as does its analysis of competitive markets, with an ideal model: a perfect contract. This contract has the following properties:

- *Individual rationality.* Economic agents have stable preferences,[6] and seek for themselves the best feasible outcome (see Chapter 1).
- *Full information.* Contract terms cover and assign responsibility for all contingencies. All parties fully understand the terms and the assignments.
- *No externalities.* No one aside from the contracting parties is effected.
- *Competitive markets.* A monopoly or cartelized market could give one party disproportionate bargaining power because the other party would have no choice with whom to contract. Bargaining power should be equal and without a chance for any party to act opportunistically.
- *Strict enforcement.* Even though a perfect contract is self-enforcing, it must exclude the potential of a third party acting to help one side extract opportunistic gain.
- *Zero transaction costs.* This condition is necessary if the contract is to be written so that all contingencies are covered.

By virtue of these conditions or properties, the perfect contract exists only in the mythical world of the Coase theorem (discussed in Chapter 4). In such a world not only are contracts complete, but all relations can be covered by them. As we saw earlier, this kind of model offers little utility beyond illustrating why such idealizations do not get us very far.

Even neoclassical economists would concede that this perfect contract model is only a starting point for understanding the source and legal treatment of real-world contract failures. Each one of the properties of the perfect contract, even from a neoclassical standpoint, falls short in the real world; and those shortfalls become potential sources of contract failure. Some people, for example, may suffer, for reasons of age or infirmity, some kind of transactional impairment. They might not have a fully transitive preference ordering; in extreme circumstances, they may not even be able to recognize whether a certain contractual term is in their self-interest. As a consequence, they may be considered legally incompetent, so that the contracts they enter into become unenforceable.

Information is not complete, and it is costly to obtain. As noted earlier, all contracts have gaps, or contingencies that are not covered; and not all of those contingencies could be covered at a finite cost. To cover *all* contingencies, contracts would have to be infinitely long and include provisions allocating the risk (among others) that a meteor might strike and disrupt business next Tuesday, next Wednesday, and every other day while the contract is in force. Information about future events that could affect contract performance is often sketchy, and it is entirely possible, as we shall see later, that both parties might be mistaken about what it is they have contracted for.

Not all gaps in contracts concern implausible events such as meteor strikes. Sometimes contracts exclude contingencies that one would expect should have been covered. In the case of *Rexite Casting Co. v. Midwest Mower Corp.*,[7] the plaintiff agreed to supply lawn mower castings to the defendant for a certain price. After signing the contract, the plaintiff demanded an increase above the contract price for its mower castings in view of an increase in metal prices that raised its production costs. It would not be illogical to suppose that firms doing a business where the cost of important inputs were subject to change from market forces would have included language to deal with such contingencies.[8] But in this case the contract did not include any such language. Not only did Rexite demand that Midwest Mower pay more than the contract called for, but it actually withheld promised shipments until Midwest Mower agreed to do so.[9] Midwest accepted the altered terms under protest, and then breached its contract with Rexite as soon as it could make alternative arrangements for lawn mower castings from another source.

Unanticipated externality problems may also render contracts imperfect. In general, externalities are covered by tort law (see Chapters 9 through 11) and government regulation (see Chapter 15 on environmental regulation), but the question of how unanticipated external costs are distributed between contracting parties is likely to be left out when the nature and magnitude of those externalities cannot be known before the contract is performed.

Also, many markets and industries are imperfect. Indeed "perfect competition" is an idealization, just like "perfect contracts."[10] In reality, some inequality in bargaining power often exists between contracting parties. Monopolization and collusion are not unknown, and outright fraud may be perpetrated within an exchange. All of these factors give rise to the potential for opportunism, coercion, and other problems that might provide reason for invalidating a contract.

Even though the United States and other developed countries have relatively impartial, strict third-party enforcement, it is by no means perfect. Corruption may lead to rulings that are biased against one party, despite legitimate contractual language favoring that party. Differences in jurisdiction, especially across state borders, may result in interpretations of contract clauses that vary according to the custom of the court. Indeed, confusion may arise as to the appropriate jurisdiction and lead to difficulty in carrying out a ruling under such circumstances. Also, as we will see, some contracts cannot be carried out regardless, so enforcement is moot.

The final element, zero transaction costs, cannot of course be approximated in the real world. True, some transactions have lower costs than others, and court rulings can raise or lower the costs of transacting. With respect to the ideal model, however, the most important concern is the cost of measuring performance and enforcing contract terms. In the case *Wood v. Lucy, Lady Duff-Gordon*,[11] for example, the plaintiff Wood had an exclusive contract to market Lady Duff-Gordon's name (a name synonymous at the time with high fashion) with respect to fashion products in the United States. The question before the court was not whether Wood had the exclusive right by contract but whether he had fulfilled his side of the bargain by making a sufficient effort to win business for Lady Duff-Gordon. This kind of measurement is not at all straightforward,[12] and before a measure could be determined the parties to the contract went through a court case and an appeals process. A measure of effort in marketing designs is different from that which would be required for a contract for 1,000 pounds of oranges. Even a contract for oranges, however, might well specify qualitative aspects (e.g., ripeness) as well as quantitative that would also be difficult and hence costly to measure.

Given the numerous ways in which actual contracts deviate from the neoclassical ideal, it is not surprising that contracts fail and that courts are asked to adjudicate. From the neoclassical perspective, the role of the court is fairly straightforward: Faced with a contract failure, the courts should endeavor to correct the imperfection and turn an imperfect contract into a perfect contract. That is, the model of the ideal contract should be used as the basis for revising imperfect contracts *ex post*. If a contingency is not specified in the contract, and consequently leads to contract failure, the court should rewrite the contract to account for that contingency, and enforce it, as revised, against the parties. The court is to make its revisions according to what, it supposes, the parties themselves would have agreed to, had they considered the contingency at contract time.

A New Institutional Model of Inevitably Imperfect Contracts

A new institutional approach begins, not by denying that the neoclassical model lacks all utility, but by showing that the gap between the neoclassical model and real contracts is unbridgeable by the best efforts of judges, so that the perfect contract cannot legitimately serve as a model for contract interpretation and enforcement. Instead, the new institutional approach focuses on the inherent limits of contracting relations. Once acknowledged, those limitations can lead to development of a more readily applicable model for decision making.

The elements of a new institutional model include the following:

- *Bounded rationality.*   People are, as neoclassical theory postulates, rational actors who seek to do the best that they can for themselves; but their abilities to calculate the outcomes of any given action or set of actions is necessarily limited. They rely on "mental models" and heuristics to guide their actions, but these shortcuts may leave them less well off than they might have been under a completely calculated decision.[13]
- *Incomplete and asymmetric information.*   No one has complete (let alone perfect[14]) information; nor can they acquire it at finite cost. Moreover, it is typically the case that one party to a contract will have better information than another party. This imbalance allows for strategic and/or opportunistic behavior.

- *Inevitable and ex ante uncertain external effects.* Contracts often have economic impacts that extend beyond the contracting parties.
- *Imperfect competition.* As already noted, no market is perfectly competitive and many markets and industries are characterized by highly imperfect competition. Monopoly power can be exercised with respect to many contracts simply because of limited availability of low-cost substitutes.
- *Costly and potentially unreliable third-party enforcement.* Even in the United States where enforcement is relatively reliable, it can be costly to initiate a claim for breach of contract and to carry the claim through the court system. Social and political factors may work against enforcement of contract terms.
- *Positive and sometimes high transaction costs.* Writing, performing, and enforcing contracts is costly. Court cases add to social costs. Indeed, not only will litigation raise the cost of a given contract, but the court decision itself may raise (or lower) the costs of subsequent contracts and contractual disputes.

These limitations apply not only to the contracting parties but also, importantly, to judges and jurors who might be asked to interpret and enforce the parties' contracts. Judges, like the rest of us, are only boundedly rational. Compared to the contracting parties, judges are likely to face even more severe limitations on information. Judges inevitably lack the specialized knowledge that the contracting parties have about their own interests. Moreover, the capacity of judges to inform themselves is limited by the rules of evidence, which restricts not only how information is presented in court but what information the court can hear. That evidence is provided by witnesses, including the parties themselves, all of whom can be expected to present biased, incomplete views of the issues at hand. Judges cannot know the parties' subjective valuations of contract performance versus nonperformance, which may well deviate from the valuations they state in court. Moreover, judges are unlikely to appreciate external effects, and may not be able to ascertain the existence, or lack of, clear substitutes. They are, therefore, unlikely to be able to envision anything like a perfect version of any incomplete contract brought before them. It is simply not possible—indeed, it is an inherent contradiction—for the court to arrive at a judgment that will lead to an ideal, Pareto efficient, exchange given that the court, a third party, is determining the outcome for the parties to the original contract.

Subject to the limitations under which courts inevitably operate, the question becomes: What can society reasonably expect courts to do in interpreting and enforcing contracts? They might, following Coase, seek to minimize the social costs of imperfect contracts. In principle, this approach would mean that any possible costs arising from a contract would be assigned to the party who could bear them at the lowest cost. This reasoning is the basic principle of the "least cost avoider" or, more accurately with respect to contractual contingencies, the lowest cost insurer against the possibility of breach.

Consider, for example, the problem that arose in the case of *Florida East Coast Railway Co. v. Beaver Street Fisheries, Inc.*[15] The defendant was to provide food to a resort, Club Med, but the plaintiff who was charged with delivery failed to ship the food safely. Without an emergency shipment of replacement food, the resort would have been left without sufficient food for its guests. The railroad was clearly liable for the damage to the cargo. But was it also liable for the costs of emergency shipment of replacement food? The question really was: Given that a contingency might arise that would prevent the delivery by Florida East Coast, who could insure food delivery to Club Med at the lowest cost? As we shall see, it is not always perfectly obvious who is the least cost insurer. But it does seem that a search to assign costs *ex post* on this basis is a more manageable decision rule than one that seeks conformity to an unrealizable ideal.

It should be noted that, in practice, the result might be the same from either the neoclassical or new institutional perspective. Under the perfect contract model, a judge would assign a cost to the lowest cost avoider on the grounds that had the parties known in advance of the contingency that disrupted the contract, they would have assigned costs in exactly that fashion. The difference lies in the expectations of the model. Under the neoclassical model, the argument is that in making that assignment the court achieves the same goal *ex post* that voluntary exchange would have accomplished *ex ante*, given more complete information. The new institutional claim is more modest: In a world of second-best outcomes, the court can seek only to minimize social costs in order to improve efficiency; the court cannot claim that its ruling is what the parties themselves would have agreed to a contracting time, if only they had thought about it. By the same token, a court applying the new institutional model could not claim that its decision unambiguously improves social welfare. Judicial decisions do not meet two of the strict conditions for Pareto efficiency: voluntary consent of all affected parties and no party left worse off. They can only be judged according to the messier test of Kaldor-Hicks.[16]

REASONS FOR CONTRACT BREACH

Some contracts, as noted earlier, should not be enforced based on economic reasons. These reasons for contract failure can be grouped generally into two categories: formation defenses and performance excuses. The former involves cases in which something improper occurred in the creation of the contract; the latter involves cases in which performance has become either impossible or undesirable. Table 8.1 lists common reasons for failure.

Formation Defenses

The category of formation defenses allows for far more reasons legally to breach a contract than does the category of performance excuses. The list of both formation defenses and performance excuses in Table 8.1 could be expanded. However, we will focus on this short list and examine the reasons why, from an economic standpoint, they might lead to the efficient *non*enforcement of contracts.

FORMATION DEFENSES	PERFORMANCE EXCUSES
Duress	Impossibility
Mutual mistake	Frustration of purpose
	Incompetence/Incapacity
Fraud	Unconscionability

Table 8.1
Reasons Justifying Breaches of Contracts

Duress

A contract is not legally binding if one party signs it under duress. An "offer he couldn't refuse" may have been enforceable by *The Godfather* (in the book and movies of that name), but it is not enforceable in a court of law. In *The Godfather*, your choice set might be restricted to signing the contract as offered or dying. This scenario hardly constitutes a voluntary exchange, and so it violates the basic economic premise that the contract is mutually beneficial and voluntary. Yet, in some cases brought to court, benefits may come from enforcement even if the particular terms were made under duress. For example, in the case of *Post v. Jones*[17] a whaling ship, *The Richmond*, ran aground and was about to sink along with its valuable cargo of whale oil. Three other ships came onto the scene and rescued the crew, but they announced that they would only save the cargo on condition that it be auctioned to them on the spot. Because the alternative was for the cargo to be a total loss, *The Richmond's* captain agreed to the terms and the cargo was sold to the rescuers at a low price. When the ships landed, however, the captain breached his agreement and took his rescuers to court, which ruled in his favor.

Although this result seems fair given that the three rescue ships appeared to take undue advantage of the situation, economic analysis does not unambiguously support this conclusion. Rescuing ships and their cargo is, one would suppose, a social good; and so it is valuable to society to provide incentives for rescue. Indeed, in cases such as this one, courts are inclined to reward rescuers, provided the reward is not excessive. Clearly this approach allows for a great deal of interpretation as to what constitutes "excessive" reward.

The judges in *Post v. Jones* made a second economic point: The buyers threatened to destroy the value of the cargo by letting it sink. It is one thing not to act so as to increase social product, but it is quite another to act in such a way as to destroy or reduce social product. Thus, *The Richmond's* captain could retain the wealth he created only by agreeing to the rescuers' terms; the alternative was to acquiesce to total loss. According to the court, a contract signed under duress poses a situation where the alternative to signing the contract is some negative consequence that would decrease social welfare and overall economic efficiency. This point is questionable. Consider the effect of the court's ruling on the incentives of future potential rescuers. Are they more or less likely to come to the aid of ships in distress? And if they are less likely to, what is the likely effect on social welfare?

Mistake

Courts may have a difficult time assessing whether a contract meets the criteria of duress, but their interpretations are even more thorny with respect to issues of mistake. The general rule is that if both parties to an agreement are mistaken as to the facts of the exchange, then the mistake is mutual and the contract need not be performed. A contract, after all, is based on mutual expectations of economic benefits. But if *both* parties were mistaken about the substance of their agreement, they can hardly be said to have entered into a viable exchange agreement. As lawyers would say, no real "meeting of minds" took place about the object of the contract. This assessment is also true if the parties are mutually mistaken as to the identity of the object(s) to be exchanged. By contrast, if one party is mistaken as to the facts and the other party is not, then the mistake is unilateral, and the contract should be enforced as written.

Actually, enforcement of such a contract is not the entire story: A unilateral mistake where one person has inside knowledge that the other cannot obtain, which leads purely to a redistribution of wealth, is not enforceable. Thus, stock market trades are not permitted where one party trades on insider information that should be disclosed. The facts must be *productive facts*.[18] That is, one party must understand through specialized knowledge something that the other party could learn only at high cost. The economic point is that the rule creates incentives for people to acquire specialized knowledge because they can be rewarded if they put that knowledge to productive use. Although one person may gain an increase in wealth at the expense of another, the gain and use of productive expertise benefits society and increases social product.

The distinction between mutual and unilateral mistakes may seem straightforward enough, but in reality the courts do not always have an easy time ascertaining who knew what, and when. In practice, the application of the rule relies on which party convinces the judges of his or her knowledge or lack thereof. Two cases follow. The first is a classic case often cited in other opinions about the issue of contract mistake. The second is an instance of the kind of evidence that convinces judges that the rule governing unilateral mistakes should apply.

Sherwood v. Walker

66 Mich. 568, 33 N.W. 919 (1887)

Morse, J.

. . . The main controversy depends upon the construction of a contract for the sale of the cow. . . . The Walkers are importers and breeders of polled Angus cattle. The plaintiff is a banker living in Plymouth in Wayne County. He called upon the defendants at Walkerville for the purchase of some of their stock. . . . A few days thereafter, he called upon one of the defendants with the view of purchasing a cow known as "Rose 2d of Aberlone." . . .

[T]he defendant introduced evidence tending to show that at the time of the alleged sale it was believed by both the plaintiff and themselves that the cow was barren and would not breed; that she cost $80, and if not barren would be worth from $750 to $1000. . . . [Later] the defendants were informed by [their employee] that in his judgment the cow was with calf, and therefore they instructed him not to deliver her to plaintiff. . . .

It appears from the record that both parties supposed this cow was barren and would not breed, and she was sold by the pound for an insignificant sum as compared to her real value as a breeder. She was evidently sold and purchased on the relation to her value for beef, unless the plaintiff had learned of her true condition and concealed such knowledge from the defendants. . . . I am of the opinion that the [lower court that first heard the case and ruled for the plaintiff] erred in holding [that the contract should have been performed as agreed upon initially]. I know that this is a close question and the dividing line between the adjudicated cases is not easily discerned. But it must be considered as well settled that a party who has given an apparent consent to a contract of sale may refuse to execute it, or he may avoid it after it has been completed, if the assent was founded, or the contract made, upon the mistake of a material fact—such as the subject-matter of the sale, the price, or some collateral fact materially inducing the agreement; and this can be done when the mistake is mutual. . . .

It seems to me . . . in the case made by this record that the mistake or misapprehension of the parties went to the whole substance of the agreement. . . . The parties would not have made the contract of sale except upon the understanding and belief that she was incapable of breeding, and of no use as a cow. . . .

The judgment of the court below must be reversed, and a new trial granted, with costs of this court to defendants. ∎

The court dismissed Sherwood's claim that the mistake was unilateral, that he knew the cow was fertile and had just made a good bargain for himself (as a lower court had ruled). Why? Judge Morse merely said, "It seems to me . . . that the mistake went to the whole substance of the agreement." Presumably, the fact that Sherwood was a banker and not a professional in the cattle business, while Walker was a cattleman, made it seem unlikely that Sherwood would know something about the cow that Walker did not. Yet a dissenting judge was equally convinced that the mistake was unilateral. He wrote, "The buyer purchased [the cow] believing her to be of the breed represented by the sellers, and possessing all the qualities stated, and even more. He believed she would breed." The case presents no objective way to resolve the issue, and many cases come down to the judgment of the court as to what was in the minds of the participants. Still, in the following case Justice Black, writing for the majority, believed it was a clear instance where the mistake was unilateral.

Harris v. Tyson
24 Pa. 347 (1855)

Black, J.

This action depends on the defendant's right to dig and take away chrome from the land of the plaintiff. The defendant claims that right under the plaintiff's deed, giving and granting it in due form. But the plaintiff asserts that the deed is fraudulent and void because, 1. The defendant suppressed the truth; 2. He suggested a falsehood; 3. He paid a totally inadequate consideration; and 4. He got the deed by means of threats which amounted to duress.

A person who knows that there is a mine on the land of another may nevertheless buy it. The ignorance of the vendor is not of itself fraud on the part of the purchaser. A purchaser is not bound by our laws to make the man he buys from as wise as himself. The mere fact, therefore, that Tyson knew there was sand chrome on Harris's land, and that Harris himself was ignorant of it, even if that were exclusively established, would not be ground for impugning the validity of the deed. But it is not by any means clear that one party had much advantage over the other in this respect. They both knew very well that chrome could be got there, which one wanted and the other had no use for. But the whole extent of it in quantity was probably not known to either of them for some time after the deed. When it was discovered that sand chrome was as valuable as the same mineral found in the rock, and that large quantities of the former could be got in certain parts of the fast land as well as by the streams, it was natural enough that the plaintiff should repent and the defendant rejoice over the contract: but this did not touch its validity. Every man must bear the loss of a bad bargain legally and honestly made. If not, he could not enjoy in safety the fruits of a good one. Besides, we do not feel sure that the contract has made the plaintiff any poorer, for it is not improbable that he would never have discovered the value of the mineral deposit on his land if he had not granted to the defendant the privilege of digging.

If the defendant, during the negotiation for the purchase, wilfully made any misstatement concerning a material fact, and then misled the plaintiff and induced him to sell it at a lower price than he otherwise would, then the contract was a cheat and the deed is void utterly. But in all cases where the evidence brings the parties face to face, the language and conduct of the defendant seem to have been unexceptionable. . . .

Mere inadequacy of price is not sufficient to set aside a deed. It is sometimes regarded as a suspicious circumstance when coupled with other strong evidence of fraud. Here it would hardly be entitled to that much consideration. . . . Judgment [in favor of the defendant] affirmed. ∎

The court gave Tyson the benefit of the doubt because, it appears, he was the expert and he deserved a reward for his personal investment in specialized knowledge. He also took some risk when he paid Harris for the mineral rights on his property because the payment was not conditional on Tyson's results. He could after all have been wrong, and Justice Black believes that the question was unsettled at the time the contract was signed.

Justice Black made a further point in noting that Harris did not lose on the bargain. It is true that *ex post* he realized he might have held out for a better deal, but he was given something by Tyson for the rights. Moreover, given the fact that Harris lacked the knowledge Tyson had, it is doubtful that on his own he would ever have uncovered as much value as Tyson was able to do. Though the court made a good argument that this example is one of unilateral mistake, in the end it came down to a judgment by the judges no different in kind from that in *Sherwood*. The only difference was that here the court convinced itself that Tyson knew something productive that Harris did not, while in the earlier case the court by a split decision decided that the mistake was mutual.

Incompetence/Incapacity

Someone who is incapable of understanding the terms of a bargain cannot be held legally responsible for upholding it. This principle seems basically sound from both the standpoint of equity and economic efficiency. Because contracts are intended for mutually beneficial and voluntary exchange, a contract made with someone who cannot understand the terms cannot be said with any certainty to be efficiency enhancing. Many incapacity cases concern parties with illnesses that allegedly impair their judgment. But incapacity cases also include those where one party is a minor. In *Cidis v. White*,[19] for example, defendant Carol Ann White, a 19-year-old woman, contracted with the plaintiff, Cidis, for the purchase of contact lenses. When her father told her not to get them, she breached the contract; but by then Cidis had already acquired the lenses for her. The court directed that Cidis be repaid for his expenses, but should not profit at White's expense. Thus, the court did not oblige White to perform the contract as agreed. White was, according to law, an "infant" (albeit "emancipated"). As such, she was considered lacking the capacity to enter into a legally binding contract.[20] She was old enough to stand trial for committing a crime, but her youth disqualified her as a contracting party; she could not be bound to her promises.

Whether this decision makes sense from an economic perspective is another question. White was old enough to be living on her own and making major decisions about her life when she made the contract; but her relative youth disqualified her as a contracting party. The strict age limit for contract responsibility seems arbitrary. Indeed, the facts of the case provide scant reason to believe that she was unable to judge the cost of the contract and the benefit she expected to receive from it.

Fraud

Misrepresentation or fraud is, for obvious reasons, grounds for breach of contract and liability (as a tort) for resulting harm. It clearly defeats any economic purpose when one person is deliberately misled into an agreement that is, in fact, not in her interest. Contracts that are designed to defraud others, even people who are outside the jurisdiction of the court, are also not legally enforceable. From an efficiency standpoint, such meretricious contracts, if allowed to stand, would create high external costs, potentially subjecting everyone to enforceable contracts to defraud consumers. If contracts to defraud were enforceable in court, it would create perverse incentives for parties to enter into such contracts.

Consider the case of *Miltenberg & Samton Inc. v. Mallor*,[21] in which the plaintiff and defendant agreed to defraud an Egyptian buyer by mislabeling cans of herring as "California mackerel." When the defendant carelessly pasted new labels over the old ones, the fraud was revealed to the Egyptian buyer. The plaintiff, who was in on the scam, sought to collect a penalty from the defendant, as provided for in their contract. The court refused to uphold the contract, declaring that to do so would be to "aid . . . in carrying out a fraudulent purpose." The plaintiff's claim was dismissed as "repugnant to public policy."

Unconscionability

A promise based on outright fraud or one gained from a person who is not competent to understand the terms are obvious examples of contracts that would, if enforced, decrease social welfare. But consider this possibility: the promisor is legally competent and the contract is not fraudulent, but the terms are difficult to understand or written in such a way as to confuse the promisor about the nature and implications of the promise. Should such contracts be upheld?

The answer to this question is ambiguous. On the one hand, individuals who sign contracts are obligated to read the terms, and if those terms are confusing, they should seek clarification. The fact that people fail to read through and gain an appreciation for the full extent of their obligations is, in a real sense, their own fault. *Caveat emptor*. Clearly a doctrine that permitted parties to opt out of contracts simply by claiming they did not understand the terms would destroy all contract enforceability. On the other hand, contract language is sometimes confusing, perhaps deliberately. Or the contract's legal implications may be unclear because of the way the contract is formed. Such contracts may fall under the doctrine (noted in the Uniform Commercial Code) of unconscionability. A contract is unconscionable, and therefore unenforceable, if its terms are determined by the court to be too onerous or ambiguous.

A most famous case of unconscionability, *Williams v. Walker-Thomas Furniture Company* (excerpted here) raises important economic as well public policy questions. Briefly stated, the story behind the case was as follows: Walker-Thomas was a company that served a poor community in the Washington, D.C. area. They offered a program for their clients to purchase furniture and appliances on credit, using a contract with a term called an "add-on" clause. The add-on clause worked something like this: Say a customer bought a sofa for $240 including interest, to be paid in monthly $10 installments over two years. Suppose that, at the end of one year, when the customer had paid off half the sofa, she returned to the store to buy a recliner, under the same terms. For the sake of simplicity, we will assume that the price of the recliner was also $240. One might assume that this purchase would increase payments per month to $20 for one year, until the sofa was paid off, after which payments for the recliner would revert to $10. With the add-on clause, the process worked differently. The consumer would owe, by the store's accounting, $360 to be paid in installments of $15 per month over the next two years. In the event of default—even if it took place in the twenty-third month, with only one month left before she had paid off both items fully— the recliner and the sofa both would be repossessed. This condition was explained in the contract in the following language and in similarly small print:

> [T]he amount of each periodic installment payment to be made by [purchaser] to the Company under this present lease shall be inclusive of and not in addition to the amount of each installment payment to be made by [purchaser] under such prior leases, bills, or account; and all payment now and hereafter made by [purchaser] shall be credited pro rata on all outstanding leases, bills, and accounts due to the Company by [purchaser] at the time each such payment is made.

The plaintiff, Mrs. Williams, a single mother of seven with little education and on public assistance, had signed 14 separate contracts with Walker-Thomas over a five-year period. Despite the fact the District of Columbia Court of Appeals deplored the idea of the add-on clause, the judges upheld the contract saying, "A careful review of the record shows the appellant's assent was not obtained by 'fraud or even misrepresentation falling short of fraud.'" And the court added, "One who signs a contract has a duty to read it and is obligated according to its terms."[22]

The district court ruling was overturned by the U.S. Court of Appeals.

Williams v. Walker-Thomas Furniture Co.

350 F. 2d 445 (D.C. Cir. 1965)

J. Skelly Wright, Circuit Judge

Appellee, Walker-Thomas Furniture Company, operates a retail furniture store in the District of Columbia. During the period from 1957 to 1962 each appellant in these cases purchased a number of household items from Walker-Thomas, for which payment was to be made in installments. The terms of each purchase were contained in a printed form contract which set forth the value of the purchased item and purported to lease the item to appellant for a stipulated monthly rent payment. The contract then provided, in substance, that title would remain in Walker-Thomas until the total of all the monthly payments made equaled the stated value of the item, at which time appellants could take title. In the event of a default in the payment of any monthly installment, Walker-Thomas could repossess the item.

The contract further provided that "the amount of each periodical installment payment to be made by [purchaser] to the Company under this present lease shall be inclusive of and not in addition to the amount of each installment payment to be made by [purchaser] under such prior leases, bills or accounts; *and all payments now and hereafter made by [purchaser] shall be credited pro rata on all outstanding leases, bills and accounts* due the Company by [purchaser] at the time each such payment is made." (Emphasis added.) The effect of this rather obscure provision was to keep a balance due on every item purchased until the balance due on all items, whenever purchased, was liquidated. As a result, the debt incurred at the time of purchase of each item was secured by the right to repossess all the items previously purchased by the same purchaser, and each new item purchased automatically became subject to a security interest arising out of the previous dealings.

Unconscionability has generally been recognized to include an absence of meaningful choice on the part of one of the parties together with contract terms which are unreasonably favorable to the other party. Whether a meaningful choice is present in a particular case can only be determined by consideration of all the circumstances surrounding the transaction. In many cases the meaningfulness of the choice is negated by a gross inequality of bargaining power. The manner in which the contract was entered is also relevant to this consideration. Did each party to the contract, considering his obvious education or lack of it, have a reasonable opportunity to understand the terms of the contract, or were the important terms hidden in a maze of fine print and minimized by deceptive sales practices? Ordinarily, one who signs an agreement without full knowledge of its terms might be held to assume the risk that he has entered a one-sided bargain. But when a party of little bargaining power, and hence little real choice, signs a commercially unreasonable contract with little or no knowledge of its terms, it is hardly likely that his consent, or even an objective manifestation of his consent, was ever given to all the terms. In such a case the usual rule that the terms of the agreement are not to be questioned should be abandoned and the court should consider whether the terms of the contract are so unfair that enforcement should be withheld.

In determining reasonableness or fairness, the primary concern must be with the terms of the contract considered in light of the circumstances existing when the contract was made. The test is not simple, nor can it be mechanically applied. The terms are to be considered "in the light of the general commercial background and the commercial needs of the particular trade or case."

. . . [R]emanded to the trial court for further proceedings. ∎

The terms of this particular contract are obscure enough so that one could make a compelling case that the court was right to nullify it. It is worth wondering how many lawyers at first reading would have understood the contract's full implications. From an economic perspective, however, most economists would conclude that a court should not deem an add-on provision, in principle, to be unconscionable. As noted in our earlier discussion of credit rate ceilings at the beginning of Chapter 3, the application of an unconscionability doctrine to add-on clauses, even the obscure clause at issue in *Walker-Thomas Furniture*, might well hurt the people the decision in that case was intended to protect: high-risk borrowers (i.e., the poor).

To understand why, consider the furniture company's reasons for inserting the add-on clause in the first place. The people the furniture company served were generally poor and hence poor credit risks. Because used furniture (other than antiques) loses much of its resale value, the company wanted to insure that it could cover the losses it sustained from customer defaults by increasing the effective collateral of each loan. This way they would be more willing to extend credit to people in Mrs. Williams's circumstances. It should be noted that firms like Walker-Thomas were not exceptionally profitable, notwithstanding such "unconscionable" programs.

In the absence of the add-on clause, or some substitute mechanism for ensuring performance, Walker-Thomas furniture might have been less willing to give credit to poor customers at all. In that case, poor customers would have been left with fewer opportunities. Standard lending agencies will not become available to the poor because they remain bad credit risks. (If they were good risks in the first place, that alternative would have been widely available, and few would have resorted to the add-on program.) In the absence of devices such as add-on clauses, firms will either refuse credit to poor customers or they will have to charge much higher interest rates on individual furniture items, which could discourage buyers and possibly increase the default rate. As the number of buyers shrinks and/or the default rate rises, the number of firms selling furniture to the poor is likely to fall. *Per se* invalidation of add-on clauses would almost certainly end up disadvantaging Mrs. Williams and other poor people.

In its decision, the appeals court gave two reasons why a contract might be unconscionable: the first reflects the confusion of the specific form of the Walker-Thomas add-on clause, with its "terms hidden in a maze of fine print." The second reason the court gave is the inequality of bargaining power between the customer and firm that may well have "negated" any "meaningful choice." This second argument is more problematic. Unequal bargaining power has been grounds for breach especially when a monopoly enterprise uses its power to impose grossly unfair terms on a customer, even when that customer is another firm.[23] It may well be that through circumstances of poverty, Mrs. Williams's choices were narrow, but the court's decision may well have narrowed them further. Moreover, consumers deal all the time with firms that have some kind of monopolistic power. Doctors and dentists in small towns may well be the only medical personnel for many miles. So might plumbers, electricians, and others with specialized skills operating in small, isolated areas. By virtue of their special skills they may possess extra bargaining power whenever their services are required. Yet, it would certainly raise transaction costs if their monopoly position made them subject to legal action any time a customer felt subjected to a bad bargain.

These problems are not raised to deny that the unconscionability doctrine may be needed in some cases for reasons of equity. It can even be argued that the use of small print and difficult-to-understand, boilerplate language in contracts reduces economic efficiency by unnecessarily increasing transaction costs and the likelihood of socially costly defaults. Still, the courts need to take care in applying the unconscionability doctrine to avoid the mistake of harming the parties they are attempting to help.

Performance Excuses

The category of performance excuses (see Table 8.1) allows fewer reasons than the category of formation defenses for legally terminating or breaching a contract. The most clear-cut excuse is where performance depends on an individual, and that individual dies before fulfilling the contractual obligation. For example, the contracts for many of the actors in the movies based on the Harry Potter children's books obligated them to perform in all seven of the planned films. But the death of Richard Harris, who played Professor Dumbledore in the first two films, negated his contractual obligation under the doctrine of impossibility.

Changes in legal rules might also render a contract "impossible" to perform. Thus, a contract to supply beer became legally "impossible" after passage of the alcohol prohibition laws (and constitutional amendment) of the 1920s. War—*force majeure*, as it is often referred to in contracts—might make a contract both physically and legally impossible to perform. For instance, the facilities required for carrying out the contract might be destroyed (which itself would be grounds for an impossibility claim), or if the contract involved a deal with someone who was now the enemy, performance might well be illegal. These barriers to performance create a potentially legitimate claim that the purpose of the contract has been destroyed or "frustrated" by events.

A defense that is *not* allowed under the common law is one of "economic impossibility." Even if performance by the promisee would bankrupt the promisee's business, it is not a legitimate excuse. However, under the Uniform Commercial Code, which has amended the common law of contracts in most states with respect to commercial contracts, "commercial impracticality" is sometimes permitted as an excuse from performance. Still, what constitutes impracticality is extremely vague. It forces the courts to draw a line between impractical performance, which is a valid performance excuse, and unexpectedly bad bargains, which are not excused. Moreover, the question remains whether self-imposed "commercial impracticality" should permit a contracting party to impose costs, resulting from their nonperformance, on the other contracting party.

Although physical impossibility may seem a far more legitimate reason for contract nonperformance, it too is not always obvious. Consider the following case in which "frustration of purpose" because of war was offered as a performance excuse, but rejected by the House of Lords, which is the highest court in the United Kingdom. The plaintiff (Tsakiroglou & Co. Ltd., a company headquartered in the Sudan) had contracted to ship peanuts to the defendant (a German firm, Noblee Thorl) by sea.[24] The shortest route, which both parties anticipated would be used, was through the Suez Canal. The contract included a standard clause that canceled the contract in the event of a war that specifically prohibited exports or imports. In fact, war did break out in the Middle East in October 1956 shortly after the contract was signed and before its terms could be performed. The war, largely between Israel and Egypt, was used as a pretext for Great Britain and France to seize the Suez Canal, which consequently remained closed for five months. This contingency undeniably complicated matters for Tsakiroglou, but did it make the performance truly impossible?

Tsakiroglou & Co. Ltd. v. Noblee Thorl G.m.b.h.

House of Lords [1962] A.C. 93

***

Lord Reid

My Lords, the appellants agreed to sell to the respondents 300 tons of Sudan groundnuts at £50 per ton c.i.f. Hamburg. Admittedly, the groundnuts had to be shipped from Port Sudan. The usual and normal route at the date of the contract was via Suez Canal. Shipment was to be November/December, 1956, but on November 2, 1956, the Canal was closed to traffic and it was not reopened until the following April. . . . The question now is whether by reason of the closing of the Suez route the contract had been ended by frustration.

The appellants' first argument was that it was an implied term of the contract that shipment should be via Suez. It is found in the case that both parties contemplated that shipment would be by that route but I find nothing in the contract or in the case to indicate that they intended to make this a term of the contract or that any such term should be implied: they left the matter to the ordinary rules of law. . . . Admittedly the ordinary rule is that a shipper must ship by the usual and customary route, or, if there is no such route, then by a practicable and reasonable route. . . .

If the appellants are right, the question whether the contract is ended does not depend on the extent to which the parties or their rights and obligations are affected by the substitution of the new route for the old. If the new route made necessary by the closing of the old is substantially different the contract would be at an end however slight the effect of the change might be on the parties. That appears to me to be quite unreasonable: in effect it means writing the old route into the contract although the parties have chosen not to say anything about the matter. On the other hand, if the rule is to ascertain the route at the time of performance, then the question whether the sellers are still bound to ship the goods by the new route does depend on the circumstances as they affect them and the buyers: whether or not they are such as to infer frustration of the contract. That appears to me much more just and reasonable and in my opinion that should be held to be the proper interpretation of the rule.

It appears to me that the only possible way of reaching a conclusion that this contract was frustrated would be to concentrate on the altered nature of the voyage. I have no means of judging whether, looking at the matter from the point of view of a ship whose route from Port Sudan was altered from via Suez to via the Cape [of Good Hope], the difference would be so radical as to involve frustration and I express no opinion about that. As I understood the argument it was based on the assumption that the voyage was the manner of performing the sellers' obligations and that therefore its nature was material. I do not think so. What the sellers had to do was simply to find a ship proceeding by what was a practicable and now a reasonable route—perhaps not a usual route—to pay the freight rind, obtain a proper bill of lading, and to furnish the necessary acuminates to the buyers. That was their manner of performing their obligations, and for the reasons which I have given I think that such changes in these matters as were made necessary fell far short of justifying a finding of frustration. I agree that the appellants cannot rely on the provisions of clause 6 of the contract regarding prevention of shipment. I therefore agree that this appeal should be dismissed. ■

***

Clearly, in this case war was an unforeseen contingency that created complications for the shipper, Tsakiroglou. But a war that creates an unforeseen contingency is not identical to one that frustrates or destroys the ability of the promisor to perform. In this case, the impossibility claim was not legally sustainable because the war did not prevent loading and shipping; it did not close down all sea and air lanes from the Sudan to Germany; and it did not destroy either the peanut crop itself or facilities that were necessary for the processing and production of the goods in question. An alternative shipping route was available around the southern tip of Africa. True, it would have added about 7,000 miles to the trip and doubled the shipping cost, but no evidence indicated that the higher cost would have been financially ruinous to Tsakiroglou; obviously it was not physically impossible. The ruling by the court in favor of the defendant was unanimous, and all the opinions (each judge in the House of Lords is entitled to offer his or her own opinion) raised the same general point that frustration in a legal sense simply had not occurred. Yet the case came to court because general legal opinion in cases of this type was not completely settled. The plaintiff had raised the precedent of *Carapanayoti & Co. Ltd. v. E. T. Green Ltd.*,[25] in which the court ruled that closure of the Suez Canal *did* amount to frustration of purpose. The Lords' opinions in *Tsakiroglou* rejected the basic thrust of the *Carapanayoto* decision, concluding that the judge in that earlier case had "erred."

But was the court's decision in *Tsakiroglou* economically efficient? The answer depends, of course, on whether the court actually imposed the burden on the least cost avoider or insurer. Certainly, a good argument can be made that Tsakiroglou was in fact the best cost avoider or lowest cost insurer. The court implicitly made this determination in assigning liability for breach of contract to the peanut shipper. Although it might be argued that neither party had an information advantage in estimating the prospects for war in the Middle East, the shipper was likely in a better position to insure against it. As a local producer and shipper, the plaintiff would likely have had (or could have acquired) specialized information on alternative shippers, rates, and routes more easily and cheaply than could an importing firm in Germany.

At the same time, Noblee Thorl had specialized knowledge of peanut sources, and even though it seems likely that the shipper was the low cost avoider, it is at least possible that Noblee Thorl could have insured more cheaply by acquiring peanuts from an alternative source, especially once it became clear that shipping prices had risen. It is at least possible to imagine other circumstances that might have made the problem more complicated and ambiguous. If Sudan's ports had been blockaded, impossibility might have been a more plausible defense even if say air routes were available; that is, the cost of shipping might well have been so high as to make it far less expensive for Noblee Thorl to engage another source of peanuts than for Tsakiroglou to have shipped. It also might have changed the designation of low cost avoider, if Noblee Thorl was itself a shipper who was acting as an intermediary for a different final user, and who therefore might have had equal or even better knowledge of shipping routes and cost. Yet, under the circumstances as presented in this case, the assignment of costs by the court seems to be well in accord with the new institutional principle that efficiency is enhanced by assigning costs to the least cost avoider.

Not all promises, even ones committed to paper or made in front of witnesses, constitute legally enforceable contracts. If, for example, an uncle announces at a family gathering that when you graduate from college he will give you $10,000, this promise of a gift in the future is generally not an enforceable promise. Still, even in this example courts will recognize that the promise has the stature of a contract *if the gift is promised in return for something—that is, for consideration.*[26] In *Hamer v. Sidway,*[27] an uncle promised his nephew $5,000 if the nephew gave up drinking, smoking, swearing, and gambling until he was 21 years old. The nephew did as the uncle requested, and on his twenty-first birthday asked his uncle for the money. The uncle agreed to give him the money, but he died before he could carry it out and the estate's executor refused to honor the claim. The court ruled in the nephew's favor because he had changed his behavior in return for the promise of the money. That is, the nephew gave valuable consideration in exchange for the uncle's promise. Consideration, the court said, includes not just money but also can be the fact that "the other abandons some legal right in the present or limits his legal freedom of action in the future, as an inducement for the promise of the first." Thus, a contract was formed. Similarly in *Ricketts v. Scothorn*[28] the court ruled in favor of a woman who had given up her job after her grandfather promised her a sum of money sufficient for her needs.

It is reasonable to ask at this point whether these bargains really were mutually beneficial. Just what did the promisors get out of them? Presumably, they raised their utility by influencing the actions of others about whom they cared. The court in *Hamer* addressed this point in passing, saying it could not know how or if the promisor benefitted personally, but "we see nothing in this record that would permit a determination that the uncle was not benefitted in a legal sense."

Promises, such as those just noted, clearly provide positive incentives for particular kinds of behavior. But even in cases where the incentive effects are evident and positive, the court may still refuse to enforce the promise as a contract. The next case is an example. Mills voluntarily, and without promise of compensation, looked after Wyman's son (then age 25). After the son died, however, Wyman wrote to Mills expressing gratitude, and promising payment for his past services. Later, when Wyman refused to make good his promise, Mills sued.

Mills v. Wyman
20 Mass. (3 Pick.) 207 (1825)

Parker, C. J.

The promise . . . in this case appears to have been made without any legal consideration. The kindness and services towards the sick son of the defendant were not bestowed at his request. The son was in no respect under the care of the defendant. He was twenty-five years old, and had long left his father's family. On his return from a foreign country, he fell sick among strangers, and the plaintiff acted the part of the good Samaritan, giving him shelter and comfort until he died. The defendant, his father, on being informed of this event, influenced by a transient feeling of gratitude, promises in writing to pay the plaintiff for the expenses he had incurred. But he has determined to break this promise, and is willing to have his case appear on record as a strong example of particular injustice sometimes necessarily resulting from the operation of general rules.

It is said a moral obligation is a sufficient consideration to support an express promise; and some authorities lay down the rule thus broadly; but upon examination of the cases we are satisfied that the universality of the rule cannot be supported, and that there must have been some preexisting obligation, which has become inoperative by positive law, to form a basis for an effective promise. . . . If moral obligation, in its fullest sense, is a good substratum for an express promise, it is not easy to perceive why it is not equally good to support an implied promise. What a man ought to do, generally he ought to be made to do, whether he promise or refuse. But the law of society has left most of such obligations to the *interior* forum, as the tribunal of conscience has been aptly called. . . .

Without doubt there are great interests of society which justify withholding the coercive arm of the law from these duties of imperfect obligation, as they are called; imperfect, not because they are less binding upon the conscience than those which are called perfect, but because the wisdom of the social law does not impose sanctions upon them.

A deliberate promise, in writing, made freely and without any mistake, one which may lead the party to whom it is made into contracts and expenses, cannot be broken without a violation of moral duty. But if there was nothing paid or promised for it, the law, perhaps wisely, leaves the execution of it to the conscience of him who makes it. . . .

For the foregoing reasons we are all of opinion that the nonsuit directed by the Court of Common Pleas was right, and that judgment be entered thereon for costs for the defendant. ∎

Though the court in *Mills v. Wyman* expressed a desire to encourage Good Samaritan acts, it found no contract to enforce. Mills acted of his own accord without expectation of payment, and with no consideration in advance of his assistance to young Wyman. While we might deplore the elder Wyman's failure to make good his later pledge, that pledge did not create a contract. It was an unenforceable promise of a future gift.[29]

CHAPTER SUMMARY

This chapter considered the economic importance of contracts, but also why contracts may fail. The courts frequently face cases in which the issues, and the effects of any remedy, are ambiguous; and rulings may not always serve economic efficiency or equity. In the next chapter we look further at the economic issues of contract law, and how legal remedies can be structured to aid economic efficiency.

QUESTIONS AND PROBLEMS

1. Compare the neoclassical and new institutional approaches to contract analysis.
2. What is meant by "consideration" in contract law?
3. Can court decisions be adjudged Pareto efficient? Why or why not?
4. Can you make an efficiency argument in support of the court's refusal to enforce the add-on clause in *Williams v. Walker-Thomas Furniture*?

5. How might a court avoid either (a) finding add-on clauses unconscionable, and thereby reducing credit availability to high-risk consumers, or (b) exposing those same consumers to the risks created by obscure and complex contract terms?

6. In *Tsakiroglou v. Noblee Thorl*, which company was likely to be the lower cost insurer against the contingency that arose, and why?

7. In *Sherwood v. Walker*, was consideration provided? What was it?

8. Compare the results in *Sherwood v. Walker* and *Harris v. Tyson*. In what ways did the decisions differ?

9. A contract is meant to be a mutually advantageous and voluntary exchange. If it turns out that one party does not benefit as expected at contract time, is it efficient for the contract to be enforced?

10. At what age should someone be considered competent to enter into a legally binding contract?

11. Should the courts provide incentives such as those displayed in *Mills v. Wyman*? Does the ruling in that case reduce social welfare?

NOTES

1. Hagley Library and Museum, Reading Railroad Archives, Box 27, #9030, dated November 3, 1847. Reprinted with permission from the Hagley Museum and Library

2. Note that if we change the assumptions of the game (except nonenforceability), the payoff matrix changes, but the overall outcome for society does not. So, if Player 2 must invest in specialized production equipment before Player 1 pays, and Player 1 later decides not to pay, Player 2 is out the investment costs. If the contract is unenforceable, Player 1 has a net gain of 0, and Player 2 has a net loss of 2X. If Player 2 is unwilling to invest in the specialized production equipment before Player 1 pays, knowing that contracts are unenforceable, no contract will be made, and both parties will realize net gains of 0.

3. Article I, Section 10 of the U.S. Constitution specifically prohibits the states from making any law "impairing the Obligation of Contracts."

4. *See* Lisa Bernstein, "Opting Out of the Legal System: Extralegal Contractual Relations in the Diamond Industry," 21 *JOURNAL OF LEGAL STUDIES* 115 (1992).

5. Note: This statement does not mean the use of standard contracts or boilerplate language is economically inefficient. In fact, the vast majority of contracts are not breached, but are performed as written. The risk of breach associated with the use of standard or form contracts is usually quite small. In highly specialized circumstances, such contracts tend not to be used. Instead, it becomes worthwhile for the parties to invest in custom contracts.

6. *Stable preferences* means that they are at a given moment in time transitive. In other words, a rational economic actor who prefers *a* to *b* and *b* to *c* must by definition prefer *a* to *c*. These preferences can, of course, change over time as tastes, income, and other factors change.

7. 267 S.W. 2d 327 (Mo. App. 1954).

8. It is true that in the 1930s deflation was a more pressing problem than inflation. However, price changes in either direction should, one would expect, have led to a consideration in the contract of how this contingency would be treated.

9. The court ruled in Midwest Mower's favor on the grounds that no consideration had been given in exchange for its promise to pay more than the original contract price.

10. Some markets, such as those for grain and beef, approximate the ideal in certain respects.

11. 222 N.Y. 88, 118 N.E. 214 (1917).

12. The measurement was, however, fairly straightforward in the *Wood* case. The allegation was that the defendant had made no effort at all to market Lady Duff-Gordon's name. The defense countered that the contract imposed no affirmative

obligation on him to do so. The court found that such an obligation was implicit in the contract; otherwise, a complete lack of effort on the defendant's part would render the contract meaningless.

13. *See* the earlier discussion of bounded rationality in Chapter 3 and its introduction to behavioral law and economics.

14. The distinction between complete and perfect information is as follows: perfect information equals omniscience. Complete information is less than omniscience. It constitutes full knowledge of *present* circumstances and opportunities. Unlike perfect information, it does not require unlimited foresight.

15. 537 So. 2d 1065 (Fla. 1989).

16. For a discussion of the Pareto and Kaldor-Hicks efficiency criteria, *see* Chapter 1.

17. 60 U.S. 19 How. 150 (1857).

18. Of course, productive facts or specialized knowledge will also likely lead to increased income, and so have distributional effects, too.

19. 71 Misc. 2d 481, 336 N.Y.S. 2d 362 (1972).

20. Exceptions to this rule include items considered "necessaries," such as food and medicine. The Court ruled, however, that contact lenses did not qualify as necessaries.

21. 1 A.D. 2d 458, N.Y.S. 2d 748 (1956).

22. 198 A.2d 914 (D.D.C. 1964).

23. *See*, for example, *Graham v. Scissor-Tail Inc.*, 28 Cal. 3d 807 (1981).

24. Why was a dispute between a Sudanese company and a German company decided by the United Kingdom's highest court? As is the custom in the industry, the parties first brought the dispute to an arbitrator from the Incorporated Oil Seed Association, a private organization headquartered in London. The arbitrator's ruling was upheld by the Association's Board of Appeal. That decision was then subject to review in the English courts, through which the case made its way up to the House of Lords.

25. 1 QB 131 (1959).

26. A large literature addresses the issue of consideration in contracting, including how much consideration is required, and whether the absence of consideration should necessarily make a promise unenforceable. Under some circumstances, courts will enforce an agreement despite the lack of consideration, for example where the promisee acts in detrimental reliance on the other party's promise. However, traditionally consideration has been deemed crucial for converting an otherwise unenforceable promise into an enforceable contract.

27. 124 N.Y. 538, 27 N.E. 256 (1891).

28. 59 Neb. 51, 77 N.W. 365 (1898).

29. A gift that is presently, intentionally, and irrevocably delivered and accepted is enforceable, not as a contract, but as a conveyance of property. Thus, had the elder Wyman actually given Mills some money or item in thanks for the care Mills gratuitously bestowed on Wyman's son, that gift immediately would have become property of Mills. However, Wyman's pledge of a *future* gift to Mills was an unenforceable, gratuitous promise.

Chapter 9

Contracts II: Remedies

As we saw in the last chapter, some contracts by virtue of their construction should not be performed or enforced, and others because of circumstances cannot be performed or enforced. Sometimes, however, breach of contract also occurs when contracts were properly constructed and no contingencies truly prevented performance. In these cases, the courts are asked to provide a remedy. This chapter examines remedies to contract breach and considers how courts might use remedies to enhance economic efficiency and create incentives for contract formation that lowers transaction costs. We will also examine instances in which courts fail to fashion efficient remedies, and leave precedents that only discourage contracting by raising the costs of deferred exchange.

TYPES OF REMEDY FOR CONTRACT BREACH

Two general types of remedies are available in the case of contract breach: *specific performance* and *money damages*. These remedies are sometimes referred to, respectively, as equitable and legal remedies. Specific performance means that the court requires the parties to perform the contract as written. However, as we saw in the last chapter, some contracts are simply unperformable. In other cases, performance after a certain time lapse would be meaningless. In both of these cases, a court has no choice but to assign money damages.

Specific Performance

Some economists argue that the equitable remedy of specific performance should be the "default" remedy for judges. Assuming performance is neither impossible nor meaningless,[1] judges should order the parties to perform their contracts as written (or as interpreted by the courts).[2] After all, a contract represents deferred exchange that, at the time of agreement, is expected to benefit both parties. The contract expresses the parties' subjective valuations of the expected net benefits of cooperation. If a contract provides that a certain car will cost $1,000, then it can be assumed that the seller valued the $1,000 at least as much and probably more than the car, and that the buyer valued the car at least as much and probably more than the $1,000. In the event of breach by either party, how could it possibly be superior to award money damages instead of enforcing the contract? If damages are awarded, the court is in effect imposing its own valuations over those of the parties as evidenced in the contract. Further, the institution of contracting, as discussed in the previous chapter, is vital to the efficient functioning of modern market economies. Arguably its institutional value is undermined, at potentially high cost to society, to the extent that promisors can use the courts as a way to renege on promises.

Economist and law professor Thomas Ulen puts it this way:

> [S]pecific performance is more likely than any form of money damages to achieve efficiency in the exchange and breach of reciprocal promises. If specific performance is the routine remedy for breach, there are strong reasons for believing, first, that more mutually beneficial exchanges of promises will be concluded in the future and that they will be exchanged at a lower cost than under any other contract remedy, and, second, that under specific performance post-breach adjustments to all contracts will be resolved in a manner most likely to lead to the promise being concluded in favor of the party who puts the highest value on the completed performance and at a lower cost than under any alternative.[3]

The crux of the argument for specific performance lies in the fact that parties presumably know what the contract is worth to them; they will not sign if the valuations do not match their goals or expectations. Costs will be saved for several reasons: First, litigation may well be reduced if parties know that in the absence of some formation problem or accepted excuse that courts will order performance, instead of altering the bargain. Second, a specific performance default rule reduces information costs for the court. As we shall see later in this chapter, assessing damages is sometimes difficult and often subject to conflicting valuations. Finally, specific performance can save on insurance costs for the parties. Parties have no guarantee that in assigning damages a court will value performance at the same price as the parties themselves, which heightens uncertainty about the cost of an eventual settlement. Therefore, all sides to an agreement in which money damages are the rule need to find other ways of protecting their individual subjective valuations. With specific performance, settlement costs are more certain, and subjective valuations are protected by the contract itself.

Specific performance often seems to be more fair as well. In the following case, the town of Muskogee, Oklahoma, signed a contract with the plaintiff by which the plaintiff was obligated to supply natural gas to the city (and to private customers as well) along a gas main that would follow a right of way already used by the town's water supply. The contract gave both parties the right to unilaterally terminate the contract on 90-days' written notice, a "reasonable time" for the company to remove its pipes and for both sides to make alternative arrangements. But more than 10 years after the contract had gone into effect, the town without notice signed a contract with another gas supplier, the Municipal Gas Company, which summarily disconnected the plaintiff's gas line. The plaintiff sued both the defendant and the city, but was denied relief, a ruling the company appealed. Later, the city finally served written notice of contract termination and declared the appeal "moot" as a result. The plaintiff, however, pursued its appeal.

Oklahoma Natural Gas Corporation v. Municipal Gas Co.
38 F.2d 444 (10th Cir. 1930)

Cotteral, Circuit Judge.

The Oklahoma Natural Gas Corporation brought this suit against the Municipal Gas Company and the city of Muskogee for a decree awarding specific performance of a contract by which the city leased to the Muskogee Gas & Electric Company, predecessor of the appellant, a certain gas line, and an injunction against interference with its customers on that line. This appeal is from a decree denying that relief without prejudice to an action at law for damages . . . .

The case was tried on June 27 and 28, 1928, and a final decree was rendered on the latter date. The Municipal Gas Company was enjoined from enforcing its five-year contracts with customers so as to prevent discontinuance of service by them, or seeking damages from them for violations of said contracts during their term, or until the further order of the court. The appellant was denied relief, its bill against the city was dismissed, and the decree in terms provided it was without prejudice to action at law against the defendants.

After the appeal was taken in this case, and on February 11, 1929, the City of Muskogee, by its council, adopted a resolution directing its manager to serve such notice as may be required by law on appellant, canceling the contract of January 26, 1917. Two days later, the resolution with notice of the termination of the contract was mailed to appellant. The notice executed by the city through its mayor recited that "the contract dated January 26, 1927 [sic], be and it is hereby cancelled . . . ."

But we cannot agree that the contract has been terminated. It provided its own method of cancellation—by 90 days' written notice, or by mutual consent. This stipulation was binding upon both parties. The contract contemplated a notice effective at the end of 90 days in the future. The object in view was doubtless precautionary to allow both parties a reasonable time to adjust themselves to the new situation. In the interim appellant would have an opportunity to arrange for the distribution of gas, through a line it might construct on its right of way acquired from the city, and thereby retain its customers, and the city would be enabled to make other arrangements to obtain gas for itself, industrial consumers, and others. Instead of giving notice, the city saw fit to commit a flagrant breach of the contract, and, after the resulting damage was done to the appellant, it sought to declare the contract terminated . . . . In our opinion, a notice would not be operative, unless the appellant is restored to the position it would have enjoyed by a 90 days' notice with its attendant privileges. As we conclude the contract has not been terminated, we must pass upon the rights and remedy claimed by appellant. The controversy is not moot, and the motion to dismiss the appeal is overruled.

There is a contention that the contract was terminated by mutual consent, consisting of a waiver of notice, but we fail to find it supported by any evidence in the record . . . .

It is true, relief by specific performance rests in the discretion of the court. But this means a sound and not an arbitrary discretion. "The remedy is only discretionary, as it depends on certain equitable conditions, and these being fulfilled, it becomes as much a matter of right as the legal relief of damages." The conditions enumerated have been met in this case. Of course, the remedy is allowed only where the complainant has no adequate remedy at law. Appellant cannot be adequately compensated in damages from the very nature of the injury it has sustained. As was said in *Griffin v. Oklahoma Gas Corporation*, decided by this court January 9, 1930: "The adequate remedy at law, which will preclude the granting of specific performance of a contract, must be as certain, prompt, complete and efficient to obtain the ends of justice as a decree of specific performance . . . ."

The decree is reversed, and the cause is remanded to the trial court, with direction to enter a decree requiring the appellees to disconnect the gas supply of the Municipal Gas Company from the line the city leased to appellant, to allow appellant to restore its connection with that line and use the same for the distribution of gas by contract with customers, and to enjoin the defendants from interference therewith or furnishing gas to customers on said line, until the contract may be terminated upon notice as stipulated by its terms after such disconnection and restoration, and with the further direction to award appellant such damages against defendants as may be susceptible to legal proof for loss of the sale of gas to the date of said decree. Reversed. ∎

Given that nothing was improper about the contract's terms or its formation, and given a flagrant breach of the agreement, the court felt that the remedy most consistent with "the ends of justice" was simply to have the contract performed as written even though it probably meant, first, reconnection of the gas lines of Oklahoma Gas, then disconnection again after 90 days, followed by a reversion of the business to Municipal Gas. The probable expense of this remedy was ameliorated by the fact that the court did not preclude an agreement whereby the city or Municipal would pay Oklahoma Gas to avoid the changeovers. In other words, the court did not prevent the parties from bargaining around its remedy to a more efficient outcome. In any case, the court's willingness to order specific performance creates incentives for contract compliance in future cases, especially in cases where money damages would not adequately compensate plaintiffs.

Despite some evident benefits of specific performance, and its clear applicability in some cases, it is not true that specific performance, even when performance is possible, is always or even likely the lowest cost remedy. It almost certainly was not the least costly remedy in the *Oklahoma Natural Gas* case. Indeed, the defendant in that case argued that specific performance would create a "harsh and unreasonable" burden because of the costs associated with multiple changeovers of the gas lines.

Even from a theoretical standpoint it can be argued that specific performance leads to higher costs. It can, for example, lead to inefficient overreliance on contracts by promisees. As the legal scholar Victor Goldberg has argued, "They [promisees] could maintain tiny inventories, build machines that require inputs from a single supplier, and so forth, knowing that the specific performance remedy would bail them out."[4] In other words, their expectation of contract performance, come what may, would lead promisees to rely on it to the exclusion of lower cost substitutes. Reliance, as well as performance itself, might in such cases be wasteful of resources.

Further, opportunities for strategic behavior might arise from a default remedy of specific performance. Say, for instance, it becomes prohibitively expensive for a promisor to perform, but she knows the court will require her to perform anyway. In that case, the promisee would be in a position to extract far more than he would have expected initially as a price for the promisor to avoid the court-ordered remedy. Sometimes incentives for actions on the part of the promisee would make it difficult for the promisor to perform, thereby inducing breach and placing the promisee in the strong, legally supported bargaining position to extract rents (excess profits). Although the actual number of litigated cases might decline with a clear default rule, the threat of litigation may raise the cost of contracting *ex ante* and of bargaining *ex post*.

Still, legal scholars would agree that many occasions call for specific performance. Indeed, as we shall see, specific performance sometimes is a clearly superior remedy to money damages.

Money Damages

Despite its conceptual and, sometimes, actual advantages over other remedies, specific performance is not the remedy courts ordinarily apply. To the contrary, it is considered an *extraordinary* remedy, to be applied only when the plaintiff cannot be "fully compensated through the legal remedy of damages."[5] Money damages are the default remedy.

In the rest of this chapter, we consider the efficiency of various kinds of money damage remedies, including expectation damages, reliance damages, restitution, and liquidated damages. But first we need to consider an important issue: Specific performance implies that courts should enforce the letter of all contracts that are not flawed in their formation or impossible to perform. Specific performance presumes, however, that in no instances would social welfare be improved by nonperformance. That presumption is challenged by the theory of efficient breach.

THE NOTION OF EFFICIENT BREACH

A central premise of our discussion so far is that contracts, as an essential element in the efficient functioning of a modern economy, should be performed as written. Consider the following scenario: Company A contracts with Company B to supply widgets. At the time of the signing of the contract, A calculates that it will cost $5,000 to make the widgets and B promises to pay $10,000 for the widgets, which it plans to sell in turn for $15,000. Subsequently, a sudden, unexpected jump in material prices, a highly unfortunate contingency, raises the cost of A's widget production run to $20,000. It is going to be a bad bargain for A to perform the contract because it will lose $10,000. Ordinarily, losing money is part of the risk one takes when making a contract, and the loss is not itself an excuse the court would accept for a breach. But suppose A breached and paid B $5,000, which is equal to B's expected profit from the contract. In this case, B is no worse off than if the contract had been performed, and

A is clearly better off. Other complicating factors might be involved. For example, B could have contractual obligations to actually deliver the widgets, which would be frustrated by A's nonperformance, putting B in breach. Assuming that is not the case, and that no other externalities stem from A's decision to pay B rather than perform the contract, then A's breach with compensation to B would appear to be Pareto superior to A's performance. A would be better off by not performing and B would be no worse off because it is fully compensated. Social welfare is unambiguously improved because the total cost is lower with the breach than with performance (given the assumption of no externalities). This scenario would be an example of what is called *efficient breach*.

Arguably a change for the better, a fortunate turn of events as it were, could likewise make a breach efficient. Suppose that Xena has a car worth $8,000 (her subjective valuation), and she agrees to sell it to Yoram for $10,000, which reflects the latter's subjective valuation of the car. Just before the transaction is completed, a third person, Zachary, offers Xena $12,000. Apparently, Zachary values the car most of all, and the efficient outcome would be for him to get the car. Because Xena has already agreed to sell the car to Yoram, the additional $2,000 profit should go to Yoram. This outcome would result if the car reached Zachary through a series of transactions: first, from Xena to Yoram; and second, from Yoram to Zachary. However, if transaction costs are relatively high, it might be more efficient to avoid a series of transactions, and simply allow Xena to sell the car to Zachary. This transaction would, of course, breach Xena's contract with Yoram, and the extent of Yoram's harm could be measured by difference between Yoram's subjective valuation of the car, $10,000 (which Yoram still has in his pocket), and the $12,000 that Zachary would have paid Yoram for the car, had Xena performed the contract. If Xena is not allowed to breach the contract with Yoram, the (presumed) high transaction costs might prevent Zachary from ever acquiring the car, which would be an inefficient outcome, given the three parties' relative, subjective valuations of the car. Thus, in theory at least, it would be efficient to allow Xena to breach.[6]

This argument has some flaws, however. In the first place, at the time the breaching party must decide to breach or perform, that party may be uncertain as to the costs of performance relative to the costs of breach, and so might be prevented from knowing whether breach would be efficient. *Ex post*, a reviewing court might have the same uncertainty. In the second place, the argument in favor of efficient breach presumes that the contract prices accurately reflect the buyers' respective valuations of the car. Just because Yoram contracts with Xena to buy her car for $10,000, and Zachary contracts with Xena to buy her car for $12,000, that does not necessarily mean that Zachary values the car more than Yoram does. It could mean, instead, that Yoram is a superior negotiator. All we know from the respective contract prices is that Yoram considered the car to be worth *at least* $10,000, and Zachary considered the car to be worth *at least* $12,000. The respective contract prices are ambiguous evidence at best that Yoram would be willing to sell Zachary the car in a subsequent transaction for $12,000.

Moreover, transaction costs might not be lower if Xena breaches her contract with Yoram. Bear in mind that Xena's breach does not, in fact, decrease the total number of transactions from two to one. Instead of two performed contracts, we have one performed contract (between Xena and Zachary) and one breached contract (between Xena and Yoram). Does the situation provide any reason to believe that the transaction costs associated with (a) two performed contracts would be greater than those associated with (b) one performed plus one breached contract? Well, search costs are presumably lower for (b) because Xena has already located both Yoram and Zachary. For (a), Yoram and Zachary would have to find one another to contract. On the other hand, the transaction costs associated with breach *could* offset the lower search costs.

It is possible, of course, that Yoram might be willing to settle with Xena for a $1,000 payment, in which case both parties are better off after Xena's breach. Instead of Yoram's $10,000, Xena has Zachary's $12,000 minus the $1,000 she paid to settle with Yoram. So, Xena is better off by $1,000. Yoram is better off too because, instead of a car he valued at $10,000, he has $11,000 in cash—the amount he was going to pay Xena for the car plus the $1,000 Xena paid him in settlement of the breach. It is worth noting, in any case, that if Yoram consents to Xena's breach in exchange for a $1,000 payment, then no breach occurs in the first place; instead, a second contract exists, whereby Xena gives Yoram $1,000 and releases Yoram from his obligations under the first contract; and Yoram, in consideration, releases Xena from her obligations under the first contract. It would not be a case of efficient breach but efficient contract termination, modification, or substitution.

The risk of litigation following a contract breach is substantial and provides reason to question whether the gains from breach exceed the costs. This issue becomes acute in cases where information is costly to acquire, facts are in dispute, or the gain from breach is relatively small. Even in the widget hypothetical, raised earlier, the widget buyer may not be immediately convinced by the seller's claim of higher material costs, and may wish to search to verify the information. Those search costs, plus other costs associated with litigation, could well be high enough to leave both parties worse off than if the contract had been performed as written.

The following case returns to the issue with which this section began: whether parties are really both better off if the contract is performed.

Neri v. Retail Marine Corporation

30 N.Y. 2d 393, 334 N.Y.S. 2d 165, 285 N.E. 2d 311 (1972)

Gibson, Judge

The plaintiffs contracted to purchase from defendant a new boat of a specified model for the price of $12,587.40, against which they made a deposit of $40. They shortly increased the deposit to $4,250 in consideration of the defendant dealer's agreement to arrange with the manufacturer for immediate delivery on the basis of "a firm sale," instead of the delivery within approximately four to six weeks originally specified. Some six days after the date of the contract plaintiffs' lawyer sent to defendant a letter rescinding the sales contract for the reason that plaintiff Neri was about to undergo hospitalization and surgery, in consequence of which, according to the letter, it would be "impossible for Mr. Neri to make any payments." The boat had already been ordered from the manufacturer and was delivered to defendant at or before the time the attorney's letter was received. Defendant declined to refund plaintiffs' deposit and this action to recover it was commenced. Defendant counterclaimed, alleging plaintiffs' breach of the contract and defendant's resultant damage in the amount of $4,250, for which sum defendant demanded judgment. . . .

Upon the trial so directed, it was shown that the boat ordered and received by defendant in accordance with plaintiffs' contract of purchase was sold some four months later to another buyer for the same price as that negotiated with plaintiffs. From this proof the plaintiffs argue that defendant's loss on its contract was recouped, while defendant argues that but for plaintiffs' default, it would have sold two boats and have earned two profits instead of one. Defendant proved, without contradiction, that its profit on the sale under the contract in suit would have been $2,579 and that during the period the boat remained unsold incidental expenses aggregating $674 for storage, upkeep, finance charges and insurance were incurred. Additionally, defendant proved and sought to recover attorneys' fees of $1,250.

The trial court found "untenable" defendant's claim for loss of profit, inasmuch as the boat was later sold for the same price that plaintiffs had contracted to pay. . . .

***

It is evident, first, that this retail seller is entitled to its profit. . . . Closely parallel to the factual situation now before us is that hypothesized by Dean Hawkland as illustrative of the operation of the rules: "Thus, if a private party agrees to sell his automobile to a buyer for $2,000, a breach by the buyer would cause the seller no loss (except incidental damages, i.e., expense of a new sale) if the seller was able to sell the automobile to another buyer for $2,000. But the situation is different with dealers having an unlimited supply of standard-priced goods. Thus, if an automobile dealer agrees to sell a car to a buyer at a standard price of $2,000, a breach by the buyer injures the dealer, even though he is able to sell the automobile to another for $2,000. If the dealer has an inexhaustible supply of cars, the resale to replace the breaching buyer costs the dealer a sale, because, had the breaching buyer performed, the dealer would have made two sales instead of one. The buyer's breach, in such a case, depletes the dealer's sales to the extent of one, and the measure of damages should be the dealer's profit on one sale. . . ."

***

It follows that plaintiffs are entitled to restitution of the sum of $4,250 paid by them on account of the contract price less an offset to defendant in the amount of $3,253 on account of its lost profit of $2,579 and its incidental damages of $674. . . . Ordered accordingly. ■

Was the court's damages remedy in *Neri* really more efficient than an alternative remedy of specific performance? Had the court ordered specific performance, Neri would have had to take possession of, and pay full price for, the boat that he had ordered. By then, of course, he was for medical reasons unable to use the boat. Consequently, he surely would have placed it for sale. This process would have entailed search costs, advertising for instance, for a buyer. The search for a buyer could also have consumed a considerable amount of time, representing opportunity costs to him. In the meantime, he would likely have borne costs associated with maintaining the boat. Given Neri's lack of expertise, in contrast to a company in the business of selling boats, the process could have dragged on for quite some time. No doubt he would eventually have sold the boat, but it would likely have been a relatively costly process.

The court's damages remedy, on the other hand, left Retail Marine with its expected profit from its sale to Neri (plus the expenses it incurred to keep the boat and resell it) and no additional boat to sell since it had managed to find another buyer for Neri's boat. Undoubtedly, Retail Marine had much greater expertise than Neri in finding that buyer. Because the second sale of Neri's boat was accomplished at relatively low cost, from the standpoint of social cost generally, the breach and court's damage award (giving Retail the expected profits from the Neri sale) was probably more efficient than specific performance.

One might take issue with this claim, however. If Neri's and Retail's legal bills and overall court costs were great, then whatever gains were achieved through breach may well have been wiped out in litigation. But the claim to efficient breach might still be valid from another perspective. If, in the future, the court's holding in the case serves as precedent for similar cases, those cases might be solved without litigation at all, but simply by settlement, with compensation equal to expected profits.

Although breach may well be efficient on some occasions, it does carry a danger that it will be applied by a court that seeks an efficient outcome without fully appreciating the meaning of efficiency. The outcome of the following case was probably thought by the judges to be efficient and grounded in solid economic reasoning. But clearly it is not, and it creates enormously perverse incentives.

Peevyhouse v. Garland Coal & Mining Company
382 P. 2d 109 (Ok. 1962)

Jackson, Justice

Briefly stated, the facts are as follows: plaintiffs owned a farm containing coal deposits, and in November, 1954, leased the premises to defendant for a period of five years for coal mining purposes. A "strip-mining" operation was contemplated in which the coal would be taken from pits on the surface of the ground, instead of from underground mine shafts. In addition to the usual covenants found in a coal mining lease, defendant specifically agreed to perform certain restorative and remedial work at the end of the lease period. It is unnecessary to set out the details of the work to be done, other than to say that it would involve the moving of many thousands of cubic yards of dirt, at a cost estimated by expert witnesses at about $29,000.00. However, plaintiffs sued for only $25,000.00.

During the trial, it was stipulated that all covenants and agreements in the lease contract had been fully carried out by both parties, except the remedial work mentioned above; defendant conceded that this work had not been done.

Plaintiffs introduced expert testimony as to the amount and nature of the work to be done, and its estimated cost. Over plaintiffs' objections, defendant thereafter introduced expert testimony as to the "diminution in value" of plaintiffs' farm resulting from the failure of defendant to render performance as agreed in the contract—that is, the difference between the present value of the farm, and what its value would have been if defendant had done what it agreed to do.

At the conclusion of the trial, the court instructed the jury that it must return a verdict for plaintiffs, and left the amount of damages for jury determination. On the measure of damages, the court instructed the jury that it might consider the cost of performance of the work defendant agreed to do, "together with all of the evidence offered on behalf of either party."

It thus appears that the jury was at liberty to consider the "diminution in value" of plaintiffs' farm as well as the cost of "repair work" in determining the amount of damages.

It returned a verdict for plaintiffs for $5,000.00—only a fraction of the "cost of performance," *but more than the total value of the farm even after the remedial work is done* [emphasis in the original].

On appeal, the issue is sharply drawn. Plaintiffs contend that the true measure of damages in this case is what it will cost plaintiffs to obtain performance of the work that was not done because of defendant's default. Defendant argues that the measure of damages is the cost of performance "limited, however, to the total difference in the market value before and after the work was performed." . . . In view of the unrealistic fact situation in the instant case, and certain Oklahoma statutes to be hereinafter noted, we are of the opinion that the "relative economic benefit" is a proper consideration here. . . .

[U]nder the "cost of performance" rule, plaintiffs might recover an amount about nine times the total value of their farm. Such would seem to be "unconscionable and grossly oppressive damages, contrary to substantial justice" within the meaning of the statute. Also, it can hardly be denied that if plaintiffs here are permitted to recover under the "cost of performance" rule, they will receive a greater benefit from the breach than could be gained from full performance. . . .

Under the most liberal view of the evidence herein, the diminution in value resulting to the premises because of non-performance of the remedial work was $300.00. After a careful search of the record, we have found no evidence of a higher figure, and plaintiffs do not argue in their briefs that a greater diminution in value was sustained. It thus appears that the judgment [for $5,000] was clearly excessive, and that the amount for which judgment should have been rendered is definitely and satisfactorily shown by the record. . . .

We are of the opinion that the judgment of the trial court for plaintiffs should be, and it is hereby, modified and reduced to the sum of $300.00, and as so modified it is affirmed. ■

The judges in this case may have thought they were making an economic improvement. After all, if people pay "too much" for goods it may lead to a waste of resources. Indeed, the court specifically refers to "economic waste" from excessively large damage awards. It substitutes the "objective" market valuation for the contract terms where enforcing those terms would lead to costs that are "disproportionate" to the benefits. In this case, the cost of performing the contract would have been $29,000 (or $25,000), and the benefit, according to the court, only $300. Although this judgment may seem "reasonable," as the court claimed, it actually shows a poor understanding of basic economic principles. If this ruling were generally followed, it would prove costly to society.

In the first place, there is no such thing as "objective" value in economics. Even market valuations are subject to change according to who is buying what when. A property may receive one valuation when appraised for tax purposes and another, very different, valuation when it is appraised for insurance or sale. The larger and more important point is that economic value is inevitably subjective. It is what a purchaser is willing to pay and a seller is willing to accept.

We know something about the Peevyhouses' subjective valuation of their own property. Specifically, we know that the owners wanted restoration to a usable (not original) condition, at a cost of $29,000. Perhaps the "high" valuation of restoration relative to any reasonable market sale price for the property reflected their love for the land. Whatever the reason, the contract stipulated a price that represented the expectation of the Peevyhouses upon completion of the contract.

We also know what the contract was worth to Garland Coal Company. Because the company agreed to the price asked by the Peevyhouses, it is evident that company executives valued the access to the minerals underneath the property at $29,000, at least. Neither party claimed that these contract valuations were either coerced or misrepresented. The parties agreed to the exchange voluntarily at a price that was acceptable to both. For the court to overturn this on the basis that a group of judges knows the "true" value was presumptuous in the extreme, and clearly inferior to the parties' agreement on any measure of efficiency. As the one dissenting judge noted in citing a previous ruling from the same court, "The law will not make a better contract for parties than they themselves have seen fit to enter into . . . the judicial function of a court of law is to enforce a contract as it is written." From an economic standpoint, specific performance or damages equal to the value of performance would have been the only efficient remedies.

In fairness to the judges, some of the evidence provided reason to doubt the value the owners, Willie and Lucille Peevyhouse, really did place on their property. At one time, the owners seemed ready to settle for the cost of a bulldozer rental simply to even out the land surface.[7] Later negotiations nearly resulted in a settlement for $3,000. And the original jury award was for $5,000. Subsequently, on appeal the Peevyhouses asked for $25,000, even though the actual damages were greater. The relevance of these post-contract valuations is questionable, however. As the dissenting judge noted, the Peevyhouses insisted on the remediation clause as a condition of signing the contract, and the defendant accepted that condition. The defendant later breached the contract, reneging on its earlier agreed obligation to remediate the property.

It is also important to consider just what effect this ruling could have on the institution of contracting. If contracting parties expect the courts to substitute their own valuations for those of the parties, no one will agree to a contract unless that person's valuation is strictly at market price and the market is fully defined. Mining companies would presumably have a more difficult time acquiring rights to mine on private lands if landowners suspect that the terms agreed to are subject to substitution by judges who presume to know more about market values than the contracting parties themselves. Landowners would likely require premining payments, escrow, or other measures to protect against the caprice of the courts before they would be willing to enter into contracts with mining companies. In all, it should make contracting both more costly and less likely, reducing economic activity and social welfare.

The general point of this section is that efficient breach may indeed be possible, and the possibility of efficient breach should be recognized by judges. However, as the *Peevyhouse* case illustrates, judges without a basic understanding of economic theory are unlikely to be able to tell the difference between efficient and inefficient (or opportunistic) breach.

THE COSTS OF RELIANCE AND PRECAUTION

As already noted, in cases of contract breach courts most often apply legal remedies, that is, money damages. The purpose is to compensate the party that has suffered from the breach. From an economic standpoint, court or other legal remedies should also provide incentives for efficient behavior of contracting parties generally. In this instance, we mean that remedies should be structured so that contracting parties take the "right" amount of precaution against contract breach and spend the "right" amount in relying on the performance of the other party.

Efficient Reliance

Consider a hypothetical contract between Alice and George. George promises to supply a customized computer program for Alice's design business. George promises it will be completed in 60 days. Alice now must decide how much to rely on George's promise. She could rely so completely that she promises her clients she can finish new design work within five days after she is due to get the program because her work will be accomplished much more quickly using George's software. She could go out and get a new computer to run the software, or other software to complement George's work. She might hire a new worker whose job will be to run the new program. If she does any or all of these things, she may well be left in the lurch if George breaches or even if he is just late in performing. Alice may wind up with contracts she cannot fulfill, equipment she cannot use, and a worker with nothing to do. Reliance on George's promise could turn out be so expensive that his breach would put her out of business.

Alternatively, Alice can sign the contract but do nothing in reliance on George's promise, refusing to make even a single expenditure until George gives her the software and proves that it runs properly. While she waits, however, she may have to turn down clients she could serve if she knew George would perform on time. In other words, opportunity costs come with *not* relying on the contract she and George signed. So, what should Alice do? She must try her best to ascertain the "right" (that is, the efficient) amount of reliance. The question is: Is it reasonable to expect her to be able to determine the correct amount of reliance?

The answer is yes, assuming that we have reason to believe Alice knows the following: the amount of revenues Alice would get if George performs as promised; the revenues she would get, including damages, if George breaches; the probability of his performance or breach; and the costs associated with different types and degrees of reliance by Alice. If she knows these values and seeks to maximize her profits—assuming that she runs her business to maximize her profits—then she should rely on George to the point where the cost of an extra dollar spent on reliance equals the expected incremental gain from his performance (which is equal to the value of his performance multiplied by the probability that he will perform). In other words, efficiency in reliance would be achieved when the marginal cost of reliance equals the expected marginal benefit. So, if Alice has any positive expectation that George will perform, then she should spend something on reliance. If damage awards were always "perfect"—accurately compensating for all damages—and she knew the exact probability of breach, she would never over-rely, and the court award would be efficient. But how likely is it that Alice will possess all of this information at the time she makes her decision about how much to rely on George's promise?

Efficient Precaution

Efficient levels of precaution are also possible. If George knows that he faces damages for breach, those damages constitute costs he must factor into his own calculations of profit maximization. He can insure against breach by hiring an extra worker, for example; or because he may be forced to breach due to illness or damage to his equipment, he can insure that at least part of the damages he would owe to Alice would be recovered. In his case, he looks to minimize costs. He faces the cost of any expenditures he makes on precaution plus the probable cost of any damages the court is likely to assess in the event that he breaches. However, he should only spend an extra dollar on precaution if that expenditure reduces his expected damages by at least $1.

We illustrate this relationship between the costs of precaution and expected liability in Figure 9-1. The defendant's expected damages equal the probability of his breach times the extent of his liability. Thus, if he reduces the expected cost of his breach by $100, for example by hiring a part-time employee for $50, he is clearly better off. We can consider each dollar increment reduction in expected liability to be his marginal benefit (MB). The fact that the MB curve on the graph is downward sloping indicates the expectation that, as he increases his level of precaution, he receives less and less incremental benefit. The cost of reducing his liability by an additional increment—hiring workers and so on—is his marginal cost (MC) of pre-caution, which is rising; that is, each additional increment of precaution is expected to cost him more. Where does George stop increasing his level of precaution? The efficient level is the point where MB equals MC. Any expenditure beyond that point lowers his expected liability by less than the amount he would have to spend to do so.

It should be noted that *both* parties can, and probably need to, invest in precaution to some extent. After all, in the event that George were to die, or because of some other contingency, performance might be excused and Alice would obtain neither software nor damages. In any case, from a Coasean perspective, the court should, in the event of breach, seek to determine which party was ex ante the least cost insurer against either party's breach. It is by no means clear the least cost insurer will always be the party that performs last, as in the preceding hypothetical case. In a notable article, Richard Posner and Andrew Rosenfeld posed the following hypothetical: a machine maker promises to build a printing machine of rather idiosyncratic specifications for a printer and to install at the latter's shop. After the machine is constructed but before installation, the

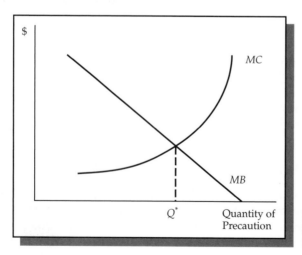

Figure 9-1 The Efficient Level of Precaution

shop is destroyed. The machine cannot be resold. It is not obvious which party in this case is the lowest cost insurer. But given a situation such as this one, it would seem that precaution should enter into the expected cost calculations of both parties.[8]

ALTERNATIVE APPROACHES TO CALCULATING DAMAGES

Contract law provides various types of legal remedies in addition to the equitable remedy of specific performance. They include expectation damages, reliance damages, restitution, and liquidated damages. In this section we will consider these alternative legal remedies, and examine cases in which damages are difficult to determine. From an economic point of view, the goal in choosing a remedy should be to generate efficient levels of reliance and precaution.

Expectation Damages

Expectation damages are likely to be the most efficient remedy for a given breach. With expectation damages, the court awards what the promisee would have expected to receive if the contract had been carried out. So, in the *Neri* case excerpted earlier, Retail Marine was awarded the profit it would have received had Neri actually purchased the boat. Similarly, in *Redgrave v. Boston Symphony*,[9] the court awarded actress Lynn Redgrave the fee she had agreed to in the contract, after the orchestra abruptly canceled her performance. If the courts routinely award full expectation damages, that should create incentives for promisors to take appropriate precautions. If the promisor knows of the requirement to pay *all* the benefits the promisee expects (that is, full expectation damages), then the promisor's precaution *must* be efficient. A promisor will insure against breach precisely up to that point where the last dollar spent on precaution will exactly equal a dollar's reduction in expected liability from breach.

However, expectation damages may lead to inefficient overreliance on the part of the promisee, who knows that the court will order compensation that meets the promisee's expectations, even if those expectations are unwarranted. A promisee has no incentive to insure or take precaution against a possible breach by the promisor. And a failure by the promisee to take precaution can be wasteful in the event that breach becomes unavoidable. Thus, the remedy that is most clearly designed to induce efficient precaution on the part of one party can lead the other to act inefficiently. It creates what is known as a "moral hazard."[10]

Indeed, the right incentives for efficient reliance come when the promisee knows that the promisor is liable for *none* of the benefits the promisee expects from the contract. In that case the promisor would have no incentives to take precaution, which would likely be inefficient. This bilateral problem is sometimes referred to as "the paradox of compensation." Remedies that create incentives for the promisor to take efficient precaution imply that the promisee will inefficiently overrely, while remedies to create incentives for promisees to engage in efficient reliance lead to inefficient underprecaution by the promisor.

The remedy of expectation damages also entails information costs that could prevent an efficient outcome. The court has to determine not only what the promisee expects but what the promisor expects the promisee to expect. Consider, once again, the case of Alice and George. When the contract is signed, George may believe that Alice will bring the software on slowly, and gain business in the future as the benefits of using the software become clearer. Alice, by contrast, may believe that the software will revolutionize the way she does business, and make substantial commitments based on the software from the day George promised completion. If George breaches, the court has to determine (a) what measure of expectations to use, and (b) the extent of George's liability for related costs stemming from the breach. For example, Alice may have made promises to her clients based on George's timely performance. His failure to perform thus may place her in breach of other contracts. The court then must decide whether George should compensate Alice for her costs associated with those breaches.

The courts have an answer that in theory should create incentives for both parties to engage in efficient precaution and reliance. The concept emerged from the following case.

Hadley v. Baxendale
9 Exch. 341, 156 Eng. Rep. 145 (1854)

At the trial before Crompton, J., at the last Gloucester Assizes, it appeared that the plaintiffs carried on an extensive business as millers at Gloucester; and that on the 11th of May, their mill was stopped by a breakage of the crank shaft by which the mill was worked. The steam-engine was manufactured by Messrs. Joyce & Co., the engineers, at Greenwich, and it became necessary to send the shaft as a pattern for a new one to Greenwich. The fracture was discovered on the 12th, and on the 13th the plaintiffs sent one of their servants to the office of the defendants, who are the well-known carriers trading under the name of Pickford & Co., for the purpose of having the shaft carried to Greenwich. The plaintiffs' servant told the clerk that the mill was stopped, and that the shaft must be sent immediately; and in answer to the inquiry when the shaft would be taken, the answer was, that if it was sent up by twelve o'clock any day, it would be delivered at Greenwich on the following day. On the following day the shaft was taken by the defendants, before noon, for the purpose of being conveyed to Greenwich, and the sum of 2l. 4s. was paid for its carriage for the whole distance; at the same time the

defendants' clerk was told that a special entry, if required, should be made to hasten its delivery. The delivery of the shaft at Greenwich was delayed by some neglect; and the consequence was, that the plaintiffs did not receive the new shaft for several days after they would otherwise have done, and the working of their mill was thereby delayed, and they thereby lost the profits they would otherwise have received.

* * *

[T]he special circumstances were here never communicated by the plaintiffs to the defendants. It follows therefore, that the loss of profits here cannot reasonably be considered such a consequence of the breach of contract as could have been fairly and reasonably contemplated by both the parties when they made this contract. For such loss would neither have flowed naturally from the breach of this contract in the great multitude of such cases occurring under ordinary circumstances, nor were the special circumstances, which, perhaps, would have made it a reasonable and natural consequence of such breach of contract, communicated to or known by the defendants. ■

The holding in this case is often referred to as the *"Hadley* rule." Expectations must be "reasonably . . . in the contemplation of both parties"; otherwise, they cannot serve as the basis for recovery. The basis for the remedy of expectation damages thus becomes *reasonably foreseeable expectations damages*. Defendants cannot be held responsible for damages that they could not reasonably foresee or were not communicated by plaintiffs.

The *Hadley* rule forces both parties to take some precautions against the defendant's possible breach. Hadley overrelied on Baxendale's performance. In the future, this ruling provides incentives for more efficient reliance. Of course, a cost is associated with creating this incentive. The administrative costs of resolving contract disputes become more expensive when courts must determine what damages are "reasonably foreseeable." The fact that "reasonably foreseeable" cannot be determined objectively, means that *Hadley* rule expectation damages are unlikely to produce efficient outcomes in terms of both precaution and reliance. At best, the rule is likely to prevent great overreliance on the part of the promisee.

Given the *Hadley* rule's approach, both parties have incentives to insure against breach. But such a result is not necessarily efficient either, particularly from a Coasean least cost avoider or insurer perspective. Even in the *Hadley* case itself, it is not clear from the information provided in the case which party could have insured at lower cost. We might assume, however, that Hadley could have made arrangements at low cost, for a temporary shaft or, as the court speculates, he might have kept an extra one on premises at low cost. Either of those options would have constituted insurance against the defendant's breach. Alternatively, as Victor Goldberg points out,[11] Hadley could have kept on hand a larger inventory of flour to meet demand in case of an unforeseen contingency. On the other hand, Baxendale too might have insured against his own breach by leasing an extra wagon and horses. So which party was the lower cost insurer? Though the court discusses this question in hypothetical terms, it did not offer an answer. If a court is seeking an efficient outcome, it needs to consider the costs of various alternatives.

Reliance Damages

The problem of determining reasonably foreseeable expectation damages makes it unlikely that the remedy of expectation damages would always achieve an efficient outcome in cases of breach of contract. Alternative remedies include reliance damages. Reliance damages compensate promisees for how much they actually spent in relying on the promise of performance. Thus, in the hypothetical case of Alice and George, if the court awarded reliance damages Alice would be reimbursed for her expenses, perhaps including the cost of advertising her new services or the wages of an employee who was hired to run the new software. The purpose of reliance damages is essentially to compensate promisees and put them in the same position *as if the contract had never been written and signed*. Arguably, it is an impossible goal to achieve because the failure of the contract represents a net loss of time and utility— costs that are difficult for courts to assess. Absent a clear measure of these opportunity costs and a metric to determine reasonable expectations, however, reliance damages are often the best the court can do.

The utility and limitations of reliance damages are illustrated in the case of *Security Stove & Mfg. Co. v. American Railway Express Co.* American Railway Express (the A.R.E. as it was often called) was the FedEx of its day (the 1920s). It provided fast, reliable, and insurable transport with pickup and delivery. In one way the A.R.E. was distinctly different from FedEx: It was a government-regulated monopoly without any meaningful competition. Still, a promise to deliver by the A.R.E. provided the basis for an enforceable contract.

Security Stove & Mfg. Co. v. American Railway Express Co.

227 Mo. App. 175, 51 S.W. 2d 572 (1932)

Bland, J.

This is an action for damages for the failure of defendant to transport, from Kansas City to Atlantic City, New Jersey, within a reasonable time, a furnace equipped with a combination oil and gas burner. The cause was tried before the court without the aid of a jury, resulting in a judgment in favor of plaintiff in the sum of $801.50 and interest, or in a total sum of $1,000. Defendant has appealed.

The facts show that plaintiff manufactured a furnace equipped with a special combination oil and gas burner it desired to exhibit at the American Gas Association Convention held in Atlantic City in October, 1926. The president of plaintiff testified that plaintiff engaged space for the exhibit for the reason "that the Henry L. Dougherty Company was very much interested in putting out a combination oil and gas burner; we had just developed one, after we got through, better than anything on the market and we thought this show would be the psychological time to get in contact with the Dougherty Company;" that "the thing wasn't sent there for sale but primarily to show;" that at the time the space was engaged it was too late to ship the furnace by freight so plaintiff decided to ship it by express, and, on September 18, 1926, wrote the office of the defendant in Kansas City, stating that it had engaged a booth for exhibition purposes at Atlantic City, New Jersey, from the American Gas Association, for the week beginning

October 11th; that its exhibition consisted of an oil burning furnace, together with two oil burners which weighed at least 1,500 pounds; that, "In order to get this exhibit in place on time it should be in Atlantic City not later than October the 8th. What we want you to do is to tell us how much time you will require to assure the delivery of the exhibit on time." . . .

Plaintiff's president made arrangements to go to Atlantic City to attend the convention and install the exhibit, arriving there about October 11th. When he reached Atlantic City he found the shipment had been placed in the booth that had been assigned to plaintiff. The exhibit was set up, but it was found that one of the packages shipped was not there. This missing package contained the gas manifold, or that part of the oil and gas burner that controlled the flow of gas in the burner. This was the most important part of the exhibit and a like burner could not be obtained in Atlantic City.

Wires were sent and it was found that the stray package was at the "over and short bureau" of defendant in St. Louis. Defendant reported that the package would be forwarded to Atlantic City and would be there by Wednesday, the 13th. Plaintiff's president waited until Thursday, the day the convention closed, but the package had not arrived at the time, so he closed up the exhibit and left. About a week after he arrived in Kansas City, the package was returned by the defendant . . . .

Plaintiff asked damages, which the court in its judgment allowed as follows: $147 express charges (on the exhibit); $45.12 freight on the exhibit from Atlantic City to Kansas City; $101.39 railroad and pullman fares to and from Atlantic City, expended by plaintiff's president and a workman taken by him to Atlantic City; $48 hotel room for the two; $150 for the time of the president; $40 for wages of plaintiff's other employee and $270 for rental of the booth, making a total of $801.51.

Defendant contends that plaintiff is endeavoring to achieve a return of the *status quo* in a suit based on a breach of contract. Instead of seeking to recover what he would have had, [i.e., expectations damages] had the contract not been broken, plaintiff is trying to recover what he would have had, had there never been any contract of shipment;" that the expenses sued for would have been incurred in any event . . . .

The case at bar was to recover damages for loss of profits by reason of the failure of the defendant to transport the shipment within a reasonable time, so that it would arrive in Atlantic City for the exhibit. There were no profits contemplated. The furnace was to be shown and shipped back to Kansas City. There was no money loss, except the expenses, that was of such a nature as any court would allow as being sufficiently definite or lacking in pure speculation. Therefore, unless plaintiff is permitted to recover the expenses that it went to, which were a total loss to it by reason of its inability to exhibit the furnace and equipment, it will be deprived of any substantial compensation for its loss. The law does not contemplate any such injustice. It ought to allow plaintiff, as damages, the loss in the way of expenses that it sustained, and which it would not have been put to if it had not been for its reliance upon the defendant to perform its contract. There is no contention that the exhibit would have been entirely valueless and whatever it might have accomplished defendant knew of the circumstances and ought to respond for whatever damages plaintiff suffered. In cases of this kind the method of estimating the damages should be adopted which is the most definite and certain and which best achieves the fundamental purpose of compensation . . . .

While, it is true that plaintiff already had incurred some of these expenses, in that it had rented space at the exhibit before entering into the contract with defendant for the shipment of the exhibit and this part of plaintiff's damages, in a sense, arose out of a circumstance which transpired before the contract was even entered into, yet, plaintiff arranged for the exhibit knowing that it could call upon defendant to perform its common-law duty to accept and transport the shipment with reasonable dispatch. The whole damage, therefore, was suffered in contemplation of defendant performing its contract, which it failed to do, and would not have been sustained except for the reliance by plaintiff upon defendant to perform it. It can, therefore, be fairly said that the damages or loss suffered by plaintiff grew out of the breach of the contract, for had the shipment arrived on time, plaintiff would have had the benefit of the contract, which was contemplated by all parties, defendant being advised of the purpose of the shipment.

The judgment is affirmed. All concur. ■

Security Stove did not seek expectations damages in this case, even though it surely expected that demonstration of its stove at the trade show would lead to sales. Any number, including the value of just one sale, would have been speculative and, therefore, not reasonably foreseeable by the defendant. Under the circumstances, reliance damages were the best it could hope to receive. Security Stove's expenses in reliance on the contract with A.R.E. were readily ascertainable, and were considered reasonable expenditures in anticipation of the defendant's commitment to perform.

A question arises nonetheless: Did Security Stove overrely? Although few other transport options were available—air freight was not an option in 1926 and the interstate highway system did not then exist—it seems nevertheless that at least some other precautions might have been taken by the company. If the one part, the gas manifold, was so crucial to the whole mechanism, perhaps the plaintiff's president should have carried a spare with him when he traveled to Atlantic City. It is also possible that after the A.R.E. breached by failing to deliver on October 11th, Security Stove could have dispatched its own worker to deliver a manifold which, if carried by train, could have reached Atlantic City by the 12th. Attempting to recontract with the A.R.E. to deliver on the 13th compounded the delivery company's failure, but also left the plaintiff without a product. Presumably, companies such as the plaintiff would in the future take greater precaution given the problems that resulted from breach. At the time, however, Security Stove evidently felt that its expressions of urgency to the A.R.E. were sufficient, and that the carrier was the best placed to insure against nonperformance at lowest cost.

Restitution

In some cases, neither expectation nor reliance damages seem appropriate, and specific performance is not possible. In these cases, the courts tend to resort to the remedy of restitution.

Consider the following case, in which the defendants, a music group, failed to appear, as they were bound to do by contract, to play at the plaintiffs' wedding reception. The defendants argued that they only owed the plaintiffs an apology and "restitution," a return of the $65 deposit the plaintiffs had given as consideration. The plaintiffs argued for full reliance damages amounting to the full cost of their wedding reception, $2,643.59, which they considered a "total loss" because of the band's breach. Expectation damages were not an option in the case because the plaintiffs never contemplated earning a profit on their wedding reception. Specific performance was obviously not an option either because the reception was already done and over. So, the court's only choice was between the plaintiffs' preferred reliance damages and the defendant's preferred restitution damages.

Deitsch v. Music Company

6 Ohio Misc. 2d 6, 453 N.E. 2d 1302 (1983)

Painter, J.

This is an action for breach of contract. Plaintiffs and defendant entered into a contract on March 27, 1980, whereby defendant was to provide a four-piece band at plaintiffs' wedding [reception on November 8, 1980]. The reception was to be from 8:00 p.m. to midnight. The contract stated "wage agreed upon $295.00," with a deposit of $65, which plaintiffs paid upon the signing of the contract.

Plaintiffs proceeded with their wedding, and arrived at the reception hall on the night of November 8, 1980, having employed a caterer, a photographer and a soloist to sing with the band. However, the four-piece band failed to arrive at the wedding reception. Plaintiffs made several attempts to contact defendant but were not successful. After much wailing and gnashing of teeth, plaintiffs were able to send a friend to obtain some stereo equipment to provide music, which equipment was set up at about 9:00 p.m. . . . Counsel for both parties have submitted memoranda on the issue of damages. However, no cases on point are cited. Plaintiffs contend that the entire cost of the reception, in the amount of $2,643.59, is the correct measure of damages. This would require a factual finding that the reception was a total loss, and conferred no benefit at all on the plaintiffs. Defendant, on the other hand, contends that the only measure of damages which is proper is the amount which plaintiffs actually lost, that is, the $65 deposit. It is the court's opinion that neither measure of damages is proper; awarding to plaintiffs the entire sum of the reception would grossly overcompensate them for their actual loss, while the simple return of the deposit would not adequately compensate plaintiffs for defendant's breach of contract.

Therefore, we have to look to other situations to determine whether there is a middle ground, or another measure of damages which would allow the court to award more than the deposit, but certainly less than the total cost of the reception.

It is hornbook law that in any contract action, the damages awarded must be the natural and probable consequence of the breach of contract or those damages which were within the contemplation of the parties at the time of making the contract.

Certainly, it must be in the contemplation of the parties that the damages caused by a breach by defendant would be greater than the return of the deposit—that would be no damages at all . . . .

[A] similar situation would be the reservation of a room in a hotel or motel. Surely, the damages for the breach of that contract could exceed the mere value of the room. In such a case, the Hawaii Supreme Court has held the plaintiff was "not limited to the narrow traditional contractual remedy of out-of-pocket losses alone."

The court holds that in a case of this type, the out-of-pocket loss, which would be the security deposit, or even perhaps the value of the band's services, where another band could not readily be obtained at the last minute, would not be sufficient to compensate plaintiffs. Plaintiffs are entitled to compensation for their distress, inconvenience, and the diminution in value of their reception. For said damages, the court finds that the compensation should be $750. Since plaintiffs are clearly entitled to the refund of their security deposit, judgment will be rendered for plaintiffs in the amount of $815 and the costs of this action. ■

The court awarded the plaintiffs $750 in recognition of their "distress, inconvenience, and the diminution in value of their reception." The court doesn't say where that number came from. Perhaps it just seemed fair in some sense; perhaps it was based on an estimate of how much less enjoyment the couple received from the reception because of the band's breach. It certainly seems arbitrary.

The court might have done better. They had at least one measure of the band's value to the Deitsches: the plaintiffs had agreed to pay the $295 for its performance. Although the judges specifically ruled out expectation damages, the contact price is the one revealed measure of the value of the band's presence to the plaintiffs. But was that amount an upper bound, a lower bound, or a median amount of their willingness to pay for live music? Had they considered hiring other bands that charged more or less, that might have been evidence as to the subjective value the couple placed on *this* band's performance. Another way of determining a value would have been for the court to examine the average cost for wedding receptions featuring live music. But courts seldom consider such evidence, especially when it is not presented by the parties appearing before it. Of course, once the court seeks to include costs of distress and inconvenience, then no price is readily obtainable, and no measure fully applies.

Even if restitution was inappropriate in the *Deitsche* case, it may be an appropriate remedy in other circumstances. Consider the following hypothetical case: Martin and Carol enter into a contract on September 1 whereby Carol promises to begin painting Martin's house on September 20 and finish on September 21. Martin, in turn, promises to pay Carol $1,000, after Carol has finished painting the house. In addition, Martin immediately pays Carol $200 as a deposit. On September 3, just two days after signing the contract, Carol phones Martin to inform him that she has broken her leg in an accident, which will prevent her from fulfilling the contract. Assume that several other house painters in town would be willing to paint Martin's house on the same terms. Under these circumstances, restitution—the return of the $200 deposit—is arguably the most efficient, as well as the fairest, remedy for Carol's breach.

Liquidated Damages/Penalty Clauses

With liquidated damages, contracting parties themselves write into their contract the nature and extent of damages in the event of a breach. This remedy would seem on the surface to be the most efficient approach. Both parties voluntarily agree how to assess damages in the event of breach; presumably rational economic actors would not enter into such an agreement if their expected benefits did not exceed their costs. It would also seem likely that such contract clauses would lower transaction costs. If the parties know their obligations beforehand, they would seem less likely to engage in lawsuits to assess damages in the event of breach. The court's only role would be enforcement of the terms. By keeping remedies to breach in contracts and out of courts, social costs should be lower while leaving the institution of contracting no less effective.

But such contract provisions do not in fact avoid litigation. First, liquidated damages are generally disallowed if they are deemed punitive, in which case they are referred to as a "penalty clause." As Judge Posner noted in his opinion on *Lake River Corporation v. Carborundum Company*,[12] under law "a liquidation of damages must be a reasonable estimate at the time of contracting of the likely damages from breach, and the need for estimation at that time must be shown by reference to the likely difficulty in measuring the actual damages from a breach of contract after the breach occurs." In other words, liquidated damages should approximate expectation damages, but it also must be shown that it would be costly for the court to have estimated those damages ex post.

Sound economic reasons support this judicial preference. First, if stipulated damages are punitive they will be likely to exceed the benefits a promisee would get from performance of the contract by the promisor. This scenario will create perverse incentives for the former to induce breach by the latter. In the event this inducement succeeds, it reduces economic activity that presumably had social value or else the contract would not have been entered into the first place. Moreover, as one party expends effort to induce breach it will likely raise the costs for the other to avoid it.

Even without an inducement to breach, a penalty clause can lead to inefficiency. Ordinarily, if it costs more to perform rather than breach and pay expectation damages, the latter course is more efficient. But a penalty for nonperformance may force a promisor to undertake wasteful performance because that would be less costly than breach under the penalty clause.

Finally, penalty clauses may reflect a great inequality of bargaining strength that raises questions of unconscionability. Even though we assume contracts are entered into voluntarily for mutual gain, a party contracting with another who has disproportionate power may have to accept punitive clauses as a precondition for doing any business at all. Consider, again, the "offer you cannot refuse."

These problems mean that liquidated damage cases often come before the courts, and even liquidated damages provisions that seem reasonable may be challenged as penalty clauses.[13] Still, liquidated damages are a remedy that can potentially lower costs and increase certainty for both parties to a contract.

CHAPTER SUMMARY

We began the preceding two chapters on contracts by noting the crucial role that contracting, and hence contract law, plays in the life of a modern economy. This point bears reiterating. The search for law and remedy does (and should) have behind it an intention to strengthen the institution of enforceable contracting, and an economic analysis is central to that endeavor. To the extent clarity can replace ambiguity, and certainty can replace uncertainty in contract relations, we achieve greater efficiency in the law. This efficiency, in turn, lowers social costs and raises the social product, a clear example of the profound impact of the law on economic life.

This chapter considered various remedies for contract breach, as well as the theory of efficient breach. No remedy (including the no-remedy option) is uniquely well suited for every breach. Courts do not always succeed in selecting the most appropriate (i.e., efficient) remedy for the case. In some cases, judicial carelessness (or ignorance of economic theory) in fashioning remedies can create perverse incentives that can significantly raise the costs of contracting.

QUESTIONS AND PROBLEMS

1. What, if anything, is wrong with the court's economic analysis in *Peevyhouse*?
2. When is restitution an appropriate remedy from an economic point of view?
3. Is the *Hadley* rule efficient?
4. Compare the incentive effects of expectation and reliance damages.
5. Why might it be inefficient to rely completely on contract performance?
6. Is precaution ever excessive?
7. Some legal authorities criticize penalty clauses. However, if the clauses are agreed to voluntarily by contracting parties, why shouldn't courts uphold them?
8. What is the economic argument for specific performance? What incentives would be created if it became the default remedy in contract cases?
9. If, in the *Oklahoma Gas* case, the court had awarded expectation damages, how would it have calculated them?
10. In the *Neri* case, the appellant signed a contract to buy a boat. Give reasons why specific performance should or should not have been the remedy.

NOTES

1. As we shall see in the next section, performance in some instances clearly would be Pareto inferior to breach.

2. Actually, specific performance is an order by the court for the parties to perform. However, the parties are free to work out some alternative arrangement.

3. Thomas Ulen, "The Efficiency of Specific Performance: Toward a Unified Theory of Contract Remedies," 83 *MICHIGAN LAW REVIEW* 341, 343–4 (1984).

4. "Relational Exchange, Contract Law and the Boomer Problem," in Victor Goldberg (ed.), *Readings in the Economics of Contract Law* (Cambridge: Cambridge University Press, 1989), pp. 126–27.

5. *Madariaga v. Morris*, 639 S.W. 2d 709, 711 (Tex. App. 1982).

6. On the other hand, if Xena breaches her agreement with Yoram, she may be viewed by Zachary and others as an unreliable contracting partner. Zachary may refuse to deal with her, resulting in a deadweight loss to society from failure to exploit potential gains from trade. Parties that breach may, thus, raise their own costs with respect to subsequent agreements.

7. Judith L. Maute, "*Peevyhouse v. Garland Coal* Revisited: The Ballad of Willie and Lucille," 89 *NORTHWESTERN UNIVERSITY LAW REVIEW* 1341, 1369–70 (1995).

8. Richard A. Posner and Andrew M. Rosenfield, "Impossibility and Related Doctrines in Contract Law: An Economic Analysis," 6 *JOURNAL OF LEGAL STUDIES* 83 (1977).

9. 602 F. Supp. 1189 (D. Mass. 1985).

10. The concept of *moral hazard* is discussed in detail, in the context of insuring against accidents, in Chapter 10.

11. Victor P. Goldberg (ed.), *Readings in the Economics of Contract Law* (1989), p. 99.

12. 765 F. 2d 1284 (1985).

13. *See, for example, Aruini v. Board of Education*, 93 Ill. App. 3d 925, 418 N.E. 2d 104 (1981).

Chapter 10

Torts I: Negligence

PROLOGUE: ACCIDENTS HAPPEN

On a winter evening, Mary is walking her dog through her residential neighborhood. She is bundled up tight against the cold in a black parka with hood, black leggings over her blue jeans, and black, fleeced-lined boots. On this dark, dreary evening, she cannot be seen by anyone from more than a few feet away.

Robert is driving home late, as usual, from work. He is tired and hungry. As he turns his car into the neighborhood where he lives with his wife and two kids—the same neighborhood where Mary is presently walking her dog—Robert slows his car down. It peeves him, the way some people drive through the neighborhood, completely disregarding the fact that there are small kids who might run out into the street at any moment. The posted speed limit is 25 miles per hour. Some people drive through as fast as 40; Robert slows his own vehicle to 30.

As Robert turns down Oak Lane, he does not see Mary walking her dog approximately fifty feet in front of him. Nor does he see her when his car is just 20 feet away from her. He does not see her at all until just before the thud. Robert noticed Mary less than a second before he hit her. He tried to swerve to avoid her, but it was too late. His car grazed Mary, throwing her onto the grass next to the road.

Mary, as it turned out, never saw Robert, either; her head had been turned to the side to keep the cold wind off her face.

Fortunately, Mary's injuries were less severe than they might have been. She suffered only a compound-fracture of her right leg. The total cost of Mary's injuries amounted to $15,000, including the trip by ambulance to the emergency room, surgery to repair the fracture, two nights in the hospital, and follow-up visits to her doctor. Robert was uninjured, but there was a small dent on the front, right side of his car to remind him of the sickening experience of hitting a pedestrian. The cost of repairing the dent was $750.

Who should bear the costs arising from this accident? Should Robert bear all the costs? Should Mary bear all the costs? Should they each be responsible for their own costs? The "tort system" is designed to resolve such questions.

WHAT IS A TORT?

Civil Wrongs

One person does something, intentionally or by accident, that causes harm to another. This event is the essence of a *tort*, a French word derived from the Latin *tortus*, which literally means "twisted." Torts are wrongs committed against individuals or, in some cases, groups. They are addressed in the civil justice system through private litigation. Torts are distinguished from *crimes*, which are wrongs committed against society, and prosecuted by the state in a distinct criminal court system. The criminal law and its courts are addressed in Chapter 13.

The Common Law of Torts

Tort doctrine evolved over the centuries within the common law. It is, for the most part, judge-made law. Courts decide, from case to case, what constitutes an actionable tort. As Oliver Wendell Holmes wrote, "The business of the law of torts is to fix the dividing line between those cases in which a man is liable for harm which he has done, and those in which he is not."[1]

The common law elements for determining liability for a tort include *breach* of a noncontractual[2] *duty* owed to the plaintiff(s), which *causes*, both legally and in fact, *harm* to the plaintiff(s).

Breach of Duty

Not all duties arise through voluntary contracting. Some duties exist simply by virtue of coexisting with others in a community. For example, Jones owes Smith the duty of not punching Smith in the nose (except, perhaps, in self-defense). If Jones does punch Smith, Jones violates a duty, which may result in a tort claim. Many tort duties are of this clear, straightforward variety. Many others are not. For example, Jones has no duty to Smith to avoid taking away Smith's business, to Smith's economic detriment, through fair competition. Jones *does* have a duty to Smith not to take away Smith's business through unfair competition. Two obvious issues arise: (1) Who decides what duties are owed? And (2) how do they decide what duties are owed?

For the most part, the courts decide what extracontractual duties are owed to others in society. Increasingly, so too do legislatures through statutory impositions of duties.

Judges have utilized various mechanisms for determining what constitutes a duty. The chief duty—the one upon which all specific, noncontractual legal obligations are based—is the duty to act "reasonably" under the circumstances. In determining the scope of duties and whether some breach has occurred, courts will ask whether the defendant acted as a reasonable person would have acted. The existence of a duty depends on the court's finding that reasonable people—or the community as a whole—would legitimately expect an individual to behave in a certain way by doing *x* or not *x* in a given set of circumstances. A violation of the reasonable-person standard constitutes a breach of the duty, potentially exposing the violator to liability for resulting harm.

Reasonableness is, to be sure, a vague standard by which to determine duties and breaches of them. The "reasonable person" that courts hold up as the standard for the rest of us to meet may seem unrealistic. The great torts scholar William Prosser referred to the reasonable person as "a fictional person who has never existed on land or sea."[3] The "Reasonable Man," as Lord A. P. Herbert famously caricatured him,

> is always thinking of others; prudence is his guide, and "Safety First" is his rule of life. He is one who invariably looks where he is going and is careful to examine the immediate foreground before he executes a leap or bound; who neither star-gazes nor is lost in meditation when approaching trap-doors or the margin of a dock; who records in every case upon the counter-foils of checks such ample details as are desirable, who never mounts a moving omnibus, and does not alight from any car while the train is in motion; who investigates exhaustively the *bona fides* of every mendicant before distributing alms, and will inform himself of the history and habits of a dog before administering a caress; who believes no gossip, nor repeats it, without firm basis for believing it to be true; who never drives his ball till those in front of him have definitely vacated the putting-green which is his own objective; who never from one year's end to another makes an excessive demand upon his wife, his neighbors, his servants, his ox, or his ass; who in the way of business looks only for that narrow margin of profit which twelve men such as himself would reckon to be "fair," and contemplates his fellow-merchants, their agents, and their goods, with that degree of suspicion and distrust which the law deems admirable; who never swears, gambles, or loses his temper; who uses nothing except in moderation, and even while he flogs his child is meditating only on the golden mean.[4]

It is tempting to compare the reasonable person of tort law and the rational man of economic theory.[5] Neither seems wholly realistic; yet each is a useful device for, respectively, legal and economic analyses.

Causation

In tort law, defendants are not liable simply for breaching some duty owed to others. Plaintiffs must also establish that the defendant's breach *caused* harm. Causation is rarely as straightforward and simple a matter as we might suppose. Even in the realm of the natural sciences, proving causation is a tricky business. It is trickier still in the law of torts, which requires proof of both causation-in-fact and "proximate cause."

Causation-in-fact represents a fairly conventional understanding of the term *causation*: Harm to the plaintiff would not have occurred "but for" the defendant's conduct. If the defendant did not do what she did, when she did it, the plaintiff would not have suffered the harm that he suffered, when he suffered it. This "but for" test may not be foolproof—it may be possible to conceive of cases where the plaintiff would have suffered the same harm from some independent source, had the defendant not done what she did—but for the vast majority of cases, the test works well enough to establish causation-in-fact.

However, any harm will have many in-fact causes. Suppose Roger injures Stanley because Roger drives through a red light and collides with Stanley's car, while Stanley is driving with the right of way through the intersection. We are interested in determining Roger's potential tort liability to Stanley. To that end, we can say with confidence, based on the facts, that Roger's driving through the red light was a cause-in-fact of Stanley's harm. "But for" Roger's breach of the duty to obey the rules of the road, Stanley would not have suffered injury. It can also be said, with utmost confidence, that Stanley would not have been injured "but for" his own act of driving through the intersection at the very time that Roger was running the red light. Thus, Stanley's driving was a cause-in-fact of his own injuries. For that matter, the accident would not have occurred had Stanley never been born. So, Stanley's parents are also a cause-in-fact of Stanley's injury under the "but for" test.

Because any accident is likely to track back to many, many "but for" causes-in-fact, the courts impose an additional causation test designed to determine whether the particular "but for" cause attributable to the defendant warrants the imposition of legal liability. This test is referred to as "proximate cause," and it determines the *legal* cause—the cause recognized by law—of the harm. As generations of law students have discovered, proximate cause is a much more difficult concept to comprehend than causation-in-fact. The rule basically is that the defendant will not be held liable in tort, even if his action was a "but for" cause of the harm, if that action was so remote in time or space that it would be unfair and possibly inefficient to hold that defendant responsible to the plaintiff.

In the famous case of *Palsgraf v. Long Island Railway Co.*[6] for example, New York State's highest court ruled that the railroad was not liable when Mrs. Palsgraf was struck and injured by heavy weight scales that fell on the railway platform. The scales fell because of the shock of an explosion that occurred at the other end of the platform when someone dropped a box of fireworks on the tracks, while attempting, with the assistance of the railway's employees, to board a moving train. The railroad employees accidently dislodged the box of fireworks from the man's hands, as they, respectively, pushed and pulled him onto the train. The court concluded that the railway employees' actions were too remote to constitute the legal cause of the plaintiff's injuries. Without question, "but for" the railway employees' actions, the explosion would not have occurred, which resulted in harm to Mrs. Palsgraf. Their actions, however careless, were not the proximate cause of her injuries.

Harm

After dealing with the element of causation, the element of harm is refreshingly straightforward: no tort liability occurs in the absence of harm. However, what constitutes compensable harm is not so clear. Financial losses, personal injuries, and harm to property always count. Less tangible injuries are more difficult to quantify, such as harm to the psyche, increased risk of disease, and fear. The judicially recognized *types* of harm have expanded over the past century or so.

Types of Torts

The two main types of torts are fault-based and non-fault-based. These terms can be misleading. *Fault-based* means that the defendant's liability turns on whether the court finds that the defendant is at fault. The term *non-fault-based* describes torts for which defendants are liable regardless of their level of fault or blameworthiness. Among these torts are the so-called strict liability offenses, which are introduced in this chapter and addressed in more detail in the next. Fault-based torts include intentional torts and the vast doctrine of negligence law.

Intentional Torts

Torts are distinguished between those—such as negligence—in which intent is not an important component of the breach of duty and those in which the intent of the defendant is vitally important. An intentional tort is one where the defendant intends to act in such a way as to interfere with rights belonging to the plaintiff. The defendant does not need to intend to cause any real harm; nor does the defendant have to be hostile or mean-spirited. A practical joker can be guilty of an intentional tort, if the plaintiff suffers harm as a direct result.

The category of intentional torts is large, encompassing all kinds of actions from battery (intentional inference with another's right to be free from nonconsensual bodily contacts) and false imprisonment (intentional interference with another's right to freely move from one place to another by direct and complete constraint or confinement) to conversion (the intentional misappropriation of another's personal property) and malicious prosecution, also called abuse of process (subjection to unjustifiable litigation). If found guilty of committing an intentional tort, the "tortfeasor" is liable for any and all resulting harm.[7] From an economic point of view, strict liability for intentional torts is generally efficient. When one person does something *intentionally* that causes harm to another, the tortfeasor is overwhelmingly likely to be the least cost avoider. For this reason, intentional torts are fairly uncontroversial among law and economics scholars. Most of the law and economics literature on torts focuses, instead, on the law of accidents (unintentional torts), where various approaches to liability as well as the economic justifications are quite different and far more controversial.

Unintentional Torts: Negligence and Strict Liability

The largest part of tort law concerns not intentional wrongs committed by one person against another, but unintentional accidents in which one or more people are hurt. In these cases, the question arises: Who should bear the costs of the harm? Holmes asserted as a "general principle of our law" that "loss from accident must lie where it falls."[8] This assertion hardly seems accurate today, when "victims" of accidents almost invariably seek to recover from someone (preferably someone with "deep pockets") who is legally liable. Yet, Holmes remains undeniably right that, in many, many cases, the legal system does leave the costs of accidents where they fall. Risk is ubiquitous in the world, and the legal system does not make tort defendants the general insurers of tort plaintiffs against all harms that might befall them.

The predominant legal doctrine governing liability for accidents is the law of negligence. Under the law of negligence, the defendant is legally liable for the plaintiff's harm only if the plaintiff establishes that the defendant, who allegedly caused the accident, failed to act reasonably, or failed to take reasonable precautions to prevent the accident. Society's courts do not expect individuals to avoid accidents *at all costs*; we are only expected to act reasonably under the circumstances. If we act reasonably, we will not be at "fault" for the accident, and therefore not liable for negligence. Acting reasonably means that some, but not all, accidents will be avoided. The costs of those accidents that occur in spite of reasonable precautions are left where they fall.

Negligence, although the dominant legal doctrine for allocating the costs of accidents, is not the only doctrine. It competes with *strict liability*, which governs the allocation of accident costs in certain kinds of cases. For example, where someone is harmed because of a defectively designed or manufactured product, the courts resolve the case not under negligence law but pursuant to special legal rules governing *products liability*. Liability for product defects is determined not by the fault-based reasonableness standard of negligence law. Instead, liability is strict, which means that the defendant—the maker of the defective product—is liable to compensate the plaintiff for harm done *regardless of fault,* and no matter how many precautions the manufacturer took to prevent such accidents from occurring. We consider some of the economic implications of the legal choice between strict liability and negligence in the next chapter.

An Economic Approach to Torts

Why Accidents Happen

From a Coasean economic point of view, torts represent an inability or failure to contract. Torts would not occur in the world of the Coase theorem because complete information would lead all would-be tortfeasors and "victims" to contract costlessly over the risks—defined as the expected harm multiplied by the probability of that harm occurring—associated with the would-be tortfeasor's conduct. Even if it were possible that tort disputes could arise, they would by definition be immediately and costlessly resolved without the need for any third-party (e.g., judicial) involvement. The very existence of tort disputes, and the existence of courts to resolve them, reminds us that the real world is characterized by ubiquitous, and often quite high, transaction costs.

In the real world of positive transaction costs, torts occur for various reasons. First and foremost, people do not have complete information about the risks created by their conduct. Even when the risks are known, people sometimes do not calculate them correctly because of bounded rationality (see Chapter 3); or they fail to act on the basis of accurate risk calculations because the risks created by their conduct are externalized to some third party. Thus, externalities play an important role in the occurrence of accidents and the commission of torts.

To live in a society with others is to live with the risk that someone else will cause you harm, either intentionally or accidentally. In deciding who is responsible for bearing the costs associated with harms of various types, the law of torts allocates risk. However, it does not—nor should it, from an economic point of view—seek to eliminate risk. Any effort to eliminate all risks from the world would be both inefficient and futile; it could not be achieved at any finite cost. The proper goal of tort law, from an economic point of view, is to create incentives for individuals to keep risks to "reasonable" (in legal terms) or "efficient" (in economic terms) levels.

Why Society Compensates Accident Victims

Law professors often state that a primary purpose of the tort system is to make tort victims "whole," by compensating them for the injuries they have suffered as a result of tortfeasors' unreasonable actions. An economic rationale for the legal concept of compensation can be illustrated by a graphical analysis of indifference curves. Indifference curves show a level of utility (or satisfaction) that a person gains from a combination of consumption possibilities.

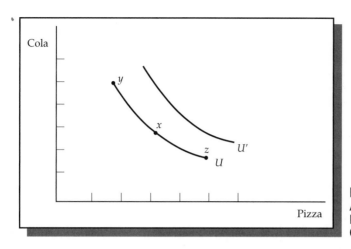

Figure 10-1
A Consumer's
Indifference Curve:
Colas Versus Pizza

Consider, for example, Figure 10-1. The indifference curve U shows a constant level of satisfaction given various combinations of cola and pizza slices per week. That is, a given consumer gains the same amount of overall utility by consuming three colas and three pizza slices (point x) as from consuming five colas and two pizza slices (point y) or five pizza slices and two colas (point z). Note that the consumer requires proportionally more cola for every pizza slice forgone and proportionally more pizza for every cola forgone. This relationship is based on the assumption that consumers prefer variety and get increasingly less utility from consumption of additional units of a single good (decreasing marginal utility). The consumer is willing to trade off some of one good for more of another with a constant level of utility. To get a higher level of overall utility, the consumer will require a larger bundle of both goods, as shown by indifference curve U'.

How does this analysis apply to tort compensation? We can assume that an injury caused by an accident results in a loss of utility, but that the injured party can gain a higher level of utility through compensation. Figure 10-2 depicts the effects on utility of someone who is injured in an accident and loses 50 percent of the function of his left arm. Before the accident, at U_1, he had 100 percent use of his arm and no compensation. After the accident, he is at U_2, with only 50 percent use of his arm and no compensation. He may never regain complete use of his arm, but he can have at least some of his lost utility restored through compensation. The figure suggests that if he receives $100,000 in compensation and maintains 50 percent of the use of his injured arm, he will have the same utility that he had before the accident, when he had no compensation but 100 percent use of his arm. Note also U_3, which shows that the victim would attain the same level of utility from a combination of $50,000 in compensatory damages and 75 percent arm function.

This analysis does not presume that the injured party would have traded the full use of his left arm for $100,000 before the accident. Given the fact of the accident, however, some level of compensation is likely to restore the injured party to something approximating the same level of utility as he had before—or as lawyers say, to "make him whole."

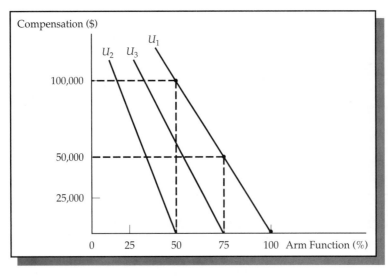

Figure 10-2
Tort Victim's Indifference Curve: Compensation Versus Arm Function

LEGAL AND ECONOMIC FUNCTIONS OF TORT LAW

Scholars have claimed various purposes for tort law, providing many distinct reasons why the law should permit victims to recover compensation from "tortfeasors."

Corrective Justice

Most legal scholars view the purpose of tort recovery to be *corrective justice*. If the defendant acted unreasonably and consequently harmed the plaintiff, justice dictates that the defendant should make the plaintiff whole. The defendant should bear all the costs associated with unreasonable behavior.

Corrective justice is a moral theory of torts, but it can be rationalized in economic terms. Defendants are presumed to be rational actors (in the sense described in Chapter 1); they can be expected to act in ways that they perceive will enhance their utility, welfare, or well-being. From their own subjective point of view, they always act reasonably. But from a larger, social point of view, their conduct may not always be reasonable. They may sometimes be able to maximize their utility by satisfying their own preferences only at a high cost to someone else. If the costs to those others are deemed, through some formal or informal cost-benefit analysis, to be high enough, the courts will conclude that the defendant has acted unreasonably. This conclusion is brought home to the defendant by the full internalization of the costs associated with the defendants' conduct. Thus, corrective justice is attained by internalizing externalities.

Deterrence Through Internalization of Externalities

Cost internalization not only corrects the injustice of torts; it also sends price signals to tortfeasors, creating incentive effects that should, if those price signals are accurate, minimize the occurrence of inefficient torts. By forcing tortfeasors to bear the costs associated with their torts, they will, if they are rational, continue to commit torts only when the benefit to them of engaging in the conduct outweighs the costs, including compensating plaintiffs.

This economic approach to torts is correct as far is it goes, but it does not go far enough. Specifically, it neglects the role of victims in creating or avoiding torts. As we learned in Chapter 4 on Coase's "The Problem of Social Cost," legal disputes invariably constitute joint cost problems. The problems arise not from the action of one party, but from the combined and conflicting actions of both parties. Thus, to maximize efficiency the law must create appropriate incentives for both tortfeasors and tort victims to take efficient precautions to avoid harm. We will see how the tort system has attempted to create appropriate incentives in the next section of this chapter, which concerns the law of negligence.

Punishment

It is sometimes said, mistakenly, that a basic purpose of tort law is to punish wrongdoers. That view is part and parcel of the more general confusion of torts and crimes. Criminal law punishes; tort law compensates. In most tort cases, the courts seek only to remedy plaintiffs' injuries—to "make them whole"—and to deter defendants from creating additional harm through unreasonable conduct. Actual damage awards serve both of these functions, but they are not punitive.

An additional, extraordinary tort remedy—the *punitive damages* award—is designed, at least in part, to punish the tortfeasor. The word *punitive* implies punishment. Yet, some scholars and judges argue that punishment is not even the primary purpose of this remedy. Its purpose, rather, is to create additional deterrent effects where an actual damages remedy is deemed insufficient to induce the efficient level of deterrence. For example, in the case of *Taylor v. Superior Court*,[9] California Supreme Court Associate Justice Clark dissented from a ruling allowing a plaintiff to seek punitive damages against a drunk driver, relying in part on the following argument:

> [A]lthough situations do exist where punitive damage awards have a substantial deterrent effect, others exist in which deterrence is marginal at best. Because restitution [of actual damages] only requires a wrongdoer give up his unjustified gains, compensatory damages will not always constitute deterrence. If the conduct while clearly wrongful is not criminal, a punitive award may be necessary to deter. Otherwise persons contemplating the wrongful conduct may feel they are in a no-lose situation, only gaining by the wrongful conduct. . . .
>
> On the other hand, deterrent effect of a punitive award may be minimal or marginal where the conduct already constitutes a crime and the criminal statute is regularly and effectively enforced. Deterrence by a punitive award is also marginal where wrongful conduct is as likely to result in injury to the wrongdoer as to others.

Consequently, Justice Clark concluded, adding a punitive damages remedy to already available tort and criminal remedies would have little significant, positive effect on the behavior of drunk drivers.

In other cases, however, juries award punitive damages not simply to deter but to punish. It is difficult to discern a legitimate deterrence motive behind a $4 million punitive damages award against a car company for not notifying its dealers or their customers of predelivery damages that required repairs. In 1990, Dr. Ira Gore, Jr., purchased a new BMW automobile from an authorized dealer in Birmingham, Alabama. After he took delivery of the car, Dr. Gore learned that the car had been damaged in transit from Germany to the United States, and repainted prior to delivery to his dealer. BMW notified neither the dealer nor Dr. Gore about this repair, pursuant to a company policy according to which dealers and their customers were only to be notified of predelivery damages that exceeded 3% of the value of the entire car. Dr. Gore sued BMW in Alabama state court, alleging that this failure to disclose amounted to a fraudulent misrepresentation of a material fact. He claimed that he paid for an undamaged, not-repainted "new" BMW, and what he received instead was a damaged, repainted "new" BMW, which was worth less. The jury determined that the automaker was liable, and awarded compensatory damages of $4,000, plus punitive damages of $4 million.[10] It would seem ludicrous to claim that the entire $4.4 million award was intended to deter but not punish BMW.

Because of the BMW case and several other high-profile decisions, punitive damages awards have a bad reputation. In reality, enormous punitive damages awards, although widely publicized in the press, are rare. When juries *do* award huge punitive damages, those awards typically are whittled down by higher courts.[11] In the BMW case, for example, the Alabama Supreme Court cut the jury's punitive damages award in half.[12] Subsequently, the Supreme Court of the United States threw out the punitive damages awarded entirely, finding that it was "grossly excessive," and therefore violative of the Due Process Clause of the U.S. Constitution.[13] Nevertheless, the Supreme Court expressly acknowledged in that case that the purpose of punitive damages awards is not only to deter but also to punish.[14]

Maximizing Social Welfare by Minimizing the Total Costs of Torts

The three sets of costs involved in any tort or potential tort situation are (1) the costs of taking precautions to avoid the tort; (2) the costs associated with the tort, if it occurs; and (3) the administrative costs associated with resolving tort disputes. The chief goal of tort law, according to Judge (and former Yale Law School Professor and Dean) Guido Calabresi, is to minimize the sum of these three sets of costs.[15] We already touched upon (and will discuss more extensively *inter alia*) tort costs and the costs of precaution/avoidance. A few words are in order, however, about the third set of costs: administrative costs.

Lawyers and the court system are both parts of the transaction cost economy. Lawyers are expensive, even when they are used to avoid litigation. When disputes arise and go to court, the legal costs for both parties can be enormous. Moreover, judicial resources are constrained; the courts can only deal with so many cases over a certain period of time. Thus, each filed case imposes substantial marginal costs on the court system. To a significant extent, the costs of litigation, both for parties and for the courts themselves, depend on the legal rules the courts choose for deciding cases. Some legal rules are more complicated, and therefore more costly to apply, than others. Some legal rules engender more litigation, and so are more costly than others. Consequently, if the goal of tort law is to minimize the total costs of the torts, it is not enough to focus on creating incentives for tortfeasors and tort victims to take efficient precautions. We must also pay attention to the administrative costs associated with any particular legal approach to resolving tort disputes.

THE LAW AND ECONOMICS OF NEGLIGENCE

Simple Negligence: Creating Incentives for Reasonable Behavior by Tort Defendants

A defendant is liable for negligence, an unintentional tort, if that person acted unreasonably in causing harm by breaching some (noncontractual) duty owed to the plaintiff. By holding defendants liable when their unreasonable conduct causes harm, the courts create incentives for defendants to take precautions against future accidents.

Defining What Is Reasonable: The Learned Hand Formula

In the famous case of *United States v. Carroll Towing Co.*,[16] Judge Learned Hand articulated, in algebraic terms, an economic formula for determining whether tort defendants have acted reasonably. The case concerned a barge, the *Anna C.*, which broke away from the pier to which it was tied, along with a flotilla of other barges, when the defendant, Carroll Towing, was attempting to move one of those other barges. The *Anna C.* floated uncontrolled downstream, where it collided with a tanker, which caused a breach in the *Anna C.*'s hull. The barge sank along with its cargo, including flour owned by the U.S. government, which sued along with the *Anna C.*'s owner and several other plaintiffs who owned lost cargo. In holding the owner of the *Anna C.* responsible, rather than the defendant, Carroll Towing, Judge Hand set out the following formula:

> Since there are occasions when every vessel will break from her moorings, and since, if she does, she becomes a menace to those about her; the owner's duty, as in other similar situations, to provide against resulting injuries is a function of three variables: (1) The probability that she will break away; (2) the gravity of the resulting injury, if she does; (3) the burden of adequate precautions. Possibly it serves to bring this notion into relief to state it in algebraic terms: if the probability be called P; the injury, L; and the burden, B; liability depends upon whether B is less than L multiplied by P: i.e., whether $B < PL$.

Applying the Learned Hand Formula

In the more recent case of *McCarty v. Pheasant Run, Inc.*,[17] Judge Richard Posner usefully expounded on Learned Hand's formula for determining negligence liability:

> Unreasonable conduct is merely the failure to take precautions that would generate greater benefits in avoiding accidents than the precautions would cost.

> Ordinarily . . . the parties do not give the jury the information required to quantify the variables that the Hand formula picks out as relevant. That is why the formula has greater analytic than operational significance. Conceptual as well as practical difficulties in monetizing personal injuries may continue to frustrate efforts to measure expected accident costs with the precision that is possible, in principle at least, in measuring the other side of the equation—the cost of burden of precaution. For many years to come juries may be forced to make rough judgments of reasonableness, intuiting rather than measure the factors in the Hand Formula; and so long as their judgment is reasonable, the trial judge has no right to set it aside, let alone substitute his own judgment.

Judge Posner's point seems to be that, even though we can derive a mathematical formula for determining what constitutes reasonable conduct so as to minimize the sum of accident and accident-avoidance costs, it is not easy to apply that formula in actual cases because of transaction costs: information about accident and accident-avoidance costs is itself costly and often lacking in court. It is simply not possible for the trier-of-fact accurately to determine the burden of precaution, if both the probability and the magnitude of the harm are significantly uncertain. The following case exemplifies the kind of "rough judgments" that Judge Posner concludes are inevitable.

Winn Dixie Stores, Inc. v. Benton

576 So. 2d 359 (1991)

Stone, J.

The appellee was injured in a slip and fall in appellant's market. We affirm a final judgment, entered following a jury verdict for the plaintiff.

***

At the point of the fall there was a puddle of milk, five to eight inches long and three to four inches wide. There were also milk drops on the floor in a thirty foot trail from the milk container case to the puddle and for another fifty feet from the puddle to the checkout lines. The drops were in an even pattern, one to one and a half feet apart. A leaky half gallon or gallon milk carton, one quarter empty, was found at the checkout area immediately after the fall. The appellant asserts that the store is normally busy at the time of the accident but appellee argues that this is refuted by the evidence that there were no other customers in the dairy aisle. The floor had not been swept for more than one-half hour prior to the incident. There was evidence that the store manager did not conduct his customary floor inspection that afternoon, and the manager's

testimony that he had "inspected" that particular aisle fifteen minutes before the accident was questioned by plaintiff's challenges to the credibility of the witness.

***

It was plaintiff's burden to prove that the milk was on the floor sufficiently long to charge Winn Dixie with notice. Notice may be proved by circumstantial evidence. It has frequently been recognized that the condition of the floor, the nature of the substance on the floor, and the surrounding circumstances, may be sufficient to support an inference by the jury that a dangerous condition existed long enough for the store employees to know, or that they should have known, of the condition. Under such circumstances the issue is for the jury to resolve even where the evidence may be susceptible of more than one reasonable inference.

***

It was within the province of the jury to decide whether the milk had been dripping for a sufficiently long period to be discovered in the exercise of reasonable care.

Warner, J., dissenting.

In my view the evidence shows that a maximum of five to ten minutes passed between the last time a store employee walked down the aisle and the injury to appellee occurred. The milk puddle was fresh and there were no tire tracks through it. The evidence is insufficient to show that the management knew or should have known that the dripping milk was on the floor for a sufficient time to be discovered. ■

***

The defendant in *Winn Dixie* was liable not simply because the plaintiff slipped on milk that had been spilt on its floor but because the jury found it to be at *fault* for the injuries the plaintiff sustained because it had not mopped up the spilt milk quickly enough. The appellate court does not specify just how quickly it expected the defendant to mop up the spill; it only finds that the jury was reasonable in concluding that the store was negligent for not mopping up the spill sooner than it actually did. The store's delay was unreasonable. However, Justice Warner, in dissent, asserts that there was insufficient evidence for the jury to conclude that Winn Dixie was unreasonable.

The Incentive Effects of Negligence Liability for Tort Defendants

Whether you agree with the majority or the dissent in *Winn Dixie*, consider the incentive effects the decision creates for Winn Dixie and other grocery stores. The jury's finding that the store was negligent and legally responsible for the plaintiff's injuries because of its failure to mop up the spilt milk within a reasonable amount of time, and its award of damages to the plaintiff, has created economic incentives for the store to be more careful in the future. But how careful? Well, we wouldn't expect the store immediately to take any and all precautions to prevent future accidents from slippage on spilt milk. We would only expect that Winn Dixie would take precautions up to that point where the costs of any further precaution would exceed the expected benefits. Those expected benefits would equal reductions in the expected liability stemming from a future accident, such as occurred in the *Winn Dixie* case. The store will engage in a cost-benefit analysis to determine the efficient level of precaution, given its calculations of the probability and magnitude of future accidents. In other words, it will act in such a way as to minimize the sum of its own accident and accident-avoidance costs.

This calculation does not necessarily mean, however, that the simple negligence rule ensures an efficient outcome. From an economic point of view, two factors are missing from the analysis: (1) the plaintiff's conduct, which can affect the costs of accidents every bit as much as the defendant's conduct; and (2) the administrative costs of implementing and enforcing the legal rule in the court system. We will defer consideration of administrative costs until later in this chapter. Next, we consider how the conduct of plaintiffs can be incorporated into a social cost-benefit analysis designed to minimize the sum of accident and accident-avoidance costs.

Influencing Plaintiffs' Incentives: Defenses to Negligence

Negligence law accounts for the costs generated by the conduct of plaintiffs in two main ways. First, it defines what constitutes "reasonable" behavior for purposes of determining liability. Under a simple negligence rule, if the court finds the defendant acted reasonably, then the defendant is not liable, which means that the plaintiff is left bearing the costs. To the extent tort plaintiffs must bear costs from tort defendants' "reasonable" conduct, they will have an incentive to take efficient precautions to prevent or minimize those costs. Courts can adjust the incentive effect for both plaintiffs and defendants by increasing or decreasing the scope of what counts as "reasonable" conduct for negligence defendants.

However, attempting to adjust plaintiffs' and defendants' incentives merely by defining or redefining what constitutes "reasonable" behavior is insufficient, by itself, to create incentives for *both* parties to take efficient precautions because it requires a winner-take-all outcome: either the defendant acted reasonably and the plaintiff bears all the costs, or the defendant acted unreasonably and the plaintiff bears none of the costs. In a case where *both* parties failed to take efficient precautions—not at all a rare case—the court cannot create incentives for both parties, at the same time, to take additional precautions merely by playing with the definition of "reasonable" conduct.

However, courts use other mechanisms to affect the incentives of both parties, namely, negligence *defenses*. When a plaintiff brings a negligence claim against a defendant, the defendant is permitted to raise certain defenses that may allow it to avoid or minimize its liability. These defenses all concern the conduct of the plaintiff. They include, most prominently, contributory and comparative negligence.

Contributory Negligence

Reasonable people should realize that "there will be a certain amount of negligence in the world." As a consequence, they have a "duty to take precautions against the negligence of others."[18] This duty is the basis for the contributory negligence defense, which focuses on the reasonableness of the plaintiff's own conduct. In states (fewer and fewer) that recognize this defense, the defendant can avoid liability entirely by showing that the plaintiff did not act reasonably under the circumstances.

In the famous English case of *Butterfield v. Forrester*,[19] the plaintiff was injured when the horse he was riding collided with an obstruction that the defendant had placed in the road. The collision occurred at twilight, when the obstruction could not be seen from more than 100 yards away. Someone riding slowly and with care might have seen the obstruction and avoided it, but the plaintiff had been riding "violently," and did not see the obstruction before he collided with it. The defendant was negligent in placing the obstruction in the road. But the court determined that the plaintiff, too, was negligent in riding without "reasonable and ordinary care." Under the rule of contributory negligence, the plaintiff's negligence absolved the defendant of legal responsibility for the harm.

It is easy to see how the defense of contributory negligence creates incentives for plaintiffs that are equivalent to the incentives created for defendants by the simple negligence rule. If plaintiffs know that they cannot recover for injuries they suffer as the result of defendants' negligent conduct, unless they act reasonably themselves, they will (in theory at least) take reasonable precautions.

The contributory negligence defense, thus, seems to resolve the problem of factoring the conduct of plaintiffs into the equation, but it does so only at the cost of ignoring the defendant's negligence. If the defendant is negligent but the plaintiff is not at all negligent, then the defendant is liable under the rule of simple negligence.

If the plaintiff is also negligent, then, under the rule of contributory negligence, the defendant is off the hook, even if the plaintiff is only slightly negligent and defendant is very negligent. This contributory negligence rule reduces the incentives of defendants to take reasonable precautions, at least in cases where plaintiffs are likely to be at least slightly negligent. Moreover, the fact that the plaintiff is negligent does not automatically mean that the plaintiff could have avoided the accident at less cost than the defendant. When defendants who are least cost avoiders are insulated from liability by the rule of contributory negligence, the likely result is inefficient underprecaution by potential defendants and inefficient overprecaution by potential plaintiffs. The contributory negligence defense is also widely perceived to be unfair to worthy, even if slightly negligent, plaintiffs, which may explain why this rule is in decline.

To ameliorate the perceived unfairness to plaintiffs, courts experimented with various legal devices for avoiding the contributory negligence defense. Some courts resorted to the very policies that underlay contributory negligence to avoid applying the rule. In *Levi v. Southwest Louisiana Electric Membership Cooperative*,[20] the plaintiff, an oil-field worker, was electrocuted while he was on the mast of a truck. The mast either touched or came close to touching the high-power lines. The court held the defendant liable despite the plaintiff's clear contributory negligence, noting that "the ordinary reasonable person, and even more so the power company, is required to realize that there will be a certain amount of negligence in the world." In other words, if potential tort plaintiffs must foresee and take reasonable precautions against the occasional negligence of potential tort defendants, so must tort defendants foresee and take reasonable precautions against the occasional contributory negligence of tort plaintiffs.[21]

Other courts adopted a rule known as Last Clear Chance as a means of ameliorating the perceived unfairness to plaintiffs under the contributory negligence defense. Under this rule, the defendant remains liable, despite the plaintiff's contributory negligence, if the defendant had the last clear chance to avoid the accident by the exercise of ordinary care.[22] Returning to the facts of the *Butterfield v. Forrester* case, if the defendant had noticed the plaintiff riding quickly toward the obstruction the defendant had placed in the road, and had the time and ability to forewarn the plaintiff, but did not, the defendant would likely have been liable under the rule of Last Clear Chance, despite the plaintiff's contributory negligence. In jurisdictions applying this rule, the entire burden is shifted back and forth between the defendant and the plaintiff in serial fashion: if the defendant was negligent, he bears all the costs, unless the plaintiff was at all contributorily negligent, in which case the plaintiff bears all the costs, unless the defendant had the last clear chance to avoid the accident through the exercise of reasonable case, in which case the defendant bears all the costs.

The courts' best efforts to avoid the undesirable consequences of the contributory negligence defense have not, however, managed to resolve the basic economic problem, which is to minimize the sum of accident and accident-avoidance costs. This issue requires the creation of appropriate incentives for both tort plaintiffs and defendants to take efficient, but not excessive, precautions. And that goal cannot be accomplished, in cases where both parties acted unreasonably, by focusing on the conduct of plaintiffs and defendants, one at a time, in serial fashion.

The economic problem of contributory negligence was well expressed by Justice James Hardin Faulkner of the Alabama Supreme Court in *Golden v. McCurry*:

> The question of whether contributory or comparative negligence should be adopted in this state is riddled with economic considerations. Judge Learned Hand formulated an algebraic equation to determine negligence: The defendant is liable if the loss (injury) caused by the accident multiplied by the probability of its occurrence is greater than the cost of avoiding the accident. . . . The economically efficient solution, therefore, is to require the smaller cost to be incurred if it will prevent the larger accident cost. . . .
>
> In application to contributory negligence, if the plaintiff can prevent a $1000 accident at a cost of $50 and the defendant's avoidance cost is $100, the economically efficient solution is to refuse the plaintiff any recovery for failure to avoid the total loss at the lesser cost. If the defendant is liable in all instances without regard to the precautionary measures the plaintiff could have taken, there is no economic incentive for the plaintiff to avert the accident.
>
> On the other hand, if the defendant is able to avoid the $1000 loss at a cost of $50 and the plaintiff's cost is $100, the defense of contributory negligence (assuming it is applicable) still mandates that the plaintiff cannot recover at all. In essence, therefore, this defense sanctions the least economically efficient solution because it provides no incentive for the defendant to spend the lesser avoidance cost cognizant that, if the plaintiff contributed even a little bit, the defendant will incur no liability (expense) at all.[23]

Comparative Negligence

Because of the perceived unfairness, but also the inefficiency, of the contributory negligence defense, virtually all states have by now replaced it with the rule of comparative negligence.

Like contributory negligence, the rule of comparative negligence examines the reasonableness of the plaintiff's conduct, but not in isolation from the defendant's conduct. Rather, it compares the parties' respective reasonableness or negligence. Most importantly, the outcome under comparative negligence, unlike contributory negligence or simple negligence, is not necessarily a winner-take-all game, in which either the plaintiff or the defendant is responsible for all the costs. Under comparative negligence, legal responsibility and economic costs can be shared, as the following case demonstrates.

Scott v. Alpha Beta Company
104 Cal. App. 3d (1980)

Ashby, J.

Plaintiff Phameline Scott slipped and fell in a grocery store of defendant Alpha Beta Company. A jury found defendant 60 percent negligent and plaintiff 40 percent negligent and awarded plaintiff $120,000 damages after reduction on account of her negligence. . . . Defendant appeals from the judgment . . .

contending there is no substantial evidence of negligence on its part. Plaintiff also appeals from the judgment, contending there is no substantial evidence of contributory negligence on her part.

At about 7 p.m. on September 10, 1976, plaintiff walked into defendant's grocery store at 3581 Century Boulevard in Lynwood. It was raining "kind of heavy" at the time, and had been raining all day.

Defendant's employees had placed a 20-foot long rubber mat inside the entrance to the store, because defendant's terrazzo floor was known to become slippery when wet. Normally the store has about 2,000 customers per day.

When plaintiff stepped off the rubber mat, she slipped; her leg went out from underneath her and she fell down. Lying on the floor, plaintiff noticed that the floor was wet.

Plaintiff suffered injury to her left knee and had surgery shortly after the accident. Her knee will never be normal and she may require further surgery or an artificial knee in the future.

***

Dr. Silver testified on behalf of defendant that based upon a review of plaintiff's medical records in his opinion plaintiff had a weakness of the left leg and a "trick knee" prior to the accident, and that such condition was compounded by plaintiff's obesity. In his opinion it was possible plaintiff's knee gave out on her to cause her fall.

This evidence is relevant not only on the issue of proximate cause but also on the issue of contributory negligence, the theory being that persons with known handicaps may have to exercise a greater degree of care in particular circumstances than other persons.

It was raining rather heavily and according to the defense witnesses plaintiff was wearing pink furry house slippers. A person in plaintiff's position might reasonably be expected to know that the floor adjacent to the mat could be wet, even without negligence on defendant's part, or that her slippers might remain wet when she reached the end of the mat. In her testimony plaintiff made no claim to having taken any special cautions in stepping from the mat to the floor. The jury might have thought plaintiff should have seen water on the floor. Under all the circumstances, we think the jury might reasonably conclude that plaintiff failed to exercise due care for her own safety.

The judgment is affirmed. ■

***

The facts of *Scott v. Alpha Beta* are similar to those of the *Winn Dixie* case (excerpted on pages 216–217), but the outcome is strikingly different. In *Winn Dixie*, the court applied the simple negligence rule, which focused only on the conduct of the defendant. Because the defendant was negligent, the store was liable for all of the plaintiff's injuries, regardless of any negligence on the plaintiff's part. If the plaintiff had been negligent in *Winn Dixie*, and the court had applied the rule of contributory negligence, then the defendant would not have been liable at all, no matter how negligent its conduct. In *Scott*, under the rule of comparative negligence, the court was able to compare the respective negligence of both plaintiff and defendant, and the outcome of the case apportioned responsibility between them.

In the *Scott* case, the plaintiff's injuries totaled $200,000. The court held the defendant 60 percent responsible for those injuries, and therefore required it to pay $120,000 in damages. The plaintiff was unable to recover the balance of $80,000 that the jury concluded was due to her own negligence. Recall that under a simple negligence rule, with no defenses, the plaintiff would have recovered the entire $200,000, providing her with no incentives to take more care in the future. On the other hand, under a contributory negligence regime, the plaintiff would have recovered nothing from the defendant, once the jury determined that the plaintiff failed to exercise due care. So, the defendant would have had no incentive to exercise greater care in the future. In a comparative negligence jurisdiction, the plaintiff's own negligence usually is not a complete bar to recovery.

Consider the incentive effects for both parties of the comparative negligence rule, as applied in *Scott v. Alpha Beta*. Prior to the court's ruling, the plaintiff suffered a loss of $200,000. This loss created a huge incentive for her to be more careful in the future. But the store, prior to the determination that it was liable, had no incentive to take any additional steps (beyond those it had already taken) to avoid slippery-floor accidents. After the court's ruling, both parties faced added incentives to economize on costs. The court's ruling left the plaintiff with $80,000 in costs (assuming no insurance coverage[24]), creating a substantial inducement for the plaintiff to be substantially more careful in the future. At the same time, the court required the defendant to pay 60 percent of the plaintiff's total costs or $120,000. This substantial liability created an incentive for the defendant to be more careful than previously to mop up slippery spots on its floor.

Under the assumption of rational behavior, the defendant can be expected to invest in precaution up to that point where the cost of the next unit of precaution (marginal cost) exceeds the consequent reduction in expected liability (marginal benefit). Expected liability, in this case, would be equal to the discounted value of future harm multiplied by the probability that the store would be held liable the next time a customer slips on the floor.

The key point is that application of the comparative negligence doctrine provides both parties with incentives to minimize the sum of accident costs and avoidance costs. This presumes, of course, that courts are able to apportion fault accurately between the parties. At least in cases where both parties acted unreasonably, comparative negligence is arguably superior, from the perspective of economic efficiency, to other fault-based tort regimes that treat cost allocation as an all or nothing proposition, imposing financial responsibility on only one party—the defendant *or* the plaintiff.

By comparing the behavior of the plaintiff with that of the defendant, the rule of comparative negligence supposedly creates incentives for both parties to take precautions. Still, it is not obvious that plaintiffs always will take reasonable precautions if defendants have already done so. Presumably, plaintiffs would allow defendants to bear all the costs of precaution only if they could be confident that the defendants' precautions reduced the product of risk of harm times the magnitude of harm from a potential accident below the marginal cost of the plaintiff's first unit of precaution. It is unlikely, however, that the plaintiff could ever be so confident because of information constraints and asymmetries (transaction costs). Plaintiffs, generally, will not be in a position to know (1) how much, if any, precaution the defendant has taken; (2) the expected value of the defendant's precautions, in terms of reducing the probability or magnitude of future harm; or (3) whether a court, in future litigation, would consider the defendant's precautions to be "reasonable" under the circumstances, so that the defendant would be relieved of liability. In the absence of this information, potential plaintiffs have reason not to rely much on the accident-avoidance measures of potential defendants. Most significantly, if an accident does occur after the defendant has taken precautions, and those precautions are deemed "reasonable" in court, the defendant will not be liable at all; the plaintiff will be left to bear all the costs.

Throughout this discussion, we have treated comparative negligence as a unitary regime for allocating the costs of accidents. In fact, several varieties of comparative negligence are used. The variety we have been discussing is known as "pure" or "apportioned" comparative negligence, in which damages are apportioned between the parties based on their respective contributions to the accident, as determined by the trier-of-fact. Another variety, far and away the most popular among states that have abandoned contributory negligence, is known as "modified" comparative negligence. Under this doctrine, responsibility is apportioned, as under the "pure" rule, but the plaintiff cannot recover at all from the defendant if the plaintiff's negligence either equals (the "Wisconsin rule") or exceeds (the "New Hampshire rule") the defendant's negligence. A final variety of comparative negligence, known as the "slight-gross system," disallows any recovery by the plaintiff whose own negligence is more than slight in comparison to the defendant's. These variations in the allocation of costs between negligent plaintiffs and defendants, depending on the apportionment of responsibility for the harm, can be expected to affect the respective incentives of the parties to undertake precautions to avoid future accidents.

THE ROLE OF INSURANCE IN NEGLIGENCE LAW

To the extent that negligence law is concerned with creating incentives for defendants and plaintiffs to take reasonable or efficient precautions, a significant problem arises. It is one thing to judge in hindsight—after an accident has already occurred—whether a party exercised reasonable care. Precautionary decisions are made *ex ante*, before the fact of an accident. At that time, substantial uncertainty would reflect high information costs about the probability and magnitude of the harm, the range of available precautions, and their respective costs and benefits.[25] In this circumstance, it seems unlikely that the Learned Hand Formula (defendant is liable if B is less than P * L) could function. Courts could not expect potential tort plaintiffs and defendants to achieve efficient levels of precautions under substantial *ex ante* uncertainty.

Here is where the insurance industry enters the picture. Insurance—in particular, the premiums that individuals pay for accident, liability, and health insurance—provides much of the information individuals require to calculate *ex ante* the costs of accidents and the benefits and costs of precautions designed to avoid or minimize the harm from accidents. The insurance premiums individuals pay are based on the insurance companies' assessments of probabilities and magnitudes of harm (expected costs) stemming from all manner of accidents, based on massive statistical information the industry collects about types, rates, and costs of accidents. It is worthwhile for the insurance industry, but not individuals, to engage in this costly process of information collection and analysis because the industry can spread the costs among all its customers. Meanwhile, through the different rates they charge on individual policies for various levels of coverage, insurance companies send appropriate price signals to their customers about the expected costs of differential levels of risk, *regardless of what amount, if any, of insurance any given individual actually purchases.*

The cost schedule of premiums for different levels of coverage, in effect, quantifies much (if not all) of the information individuals need to know about the expected costs of accidents and the expected benefits of different levels of precaution. This places individuals in a position to determine *ex ante* the reasonable (or efficient) level of precaution. Thus, the existence of insurance markets allows the Learned Hand formula to function before the fact of harm (and before the fact of litigation), as well as in judicial hindsight. For this reason, laws that require insurance for engaging in certain activities, such as driving an automobile or operating a hazardous waste facility, may be efficient.[26] Such laws, in essence, force individuals to acquire the information needed to determine what level of precaution to take. On the other hand, insurance can lead to an increase in accidents because of two problems known as *moral hazard* and *adverse selection*. Evidence suggests, for example, that automobile insurance leads drivers to be *less* careful than they otherwise would be. This problem is known as moral hazard. A driver without insurance might be expected to drive more carefully, on average, than a driver with insurance because, if an accident occurs for which no one else is liable, the driver without insurance must bear the costs of damage to the car and possible personal injury. The driver with insurance is unlikely to be so careful, however, because, in case of an accident, the driver will not bear the costs personally; rather, the costs will be borne by the insurance company and, ultimately, spread among that company's policy holders.

The associated problem of adverse selection reflects the fact that even though insurance companies are adept at accumulating and assessing statistical information, they are not in a good position to determine *ex ante* the risk profile of each individual to whom they provide coverage. The insurance premiums companies charge will be based on the average (statistical) probabilities and magnitudes of harm from accidents. Among all those who pay the premiums—the insured—some will be risk-averse and others will be risk-takers. At the outset, the insurance company does not know who belongs to which category, but risk-takers know who they are and why they want insurance. They are likely to be the first to insure against their own risky behavior. As they engage in that risky behavior, they have more accidents, which the insurance company is obliged to cover. Consequently, the risk-takers drive up the costs of coverage not only for themselves but for all policy holders. Premiums will increase. Risk-averse individuals, however, will not be willing to pay as much for insurance as the risk-takers because their own chances of having an accident are lower to begin with precisely because they are risk-averse. Over time, as premiums increase, it becomes increasingly likely that the bulk of the insured will be the risk-takers.

Insurance companies use several mechanisms for dealing with problems of moral hazard and adverse selection. For one, they try as best they can to differentiate premiums based on the risk profiles of different groups of consumers. It is well known, for example, that young, inexperienced drivers have higher rates of accidents than older drivers; therefore, insurance premiums are higher for younger drivers. Those who drive sports cars (signaling that they are, relatively speaking, risk-takers) also pay higher premiums than those who drive family cars (and are, therefore, presumed to be more risk-averse). Those who drive cars with extra safety features often get a discount because, by taking the precaution of spending more on a car to acquire the extra safety devices, the driver is reducing the expected magnitude and, perhaps, the probability of a potential accident, thereby reducing the expected costs to the insurance company. The insurance company, which wants to encourage this kind of activity, will pass on some of the expected cost savings to the individual driver in the form of a reduced or discounted premium.

Insurance companies also tailor their premiums to the past experiences of individual drivers. If you have more than one accident, chances are your insurance premium is going to increase; too many accidents and your coverage may be dropped entirely, in which case you will have to find another company to insure you, almost certainly at a significantly higher cost. In extreme cases, you will not be able to find insurance at any price, in which case you drive at your own risk, including the risk of having your diver's license suspended for driving without insurance.

Another mechanism that insurance companies use to ameliorate the moral hazard problem is the *deductible*, which is a fixed dollar amount the driver must pay toward the cost of repair or liability before the insurance company becomes financially responsible. It is quite common, for example, for drivers to carry automobile insurance with a $500 deductible, so that they must pay the first $500 of any repair, unless they can prove that someone else was entirely responsible for the accident.

Insurance is relevant to the tort system in one further, extremely important, respect: It provides an alternative to tort liability. Even if accident law were abolished entirely, the insurance industry would provide an alternative mechanism for compensating tort victims. We would also expect potential tort victims to compensate for the abolition of the tort system by purchasing more insurance. In fact, insurance has replaced the tort system as the primary mechanism of compensation for automobile accidents in states that adopted a so-called "no-fault" system. In this system, all parties to automobile accidents are compensated by their own insurance companies for the harms they suffered, unless they can clearly establish that others were at fault.[27]

CHAPTER SUMMARY

This chapter focused on negligence, which is the dominant legal regime for resolving accident disputes. Various negligence rules seek to create incentives for tort plaintiffs (victims) and defendants (tortfeasors) to take efficient precautions to avoid accidents *and* minimize administrative costs for the courts in order to minimize the total costs of accidents in society.

Although the negligence rule predominates, it has not displaced all other rules for assessing tort liability. Strict liability retains a strong hold over certain types of torts. Debate also continues in the law and economics literature about whether negligence or strict liability is preferable (i.e., more efficient) as a mechanism for resolving disputes over accidents. Chapter 11 surveys the law of strict liability and compares strict liability with negligence. Chapter 12, then, addresses contemporary debates over the merits of measures to reform the current tort system

QUESTIONS AND PROBLEMS

1. What is the goal of the tort system?
2. Would a "tort system" be necessary if the standard assumptions of neoclassical economic theory all held true (i.e., in the world of the Coase theorem)? Why or why not? ⬥
3. Is the "reasonable person" of tort law similar to, or different from, the rational actor of economic theory?
4. Why would a simple negligence rule be inefficient, if negligence defences were not available?
5. Why has the rule of contributory negligence been replaced in nearly all U.S. jurisdictions by the rule of comparative negligence?

6. How does the Learned Hand Formula seek to allocate tort liability? What problems tend to render it ineffectual?

7. Why aren't tort defendants liable for any and all harms that befall plaintiffs as a result of defendants' actions?

8. Many law and economics scholars would amend the Learned Hand Formula to equate the marginal cost of harm with the marginal benefit of precaution. How, if at all, would this amendment change the analysis of a case such as *Winn Dixie*?

9. How are economic rationales for tort compensation consistent with the Kaldor-Hicks efficiency criterion?

10. How does the insurance industry affect the tort system?

NOTES

1. Oliver Wendell Holmes, *The Common Law* (Boston: Little Brown, [1881], 1923), p. 23.

2. If the duty is contractual, then the dispute is dealt with under the law of contract, rather than tort.

3. William L. Prosser, *Law of Torts* (Minneapolis, MN: West Publishing, 1971), p. 150.

4. Lord Herbert also caricatures "Economic man, whose every action is prompted by the single spur of selfish advantage and directed to the single end of monetary gain." *Uncommon Law* (London: Methuen Publishing Ltd., [1935], 1969), p. 2.

5. Lord A. P. Herbert, *Uncommon Law* (London: Methuen Publishing Ltd. [1935], 1969), pp. 1–3.

6. 248 N.Y. 399, 162 N.E. 99 (1928).

7. Consequently, the analysis of strict liability law, in the next chapter, applies in large measure to intentional torts.

8. Oliver Wendell Holmes, *The Common Law*, (Boston: Little Brown, [1881], 1923), *supra* note 1, p. 94.

9. 24 Cal. 3d 890, 901–3 (1979) (Clark, J., dissenting).

10. *See BMW of North America v. Gore*, 517 U.S. 559, 565 (1996).

11. Punitive damage awards are a central issue in debates about tort reform, which is the subject of Chapter 12.

12. *BMW of North America v. Gore*, 646 So. 2d 619 (Ala. 1994).

13. 517 U.S. 559, 574 (1996).

14. *Ibid.*, at 567, *citing Gertz v. Robert Welch, Inc.*, 418 U.S. 323, 350 (1974).

15. Guido Calabresi, *The Costs of Accidents: A Legal and Economic Analysis* (New Haven, CT: Yale University Press, 1970), pp. 26–29.

16. 159 F. 2d 169, 173 (2d Cir. 1947).

17. 826 F. 2d 1554, 1557 (7th Cir. 1987).

18. William L. Prosser, *Law of Torts* (1971), pp. 171–72.

19. 11 East's Rep. 59, 103 Eng. Rep. 926 (1809).

20. 542 So. 2d 1081, 1086 (La. 1989).

21. Note how this kind of analysis can lead to a *reductio ad absurdem*: Must tort plaintiffs foresee that tort defendants will sometimes negligently fail to act in view of the foreseeable negligence of tort plaintiffs?

22. *See, for example, Davies v. Mann*, 152 Eng. Rep. 588 (1842); *Perin v. Nelson & Sloan*, 119 Cal. App. 2d 560 (1953).

23. 392 So. 2d 815, 819–20 (Ala. 1980), (Faukner, J., concurring in part and dissenting in part).

24. The role of insurance in the tort system is addressed in the next section of this chapter. Even with insurance, plaintiffs will have to bear the costs of deductibles, plus possible increases in premiums.

25. Uncertainty is not always the case. Even in the absence of insurance, individuals today possess a good deal of information about certain risks, such as the hazards of cigarette smoking or heavy drinking. Many of the risks associated with everyday life in society do not stem from such volitional, individual decisions. About those risks, individuals are more likely to be underinformed compared to insurance companies. In addition, studies show that individual assessments of risk often differ markedly from expert risk assessments. Individuals overestimate some risks and underestimate others.

26. Judge Posner argues, to the contrary, that such laws are not efficient because insurance itself

reduces the deterrent effect of the tort system. *See* Richard A. Posner, *An Economic Analysis of Law* (1998), p. 221. He goes on to note, however, that liability insurance does not necessarily render the tort system inefficient (p. 222). He further notes that it need not blunt the deterrent effect of tort law at all, if insurance companies efficiently monitor the safety records of those they insure (p. 222, n. 3). He cites no reason to believe that insurance companies lack sufficient incentive to engage in such monitoring.

27. "No-fault" insurance, as an alternative to the tort system, is examined in greater detail in Chapter 12.

Chapter 11

Torts II: Strict Liability

AN ALTERNATIVE TO NEGLIGENCE

For certain kinds of torts, courts reject the fault-based analysis of negligence law in favor of the rule of strict liability, which holds defendants liable for the harm their actions cause plaintiffs no matter how many precautions the defendants took. The most prominent types of strict liability torts include trespass (previously addressed in Chapter 6), abnormally dangerous or ultrahazardous activities, public nuisances, and products liability—harm resulting from defectively designed or manufactured products.

Strict liability is no recent development in the common law; its roots extend back at least to the fourteenth century. For modern applications of the rule of strict liability, the common point of departure is the nineteenth-century English case of *Rylands v. Fletcher*.[1] In that case, the plaintiff sought to recover damages for harm to his mining operations, when a reservoir defendants were constructing on their land flooded the plaintiff's mine shafts and colliery. The court ruled in the plaintiff's favor but not because of any negligence on the defendant's part. Writing for the court, Lord Cairns, the Lord Chancellor, quoted from an earlier ruling by Justice Blackburn of the Court of Exchequer Chamber:

> We think that the true rule of law is, that the person who, for his own purposes, brings on his land and collects and keeps there anything likely to do mischief if it escapes, must keep it at his peril; and if he does not do so, is prima facie answerable for all the damage which is the natural consequence of its escape. He can excuse himself by shewing that the escape was owing to the Plaintiff's default; or, perhaps, that the escape was the consequence of vis major, or the act of God; but as nothing of this sort exists here, it is unnecessary to inquire what excuse would be sufficient. The general rule, as above stated, seems on principle just. The person whose grass or corn is eaten down by the escaping cattle of his neighbour, or whose mine is flooded by the water from his neighbour's reservoir, or whose cellar is invaded by the filth of his neighbour's privy, or whose habitation is made unhealthy by fumes and noisome vapours of his neighbour's alkali works,

is *damnified without any fault of his own*; and it seems but reasonable and just that the neighbour who has brought something on his own property (which was not naturally there), harmless to others so long as it is confined to his own property, but which he knows will be mischievous if it gets on his neighbour's, should be obliged to make good the damage which ensues if he does not succeed in confining it to his own property.

Lord Cranworth concurred: "If a person brings, or accumulates, on his land anything which, if it should escape, may cause damage to his neighbour, he does so at his peril. If it does escape, and cause damage, *he is responsible, however careful he may have been, and whatever precautions he may have taken to prevent the damage.*"[2]

The Elements of Strict Liability

Guille v. Swan
19 Johns. 381 (1822)

[The defendant landed a hot air balloon in the plaintiff's vegetable garden. The plaintiff sued the defendant for the harm to the vegetable garden caused by his balloon and by the crowd that assembled to see him land it.]

Spencer, CH. J., delivered the opinion of the court:

***

The intent with which an act is done, is by no means the test of the liability of a party to an action of trespass. If the act cause the immediate injury, whether it was intentional, or unintentional, trespass is the proper action to redress the wrong.

***

I will not say that ascending in a balloon is an unlawful act, for it is not so; but it is certain that the aeronaut has no control over its motion horizontally; he is at the sport of the winds, and is to descend when and how he can; his reaching the earth is a matter of hazard. He did descend on the premises of the plaintiff below, at a short distance from the place where he ascended. Now, if his descent, under

such circumstances, would, ordinarily and naturally, draw a crowd of people about him, either from curiosity, or for the purpose of rescuing him from a perilous situation; all this he ought to have foreseen, and must be responsible for. Whether the crowd heard him call for help or not, is immaterial; he had put himself in a situation to invite help, and they rushed forward, impelled, perhaps, by the double motive of rendering aid, and gratifying a curiosity which he had excited. Can it be doubted that if the [the defendant] had beckoned to the crowd to come to his assistance, that he would be liable for their trespass in entering the enclosure? I think not. In that case, they would have been co-trespassers, and we must consider the situation in which he placed himself, voluntarily and designedly, as equivalent to a direct request to the crowd to follow him. In the present case, he did call for help, and may have been heard by the crowd; he is, therefore, undoubtedly, liable for all the injury sustained.

Judgment affirmed. ■

Guille v. Swan, according to Judge Posner,

> is a paradigmatic case for strict liability. (a) The risk (probability) of harm was great, and (b) the harm that would ensue if the risk materialized could be, although luckily was not, great (the balloonist could have crashed into

the crowd rather than into the vegetables). The confluence of these two factors established the urgency of seeking to prevent such accidents.

(c) Yet such accidents could not be prevented by the exercise of due care; the technology in ballooning was insufficiently developed. (d) The activity was not a matter of common usage, so there was no presumption that it was a highly valuable activity despite its unavoidable riskiness. (e) The activity was inappropriate to the place in which it took place—densely populated New York City. The risk of serious harm to others (other than the balloonist himself, that is) could have been reduced by shifting the activity to the sparsely inhabited areas that surrounded the city in those days.

(f) Reinforcing (d), the value to the community of the activity of recreational ballooning did not appear to be great enough to offset its unavoidable risks.

Each of these factors, Judge Posner continues, "is a different facet of a common quest for a proper legal regime to govern accidents that negligence liability cannot adequately control."[3]

Why Strict Liability?

The existence of strict liability, as an alternative to negligence and other fault-based rules, reflects a judicial perception that in some circumstances—involving "extraordinary risk whose existence calls for such special responsibility"[4]—torts defendants should be held liable even though they are not negligent or otherwise at fault for the plaintiff's harm.[5] Liability, in such cases, is based simply on the fact that defendants engaged in conduct that caused harm to the plaintiff. The plaintiff still must prove that the defendant acted in such a way as to cause—both in fact and proximately—their harm. Once it is proven, the defendant's liability is assured, regardless of any efforts to avoid the harm.

Courts and scholars have advanced several positive and normative reasons for preferring strict liability in at least some kinds of cases. The positive reasons include the following: (1) defendants are, in most cases involving "extraordinary risk," the least cost avoiders or insurers of the plaintiffs' harm; (2) defendants are better able to spread the costs associated with the risks created by their conduct; and (3) defendants are better able than the plaintiffs to afford the losses. The normative argument for strict liability is that defendants should internalize the costs associated with their conduct. Whether any or all of these reasons withstand scrutiny remains to be seen.

Defendants as Least Cost Avoiders/Insurers

When the Supreme Court of Wyoming adopted strict liability for defective products in 1986, Justice Cardine wrote in the case of *Ogle v. Caterpillar Tractor, Co.,*

> When a defective article enters the stream of commerce and an innocent person is hurt, it is better that the loss fall on the manufacturer, distributor or seller than on the innocent victim. This is true even if the entities in the chain of production and distribution exercise due care in the defective product's manufacture and delivery. They are simply in the best position to either insure against the loss or spread the loss among all the consumers of the product.[6]

Six years later, the same court reiterated this language and noted that "[t]he risk allocation theory stated in *Ogle* may also be termed a 'cheapest cost-avoider' criterion for strict liability. . . . Under this theory, the 'cheapest cost-avoider' is the person who could avoid the accident at the lowest cost."[7] Similarly, in a concurring opinion in *Escola v. Coca-Cola Bottling, Co.,* California Supreme Court Justice Roger Traynor wrote that manufacturers ought to be subject to strict liability for product defects, in part, because "the manufacturer is best situated to afford such protection."[8]

It seems unlikely, however, that defendants are *always* the best cost avoiders in cases governed by strict liability. In cases where the plaintiff is the best cost avoider, it is inefficient to impose strict liability on the defendant. However, defendants may be the best cost avoiders often enough that imposing liability on defendants as a matter of course is efficient across the run of cases. If defendants are the least cost avoiders in 90 percent of the cases governed by strict liability, then the rule may well be efficient.[9] Moreover, for the other 10 percent of cases, defendants may avail themselves of affirmative defenses to strict liability that might excuse them from liability. Those defenses will be addressed in due course.

Cost-Spreading Effects of Strict Liability

Courts have expressly recognized that cost spreading is among "the fundamental reasons underlying the imposition of strict liability." By imposing strict liability on the defendant, the court "spread[s] the cost of injury from the plaintiff to the consuming public, which will pay a higher price for the product to reflect the increased expense of insurance to the manufacturer resulting from its greater exposure to liability."[10] Still, strict liability is subject to limits, as Judge Kane suggests in his dissent in the following case, a products liability suit against Ford Motor Company for an allegedly defective door lock.[11]

Shepard v. Superior Court of Alameda County
76 Cal. App. 3d 16 (1977)

Kane, J. I dissent.

***

To start with, it is noted that the avowed purpose of imposing strict liability upon the manufacturer is twofold: (1) loss-distribution or risk-spreading and (2) injury-reduction by enhanced safety. The first rationale, risk-spreading, holds the manufacturer liable for injuries resulting from the use of his product because he is in the best position to distribute the loss either by insurance or by increasing the price of

his product. . . . [T]he purpose of strict tort liability is to insure that the costs of injuries resulting from defective products are borne by the manufacturers who put such products on the market rather than by the injured persons who are powerless to protect themselves. . . . [S]trict liability on the manufacturer affords protection to the injured person and works no injustice because the manufacturers can protect themselves through obtaining insurance and dispersing the cost through the prices of the products. The second rationale, the theory of injury reduction, holds the manufacturer liable because he is in the best position to discover and correct the dangerous aspects of his products before any injury occurs. Again, the manufacturer may pass on to the consumer the increased product costs by incorporating them in the purchase price of the merchandise.

Although since its inception the courts have generally tended to broaden the scope of products liability, there are few cases, if any, which have embarked on a thorough and delicate analysis to explore whether the above stated policy goals are indeed promoted by the ever-expanding scope of enterprise liability. It is time for such an examination.

The basic facts of economy teach us that the fashionable trend of a wholesale extension of strict liability proves to be counterproductive in many instances by hampering and arresting, rather than promoting, the policy objectives underpinning the doctrine. Thus, it requires no special economic expertise to realize that the double demand posed by the law, i.e., to make the product absolutely safe on the one hand, and to spread the cost of the ever increasing insurance premiums together with the expense of safety measures to the consumer on the other, becomes increasingly difficult, if not entirely impossible, to meet. It is well to remember that economic forces do not work in a vacuum, but rather in a strict and realistic economic environment where prices of merchandise are greatly influenced (if not entirely determined) by economic rivalry and competition. Under these circumstances, the fundamental assumption of spreading the risk of the enterprise to the consumers at large cannot be attained and materialized. While some portion of the ever growing safety and insurance cost may pass directly to the consumer by way of a higher dollar price, the remainder will take the form of decreased quality not affecting safety and decreased profits. The decreased profits affect the manufacturers first (among them mainly the large segment of small businessmen with limited or marginal capital who have to shoulder the strict enterprise liability side

by side with the huge corporations), then society as a whole. The motion and realistic operation of economic forces have been graphically described by one observer as follows: *"Decreased profits, however, do not stop with the manufacturer.* He distributes them to the shareholders of his corporation, just as he distributes increased prices to the consumers of his product. Moreover, decreased profits do not stop with the shareholders. *Rather, in more or less attenuated form, they pass on to other, broader classes.* The major distribution of decreased profits occurs when shareholders switch their investment to other, more profitable enterprises. When this happens, the liability-bearing manufacturer's enterprise loses its ability to attract investment capital, resulting in decreased industrial activity. *This decreased activity results in losses to several categories. First, the consumer will feel the loss because the manufacturer's ability to produce a better, safer product will diminish. Second, reduced industrial activity will affect labor. Severely diminished profits may force the manufacturer out of business. Even less drastic reductions, however, could reduce the number of new jobs. Finally, reduced economic activity will affect the entire society, in a more or less attenuated form, through lower tax revenues, lower wages, and lower profits for distribution."* . . .

Paying heed to economic realities rather than our own fancy, the courts as a matter of judicial policy must stop the further extension of the strict liability of entrepreneurs, at least to areas where, as here, the determination of damages is speculative and conjectural rather than real and definable. In doing so, we are in line with established law which holds that the manufacturer is not an insurer of the product and that the strict liability of entrepreneurs may not be equated with absolute, limitless liability. As has been emphasized time and time again, in determining the parameters of enterprise liability we must draw a proper balance between the need for adequate recovery and the survival of viable enterprises. The guiding principles to achieve these goals are judicial temperance, evenhandedness and, first and foremost, fairness to all. ■

***

"Deep Pockets"

Some courts hold defendants strictly liable simply because they perceive that defendants, as a class, are able to afford the costs of the harm better than plaintiffs. In *Richman v. Charter Arms Corp.*,[12] Judge Mentz of the Federal District Court for the Eastern District of Louisiana quoted at length from an article by Professor Clarence Morris of the University of Texas Law School:

> The financial burden of disabling personal injury overwhelms most people. While many can bear the cost of minor injury, prolonged infirmity and extended medical expense often exceed the financial competence of common men. Unless [common man] happens to be rich or covered by one of the more generous workmen's compensation plans, he will probably bear the risk less easily than Enterpriser [the defendant]. The preponderant likelihood is that Enterpriser is the better risk bearer of the two.[13]

Internalization of Externalities

Strict liability is also supported by theories of welfare economics, according to which costs must be internalized to the producers in order to ensure allocative efficiency. In the following case, the court explicitly raises this economic argument on behalf of the rule of strict liability.

Doe v. Miles Laboratories, Inc.

675 F. Supp. 1466 (D. Mary. 1987)

Ramsey, J.

A plague inflicts society and this Court is called upon to adjudicate the extent to which the effects will be visited upon its victims. The facts are tragic. In the autumn of 1983, plaintiff Jane Doe, who a week previous had given birth, sought emergency medical treatment for vaginal bleeding. During the course of treatment, the attending physician ordered the administration of 500 units of "Konyne," a blood-coagulation-factor concentrate produced by Cutter Laboratories, a division of Miles. Treatment appeared successful and plaintiff eventually was discharged.

Over the course of the months to follow, plaintiff suffered from a succession of ailments, ultimately being diagnosed as infected by the HTLV-III virus, and as having Acquired Immuno-Deficiency Syndrome-Related Complex (ARC), a predecessor of AIDS. On July 6, 1986, plaintiffs Jane and John Doe filed suit, alleging claims for strict liability in tort [among others]. . . .

***

[S]trict products liability can promote the efficient allocation of resources. Society has chosen to allow market forces to set the price for goods and thus to determine their availability and distribution. In some respects the market is very efficient. The price purchasers pay invariably reflects direct costs such as raw products, capital investment, labor, plus a reasonable rate of return. However, in other respects the market is not efficient. Prices often do not reflect indirect costs. These hidden costs can include the effects of pollution or the expenses of accidents, and are what economists refer to as "externalities."

When the price of an item does not reflect both its direct costs and its externalities, the price will be lower than its actual cost. This lower price will stimulate an inefficient allocation of resources, for persons will be encouraged to buy more of the product than they might if they were paying its true price. Society thus may increase the consumption of the very goods that create pollution, and thus have indirect cleanup costs, or that are defective, and thus have indirect accident costs. Strict products liability shifts the cost back to manufacturers, who will then reprice the goods to reflect their actual costs. Strict products liability therefore affords society a mechanism for a rational allocation of resources.[3] Absent it, the costs of externalities are thrust upon victims or upon society through its governmental welfare programs. In essence, without it there is a subsidy given to the polluting or defective products.

***

It is argued that providers of blood and blood products are promoting the general welfare by making possible improved health. It is argued that it is a fundamental social policy of the State of Maryland to promote the supply of blood and blood products. And it is argued that to allow strict products liability, which given the wide exposure to AIDS due to transfusions could create potentially substantial liability, would so raise costs of production that the supply of blood could be choked off.

The arguments are unpersuasive. . . . Those who choose to operate in the economic marketplace play by the rules applicable to all.

The arguments in favor of strict products liability apply as persuasively to blood and blood products as they do to any other product. First, there is no reason why victims of defective blood should bear the costs where victims of other defective products do not. Second, strict liability would provide the incentive to promote all possible accident prevention, for it is

a rational business decision to keep costs down. Third, the producers are in a better position to spread the costs than are individual consumers. Finally, it makes for a more efficient allocation of social resources when the price of a transfusion of blood or blood products reflects its true costs.

Entrepreneurs by their nature are risk taking individuals. To the extent they need an incentive to engage in socially beneficial activities, the law already provides it in the form of a corporate shield on personal liability. To do as defendant argues, and exempt blood from strict liability would be to subsidize the product by forcing either victims or government through its social welfare programs to bear accident costs. In the absence of a clear expression on the part of the legislature of an intent to subsidize a particular product, it is not this Court's role to create the subsidy indirectly by carving out a Judge made exemption to strict products liability.

***

Accordingly, the Court will deny defendant's motion for summary judgment on plaintiffs' claim for strict products liability. ∎

[3]The argument is often made that strict products liability has the potential to bankrupt manufacturers. Such an argument misses the salutary economic role strict products liability plays. Understood properly, it can be seen that strict liability promotes a rational market place. Society cannot make rational decisions concerning the allocation of resources unless the price reflects the true costs. When the price rises greatly, reflecting the fact the product produces either substantial direct costs or creates widespread externalities, it is rational to discourage or even abandon consumption of that product. Strict products liability thus allows the marketplace to make better informed decisions.

Judge Ramsey proves himself to be a good Pigovian, which is to say, a bad Coasean. As Coase explained in "The Problem of Social Cost," Pigou and other welfare economists were wrong to think that allocative efficiency is always maximized by internalizing externalities to the producer (in this case, the tort defendant). In cases where the victim (the tort plaintiff) is the least cost avoider, imposing liability on the defendant would not maximize allocative efficiency. Coase probably would recognize, however, that if tort defendants were overwhelmingly likely to be least cost avoiders, then a rule of strict liability might make sense as a mechanism for minimizing transaction costs. That argument, however, is not the one Judge Ramsey made in *Doe v. Miles Laboratories, Inc.*

Defenses to Strict Liability

If Coase is right about the joint or social cost nature of externality problems, and it is possible that plaintiffs, often enough, would prove to be the least cost avoiders, then it becomes important to take account of their role in creating or avoiding accidents subject to strict liability. Does a potential plaintiff have any incentive, under strict liability, to take precautions that might reduce or eliminate the expected costs? Not in the absence of defenses. If the defendant caused the harm, the defendant is liable, no matter how many precautions the defendant took, and regardless of how many precautions the plaintiff might have taken but did not in fact take.

However, the law of strict liability provides defendants with several affirmative defenses to excuse or reduce their liability. The availability of these affirmative defenses creates incentives for plaintiffs to be careful.

Comparative Negligence

Most states allow manufacturers to avoid strict liability for defective products, if they can prove that the plaintiff/consumer was comparatively negligent in using the product. So, for example, in *Daly v. General Motors*,[14] the auto maker was not strictly liable for a design defect that caused the front door to open during an accident, despite the fact that the plaintiff's husband died when he was thrown from the vehicle. The California Supreme Court found the decedent to be comparatively negligent because he failed to lock the door and wear the seat belt, either of which would have prevented him from being thrown from the car.

The addition of a comparative negligence defense to a strict liability regime does create a conceptual or semantic issue: What difference is there between strict liability with a comparative negligence defense and a plain comparative negligence regime? The California Supreme Court, in *Daly*, attempted to answer this question:

> We imposed strict liability against the manufacturer and in favor of the user or consumer in order to relieve injured consumers "from *problems of proof* inherent in pursuing negligence . . . and warranty . . . remedies. . . ." [W]e sought to place the burden of loss on manufacturers rather than " . . . injured persons *who are powerless to protect themselves.*" . . .
>
> The foregoing goals, we think, will not be frustrated by the adoption of comparative principles. Plaintiffs will continue to be relieved of proving that the manufacturer or distributor was negligent in the production, design, or dissemination of the article in question. Defendant's liability for injuries caused by a defective product remains strict. The principle of protecting the defenseless is likewise preserved, for plaintiffs recovery will be reduced *only* to the extent that his own lack of reasonable care contributed to the injury. The cost of compensating the victim of a defective product, albeit proportionately reduced, remains on defendant manufacturer, and will, through him, be "spread among society." However, we do not permit plaintiff's own conduct relative to the product to escape unexamined, and as to that share of plaintiff's damages which flows from his own fault we discern no reason of policy why it should . . . be borne by others. Such a

result would directly contravene the principle . . . that loss should be assessed equitably in proportion to fault.

Up until the last sentence of the quote, the court seems effectively to reconcile the comparative negligence defense with the theory of strict liability. Even burdened by a possible comparative negligence defense, plaintiffs benefit from two of the chief virtues of strict liability: a reduction in their burden of proof and relief from costs that they are powerless to prevent. If they are powerless to prevent the costs, then they cannot be said, in any meaningful way, to have been comparatively negligent. However, the last quoted sentence from the court's ruling seems directly to contradict the *raison d'être* of strict liability: to eliminate fault as the basis for liability. This apparent logical inconsistency—introducing considerations of fault into a liability scheme expressly designed to exclude fault considerations—is the reason a minority of states decline to recognize a comparative negligence defense in strict liability cases.[15]

Nevertheless, strict liability with a comparative negligence defense is not quite the same as a plain comparative negligence rule. Under a comparative negligence regime, the defendant is liable only if he acted unreasonably; that is, he is at fault. In such cases, the defendant is liable for the difference between the plaintiff's actual damages and the damages due to the plaintiff's own failure to take reasonable precautions. Similarly, under strict liability with a comparative negligence defense, the defendant is liable for the plaintiff's actual damages minus those damages that plaintiff might have avoided by taking reasonable precautions. The only difference arises in cases where the defendant acted reasonably. Under strict liability, the reasonableness of the defendant's conduct does not absolve him of liability for the plaintiff's harm. Under comparative negligence, the defendant's reasonableness relieves him of all liability, so that in cases where both parties act reasonably, the plaintiff is left to bear the harm. The outcome in terms of social costs is the same under both rules; the only difference is in the allocation of the costs between the parties.

Assumption of the Risk and Misuse

In jurisdictions that reject the comparative negligence defense to strict products liability, other defenses are made available to give potential plaintiffs some incentive to take reasonable precautions to prevent or minimize the costs of accidents. It is a generally accepted rule in products liability cases, for example, that plaintiffs cannot recover for damages when they have (1) used a product that was patently defective, so that they had notice of the danger, or (2) unreasonably misused a product in a way that was unintended and unforeseeable by the manufacturer. As Justice Mosk vividly explained, in dissenting from the California Supreme Court's adoption of comparative negligence as a defense to strict liability in *Daly v. General Motors*:

> If a consumer elects to use a product patently defective when other alternatives are available, or to use a product in a manner clearly not intended or foreseeable, he assumes the risks inherent in his improper utilization and should not be heard to complain about the condition of the object. One who employs a power saw to trim his fingernails—and thereafter finds the number of his fingers reduced—should not prevail to any extent whatever against the manufacturer even if the saw had a defective blade.[16]

Justice Mosk went on to assert that assumption of the risk—a total defense to strict liability—is preferable to comparative negligence, which would merely offset the plaintiff's recovery in proportion to the plaintiff's own negligence. It is difficult to see, however, how a defense to strict liability based on assumption of the risk, any more than a comparative negligence defense, avoids the logical problem of introducing fault-based considerations into a regime that is expressly designed to ignore considerations of fault. On the other hand, it surely would be inefficient to compensate plaintiffs who foolishly use a saw to trim their nails.

The question remains: If we really are interested in comparative fault, should we have a strict liability regime in the first place? One reasonable answer to this question might be that, in strict liability, we are not interested in the defendant's fault but we *are* interested in the plaintiff's fault. From the very beginning of judicial applications of strict liability theory in products liability cases, it was assumed that only plaintiffs who made "normal and proper use" of products should be able to recover for injuries sustained as a result of product defects.[17]

More difficult to answer is the following question: If it is true that strict liability applies in cases in which defendants are overwhelmingly likely to be the least cost avoider, what point is served by introducing evidence of plaintiffs' fault? The increasing availability of defenses to strict liability might suggest that the presumption—that defendants are overwhelmingly likely to be the least cost avoiders—in products liability and other strict liability cases, is incorrect. In which case, again, it becomes questionable whether strict liability should apply in the first place.

STRICT LIABILITY VERSUS NEGLIGENCE

A long-standing and ongoing debate in the courts and in the law and economics literature centers on whether negligence or strict liability should be the default rule for resolving tort disputes. This debate is reflected in a historical ebb and flow between the two rules.

Historical Context of the Debate

In the early days of the common law, in the fourteenth century, liability for all torts was strict,[18] but with defenses including *force majeur* (forces out of the control of the defendant, including natural calamities such as storms or earthquakes) and contributory negligence of the plaintiff. Just like defenses to modern rules of strict liability, these defenses introduced notions of fault into liability analysis: if the accident was due to force majeur, then it really was not the defendant's fault; the defendant could not be held legally or financially responsible for the plaintiff's harm. Likewise, if the plaintiff was contributorily negligent, the defendant really was not at fault for causing the harm. Thus, notions of fault were part of the liability analysis in tort law from the beginning. In the early, formative period of the common law, however, plaintiffs did not have to prove the defendant was at fault in order for the court to hold the defendant liable for the plaintiff's harm.

By the early nineteenth century, fault had become a more prominent consideration in common law torts cases. Even though trespass (see Chapter 6) remained a strict liability offense, negligence increasingly displaced strict liability as the rule for resolving accident and nuisance cases. In England, according to some legal historians, the main reason for the shift from strict liability to negligence for nuisances and accidents, was functional:

> One of the most striking aspects of legal change during the antebellum period is the extent to which common law doctrines were transformed to create immunities from legal liability and thereby to provide substantial subsidies for those who undertook schemes of economic development.[19]

This shift is plausible from a public choice perspective. Industrialists with substantial financial power and political connections could well have influenced legislators and judges, if not in specific cases then in general attitudes and tendencies. Business leaders, who were far more likely to be defendants than plaintiffs in tort disputes, had reason to prefer negligence to strict liability.

Other scholars dispute this functional account of the shift from strict liability to negligence. They point to evidence that the shift was already well underway by the beginning of the nineteenth century, before the explosion in accidents and accident cases that accompanied the Industrial Revolution.[20] Even if this observation is true, the shift from strict liability to negligence undoubtedly favored tort defendants. Instead of being liable for harm regardless of fault, tort defendants were held liable only for harm deemed by the courts to be unreasonable. Moreover, the switch from strict liability to negligence imposed on tort plaintiffs the additional burden of proving that defendants acted unreasonably. All else being equal, tort defendants subject to negligence rules would be held liable in fewer cases than under strict liability, resulting in potentially sizeable cost savings.

If the nineteenth century witnessed the birth of negligence, the twentieth century saw a partial return to strict liability. We already canvassed the broad application of strict liability in the modern torts field of products liability. In recent years, that same field of tort law has been moving beyond strict liability to something approaching *absolute liability*, sometimes referred to as "enterprise liability." Enterprise liability equals strict liability without the traditional defenses, including consumer misuse and contributory negligence. It is liability regardless of both defendant's fault and plaintiff's fault. If the defendant engages in some activity that causes harm to the plaintiff, the defendant is liable, period.[21] This shift back to strict liability should not be exaggerated; it has been only partial. Throughout the twentieth century, negligence (in one form or another) remained the predominant rule for resolving accident disputes.

The historical ebb and flow between strict liability and negligence fuels debates over which tort regime is generally preferable. Arguments in the debate range from ethical considerations of compensatory justice to economic claims of efficiency or inefficiency.

The Comparative Ethics of Negligence and Strict Liability

Ethical arguments can be made to favor either strict liability or negligence. A good deal depends on how torts are conceived in the first place. If torts are viewed, as they have been traditionally, as "wrongs" committed by an identifiable wrongdoer (tortfeasor) against an innocent "victim," then strict liability may be preferred as an ethical matter. The argument is especially strong in cases where the plaintiff is blameless. Between a blameless victim and a defendant who, blameworthy or not, causes the harm, a strong, intuitive sense of justice seems to demand that the defendant should bear the cost. This intuition is particularly powerful where the defendant is profiting from the activity that harms the plaintiff. In cases where the plaintiff is at fault to some extent, the ethical argument favoring strict liability is weakened.

If torts are viewed, in the first instance, not as harms imposed on presumptively innocent victims by presumptive "wrongdoers" but as Coasean, joint-cost conflicts over entitlements, then the ethical argument favoring strict liability is weak to begin with. It may even be argued that negligence rules are *more* ethical than strict liability rules because they hold tort defendants liable only in those cases in which they can legitimately be said to be blameworthy. In contrast to the rule of strict liability, negligence does not make tort defendants the general insurer of all harms that might accidentally befall potential plaintiffs in the modern world.

Comparative Institutional Analysis

Neither negligence nor strict liability is obviously more efficient across all cases, minimizing the sum of accident, avoidance, and administrative costs. For some types of cases, strict liability is more efficient than negligence. For many other types of cases, some kind of negligence regime is more efficient.

Begin by considering, once again, the similarities between proportional comparative negligence and strict liability with a comparative negligence defense. The results in all cases appear to be equally efficient under either rule, with the only significant difference being the distribution of remaining costs in cases where both parties have acted reasonably. Remaining costs, in this context, are those associated with harm the plaintiff suffered despite the fact that both parties took all reasonable precautions to avoid or minimize harm. Under strict liability, the defendant would bear the remaining costs; under negligence, the plaintiff would bear them. And it *does* matter, for purposes of economic efficiency, which party bears the remaining costs, at least in cases where one party or the other's activity level (how often or how much they engage in some activity), in addition to their level of precaution, can affect the probability or extent of harm.

Strict liability and negligence rules operate on parties' incentives in different ways, which may cause one rule to operate more efficiently in some types of circumstances but less efficiently in others. Specifically, negligence rules tend to affect how much precaution parties take, but not the extent to which they undertake the activity that causes the harm. Thus, the potential for negligence liability leads automobile drivers to drive more carefully, but does not lead them to drive less frequently. No matter how much someone drives, if they take reasonable precautions, their potential liability remains constant.[22]

Strict liability, by contrast, affects both precautions and activity levels. Defendants subject to a rule of strict liability can be expected to undertake an efficient level of precaution—up to that point where the cost of the next unit of precaution would exceed the expected savings from reduced liability—*and* they will automatically adjust their activity level in all cases where the extent of activity affects the probability of harm to some potential plaintiff. Assume, for example, that road builders can use either dynamite or bulldozers to clear off boulders, and they prefer dynamite because it is generally considered more efficient. Now suppose, realistically, that the state imposes a rule of strict liability for blasting, as an abnormally dangerous or ultrahazardous activity. This ruling may well affect the road builder's choice between using dynamite and bulldozers. All other things being equal, we would expect the strict liability rule to lead the road builder to use bulldozers more and dynamite less, especially in urban and highly developed rural areas. It is not just that they will be more careful when they blast with dynamite; they will actually seek to minimize their blasting activity in cases where bulldozing is a feasible option, so as to reduce their potential tort liability.

This example might make strict liability generally preferable to negligence, *if* society were solely concerned with defendants' levels of precaution and activity. In fact, society is equally interested—as it should be for efficiency's sake—in plaintiffs' levels of precaution and activity. As already discussed, under the rule of strict liability and in the absence of affirmative defenses, strict liability does not induce potential plaintiffs either to take reasonable precautions or to reduce their own activity level. Where affirmative defenses to strict liability, such as comparative negligence, are available, potential plaintiffs will have an incentive to undertake precautions, but they still will not have any incentive to reduce their activity levels.

Consider bicycle riders, who share the streets with automobiles, creating substantial risks of accident. Even when bicycle riders and automobile drivers both exercise reasonable care, accidents sometimes happen. Were these accidents resolved under a rule of strict liability (with or without affirmative defenses), then automobile drivers would have some incentive to adjust their activity level, but bicycle riders would not. As long as cyclists can expect full compensation for any and all accident costs, they will have no incentive to ride less often.[23] But suppose society wants cyclists to ride less, especially at night, when low visibility makes accidents more likely. To accomplish this goal, the courts would have to stop holding drivers strictly liable for accident costs. The only way to get the riders to adjust their activity level would be to leave them to bear some of the "excess costs"—the costs that remain despite the reasonable precautions of both parties. In other words, the courts would have to substitute a negligence rule for strict liability. Under a negligence regime, cyclists would bear the costs of accidents with nonnegligent drivers. They would, accordingly, marginally adjust their activity level to maximize their total utility, which is the utility they receive from cycling given the expected costs they would incur from an accident with a nonnegligent driver.

Note that the law can create incentives related to activity levels only for one party at a time. It cannot induce potential defendants (injurers) and potential plaintiffs (victims) to reduce their respective activity levels at the same time.[24] This limitation makes the selection of negligence or strict liability a matter of policy choice. In fact, every American jurisdiction employs both negligence and strict liability rules for different types of accident cases. In cases where plaintiffs' levels of care and activity make little or no contribution to the overall probability or magnitude of harm, strict liability is preferred. Abnormally dangerous and ultrahazardous activities, such as blasting, provide a good example. Such activities are subject to strict liability because defendants' precautions and levels of activity influence the costs of accidents stemming from such activities far more than plaintiffs' precautions and levels of activity. When a road builder starts blasting within a block or two of your home, you can do little, as a practical matter, to prevent or minimize the harm that might occur. You might, if you know in advance that the blasting will occur and you have reason to believe the explosions could rattle your house and its contents, take steps to protect valuable and fragile objects, by removing them from shelves and wrapping them in protective tissue or bubble wrap. The law does not even require such minor precautions, let alone more substantial changes in activity levels—society does not expect homeowners to minimize the amount of glass and china they keep in their houses in order to minimize the potential damage from rare acts of blasting in the neighborhood.

On the other hand, in cases where plaintiffs can most cost-effectively avoid or minimize harm by altering their activity levels, then defendants should not be held liable. When, for example, professional athletes are injured in the course of a sporting event, they have no right to compensation, even if their injuries were caused by the negligence of another participant.[25] Courts typically hold that injured athletes "assumed the risks" associated with their sport. In the absence of liability, they retain the options of purchasing insurance or taking up some other profession.

The difficulty in this line of reasoning, of course, is in predicting when plaintiffs' or defendants' activity levels are the more important. As a practical matter, the courts err on the side of defendants. Negligence is the default rule. A defendant who takes reasonable precautions will avoid liability; and the plaintiff will be left to bear the costs. For specific kinds of accident cases, however, such as abnormally dangerous activities, products liability, and trespass, courts have determined that defendants' activity levels are far more important than plaintiffs' activity levels. Those cases are subject to strict liability.

THE COSTS OF ADMINISTERING THE TORTS SYSTEM

So far, our analysis of tort law has focused on the costs of harm and harm avoidance. Those costs are not the only costs involved, however. The tort system itself is costly to administer. Administrative costs include the costs of physical plant construction and court maintenance as well as the costs of attorneys, judges, clerks, stenographers, and other court personnel. Finally, and most importantly for present purposes, differential costs are associated with applying and enforcing various legal rules.

Choosing the Legal Rule

Tort law is not unique in raising issues about the costs associated with choice of legal rules, but it raises them in particularly stark relief. Consider the choice between the rule of strict liability and the rule of negligence for resolving accident cases. Some law and economics scholars predict that a negligence rule would, all other things being equal, generate less litigation than strict liability, and thereby save on the costs of judicial administration. According to Richard Epstein, "A negligence rule leads to somewhat fewer lawsuits than strict liability because its conditions for liability are more restrictive. *Ceteris paribus*, fewer suits mean lower administrative costs."[26]

Empirical evidence supports the claim that strict liability leads to a greater number of legal claims: products liability lawsuits exploded in the second half of the twentieth century, after the switch from negligence to strict liability for accidents involving defective products. Not every legal claim leads inexorably to litigation, however. Because more legal claims are made under strict liability, the reasoning goes, then the increase in litigation would lead to higher administrative costs. However, the relative certainty of defendants' liability under the rule of strict liability would actually reduce the rate of litigation by encouraging prelitigation settlements.[27]

As a general rule, disputes involving fewer legal issues require less litigation. Strict liability admits fewer issues for litigation than negligence. In this respect, it is said to be a "brighter-line" rule. Generally speaking, just three questions are raised in any strict liability case: (1) Did this defendant *cause* the plaintiff's harm? (2) Did the plaintiff act reasonably? and (3) What is the extent of the harm? In negligence, a fourth question is always asked: (4) Was the defendant at fault? As a factual question, its answer is particularly prone to litigation because of the likelihood that prospective plaintiffs and prospective defendants will disagree, from case to case, about what behavior was or was not "reasonable" under the circumstances.

All other things being equal, defendants subject to strict liability (especially a rule of strict liability without affirmative defenses) should be more likely to settle out of court, thus significantly reducing administrative costs. It is not just that more cases will go to litigation under a negligence rule (assuming potential plaintiffs are not discouraged by low standards of care and high burdens of proof); it will also take longer to litigate each case, because each involves more evidence for attorneys to present and courts to assess in order to determine liability. For example, a court must be able to calculate the cost and effectiveness of different levels of care that might have reduced the probability or magnitude of harm. Such calculations are unnecessary under strict liability. So, even if the number of legal claims is higher under strict liability, the average administrative costs of resolving negligence claims may well be higher.[28]

The chief point, in any case, is that the choice and structure of the legal rule can, itself, affect the costs of administering the tort system.

The Costs of Estimating Damages

Another important administrative cost is common to both strict liability and negligence: the court must *accurately assess the damages* to the plaintiff. From an economic perspective, this assessment is a critical enterprise—perhaps even more important than the determination of liability—because the estimation of damages will substantially determine the incentive effects created for the parties by the court's ruling. Assume, for example, that the plaintiff suffered $1,000 worth of damages from an accident, but the court incorrectly estimates the total damages at $600. The court then would allocate those $600 in costs between the two parties, depending on its determination of liability under either negligence or strict liability. Whichever rule it chooses for allocating liability, the decision is virtually certain to give the parties inappropriate incentives to attain the efficient level of precaution. A defendant held liable for all the damages will have to pay the plaintiff only 60 percent of the actual damages the plaintiff suffered. Because the defendant must bear only a fraction of the actual damages, the defendant successfully *externalized* some of the costs of the conduct that caused the damages, and is likely to take too few precautions to prevent similar harm in the future. The plaintiff, meanwhile, is left to bear $400 of the costs, even though the plaintiff was not responsible for causing these costs. As a result, the plaintiff is likely to be overly cautious in the future, expending more on precaution than would be efficient. Thus, the court's underestimation of damages leads to overprecaution by the plaintiff and underprecaution by the defendant. If, by contrast, the court overestimated the harm to the plaintiff by awarding, say, $1,500 rather than the $1,000 actually suffered, the result will be the reverse: the plaintiff will have an incentive to be less cautious, and the defendant will have an incentive to be overly cautious.

Over- and undercompensation are not purely academic concerns. They are endemic problems. The real question is the extent of under- or overestimation of damages. If the court's estimation deviates from actual damages only marginally, the error should not greatly compromise the overall efficiency of the tort system.

The Costs of Evaluating *Ex Ante* Precautions and Potential Precautions

Not only must the courts accurately assess the extent of damages; they must also, in negligence cases, accurately assess the respective costs and benefits of feasible precautions that plaintiffs and defendants *might* have taken to minimize the magnitude and the probability of an accident. This analysis is necessary for the courts to be able to determine whether one or both parties are at fault for the accident. If the court cannot accurately assess the costs and benefits of feasible *ex ante* precautions, it cannot accurately determine whether one party or the other is at fault. Suppose, for example, that the defendant could have avoided, at a cost of $500, an accident that cost the plaintiff $1,000. Assume the plaintiff's avoidance cost was $600. But the evidence presented in court does not include all of this information. Instead, the available evidence leads the court to conclude that the defendant could only have avoided the accident at a cost of $1,200. This conclusion makes it appear as if the defendant acted "reasonably," when in fact the defendant did not. And the plaintiff appears to have been the least cost avoider, which is also untrue. Under any kind of negligence regime, the court is likely to hold that the defendant is not liable for the plaintiff's injuries. Of course, courts can err in the opposite direction if they underestimate the defendant's cost of avoidance; the defendant would be held liable when, in fact, the defendant took reasonable precautions.

To what extent do such information constraints impede the courts from accurately estimating actual damages and the values of *ex ante* precautions? No one really knows. But as Judge Posner asserted in *McCarty v. Pheasant Run, Inc.*, the courts, in applying the Learned Hand formula ($B = P * L$), tend to rely on "rough judgments" and intuition, more than precise measurement. Learned Hand, himself, conceded that his formula was easier to describe than apply. In the case of *Moisan v. Loftus*,[29] he recast his formula and expressed pessimism about its practical utility:

> It is indeed possible to state an equation for negligence in the form, C equals P times D, in which the C is the care required to avoid risk, D, the possible injuries, and P, the probability that the injuries will occur, if the

requisite care is not taken. But of these factors care is the only one ever susceptible of quantitative estimate, and often that is not. The injuries are always a variable within limits, which do not admit of even approximate ascertainment; and, although probability might theoretically be estimated, if any statistics were available, they never are; and, besides, probability varies with the severity of the injuries. It follows that all such attempts are illusory; and, if serviceable at all, are so only to center attention upon which one of the factors may be determinative in any given situation.

This assessment cautions economists to be modest about the potential of courts to achieve first-best, least-cost solutions to accidents and other tort disputes.

Chapter Summary

This chapter introduced the rule of strict liability as an alternative to negligence, and compared the two tort regimes. For types of disputes in which tort defendants are overwhelmingly likely to be least cost avoiders, strict liability makes sense because it dispenses with *ad hoc* factual inquiries into the defendant's blameworthiness. For other cases, where less reason exists *ex ante* to believe that the defendant would be the least cost avoider, negligence law and its *ad hoc* factual inquiries into respective fault may be the most efficient rule. It is unclear, however, which liability rule economizes on administrative costs. Moreover, endemic institutional problems, such as the calculation of damages, can have a profound effect on the efficiency of outcomes under either rule.

One critical question remains: Is the tort system, as a whole, efficient? The simple answer is that no one believes it is as efficient as it could be. Beyond that evaluation, scholars of various perspectives strongly disagree about whether proposed changes in the existing system would create net social benefits or costs. The next chapter examines the arguments for and against tort reform.

Questions and Problems

1. Is the rule of strict liability inconsistent with Coase's view of torts as joint cost problems?
2. Under what circumstances, if any, would a "pure" strict liability rule (with no affirmative defenses) likely be efficient?
3. What is the practical difference between a comparative negligence rule and a rule of strict liability with a comparative negligence defense?
4. Why are some types of torts, such as products liability, subject to strict liability, while others are subject to negligence?
5. How might *Doe v. Miles Laboratories* have been judged under a negligence rule?
6. Do rulings against defendants with "deep pockets" create a moral hazard problem (as defined in Chapter 10) for consumers?
7. Company X makes firearms in a strict liability jurisdiction. It determines an increase of $1,000 per year in precaution will reduce the harm from accidents by 1 percent. Under what circumstances will it spend that extra $1,000 per year on precaution?

1. [L.R.] 3 H.L. 330 (1868) (emphasis added).
2. [L.R.] 3 H.L. 330 (1868) (emphasis added).
3. *Indiana Harbor Belt R.R. Co. v. American Cyanamid Co.*, 916 F. 2d 1174, 1177 (7th Cir. 1990).
4. William L. Prosser, *The Law of Torts* (St. Paul, MN: West Publishing Co., 1971 p. 518.
5. As William Prosser expressed it, the defendant "is liable although he has taken every possible precaution to prevent the harm, and is not at 'fault' in any moral or social sense." William L. Prosser, *The Law of Torts* (St. Paul, MN: West Publishing Co., 1971), p. 517.
6. *Ogle v. Caterpillar Tractor, Co.*, 716 P. 2d 334, 342 (Wyo. 1986).
7. *Schneider National, Inc. v. Holland Hitch Co.*, 843 P. 2d 561, 580 (Wyo. 1992).
8. 24 Cal. 2d 453, 462 (Wyo. 1944).
9. This argument will be fleshed out later in this chapter, when the administrative costs of alternative legal rules for accident cases are addressed.
10. *Brown v. Superior Court*, 44 Cal. 3d 1049, 1062 (1988).
11. The named defendant is the Superior Court of Alameda County because it decided the case on a pretrial motion by the defendant. In this appeal, the plaintiffs were asking the appellate court to order the trial court to allow them to amend their complaint.
12. 571 F. Supp. 192, 203–4 (E.D. La. 1983).
13. Clarence Morris, "Hazardous Enterprises and Risk Bearing Capacity," 61 *YALE LAW JOURNAL* 1172, 1177 (1952).
14. 575 P. 2d 1162 (Cal. 1978).
15. *See, for example, Melia v. Ford Motor Co.*, 534 F. 2d 795, 802 (8th Cir. 1976). "[A]pplication of the Nebraska comparative negligence statute would . . . be extremely confusing and inappropriate in a strict liability case."
16. 575 P. 2d at 1185–6 (Mosk, J., dissenting).
17. *Escola*, 24 Cal. 2d at 468 (Traynor, J., concurring): "[T]he manufacturer's liability should, of course, be defined in terms of the safety of the product in normal and proper use."
18. Morris S. Arnold, "Accident, Mistake, and Rules of Liability in the Fourteenth Century Law of Torts," 128 *UNIVERSITY OF PENNSYLVANIA LAW REVIEW* 361, 274–5 (1979).
19. Morton J. Horwitz, *The Transformation of American Law, 1780–1860* (Oxford: Oxford University Press, 1992), pp. 99–101.
20. *See, for example*, Gary Schwartz, "Tort Law and Economy in Nineteenth-Century America: A Reinterpretation," 90 *YALE LAW JOURNAL* 1717 (1981).
21. The emergence of enterprise liability is reflected in cases such as *Beshada v. Johns-Manville Prods. Corp.*, 90 N.J. 191 (1982), in which the New Jersey Supreme Court held an asbestos manufacturer liable for not warning consumers about the then unknown dangers of asbestos. That's right: the defendant was liable for not disseminating to consumers information that neither it, nor anyone else, possessed.
22. This distinction results because courts, in negligence cases, only inquire into the level of precaution, not the level of activity, in determining the defendant's liability. "[T]hey do not ask," wrote Richard Posner, "when a driver is in an accident, whether the benefit of the particular trip (maybe he was driving to the grocery store to get some gourmet food for his pet iguana) was equal to or greater than the costs, including the expected accident cost to other users of the road; or whether driving was really cheaper than walking or taking the train when all social costs are reckoned in." Richard A. Posner, *Economic Analysis of Law* (New York: Aspen Publishers, Inc., 1998), p. 192. Moreover, Posner asserts, courts are unable "to determine optimal activity levels except in simple cases" (p. 193).
23. This statement assumes, of course, that the bicycle riders are indifferent between having no accidents and being fully compensated for accidents.
24. This mutual exclusiveness would not be a problem if everyone had an equal probability of being either a tort plaintiff or tort defendant. It is extremely doubtful, however, that such equal probability would actually be the case.
25. *See, for example, Ordway v. Superior Court*, 198 Cal. App. 3d (1988), which held that a professional jockey had assumed the risk that another jockey might negligently cause her to fall off of her horse. Professional athletes are, however, protected from intentional torts and from *gross* negligence, or negligence above and beyond

"common occurrences and within the parameters of the athletes' expectations."

26. Richard A. Epstein, *Torts* (New York: Aspen Publishers, Inc., 1999), p. 95. Other scholars have made essentially the same argument. *See, for example*, Thomas J. Miceli, *Economics of the Law* (Oxford: Oxford University Press, 1997), p. 44. *See also* Richard A. Posner and William M. Landes, *The Economic Structure of Tort Law* (Cambridge: Harvard University Press, 1987), p. 65.

27. This greater likelihood of settlement assumes, of course, that an alternative negligence rule would be subject to greater uncertainty, which might not always be the case. For example, a negligence rule that imposed low standards of care on defendants and high burdens of proof on plaintiffs might greatly discourage litigation, despite generating more legal issues than a strict liability rule. Of course, a rule of no liability would entail the lowest administrative costs: zero. The more closely a negligence regime is made to approximate a no liability regime, for example by combining low standards of care with high burdens of proof, the lower the administrative costs associated with that negligence regime.

28. *See* Steven Shavell, *Economic Analysis of Accident Law* (Cambridge: Harvard University Press, 1987), p. 264.

29. 178 F. 2d 148, 149 (2d Cir. 1949).

Chapter 12

Torts III: Reform

The previous chapters looked at how both negligence and strict liability rules can be, and often are, efficient. Neither rule is obviously more efficient than the other across all kinds of accident claims. But is the tort system, as a whole, efficient?

Few observers believe that the existing tort system is the best possible, or even that it is very efficient.[1] Many argue that the system produces too much litigation, overly burdens tort defendants, and consequently costs society too much. These claims have prompted numerous calls for tort reform. *Reform* is an ambiguous term, applicable to institutional changes that would either expand or narrow the scope of tort liability. The goal of the present tort reform movement is decidedly to limit the liability of tort defendants.

To some extent, the tort reform movement, and its opposition, can be explained by public choice theory: Regardless of whether the tort system really is inefficient compared to some feasible alternative, it is in the interest of tort defendants to seek reforms that would insulate them from liability. At the same time, it is in the interest of plaintiffs' lawyers and consumer organizations to oppose any efforts to restrict either the ability of "victims" to sue or the damages they are entitled to recover. Aside from such obvious political motives, meritorious arguments can be made both for and against tort reform.

This chapter presents the respective cases for and against tort reform in the form of briefs, as the proponents and opponents of tort reform themselves would present them. Those arguments are followed by an appraisal of actual tort reform efforts.

THE CASE FOR TORT REFORM

The Current Tort System Produces Net Social Costs

Proponents of tort reform argue that the existing system is inefficient, ineffective, and unfair. It is inefficient because it creates more costs for tort defendants than benefits for tort plaintiffs or for society as a whole. In particular, the transaction costs of litigation, and threatened litigation, make the tort system a poor conduit for compensating those who are injured in accidents.

In 2001, the tort system of the United States cost an estimated $205.4 billion. That figure includes both litigated cases, settlements of injury claims, and the administrative costs for insurance companies.[2] During the second half of the twentieth century, the costs of tort claims in the United States increased three times faster than the overall rate of growth of the U.S. economy.[3]

The costs created by the tort system are not all related to paying compensation to the victims of accidents. Tort reform advocates point out that the mere risk or threat of tort claims is costly. Moreover, tort defendants bear substantial legal expenses whether claims filed against them have merit or not. It can cost a physician $10,000 or more just to get a meritless malpractice claim thrown out of court. The cost of litigating worthy claims can run into the hundreds of thousands of dollars, even before the jury reaches a verdict. And the size of jury awards—particularly punitive damages awards and awards for pain and suffering—has grown out of all proportion to plaintiffs' actual injuries.

Recall the discussion in Chapter 9 of the BMW case, in which a jury awarded the plaintiff punitive damages of $4 million—1,000 times the jury's estimate of the plaintiff's *actual* damages—because the auto maker sold the car to the plaintiff as new, even though the car had been damaged in transport and repainted prior to delivery.[4] In another case, widely reported in the media as a "looney lawsuit," a New Mexico jury ordered McDonald's to pay an 81-year-old woman $2.9 million in total damages after she was severely scalded by a hot cup of McDonald's coffee.[5] Even though such astronomical punitive damage awards are subsequently reduced on appeal, W. Kip Viscusi notes that "[e]ven awards reduced on appeal can be $100 million or more."[6]

According to tort reform proponents, rising rates and costs of tort litigation, combined with skyrocketing jury awards, force insurance companies, which ultimately foot the bill for most liability claims, to raise the premiums they charge for liability insurance. For more than a decade, the rate of increase in the price of liability insurance has far exceeded the overall rate of inflation. In some states, doctors pay upwards of $100,000 per year for medical malpractice insurance. As a consequence, some have given up their practices; others have gone on strike in protest. For all kinds of businesses, big and small, the increasing costs of liability insurance represent a huge financial burden, affecting jobs, innovation, and international competitiveness.

Tort reformers allege that the current tort system amounts to a vast, invisible tax on businesses and consumers. One study estimated that this "tort tax" amounts to $1,200 per year on every American citizen.[7] And it is a regressive tax, imposing the greatest burden on the poorest citizens, who can least afford it. If the risks of tort claims increase the price of, say, a telephone by $5, that extra cost will hurt poor people more than rich people because $5 constitutes a greater proportion of their total income.[8] The example is hypothetical, but the effect of the "tort tax" is not. It does, in fact, raise the costs of consumer goods, in some cases quite significantly. One estimate, for example, claims that 55 percent of the cost of a football helmet is attributable to the risk of tort liability;[9] for stepladders, the risk of liability accounts for 15 to 20 percent of the prices consumers pay.[10] Even worse, socially desirable products are sometimes withdrawn from the market or never marketed in the first place because of the costs associated with the risk of tort claims. When those costs rise high enough, products are priced out of the market entirely, forcing plant closings and business failures, with consequent job losses. Manufacturers of textile machines, medical devices, and gymnastic equipment have all attributed plant closures to the costs of potential or actual tort liability.[11] In other cases, new and innovative products, including a substitute for asbestos, a nonchemical substitute for pesticides, and a portable kidney dialysis machine, never made it to the market at all because of the risk of tort liability.[12] According to an article in *Science* magazine, concern over potential tort liability led pharmaceutical companies to delay or abandon entirely research toward developing AIDS vaccines.[13] As Alfred Cortese and Kathleen Blaner note, "The benefits that society might have enjoyed from these new products are lost, as is the chance that the new idea encapsulated in the new product might spark another new idea leading to even more benefits."[14] Most ironically, many of these products made, or would have made, society safer.

To the extent that the risk of tort liability reduces productivity or retards increases in productivity, no one gains; potential economic gains simply go unrealized.[15] However, the money tort defendants spend directly on the tort system—attorneys fees, litigation expenses, damage awards—does not simply disappear from the economy. It must go somewhere, to someone. To tort plaintiffs? Not as much as one might suppose. Jury awards *are* large and growing ever larger, but plaintiffs ultimately receive only a fraction of the sums juries award them. It has been estimated that only 22 percent of the total costs of operating the U.S. tort system actually goes to compensating the economic losses of tort plaintiffs.[16] Most of the rest goes to the administrative costs of filing and litigating lawsuits, including attorneys fees. The tort system, as currently organized, seems tailored more to the interests of plaintiffs' lawyers (and, to a lesser extent, defendants' attorneys[17]) than to plaintiffs themselves, let alone to society as a whole.

Tort Reform Recommendations

Tort reform advocates recommend various institutional changes to reduce the incidence of, and limit the costs associated with, tort claims. Methods for reducing the incidence of tort claims include (1) shortening statutes of limitations, which are time limits for filing legal claims after some injury has occurred; (2) imposing the English "loser pays" rule, which would up the ante for plaintiffs because, under this rule, the losing party in any lawsuit is required to pay all the court costs of both parties, including attorneys' fees; (3) limiting or abolishing joint and several liability, under which a single defendant may be held liable for all the plaintiff's harm, even though that individual defendant caused only a fraction of the harm; (4) instituting a "collateral source" rule, which would reduce defendants' liability to the extent plaintiffs receive compensation from other sources such as insurance or workers' compensation; (5) imposing a "state of the art" defense, which would insulate defendants from liability if they could show that they utilized the best technologies and methods available at the time the plaintiff was injured; (6) replacing strict liability with a negligence rule for determining liability; and (7) increasing the number and scope of affirmative defenses to strict liability.

Methods for minimizing the costs of tort claims include (1) limiting recovery for nonpecuniary injuries, such as pain and suffering, to some set dollar amount or a certain multiple of economic damages; (2) capping awards for punitive damages, either nominally or as a certain multiple of economic damages;[18] (3) shifting the authority to award or not award punitive damages from the jury to the judge; and (4) limiting plaintiffs' attorneys fees, for example by limiting the percentage of damages an attorney can collect pursuant to a contingency fee agreement.

As we shall see later in this chapter, nearly all of these recommendations have been implemented in various states, with some success.

THE CASE AGAINST TORT REFORM

Tort reform is opposed primarily by consumer rights organizations and trial lawyers. These groups have a vested interest in the existing tort system, just as insurance companies and likely defendants have vested interests in tort reform. Not all arguments against tort reform are based purely on the self-interest of reform opponents, however. Just as reasoned arguments are made supporting tort reforming, other reasoned arguments are made opposing it.

Arguments against tort reform are of two basic types: They challenge the factual basis for tort reform; and they question whether the proffered "cures" might prove worse than the "disease."

Fact, Fiction, and the Tort System

Opponents of tort reform do not claim that the existing system is perfect or even very good, but they point out that claims of litigation "explosions," "looney lawsuits," and out-of-control jury awards are at least exaggerated, and in some cases outright dishonest.[19] The rate of litigation in the United States did not increase during the twentieth century, as tort reform advocates contend. Empirical studies show that, in fact, Americans today file fewer civil lawsuits on a per capita basis than they did a century ago.[20] True, tort claims increased markedly as a percentage of civil cases; but the overall per capita rate of litigation has been trending downward. As of the 1980s, litigation remained a relatively uncommon response to disputes. Fewer than 19 percent of all tort disputes ever reached the courts;[21] only 8 percent of those filed lawsuits went to trial;[22] and legal fees in a majority of those cases were below $1,000.[23] A more recent study estimated that only about 10 percent of accident victims ever file claims.[24] A 1990 report prepared by Harvard Medical School researchers for the State of New York revealed that only one out of every nine injuries due to medical malpractice leads to the filing of a malpractice claim; and actual negligence victims only seek compensation through the tort system about 6 percent of the time.[25]

Likewise, the reality of jury awards is quite different from popular perceptions, which are informed by misleading anecdotes told by tort reform advocates and repeated in the press. Even the allegedly "looney lawsuits" have outcomes that are defensible. In the BMW case, for example, it is true that the jury awarded the plaintiff $4 million in punitive damages, but that award was cut in half by the trial court judge, and ultimately thrown out by the U.S. Supreme Court.

In the McDonald's case, the plaintiff was, in fact, seriously injured by the coffee, which McDonald's served at 185 degrees, at least 20 degrees hotter than coffee at other restaurants. At that temperature, coffee can cause third-degree burns in two to seven seconds. McDonald's knew of this danger. The company admitted that victims burned by its coffee had filed more than 700 claims against it between 1982 and 1992. McDonald's also knew that people did not wait until they were out of the car to drink the coffee. Nevertheless, it declined either to reduce the temperature of its coffee or to warn its customers about the danger of severe burns. The plaintiff suffered third-degree burns to over 6 percent of her body, including her groin, thighs, and buttocks, which required skin grafts. The cost of her treatment, which caused her to spend eight days in the hospital, ran to $20,000. Tort reform advocates and the media made much of the fact that she sued and obtained a jury verdict of $2.9 million— $200,000 in compensatory damages plus $2.7 million in punitive damages (the equivalent of two days' worth of coffee sales for the corporation). However, they neglected the fact that, before suing, she offered to settle with McDonald's for nothing more than her actual medical costs. McDonald's refused. They also neglected the fact that her compensatory damages were reduced from $200,000 to $160,000 because the jury found the plaintiff to be 20 percent at fault for her own injuries. (She had balanced the cup between her knees, while she opened the lid and poured in cream and sugar. It was then that the entire contents of the cup spilled over her lap.) Finally, the trial court judge reduced the jury's punitive damages award to just $480,000. Following the jury verdict in the case, it is worth noting, the McDonald's restaurant where the plaintiff purchased her coffee lowered the temperature on its coffee makers by more than 20 degrees.

The McDonald's case is only one example of the way in which misleading media coverage distorts public perceptions of the tort system. According to a 1998 study, newspapers regularly report big jury awards against defendants, but typically ignore verdicts in their favor. Overall, a plaintiff's victory is 12 times more likely to be reported than a verdict in favor of the defendant.[26] This imbalance creates an illusion that plaintiffs win in court the vast majority of the time. In reality, plaintiffs prevail in slightly over half of all tort cases. In products liability and medical malpractice cases, which are at the top of the agenda for tort reformers, plaintiffs lose far more often than they win.[27]

The media also distort public perceptions of the size of jury awards. The typical cases covered by the media involve jury awards that exceed that of the average tort case by a factor of 10 to 20.[28] Similarly, public perceptions of "excessive" punitive damages awards are colored by media coverage of exceptional cases involving huge dollar figures. One never reads a headline about a jury's decision *not* to grant punitive damages. And yet, punitive damages are awarded only rarely, especially in tort cases. Juries are far more likely to award punitive damages in contracts or real property cases.[29] In tort cases, juries award punitive damages between 1 and 7 percent of the time, depending on the jurisdiction. And most of those cases involve intentional torts, business torts not involving personal injury, and contracts cases, rather than products liability or medical malpractice.[30] Based on his assessment of several empirical studies of jury awards, Harvard Law and Economics Professor W. Kip Viscusi concluded that "the common belief that product liability awards leads to windfall gains is erroneous. . . . The actual value of court awards and settlements is . . . often less than the actual losses suffered by the victim."[31] Nevertheless, the *perception* of jurors sticking it to big business by turning gold-digging plaintiffs into instant millionaires has proven more powerful than facts about the rate at which juries actually award punitive damages and the ultimate size of those awards.

Even members of the U.S. Supreme Court have bought into the rhetoric of rampant punitive damages awards. In her opinion dissenting from the Court's ruling in *TXO Production Corp. V. Alliance Resources Corp.*,[32] Justice Sandra Day O'Connor wrote that "[a]s little as 30 years ago, punitive damages awards were 'rarely assessed' and usually 'small in amount.' Recently, however, the frequency and size of such awards has been skyrocketing." In fact, as already noted, the frequency of punitive damages awards remains quite low. Although the size of such awards has increased significantly for the nation as a whole, they have not increased in all jurisdictions as much as tort reform advocates would have us believe. In Chicago, the mean tort award increased by 300 percent between 1985 and 1994, but in Manhattan, a part of New York City, the increase was only 11 percent during the same period. In some places, including Kings County, New York (which includes the Borough of Brooklyn), and St. Charles County, Missouri (in metropolitan St. Louis), the size of average jury awards actually fell.[33] Even where punitive damage awards have been on the rise, huge jury awards are nearly always slashed by trial or appellate court judges. To the extent that juries do award excessive damages, the problem seems largely to be resolved within the system as it is currently structured.

In sum, Professor Marc Galanter observes, "Notwithstanding occasional efforts to debunk some of the legends about the 'litigation explosion,' the regular consumer of media reports would be badly misinformed about the number of products liability and medical malpractice cases, the size of jury awards, the incidence of punitive damages, and the regularity with which corporate defendants succeed in defeating individual claimants."[34]

Still, the question remains: Do tort claims cost society too much? Proponents of tort reform are quick to point out that they cost society more than $200 billion per year. Yet they rarely address the other side of the equation: the cost to society of preventable accidents that might have been avoided if those who caused the accidents had taken adequate precautions. Even under the current tort system, a study by the Institute of Medicine of the National Academy of Sciences found as many as 98,000 preventable deaths each year occur in hospitals as a result of "medical errors."[35] And that figure does not include nonfatal injuries from medical malpractice in hospitals, occurrences of medical malpractice outside of hospitals, or injuries from other types of accidental torts. We can generally assume that a reformed tort system, restricting recovery for malpractice, might increase this number of preventable deaths and other injuries resulting from medical errors because potential defendants would have reduced incentives to take adequate precautions. In view of the social costs of accidental and preventable torts, it is not so clear that tort claims cost society too much. It might even be argued that society does not spend enough on tort liability or other mechanisms to provide the appropriate incentives for doctors and other health care workers to undertake efficient precautions.

Doctors are quick to complain about the rising costs of malpractice insurance and to seek caps on tort liability, but they are not so quick to deal with their own responsibility for the high number of medical errors. According to the consumer group Public Citizen, 60 percent of all malpractice payments in New Jersey during the 1990s were made by only 6 percent of the state's doctors.[36] The number of tort cases, the costs of tort claims, and the price of the liability premiums would all be reduced if the medical profession simply did a better job of identifying and punishing the small number of dangerously bad "repeat offenders" within their profession.

This analysis assumes, of course, that the doctors are more likely than their patients to be the least cost avoiders. This assumption seems entirely plausible in many medical malpractice settings in which doctors have far more control over, and information about, the situation than do their patients. The law of torts even has a special rule for such circumstances, known as *res ipsa loquitor* ("the thing speaks for itself"), according to which the accident itself constitutes evidence that negligence occurred. Courts will apply this rule when it infers from the fact of harm itself that the defendant's negligence was *probably* responsible for the plaintiff's harm. The effect of the rule is to relieve plaintiffs of the burden of proving that defendants acted negligently; instead, it will be left to defendants to prove that they did not act negligently. Thus, *res ipsa loquitor* shifts the burden of proof from a plaintiff to a defendant. This shift makes sense from a Coasean economic perspective in cases where the defendant (1) has significantly lower information costs than the plaintiff and, in large part because of those lower information costs, (2) is more than likely the least cost avoider.

Is the Cure Worse Than the Disease?

Opponents of tort reform point out that tort reformers, as the proponents of institutional change, bear the burden of proving that their "solutions" to problems in the existing tort system will yield net social benefits. It is not enough to provide a laundry list of problems with the existing system and to identify methods of correction. The advocates of tort reform must also show that those methods of correction would not create more problems than they would solve.

The pro-reform literature never addresses the *costs* of tort reform, as if their proposals are costless. As Neil Komesar has written, "In a setting where all institutions are and will be very far from ideal, reforms cannot be promoted by parading the horribles of the existing system while proposing substitutes on 'black box' institutions vaguely assumed to operate in an ideal fashion."[37] A more realistic assessment would require a comparison of the costs to defendants and others of the existing system versus the costs to plaintiffs and others of a more restrictive liability system, *plus* the costs of institutional change. Note that this argument does not necessarily speak against tort reform; it is merely a call to change the nature of the debate over tort reform. The problem is that reform proposals are often based on "superficial (or nonexistent) institutional analyses."[38]

Some evidence suggests that each of the approaches to tort reform discussed in the preceding section would entail significant costs. Reducing or capping punitive damage awards, for example, would surely reduce the costs of tort liability for defendants. But it might result in reduced deterrence in cases where the sum of economic damages and maximum allowable punitive damages would create insufficient incentives for efficient precaution/deterrence.

In the early 1980s, the Ford Motor Company was hit with a huge punitive damages penalty in a case involving its Pinto model. Ford designed the Pinto's gas tank in such a way that made it highly susceptible to punctures, gas spills, explosions, and fire, even in minor, low speed collisions. Substantial evidence indicated that this susceptibility could have been avoided at low cost. According to Ford's own records, the cost would have been less than $11 per vehicle. However, on Ford's cost-benefit analysis, which implicitly valued individual human lives at only $200,000, that price was too high. Subsequently, in several highly publicized accidents involving Pintos, the gas tanks exploded and engulfed the vehicles in flames. In one such case, a thirteen-year-old boy was burned over 90 percent of his body when the gas tank of the Pinto he was riding in exploded after a minor accident. He sued Ford, and the jury awarded compensatory damages of $2.5 million and 50 times that amount—$125 million—in punitive damages.[39] The trial court judge later reduced the punitive damages award to $3.5 million. Still, the jury's high punitive damages award may have been justified as reasonably necessary to send Ford the message that its cost-benefit calculations, particularly its human-life valuations, were grossly mistaken. It may have been reasonable for the jury to conclude that without a high punitive damages award, the tort system would fail to give Ford sufficient incentive to correct its cost-benefit analysis and take efficient precautions.[40]

If punitive damage awards are capped pursuant to tort reform, juries will be limited in their discretion to tailor awards to send the price signals needed to create incentives for efficient deterrence. If punitive damages are capped too low, the result could be systematic underdeterrence. It has yet to be shown *ex ante* that underdeterrence would prove less costly to society than overdeterrence. Other mechanisms, such as government regulation, may create efficient incentives in the absence of the threat of high punitive damages awards. Here too, no reason is shown to indicate *ex ante* that regulation would prove to be a lower-cost approach, all things considered. The same arguments hold for tort reforms that would cap awards for pain and suffering.

A big part of the issue here is the administrative cost of resolving tort disputes. It is the administrative problem of accurately estimating damages in order to create incentives for all concerned to take efficient precautions. With capped punitive damages (and pain and suffering awards), the risk is that jury awards would be too low, resulting in underdeterrence of tort defendants and inefficient overproduction of harmful activities. Proponents of tort reform have provided no estimates to show that limits they would place on jury awards would be sufficient to sustain incentives for tort defendants to take efficient precautions.

A different problem arises from tort reform measures that would replace joint and several liability with proportional liability. Under joint and several liability, a defendant who causes *some* of the plaintiff's harm can be made to pay for *all* the harm. This type of liability may seem grossly unfair to defendants. It might seem more fair to hold defendants liable only for that part of the plaintiff's harm actually attributable to their actions. However, this analysis is myopic because it focuses only on the fairness or unfairness to tort defendants, in disregard of plaintiffs who might be left undercompensated by a rule of proportional liability in cases where the costs of identifying all the defendants who contributed the plaintiff's injuries are quite high, and some defendants may be judgment proof. Arguably, it is less unfair to impose disproportionate costs on one of several blameworthy defendants than to impose any costs on a relatively blameless victim.

Joint and several liability may generate efficiencies that would be lost in its absence. It might be more efficient for tort plaintiffs, and for society as a whole, for plaintiffs to recover everything from one, easily identifiable defendant. Once a defendant is identified and held liable for all harm to a plaintiff, that defendant is entitled to file "contribution actions" against other defendants who contributed to the harm for which the first defendant (who now becomes a plaintiff) has paid. So, if X, Y, and Z corporations all caused plaintiff P's harm, but P sued only X and recovered all the costs of harm from that one defendant under a rule of joint and several liability, X can now seek "indemnification" from Y and Z, for their respective contributions to P's harm. Thus, the effect of joint and several liability is to shift the responsibility for identifying and suing other responsible defendants from P to X. The question is whether this is a more or less efficient allocation of that responsibility. It may be more efficient, as well as more fair, if the original defendant (X) is more likely than the plaintiff (P) to know the identities of the other parties (Y and Z) responsible for harming P.

Finally, it is not good enough for tort reform advocates to point to deficiencies in the existing tort system and offer alternatives that are presumed to solve those deficiencies. It must be recognized that all alternative approaches to resolving accident claims have advantages (benefits) and disadvantages (costs). Once costs and benefits are identified, it becomes obvious that a comparative institutional analysis is needed to choose between alternative approaches. Many alternatives have been promoted, but to date few serious comparative institutional analyses have been offered.

EXPERIENCES IN TORT REFORM

The information on which comparative institutional analyses might be based has been increasing in recent years, as states have enacted various tort reform measures. Empirical analyses of the effects of those reform efforts are not voluminous, but are growing in number. They provide at least some basis for comparing the operation of reformed and unreformed tort systems.

A majority of states have enacted some type of tort reform since the mid–1980s, and the pace of reform is increasing. Most of the reforms come from state legislatures; courts show more reluctance to reform their own rules, even to the point of foiling, through judicial review, some legislative reform efforts. Nevertheless, many of the reforms implemented include several of the methods discussed earlier in this chapter.

Caps on Punitive Damages

Many states have enacted punitive damage laws that cap or affect the distribution of punitive damages. A 2000 Georgia statute, for example, limits punitive damages to $250,000, unless the plaintiff can demonstrate by clear and convincing evidence that the defendant acted with specific intent to cause the harm.[41] A 1995 Indiana law caps punitive damages at $50,000 or three times the amount of compensatory damages, whichever is greater, and requires that 75 percent of punitive damages awards be paid into a state fund rather than to the plaintiff.[42] Florida, which seemingly has enacted more tort reform measures than any other state, imposes different caps on punitive damages, depending on the nature and extent of the defendant's wrongful conduct. In all cases, to collect any punitive damages plaintiffs must prove by clear and convincing evidence that defendants acted with intentional misconduct or were grossly negligent. In most such cases, punitive damages are limited to the lesser of three times compensatory damages or $500,000. In cases where the defendant's wrongful conduct was motivated by unreasonable financial gain, and the defendant knew that injury was likely to result, the cap is raised to the lesser of four times compensatory damages or $2 million.

In addition to state statutory limitations on punitive damages, the U.S. Supreme Court recently attempted to constrain jury awards of punitive damages under the Constitution's Due Process Clause. In the infamous BMW case discussed in Chapter 10,[43] the Court established that punitive damage awards should be proportionate to (1) the reprehensibility of the defendant's conduct, (2) the extent of actual damages, and (3) damage awards in similar cases.[44] More recently, in *State Farm Mutual Automobile Insurance Co. v. Campbell,* the Court ruled that "courts must ensure that the measure of punishment is both reasonable and proportionate to the amount of harm to the plaintiff and to the general damages recovered."[45] The court declined to impose a "bright-line ratio" between actual damages and permissible punitive damages awards. However, it noted that existing precedents establish that "in practice, few awards exceeding a single-digit ratio [that is, 9 to 1] between punitive and compensatory damages . . . will satisfy due process. . . . Single digit multipliers are more likely to comport with due process, while still achieving the State's goals of deterrence and retribution, than awards with ratios of 500 to 1."[46] Only in cases combining "particularly egregious acts" and slight actual harm would the Court tolerate larger ratios between compensatory and punitive damages. On the other hand, the Court might permit only a one-to-one ratio between such damages in cases where compensatory damages are "substantial."[47]

But how much does the Supreme Court's ruling in *State Farm* really constrain the size of punitive damages awards? In a recent post-*State Farm* case, the 7th Circuit U.S. Court of Appeals upheld a jury verdict of punitive damages that were more than 37 times actual damages. In his opinion for a unanimous panel, Judge Richard Posner both explained and distinguished the Supreme Court's decision in *State Farm v. Campbell,* while providing a history lesson about the purposes of punitive damage awards.

Mathias v. Accor Economy Lodging, Inc.

347 F. 3d 672 (7th Cir. 2003)

Posner, Circuit Judge.

***

The plaintiffs claim that in allowing guests to be attacked by bedbugs in a motel that charges upwards of $100 a day for a room and would not like to be mistaken for a flophouse, the defendant was guilty of "willful and wanton conduct" and thus under Illinois law is liable for punitive as well as compensatory damages. . . . The jury agreed and awarded each plaintiff $186,000 in punitive damages though only $5,000 in compensatory damages. The defendant appeals, complaining primarily about the punitive-damages award. . . .

***

There was . . . sufficient evidence of "willful and wanton conduct" within the meaning that the Illinois courts assign to the term to permit an award of punitive damages in this case.

But in what amount? In arguing that $20,000 was the maximum amount of punitive damages that a jury could constitutionally have awarded each plaintiff, the defendant points to the U.S. Supreme Court's recent statement that "few awards [of punitive damages] exceeding a single-digit ratio between punitive and compensatory damages, to a significant degree, will satisfy due process." *State Farm Mutual Automobile Ins. Co. v. Campbell, 155 L. Ed. 2d 585, 123 S. Ct. 1513, 1524 (2003)*. The Court went on to suggest that "four times the amount of compensatory damages might be close to the line of constitutional impropriety." . . . Hence the defendant's proposed ceiling in this case of $20,000, four times the compensatory damages awarded to each plaintiff. The ratio of punitive to compensatory damages determined by the jury was, in contrast, 37.2 to 1.

The Supreme Court did not, however, lay down a 4-to-1 or single-digit-ratio rule—it said merely that "there is a presumption against an award that has a 145-to-1 ratio"—and it would be unreasonable to do so. We must consider why punitive damages are awarded and why the Court has decided that due process requires that such awards be limited. The second question is easier to answer than the first. The term "punitive damages" implies punishment, and a standard principle of penal theory is that "the punishment should fit the crime" in the sense of being proportional to the wrongfulness of the defendant's action, though the principle is modified when the probability of detection is very low (a familiar example is the heavy fines for littering) or the crime is potentially lucrative (as in the case of trafficking in illegal drugs). Hence, with these qualifications, which in fact will figure in our analysis of this case, punitive damages should be proportional to the wrongfulness of the defendant's actions.

Another penal precept is that a defendant should have reasonable notice of the sanction for unlawful acts, so that he can make a rational determination of how to act; and so there have to be reasonably clear standards for determining the amount of punitive damages for particular wrongs.

And a third precept, the core of the Aristotelian notion of corrective justice, and more broadly of the principle of the rule of law, is that sanctions should be based on the wrong done rather than on the status of the defendant; a person is punished for what he does, not for who he is, even if the who is a huge corporation.

What follows from these principles, however, is that punitive damages should be admeasured by standards or rules rather than in a completely ad hoc manner, and this does not tell us what the maximum ratio of punitive to compensatory damages should be in a particular case. To determine that, we have to consider why punitive damages are awarded in the first place. . . .

England's common law courts first confirmed their authority to award punitive damages in the eighteenth century . . . at a time when the institutional structure of criminal law enforcement was primitive and it made sense to leave certain minor crimes to be dealt with by the civil law. And still today one function of punitive-damages awards is to relieve the pressures on an overloaded system of criminal justice by providing a civil alternative to criminal prosecution of minor crimes. An example is deliberately spitting in a person's face, a criminal assault but because minor readily deterrable by the levying of what amounts to a civil fine through a suit for damages for the tort of battery. Compensatory damages would not do the trick in such a case, and this for three reasons: because they are difficult to determine in the case of acts that inflict largely dignatory harms; because in the spitting case they would be too slight to give the victim an incentive to sue, and he might decide instead to respond with violence—and an age-old purpose of the law of torts is to provide a substitute for violent retaliation against wrongful injury—and because to limit the plaintiff to compensatory damages would enable the defendant to commit the offensive act with impunity provided that he was willing to pay, and again there would be a danger that his act would incite a breach of the peace by his victim.

When punitive damages are sought for billion-dollar oil spills and other huge economic injuries, the considerations that we have just canvassed fade. As the Court emphasized in *Campbell*, the fact that the plaintiffs in that case had been awarded very substantial compensatory damages—$1 million for a dispute over insurance coverage—greatly reduced the need for giving them a huge award of punitive damages ($145 million) as well in order to provide an effective remedy. Our case is closer to the spitting case. The defendant's behavior was outrageous but the compensable harm done was slight and at the same time difficult to quantify because a large element of it was emotional. And the defendant may well have profited from its misconduct because by concealing the infestation it was able to keep renting rooms. . . . The award of punitive damages in this case thus serves the additional purpose of limiting the defendant's ability to profit from its fraud by escaping detection and (private) prosecution. If a tortfeasor is "caught" only half the time he commits torts, then when he is caught he should be punished twice as heavily in order to make up for the times he gets away.

Finally, if the total stakes in the case were capped at $50,000 (2 × [$5,000 + $20,000]), the plaintiffs might well have had difficulty financing this lawsuit. It is here that the defendant's aggregate net worth of $1.6 billion becomes relevant. A defendant's wealth is not a sufficient basis for awarding punitive damages. . . . That would be discriminatory and would violate the rule of law, as we explained earlier, by making punishment depend on status rather than conduct. Where wealth in the sense of resources enters is in enabling the defendant to mount an extremely aggressive defense against suits such as this and by doing so to make litigating against it very costly, which in turn may make it difficult for the plaintiffs to find a lawyer willing to handle their case, involving as it does only modest stakes, for the usual 33–40 percent contingent fee.

In other words, the defendant is investing in developing a reputation intended to deter plaintiffs. It is difficult otherwise to explain the great stubbornness with which it has defended this case, making a host of frivolous evidentiary arguments despite the very modest stakes even when the punitive damages awarded by the jury are included.

***

All things considered, we cannot say that the award of punitive damages was excessive, albeit the precise number chosen by the jury was arbitrary. It is probably not a coincidence that $5,000 + $186,000 = $191,000/191 = $1,000: i.e., $1,000 per room in the hotel. But as there are no punitive-damages guidelines, corresponding to the federal and state sentencing guidelines, it is inevitable that the specific amount of punitive damages awarded whether by a judge or by a jury will be arbitrary. (Which is perhaps why the plaintiffs' lawyer did not suggest a number to the jury.) The judicial function is to police a range, not a point. . . .

But it would have been helpful had the parties presented evidence concerning the regulatory or criminal penalties to which the defendant exposed itself by deliberately exposing its customers to a substantial risk of being bitten by bedbugs. That is an inquiry recommended by the Supreme Court. . . . But we do not think its omission invalidates the award. We can take judicial notice that deliberate exposure of hotel guests to the health risks created by insect infestations exposes the hotel's owner to sanctions under Illinois and Chicago law that in the aggregate are comparable in severity to that of the punitive damage award in this case.

***

Affirmed. ■

According to Judge Posner, the Supreme Court, in *State Farm v. Campbell*, did not set an absolute ceiling on punitive damages awards, but merely created a rebuttable presumption that a punitive damages award exceeding actual damages by a factor of 10 or more would be unreasonable and a violation of due process. The presumption of unconstitutionality can be rebutted, however, if the award is proportional to the defendant's culpability, as the 7th Circuit found in the *Mathias* case. Moreover, Judge Posner provided economic reasons why it would be a bad idea for the Supreme Court to impose an absolute ceiling on punitive damages awards in some future case.[48]

Limitations on Joint and Several Liability

In addition to judicial and legislative efforts to cap punitive damages, most states have enacted reforms to limit or eliminate joint and several liability. In 1986, the State of California, pursuant to public referendum (Proposition 51), barred recovery of noneconomic damages under joint and several liability.[49] A year later, in 1987, the Arizona legislature banned joint and several liability in all cases except those involving intentional torts and hazardous waste.[50] New York's legislature similarly limited the application of joint and several liability in 1986, though with more exceptions than Arizona provided in its ban.[51] Indiana has imposed a complete ban on joint and several liability, without exception.[52]

Ceilings on Malpractice Liability

Another favorite reform measure among the states has been to limit the malpractice liability of doctors. The State of Indiana limits the total amount recoverable in medical liability cases, including awards for pain and suffering and punitive damages, to $1.25 million.[53] New York imposes no such cap on medical liability, but limits contingent fee arrangements between plaintiffs and their lawyers.[54] California caps noneconomic damages at $250,000 *and* limits contingent fee agreements to 40 percent for the first $50,000, 33 percent for the next $50,000, and 15 percent for any amount in excess of $600,000.[55]

Collateral Source Rules

More and more states have enacted *collateral source rules*, which reduce tort recoveries to the extent that plaintiffs are compensated from other sources, such as insurance companies or workers' compensation funds.[56] States have not been in a hurry, however, to reform products liability; the reforms enacted in that field are relatively modest. None seeks to replace strict liability with negligence law's rule of reasonableness. California raised the burden of proof to establish liability from a preponderance of the evidence to clear and convincing evidence.[57] The State of Kansas limits, by statute, the useful safe life of products to 10 years, reduces the duty of sellers and manufacturers to warn customers about product defects, and creates a rebuttable presumption that products are safe if they meet certain regulatory standards.[58]

Federal Tort Reforms

Tort reform is not just for the states. The federal government has been engaged in tort reform at least since 1957, when Congress enacted the Price-Anderson Act, which capped total liability for a single nuclear accident at any privately-owned, publicly-regulated nuclear power plant to $560 million.[59] Most recently, in 2002 the Bush Administration proposed reforms to medical malpractice liability following a series of highly publicized strikes by doctors, who were protesting high medical malpractice insurance premiums. The Bush Administration's reform proposals included a shortened statute of limitations for filing medical malpractice claims; caps on punitive damages; limitations on contingent fee arrangements between plaintiffs and their attorneys; and imposition of a collateral source rule.

ECONOMIC CONSEQUENCES
OF TORT REFORM

As of yet, few studies have looked at the effects of tort reform. The studies that do exist seem to focus exclusively on the consequences of tort reform for productivity, economic growth, and employment. No studies have accounted for the costs of tort reforms, including losses suffered by plaintiffs, to determine whether those reforms are providing *net* benefits for society as a whole. Nevertheless, the studies provide at least some evidence that tort reform can provide substantial *gross* economic benefits.

A 1995 empirical study for the National Bureau of Economic Research found that tort reforms that reduced liability exposure increased output per worker by 3.1 percent in retail trades, 7.6 percent in repair services, and 8.9 percent in the amusement and recreation industry. Observed productivity effects were smaller in health care and manufacturing industries.[60] With respect to employment, the same study found that liability-reducing reforms were associated with higher employment, "in a broad range of industries."[61] States with a greater number of liability-reducing reforms were found to have higher levels of productivity growth.[62] Interestingly, the authors also studied changes in tort rules that increased the probability and magnitude of liability, and found that those changes were "associated with lower productivity and employment."[63]

In 1994, W. Kip Viscusi and Patricia Born published a study of the effects of general liability and medical malpractice reforms from 1985 to 1987. Among their most interesting findings: "There was a clear-cut relationship between the state's liability insurance performance and the adoption of liability reform. States in which losses greatly exceeded premiums, so that liability insurance was particularly unprofitable, adopted reforms earlier than states whose firms had a better record of profitability."[64] As for post-tort reform effects, Viscusi and Born found "substantial improvements in the profitability of both general liability and medical malpractice insurance."[65] They also predicted that insurance customers would ultimately benefit from lower premiums. However, in a subsequent study, the same authors found only slight (statistically insignificant) evidence that the gains from medical malpractice reforms in Colorado were being passed along to insurance customers.[66] An unrelated *Wall Street Journal* report on medical malpractice reform in Colorado estimated that a 30 percent increase in industry profitability led to only a 9 percent reduction in liability insurance premiums.[67] More recently, a survey published in the trade publication *Medical Liability Monitor* found that limitations on medical malpractice liability in 25 states did not lead to any reductions in insurance premiums.[68]

Nor do tort reforms necessarily reduce lawsuits. For example, restrictions on joint and several liability proved ineffective in reducing the rate of litigation. A 1994 study found "[o]nly weak support for an overall reduction in filings."[69]

Finally, Viscusi and Born conclude one of their studies with an important cautionary note: "In the absence of a more detailed assessment of the desirability of the reforms *and their effects on injured parties*, it would be premature to conclude that reform efforts that were successful in enhancing insurance market profitability should be judged a success from the standpoint of advancing social welfare."[70] In the absence of comparisons of the costs as well as the benefits of tort reform, it is impossible to determine whether capping jury awards, raising burdens of proof, replacing joint and several liability with proportional liability, and other mechanisms improve the overall efficiency of the tort system. On the other hand, no evidence shows that unreformed tort liability systems maximize social welfare. Legal policy choices in this area remain subject to substantial uncertainty. The same cannot be said for the political contests over tort reform, which are absolutely certain to continue.

THE NO-FAULT ALTERNATIVE

Even as American states experimented with various incremental reforms to the tort systems, none seriously considered abandoning tort law entirely in favor of something radically different, such as a comprehensive system of no-fault accident insurance. Elsewhere in the world, however, a few countries, including New Zealand, Sweden, and Finland, have done just that. In this section, we assess the advantages and disadvantages of the no-fault alternative to torts.

The idea of no-fault insurance, as an alternative to the tort system, is simple enough in theory. Instead of using tort law to establish fault and require compensation from some legally responsible party, victims of accidental injuries receive compensation from a public or private insurance fund. This approach removes disputes over accidents from the legal system, presumably saving on court costs (including delayed compensation because of time lags in the litigation process) and lawyers' fees.

Workers' Compensation and No-Fault Auto Insurance in the United States

The no-fault insurance approach is not unfamiliar in the United States. States have long relied on it for compensating victims of certain kinds of accidents. In most states, employees injured at the *workplace* cannot sue their employers for tort, even if the injury resulted from the employers' negligence. Instead, injured workers are compensated out of state-controlled workers' compensation funds, which are financed by payroll taxes. In some states, injured workers can sue their employers for negligence if the workers are less than fully compensated for their injuries by workers' compensation. In some other states, workers can choose between suing in tort or receiving workers' compensation. In most states, workplace accident victims have no choice; their only recourse is to the state's workers' compensation fund.

In addition to workers' compensation laws, several American states (though none since 1976[71]) have enacted no-fault insurance legislation to compensate victims of automobile accidents. In this context, however, the label *no-fault* is something of a misnomer. Under a pure no-fault rule, auto accident victims would be compensated for their injuries by their own insurance company, regardless of who was at fault. No state follows this pure rule. Instead, they create hybrid regimes in which both insurance and the tort system play roles in compensating auto accident victims. Insurance is the exclusive source of compensation up to some preset limit, beyond which the victim can sue to recover from a negligent party. Note that in contrast to workers' compensation laws, no-fault automobile insurance schemes are neither funded by taxes nor publicly managed; they are private insurance systems.

Is the shift from tort law to no-fault automobile insurance socially efficient? That is, does it reduce the total costs of accidents, accident avoidance, and administration? Empirical studies yield inconclusive results. As one such study explains, "The results indicate that no-fault can yield substantial savings over the traditional [tort] system, or may increase costs significantly, depending on the no-fault plan's provisions." However, the same study found that all no-fault plans, regardless of plan provisions, do the following: reduce transaction costs by up to 80 percent; match compensation more closely with economic loss by increasing the fraction of economic losses actually compensated; reduce the amounts paid in compensation for noneconomic loss for less seriously injured people, for example, by excluding recovery for pain and suffering; and speed up compensation by an average of two months.[72]

On the other hand, a study prepared by the public interest group Public Citizen and California's Proposition 103 Enforcement Project found that auto insurance premiums rose 25 percent faster in no-fault states than in tort states between 1989 and 1995. Indeed, drivers in no-fault states paid the highest average auto liability premiums. Meanwhile, drivers in states that repealed no-fault auto insurance laws and returned to the tort system saw their insurance rates fall.[73]

One perceived drawback of no-fault auto insurance regimes concerns the incentives of drivers who would be legally liable for fewer—and in a *pure* system, none—of the costs resulting from careless driving. Does no-fault create a moral hazard—an incentive for people to drive with less care?[74] Again, empirical studies yield mixed results. Some find an increase in traffic fatalities in states that adopted no-fault auto insurance,[75] but others find no such relation.[76] In one recent study, empirical evidence supported the researcher's hypothesis that the effect of no-fault on fatal accident rates is "ambiguous:" "[I]f negligence assignment under tort is sufficiently responsive to care levels undertaken by drivers, then no-fault is likely to be associated with higher fatality rates." The evidence suggested the existence of a "trade-off between the advantages of no-fault as an accident compensation system and its adverse effects on incentives."[77]

Comprehensive No-Fault Insurance in New Zealand

While some American states instituted no-fault insurance systems to cover certain kinds of accidents, New Zealand went much farther, replacing its tort system with a state-sponsored regime of no-fault insurance for virtually all accidental injuries.[78] In 1972, New Zealand's parliament enacted the Accident Compensation Act,[79] which was designed as a thoroughgoing substitute for the tort system as a conduit for compensating accident victims. In fact, the act threw out the tort system by terminating victims' rights to sue for personal injuries resulting from accidents.[80] In its place, New Zealand's parliament erected a cradle-to-grave scheme of no-fault accident insurance to compensate and rehabilitate accident victims. This scheme was based on five principles established in 1967 by the Royal Commission on Compensation for Personal Injury in New Zealand: community responsibility, comprehensive entitlement, complete rehabilitation, real compensation, and administrative efficiency.[81]

Under New Zealand's Accident Compensation Act, as originally implemented, accident victims had no choice but to seek compensation from a state-funded and -managed accident compensation/insurance fund,[82] regardless of who was at fault for the accident. The compensation fund was financed by taxes on payrolls and motor vehicles, supplemented by general government revenues. Victims could make claims against the compensation fund for (a) all reasonable medical expenses, including costs of any necessary rehabilitation; (b) up to 80 percent of lost earnings to a maximum of NZ$200 per week for the entire period of disability,[83] or up to 80 percent of lost earning capacity for permanent disabilities; (c) lump-sum payments of up to NZ$5,000 for noneconomic losses including impaired bodily functions or lost body parts, plus a maximum of NZ$7,000 for pain and mental anguish; and (d) other related and necessary expenses.[84] In addition to compensating accident victims, the act also sought to protect their dependents (spouses and children) in case of accidental death or incapacitating injury.[85]

As a result of the switch from tort-based compensation to no-fault insurance, New Zealand reduced to zero the costs associated with filing, defending, and litigating tort claims. Instead, it accepted the costs associated with funding and administering a state-based comprehensive insurance fund. The New Zealand government was betting that the total costs of its new comprehensive no-fault system would be lower than the total costs associated with its preexisting tort system. As Geoffrey Palmer, an early proponent of the Accident Compensation Act who later became prime minister of New Zealand, explained, the shift to state-funded no-fault insurance was expected to provide broader and surer coverage at the same or lower cost than tort compensation. In the tort system, "a large percentage of the premium dollar did not reach the accident victim." Under New Zealand's Accident Compensation Act, by contrast, "[b]etter use was to be made of existing money by delivering a greater proportion of the money to the injured. Insurance companies were cut out of the business, the adversary process abolished, and administrative costs drastically reduced."[86]

In 1979, Palmer judged New Zealand's experiment a clear (if not unalloyed) success:

> The administration of the Act in New Zealand has not matched the vision of the original blueprint. The style of administration has too often been characterized by an abundance of caution, a stubborn inflexibility, and an undue sensitivity to public criticism. Notwithstanding the conservative style of administration, the Accident Compensation Act has worked in New Zealand for four years without much sign of public dissatisfaction. . . .
>
> Against the difficulties encountered must be matched the achievements of the new scheme. There is much less room for argument under the new scheme than there was under the common law. Everyone who is incapacitated is paid and paid quickly in most cases. The social problem posed by the uncompensated victim has disappeared. Rather than providing a brake on rehabilitation the new scheme promotes it. The removal of the right to sue has been accompanied by no floods of protests. The common law action for personal injury in New Zealand has been buried and there is no demand for its exhumation. The unnecessary waste and expense of the old

systems has been cut away. Uncertain, uncoordinated, and capricious remedies have been replaced by an integrated and comprehensive scheme offering compensation which is usually swift and sure.[87]

Other observers have been less impressed by the design and performance of New Zealand's Accident Compensation Act. According to one source, by the late 1990s there was a consensus in New Zealand that the comprehensive no-fault system of accident insurance "failed to meet expectations."[88] Indeed, the Accident Compensation Commission acknowledged that already in the 1970s, a "growing dissatisfaction with the overall cost of the scheme," appeared especially among employers who financed the lion's share of the compensation funds through payroll taxes.[89] The mere fact that New Zealand's parliament has substantially amended the Accident Compensation Act at least a dozen times since 1974 suggests serious design and/or implementation problems.

The sheer rate of institutional change itself constitutes a potentially serious problem. In 1998, for example, New Zealand's parliament enacted an Accident Insurance Act, which allowed employers to choose between the state's no-fault scheme and private workers' compensation insurance. The idea was to introduce greater competition into the insurance market, with the expectation that competition would lower the cost of coverage. Then, just two years later, the Accident Insurance Act was repealed, as New Zealand's Accident Compensation Commission was made the sole insurer of workplace injuries once again. Such changes could not help but generate public and administrative confusion, which itself is costly.

As with no-fault auto insurance programs in the United States, critics of New Zealand's comprehensive no-fault accident insurance programs point out that "the virtual absence of any external incentive to avoid accidents" creates a sizeable moral hazard. As Richard Miller has noted, "Other than their own moral values or a desire to maintain or create a reputation for safety, most companies, landlords, health care providers, and manufacturers of products . . . have no incentive to invest in accident prevention and safety."[90] The simple reason is that they are not financially responsible if anyone is injured due to their carelessness. New Zealand's social insurance system for compensating accident victims externalizes the risks of accidents from those who create them to all New Zealanders who contribute, in one way or another, to the state's compensation fund. The question is whether it is an efficient externality (as defined in Chapter 1). That is, does it reduce overall accident costs for society?

Economists would predict that the moral hazard created by the Accident Compensation Act would lead to an increase in the rate and possibly the magnitude of accidental injuries. Empirical tests have not borne out this prediction. A 1989 study of automobile accidents in New Zealand found that "the abolition of the right to sue for personal injury is an important factor in promoting road safety. The ability to obtain noneconomic loss compensation by meeting court care standards appears to be an important factor in encouraging driver care."[91] A less rigorous 1985 study, by contrast, found that "the removal of tort liability for personal injury in New Zealand has apparently had no adverse effect on driving habits. In fact, statistics show a decline in accident and fatality rates."[92] This study did not, however, control for several exogenous explanatory factors including increasing gasoline prices; technological improvements in automobile safety; new government regulations that mandated use of seat belts in 1972, reduced speed limits in 1973, and lowered the legal limit of drivers' blood-alcohol levels; and increased government enforcement of these and other automobile regulations.[93] Most recently, a 2003 study found the following:

> Overall fatal accident rates do not appear to be sensitive to the existence of liability. There is no evidence of a discontinuity in accident rates when New Zealand abolished tort liability for injury in 1974. At most, there has been a modest long run trend effect in increasing fatal accident rates over what they would otherwise have been. Data on industrial injury trends and rotary wing aircraft accidents provide some support for believing that the abolition of tort liability for personal injury has led to a net reduction in incentives to reduce accident-generating behavior.[94]

With respect to accidental injuries resulting from other activities, such as medical malpractice, the evidence from New Zealand is more mixed. It should be noted, however, that empirical analyses are hampered by a lack of adequate data collection and dissemination by New Zealand's Accident Compensation Commission, which is particularly surprising given that New Zealand's government-controlled compensation system should have made data collection and dissemination relatively easy (i.e., inexpensive).[95]

Finally, critics discount the significance of claims that New Zealand's no-fault system minimizes administrative costs. It may be true, as the system's proponents claim, that overhead costs are only 10 percent of total expenditures, so that more funds can be paid directly to accident victims. However, Patricia M. Danzon observes that low overhead does not necessarily signify efficiency. The Accident Compensation Commission, she notes, accepts more than 80 percent of claims as filed, assuming that physicians would not falsely or fraudulently certify a personal injury claim:

> But physicians have no incentive to oppose claims; indeed, until recently physicians could benefit from certifying a claim. . . . Thus this mechanism of claims adjudication may have saved overhead costs but has contributed to the rapid escalation of total claims costs. . . . [S]uch economizing on overheads may be 'penny wise but pound foolish', skimping on budget costs but with higher real social costs. . . .
>
> [I]n New Zealand the very low overhead percentage reflects the rapid increase in claims payments (the denominator) owing to minimal claims investigation. The true overheads of an insurance or accident compensation scheme include not only the measured overheads, but also the deadweight loss from unnecessary injuries and inappropriately compensated claims. Unfortunately this is not observable, but in the [Accident Compensation Commission] it is likely to be very high.[96]

In the final analysis, the existing empirical evidence does not permit a conclusion that New Zealand's comprehensive no-fault scheme for accident compensation is either a thoroughgoing success or an outright failure. It certainly has saved on some of the costs associated with a traditional tort system, while increasing other costs, including the costs associated with constant legislative tinkering with the system. Whether the total gains exceed the total costs is uncertain.

In any case, New Zealand's no-fault system is not a model that other countries are likely to follow. American states continue to actively debate the value of marginal reforms to their tort systems, but none seems likely to scrap its tort system entirely, as New Zealand has done, in favor of a comprehensive no-fault insurance scheme. At the same time, although New Zealand continually tinkers with its no-fault system, a quick return to tort law seems unlikely.

CHAPTER SUMMARY

This chapter explored the ongoing public policy debates over tort law, including whether the current system costs society too much money compared to some reformed tort system that (among other things) would reduce the potential liabilities of tort defendants. Both sides in the debate present some strong arguments, and it is not obvious that one side should prevail. Unfortunately, not enough solid research exists comparing the costs and benefits of the current system with the costs and benefits of various reforms.

This chapter also examined a more thoroughgoing alternative to the tort system of compensating accident victims: no-fault insurance. This insurance-based compensation system has seen limited use in the United States and more comprehensive use in New Zealand (and a few other countries). Although no-fault insurance surely avoids some of the costs associated with the tort system, it has problems of its own, including moral hazard problems. Whether it is superior, all things considered, to a tort-based compensation regime remains unanswered.

QUESTIONS AND PROBLEMS

1. How would various tort reform proposals reduce the incidence and the costs of tort claims?
2. Who do you think was the best cost avoider in the McDonald's coffee case, and why?
3. Should state legislatures cap punitive damages awards and awards for pain and suffering? Why or why not?
4. How likely is it, in any case, that state legislatures will enact tort reforms that cap punitive damages at an efficient level, in order to avoid both under- and overdeterrence of economic activities that create risks of harm? What might a public choice theorist expect of tort reform legislation?
5. What are some advantages and disadvantages of no-fault insurance as a substitute for the tort system?
6. Why might economists expect traffic fatalities to rise after a switch from tort-based compensation to no-fault insurance? And why might the empirical evidence fail to confirm those expectations?
7. Why might an absolute cap on punitive damages be a bad idea from an economic point of view?

NOTES

1. *See* William M. Landes and Richard A. Posner, *The Economic Structure of Tort Law* (Cambridge: Harvard University Press, 1987), p. 312, which claims that *most* common law tort rules are efficient.

2. Tillinghast-Towers Perrin, *U.S. Tort Costs 2000 Update: Trends and Findings on the Costs of the U.S. Tort System* (2002), p. 13. It does not include, however, the costs associated with administering the state and federal courts or "indirect" costs, such as the costs to society of duplicative and unnecessary tests that doctors sometimes order out of fear of possible malpractice exposure (p. 18).

3. Tillinghast-Towers Perrin, *U.S. Tort Costs 2000 Update: Trends and Findings on the Costs of the U.S. Tort System* (2002), p. 9.

4. *BMW of North America v. Gore*, 517 U.S. 559 (1996).

5. For more on this case, *see* page 251.

6. W. Kip Viscusi, *The Blockbuster Punitive Damages Award*, Harvard Law School, John M. Olin Center for Law, Economics, and Business, Discussion Paper No. 473 (April 2004), p. 22.

7. John Lewis and Raquel Becerra, *A Study of the United States and Illinois Tort System* (Center for Governmental Studies, Northern Illinois University,1995), p. 2.

8. *See* William A. Worthington, "The 'Citadel' Revisited: Strict Tort Liability and the Policy of Law," 36 SOUTHERN TEXAS LAW REVIEW 227, 250 n. 108 (1995).

9. *See* Man C. Maloo and Benjamin A. Neil, *Product Liability Exposure: The Sacrifice of American Innovation*, 13 JOURNAL OF PRODUCTS LIABILITY 361, 368-9 (1991).

10. W. Kip Viscusi, *Reforming Products Liability* (Cambridge: Harvard University Press, 1991), p. 8.

11. *See* Alfred W. Cortese, Jr. and Kathleen L. Blaner, "The Anti-Competitive Impact of U.S. Product Liability Laws: Are Foreign Businesses Beating Us at Our Own Game?" 9 JOURNAL OF LAW AND COMMERCE 167, 194, 201 (1989).

12. Alfred W. Cortese, Jr. and Kathleen L. Blaner, "The Anti-Competitive Impact of U.S. Product Liability Laws: Are Foreign Businesses Beating Us at Our Own Game?" 9 JOURNAL OF LAW AND COMMERCE 196 (1989).

13. "Is Liability Slowing AIDS Vaccines?" SCIENCE, April 10, 1992, pp. 168–69.

14. Alfred W. Cortese, Jr. and Kathleen L. Blaner, "The Anti-Competitive Impact of U.S. Product Liability Laws: Are Foreign Businesses Beating Us at Our Own Game?" 9 JOURNAL OF LAW AND COMMERCE 195–96 (1989).

15. Economists refer to such unrealized gains as "deadweight losses."

16. Tillinghast-Towers Perrin, *U.S. Tort Costs 2000 Update: Trends and Findings on the Costs of the U.S. Tort System* (2002), p. 17.

17. Accounts of the existing tort system typically neglect that defendants' attorneys also have a substantial interest in perpetuating the status quo. Unlike plaintiffs' attorneys, they do not directly benefit from high damages awards (although the magnitude of potential tort damages should, all else being equal, lead potential defendants to invest more in tort defense). However, defense attorneys do have a direct stake in the rate of claims/litigation. To the extent tort reform proposals are designed to reduce the number of claims, potential defendants can be expected to hire fewer in-house lawyers and invest less in outside counsel to deal with tort claims.

18. For an economic argument that punitive damages should be capped as a multiple of compensatory damages, rather than set at some certain level unrelated to compensatory damages, *see* Gary Becker, "How to Put the Right Cap on Punitive Damages," *Business Week,* September 15, 2003, p. 28.

19. A useful overview is found in Marc Galanter, "Real World Torts: An Antidote to Anecdote," 55 *MARYLAND LAW REVIEW* 1093 (1996).

20. *See* Molly Selvin and Patricia A. Ebener, *Managing the Unmanageable: A History of Civil Delay in the Los Angeles Superior Court* (Santa Monica: Rand Corp. 1985), pp. 32–34. A "trough" occurred from roughly 1930 through 1960, when the rate of litigation fell significantly. That "trough," it has been suggested, became a somewhat unrealistic baseline for those who, after 1960, perceived a litigation explosion. *See* Marc Galanter, "The Turn Against Law: The Recoil Against Expanding Accountability," 81 *Texas Law Review* 285, 285–6,

295 (2002). According the statistics gathered by the U.S. Department of Justice, the level of tort litigation has been stable since 1986, and actually declined since 1990. *See* Steven K. Smith et al., U.S. Dept. of Justice, Bureau of Justice Statistics Special Report: Civil Justice Survey of State Courts, 1992; Tort Cases in Large Counties 2 (1995); Court Stat. Project, Examining the Work of State Courts, 1994: A National Perspective from the Court Statistics Project (1995).

21. David M. Trubek et al., "The Cost of Ordinary Litigation," 31 *UCLA Law Review* 72, 87, Table 1 (1983).

22. David M. Trubek et al., "The Cost of Ordinary Litigation," 31 *UCLA Law Review* 89 (1983).

23. David M. Trubek et al., "The Cost of Ordinary Litigation," 31 *UCLA Law Review* 92 (1983). In only 8 percent of cases did legal fees exceed $10,000.

24. Deborah H. Hensler et al., *Rand Inst. for Civil Justice, Compensation for Accidental Injuries in the United States* (1991), p. 19.

25. *Patients, Doctors, and Lawyers: Medical Injury, Malpractice Litigation, and Patient Compensation in New York: The Report of the Harvard Medical Practice Study to the State of New York* (1990), p. 7.

26. Steven Garber, "Products Liability, Punitive Damages, Business Decisions and Economic Outcomes," 1998 *Wisconsin Law Review* 237, 277.

27. Erik Moller, *Trends in Civil Jury Verdicts Since 1985* (Rand Corporation, 1995), p. xv, which noted that plaintiffs prevail in only 33 percent of medical malpractice cases and 44 percent of products liability cases. Interestingly, when plaintiffs prevail in products liability and medical malpractice cases, the average jury awards are relatively high. Thus, defendants have a lower probability of being held liable for defective products or medical malpractice, but the magnitude of expected damages is higher.

28. Marc Galanter, "Real World Torts: An Antidote to Anecdote," 55 *Maryland Law Review* 301 (1996).

29. Kenneth D. Kranz, "Tort Reform 1997–98: Profits v. People?" 25 *Florida State University Law Review* 161, 178 (1998).

30. Erik Moller, *Trends in Civil Jury Verdicts Since 1985* (Rand Corporation, 1995), p. xviii. *Also see* Carol J. DeFrances et al., "Civil Jury Cases and Verdicts in Large Counties," Bureau of Statistics Special Rep. NCJ–154346 Tables 4, 6, and 8 (July 1995), which reported that juries in 12,026 cases in the 75 largest American counties in 1992 awarded punitive damages in 5.9 percent of all cases, 12.2 percent of contract cases, 18.5 percent of intentional tort cases, and just 3.4 percent of nonintentional tort cases. Theodore Eisenberg et al., "The Predictability of Punitive Damages," 26 *Journal of Legal Studies* 623 (1997), which found that punitive damage awards are awarded only rarely and most often in business and contract cases. The Eisenberg et al. study's findings and interpretation have been challenged in A. Mitchel Polinsky, "Are Punitive Damages Really Insignificant, Predictable, and Rational? A Comment on Eisenberg et al.," 26 *Journal of Legal Studies* 663 (1997).

31. W. Kip Viscusi, "Toward a Diminished Role for Tort Liability: Social Insurance, Government Regulation and Contemporary Risks to Health and Safety," 6 *Yale Journal on Regulation* 65, 95–6 (1989).

32. 509 U.S. 433, 500 (1993).

33. Erik Moller, *Trends in Civil Jury Verdicts Since 1985* (Rand Corporation, 1995), pp. 20–23.

34. Marc Galanter, "Real World Torts: An Antidote to Anecdote," 55 *Maryland Law Review* 301 (1996).

35. Linda T. Kohn et al., *To Err Is Human: Building a Safer Health System* (Washington, DC: National Academy Press, 2000).

36. "Medical Misdiagnosis in New Jersey: Challenging the Medical Malpractice Claims of the Doctor's Lobby," *Public Citizen*, January 2003.

37. Neil Komesar, "Injuries and Institutions: Tort Reform, Tort Theory, and Beyond," 65 *New York University Law Review* 23, 24 (1990).

38. Neil Komesar, "Injuries and Institutions: Tort Reform, Tort Theory, and Beyond," 65 *New York University Law Review* 70 (1990).

39. *Grimshaw v. Ford Motor Co.*, 119 Cal. App. 3d 757 (1981).

40. *See* Neil Komesar, "Injuries and Institutions: Tort Reform, Tort Theory, and Beyond," 65 *New York University Law Review* 64–5 (1990).

41. Ga. Code Ann. § 51-12-5.1.

42. Ind. Code Ann. § 34-51-3-4.

43. *See* page 214.

44. *BMW of North America, Inc. v. Gore*, 517 U.S. 559, 575 (1996)

45. 538 US 408, 123 S.Ct. 1513, 1524 (2003).

46 *Ibid.*

47. *Ibid.*

48. The *State Farm* precedent is, however, having some effect on punitive damages awards in other courts. In *Romo v. Ford Motor Co.*, 113 Cal. App. 4th 738 (2003), for example, the California Court of Appeals repeatedly cited *State Farm* in reducing a jury's punitive damages award from a ratio of 54.7:1 (punitive damages to compensatory damages) to a ratio of only 5:1. On the other hand, it was hardly unusual, even before *State Farm*, for appeals courts to slash punitive damages awards. So, it is difficult to assess the precise impact of the Supreme Court's decision on lower court behavior (at least at this early date). In a recent study of "blockbuster" punitive damage awards (in excess of $100 million), W. Kip Viscusi found that 96 percent of punitive damages awards in state courts are within the 9:1 (punitive damages to compensatory damages) ratio authorized by the U.S. Supreme Court in *State Farm*. W. Kip Viscusi, *The Blockbuster Punitive Damages Award*, Harvard Law School, John M. Olin Center for Law, Economics, and Business, Discussion Paper No. 473 (April 2004), p. 18.

49. Cal. Civ. Code § 1431.2.

50. Ariz. Stat. § 12-2506.

51. N.Y. Civ. Prac. L. & R. §§ 1601–1602.

52. Ind. Code Ann. § 34-51-2-8.

53. Ind. Code Ann. § 34-18-14-3. The $1.25 million cap is for acts occurring after July 1, 1999. For acts occurring before that date, liability is capped at $750,000.

54. N.Y. Jud. Law. § 474-a.

55. Cal. Bus. & Prof. Code §§ 333.2 and 6146(a).

56. *See, for example*, Ind. Code. Ann. § 34-44-1-2; N.Y. C.P.L.R. § 4545(a); Cal. Civil Code § 3333.1; Ariz. Rev. Stat. §12–565; 735 Ill. Comp. Stat. Ann. § 5/2-1205.

57. Cal. Civ. Code § 3294(a).

58. Kan. Stat. Ann. §§ 60-3301 to 60-3304.

59. 42 U.S.C. § 2210.

60. Thomas J. Campbell, Daniel P. Kessler, and George B. Shepard, "The Causes and Effects of Liability Reform: Some Empirical Evidence," Working Paper No. 4989, National Bureau of Economic Research (January 1995), p. 19.

61. Thomas J. Campbell, Daniel P. Kessler, and George B. Shepard, "The Causes and

Effects of Liability Reform: Some Empirical Evidence," Working Paper No. 4989, National Bureau of Economic Research (January 1995), p. 28.

62. *Ibid.*

63. Thomas J. Campbell, Daniel P. Kessler, and George B. Shepard, "The Causes and Effects of Liability Reform: Some Empirical Evidence," Working Paper No. 4989, National Bureau of Economic Research (January 1995), p. 27.

64. W. Kip Viscusi and Patricia Born, "The National Implications of Liability Reforms for General Liability and Medical Malpractice Insurance," 24 *Seton Hall Law Review* 1743, 1764–5 (1994).

65. *Ibid.*

66. W. Kip Viscusi and Patricia Born, "Medical Malpractice Insurance in the Wake of Liability Reform," 24 *Journal of Legal Studies* 463, 466, 488–90 (1995).

67. Milo Geyelin, "Tort Reform Test: Overhaul of Civil Law in Colorado Produces Quite Mixed Results," *The Wall Street Journal*, March 3, 1992, p. A1.

68. "2002 Rate Report," *Medical Liability Monitor*, 2002.

69. Han-Duck Lee, Mark J. Browne, and Joan T. Schmidt, "How Does Joint and Several Tort Reform Affect the Rate of Tort Filings? Evidence from the State Courts," 61 *Journal of Risk & Insurance* 295 (1994).

70. W. Kip Viscusi and Patricia Born, "The National Implications of Liability Reforms for General Liability and Medical Malpractice Insurance," 24 *Seton Hall Law Review* 1765–6 (1994) (emphasis added).

71. Since 1989, four states have repealed no-fault insurance schemes for auto accidents, returning to tort law-based compensation. *See* Public Citizen, "The Absolute Failure of No-Fault: Premium Trends in No-Fault States," at http://www.citizen.org/congress/civjus/no_fault/articles.cfm? ID=867.

72. Stephen J. Carroll and James S. Kakalik, "No-Fault Approaches to Compensating Auto Accident Victims," 60 *Journal of Risk & Insurance* 265, 265, 286 (1993).

73. Public Citizen, Congress Watch, "The Absolute Failure of No-Fault: Premium Trends in No-Fault States," available at http://www.citizen.org/congress/civjus/no_fault/articles.cfm?ID=867.

74. On the concept of moral hazard, see Chapter 6. The same question applies, as we shall see, to New Zealand's comprehensive no-fault insurance scheme for compensating victims of all types of accidents.

75. *See, for example*, Elizabeth Landes, "Insurance Liability and Accidents: A Theoretical and Empirical Investigation of the Effect of No-Fault Accidents," 25 *JOURNAL OF LAW & ECONOMICS* 49 (1982).

76. *See* Paul S. Kochanowski and Madelyn V. Young, "Deterrent Aspects of No-Fault Automobile Insurance: Some Empirical Findings," 52 Journal of Risk & Insurance 269 (1985); Paul Zador and Adrian Lund, "Reanalyses of the Effects of No-Fault Auto Insurance on Fatal Crashes," 53 *JOURNAL OF RISK & INSURANCE* 226 (1986).

77. J. David Cummins, Richard D. Phillips, and Mary A. Weiss, "The Incentive Effects of No-Fault Automobile Insurance," 44 *JOURNAL OF LAW & ECONOMICS* 427, 454–5 (2001).

78. Tort law still governs *intentional* torts such as assault and battery in New Zealand. Also, it should be borne in mind that while the tort system from which New Zealand converted to no-fault was similar to the U.S. tort system, it was not precisely the same. For example, New Zealand's common law never developed a rule of strict liability for defective products; no contingency fees were permitted; and judges were allowed to comment, before the jury, on the quality of the evidence. These characteristics reflect the jurisdiction-specific nature of the common law, as discussed in Chapter 2.

79. Accident Compensation Act 1972, No. 43. This act was substantially amended twice before it took effect in 1974.

80. The act did *not*, however, terminate the right to sue for punitive damages.

81. *Report of the Royal Commission of Inquiry into Compensation for Personal Injury in New Zealand* (1967), p. 20. *See also* Bryce Wilkinson, "New Zealand's Failed Experiment with State Monopoly Accident Insurance," 2 Green Bag 2D 45, 49 (Fall 1998).

82. In fact, three distinct funds were established: an "earners' fund," a "motor vehicle fund," for non-work-related automobile accidents, and a "supplemental fund."

83. If the accident occurred in the course of employment, the employer was obligated to pay wages for the first week following the accident; the compensation fund would begin paying out in the second week of disability. To protect against losses above 80 percent of $200, individuals had to privately insure.

84. To account for inflation and in response to other social pressures, New Zealand's Parliament raised, from time to time, compensation limits under the Accident Compensation Act. For example, by the early 1990s, the compensation limit was 80 percent of lost wages up to NZ$1,179 per week (or NZ$61,308 per year). *See* "Beyond Compensation: The New Zealand Experience," 15 *HAWAII LAW REVIEW* 621, 627 (1993).

85. For more on the 1972 Accident Compensation Act, as it took effect in 1974, *see, for example,* D.R. Harris, "Accident Compensation Law in New Zealand: A Comprehensive Insurance System," 37 *MODERN LAW REVIEW* 361 (1974).

86. Geoffrey W. R. Palmer, *Compensation for Incapacity: A Study of Law and Social Change in New Zealand and Australia* (Oxford: Oxford University Press, 1979), p. 365.

87. Geoffrey W.R. Palmer, *Compensation for Incapacity: A Study of Law and Social Change in New Zealand and Australia* (Oxford: Oxford University Press, 1979), pp. 404–05.

88. Bryce Wilkinson, "New Zealand's Failed Experiment with State Monopoly Accident Insurance," 2 Green Bag 2D 45, 50 (Fall 1998).

89. *See* http://www.acc.org.nz/about-acc/history-of-acc/index–3.html.

90. "Beyond Compensation: Comments: The New Zealand Experience," 15 *HAWAII LAW REVIEW* 621, 630 (1993).

91. R. Ian McEwin, "No-Fault and Road Accidents: Some Australasian Evidence," 9 *INTERNATIONAL REVIEW OF LAW & ECONOMICS* 13, 23–4 (1989).

92. Craig Brown, "Symposium: Alternative Compensation Schemes and Tort Theory: Deterrence in Tort and No-Fault: The New Zealand Experience," 73 *CALIFORNIA LAW REVIEW* 976, 1001–2 (1985).

93. For an explanation of why multivariate analyses of fatality rates are required to reveal relations between no-fault systems and fatalities, *see* J. David Cummins, Richard D. Phillips, and Mary A. Weiss, "The Incentive Effects of

No-Fault Automobile Insurance," 44 *JOURNAL OF LAW & ECONOMICS* 427, 452-3 (2001).

94. John C. Hause, "Fatal Encounters: An Economic Theory of Accidental Injury with Application to New Zealand's No-Fault System," University of Chicago Center for the Study of the Economy and the State, Working Paper (July 1995), p. 116.

95. Many observers, including staunch proponents of New Zealand's no-fault system, have commented on the government's deplorable failure to gather and publish statistics on accidental injuries. *See, for example*, Geoffrey W. R. Palmer, *Compensation for Incapacity: A Study of Law and Social Change in New Zealand and Australia* (Oxford: Oxford University Press, 1979), p. 405. It is worth wondering whether it might not be in the government's interest *not* to gather and publish information that might provide ammunition to critics of the government-run system.

96. Patricia M. Danzon, "Tort Reform: The Case of Medical Malpractice," 10 *OXFORD REVIEW OF ECONOMIC POLICY* 84, 92–3 (1994).

Chapter 13

Crime and Punishment

CRIMINAL WRONGS

Crime and Criminal Law

A crime is simply a tort—a wrong—committed against both the individual victim (if there is one) *and* the larger society. This distinction raises an immediate question about the need for a separate body of law, known as criminal law, in addition to the law of torts. Several ethical and economic reasons explain the need to treat public wrongs (crimes) differently from private wrongs (torts). Some acts are considered so wrongful (or socially inefficient) that the law prohibits them with few or no exceptions. Such acts should not be committed, even if the perpetrator is willing to pay compensation. Murder is a good example. If murder were simply a tort, society presumably would be willing to tolerate murders as long as perpetrators were willing to compensate victims' families. Instead, every society on earth has ultimately concluded that murder should not be allowed regardless of compensation. Murder is everywhere a crime.

Let's assume for a moment that murder is simply a tort, subject to compensation. Suppose a murderer could not afford to fully compensate the victim's family. One purpose of the criminal law is to generate additional deterrent effects—through the threat of imprisonment and, in some cases, capital punishment—where tort damages are likely to be insufficient. Richard Posner suggests that this scenario is most likely where the perpetrator of the crime is nonaffluent, and therefore more likely to be judgment proof. Those who cannot pay tort judgments will not be deterred by tort judgments. More affluent individuals, by contrast, "are kept in line, for the most part, by tort law."[1]

Additional deterrence is not the only purpose of the criminal law. Another is to punish. It would be myopic to suppose, from a naive economic instrumentalism, that criminal sanctions against rape are designed merely to ensure an "optimal level" of deterrence and, by the same token, an "optimal level" of rape. Society criminalizes rape *because rape is a wrong* against all society. Rapists are imprisoned not because their acts are economically inefficient, although they may well be that; and punishments for rape are not designed with the purpose of setting a price on rape, though that is certainly one effect. As Lawrence Friedman has written, "*All* criminal justice, whatever else can be said about it, is economic in one crude, primary sense: its rules are attempts to fix prices or ration behavior."[2]

Criminal Procedure

The immediately obvious difference between criminal law and the law of torts concerns remedies. Convicted criminals are subject to more serious penalties than tortfeasors. Both may be liable for monetary payments in the form of damages for torts and fines for crimes. Unlike tortfeasors, however, convicted criminals may also forfeit their liberty and, in some cases, their lives.

Because the stakes are higher for criminal defendants, the U.S. Constitution imposes special requirements that govern the process whereby defendants are convicted and sentenced. Among them are the following:

- No one can be criminally convicted for an act that was not legally designated a crime before they committed the act.
- Criminal prosecutions are initiated not by those who may have been harmed by the defendant's act but by government prosecutors on behalf of the public at large.
- Alleged perpetrators of crimes are tried in specialized criminal courts in accordance with various constitutional protections against arbitrary or otherwise wrongful arrests, unfair trials, and cruel and unusual punishments.

Special protections include the following:

- Criminal defendants are entitled to legal representation, if necessary at state expense.
- They have a right to trial by jury; the prosecution must prove their guilt not only by a preponderance of the evidence (the standard "burden of proof" in civil trials) but "beyond a reasonable doubt."
- The prosecution may only present evidence obtained through legally warranted searches or seizures; and criminal defendants cannot be required to testify against themselves.

These protections (and others) are designed to prevent abuses of state power, and to minimize the prospects for mistakes that would result in the wrongful conviction of innocent people.

Society Criminalizes Certain Wrongful Acts, But Not Others

Harm ≠ Crime

Not every wrongful or harmful act is a crime. Two boxers in a state-sanctioned fight might beat one another into bloody pulps without being criminally liable. Similarly, negligent behavior, although wrongful, is not ordinarily criminal; it can lead to civil liability but not criminal punishment. On the other hand, some acts are crimes even if no one is actually harmed by them. Attempted murder is one example; conspiracy is another. So it is not the mere fact that harm is done that signifies a crime. Instead, it is the type of act, the degree of wrongfulness of the conduct, or the bad intent of the person causing the harm that leads society to criminalize certain behavior. Criminalization is, ultimately, a matter of public choice.

Criminal Acts, Criminal Intent

Some acts are deemed criminal by their very nature: taking another's property without permission, or pointing a gun at someone and pulling the trigger (without an exculpatory reason such as self-defense). In other cases, it is the extent of wrong-fulness that distinguishes a crime from a mere tort. Simple negligence is almost never punished as a crime, but *gross* negligence (or recklessness) is sometimes criminalized. As the Alabama Court of Appeals explained in *French v. State,*

> It has been repeatedly held . . . that criminal negligence may not be predi-cated upon mere negligence or carelessness, but only upon that degree of negligence or carelessness which is denominated "gross," and which consti-tutes such a departure from what would be the conduct of an ordinarily careful and prudent man under the same circumstances as to furnish evi-dence of that indifference to consequences which in some offenses takes the place of criminal intent.[3]

So, gross negligence becomes a substitute for criminal intent. In cases where the defendant acts with gross negligence or recklessness, the prosecution need not prove that he intended either the act or its consequences.

The same is true when the defendant commits a so-called strict liability crime, such as statutory rape. If a man has sexual intercourse with a woman who is younger than the statutory age of consent, he is guilty of statutory rape, even though he may never have intended to have sex with a minor. He is guilty regardless of his lack of intent to commit the crime, and regardless of his lack of knowledge that the woman was too young.

For most crimes, however, intent is a critical element. Criminal intent can be either general (intent to perform a proscribed act) or specific (intent that performance of the proscribed act will lead to a certain outcome). The crime of simple assault—defined as the use or threatened use of force directed against another, causing a well-founded fear of injury or unwanted touching—is an example of a general intent offense. Assault with intent to murder is a specific intent offense. You might think that such intent would always be difficult to prove beyond a reasonable doubt, yet the law allows a defendant's intent to be presumed from the circumstances. As the California Court of Appeals explained in *People v. Peak,*

> Where the act is both unlawful and wrongful, and well calculated to inflict serious personal injury, the law will imply malice and an unlawful intention and override any actual intention existing in the mind of the aggressor. Thus, while it is not an assault to fire a gun in the air for the purpose of frightening another, it is an assault, without regard to the aggressor's inten-tion, to fire a gun at another or in the direction in which he is standing. The law will not tolerate such a reckless disregard for human life.[4]

Many criminal offenses are uncontroversial: Murder has been a crime in nearly every society that has existed since biblical times. On the other hand, states sometimes criminalize acts for reasons that are best explained by public choice theory. One infamous example is the widespread criminalization of oleomargarine, a butter substitute, which was invented in the 1860s. By the mid–1880s, dairy interests had successfully lobbied for laws in nine states making it a crime to sell Oleo; 34 other states or territories enacted elaborate labeling and other regulatory requirements. Congress got into the act in 1886, when it regulated and taxed the sale of margarine. This state of affairs lasted until the middle of the twentieth century, when the political power of dairy farmers began to subside. Federal taxes and regulations on margarine were repealed in 1950; and the substance was gradually decriminalized in the states. The last holdout, Wisconsin, legalized the sale of butter-colored margarine in 1967.[5]

Crimes as Well as Torts

The fact that an act has been criminalized does not mean it has been removed from the civil liability system of tort law. A single act may be both a tort against a private individual or group and a crime against the state. Thus, in 1996–1997 the former football star O.J. Simpson was subject to both criminal prosecution and civil liability after he allegedly murdered his wife Nicole Brown Simpson and her friend Ron Goldman. After a lengthy criminal trial, the jury found Simpson "not guilty." In a separate civil proceeding, a different jury held him liable in tort for the "wrongful deaths" of Ron and Nicole, and awarded their surviving families a total of $33.5 million in compensatory and punitive damages.

Firms Commit Crimes Too

Not all crimes are committed by individuals. Corporations, too, may be subject to criminal prosecution. A firm that intentionally pollutes a stream, for example, may be criminally liable under federal environmental protection laws. A crucial difference characterizes corporate criminal liability, however. A corporation, unlike a real individual, cannot be imprisoned. For the most part, criminally convicted firms are subject only to fines.[6] It is important to recognize, however, that those fines are not in the nature of compensation; they are penalties akin to punitive damages in civil litigation.

In many cases of corporate criminal liability, prosecutors will seek to identify corporate officials who may be held personally responsible for the corporation's crimes. It is not uncommon for corporate officers who violate, for example, environmental or securities laws, to face imprisonment as well as fines.[7]

THE ECONOMICS OF CRIME

Crime and Its Economic Consequences in the United States

In the year 2000, 25.9 million crimes were reported in the United States.[8] That number represents a crime rate of 4,124 crimes per 100,000 inhabitants. If this rate seems disturbingly high, consider that it amounts to a 25 percent decrease from the 1979 crime rate. The rate of crime in the United States fell throughout the 1990s. The vast majority, or about 88 percent of all reported crimes in 2000, were nonviolent property crimes, mostly burglary and theft. Among violent crimes, homicide and rape were rare, accounting for only 1 and 6.3 percent of cases, respectively. Assaults (63.9 percent) and robberies (28.6 percent) were the most common violent crimes.[9] But percentages may be misleading. Throughout the United States, 15,517 murders or nonnegligent homicides, 92,440 rapes, 54,720 attempted rapes, and 113,790 cases of sexual assault (including threatened rape) were reported in 2000.[10] It is important to bear in mind that such incidents are notoriously underreported to the authorities. The true numbers are unknown but certainly higher than officially reported statistics.

Crimes impose significant costs on American society. The U.S. Department of Justice estimates that the gross economic costs of all reported crimes in 2000 amounted to nearly $13.4 billion.[11] This figure is *not*, however, an estimate of the total costs of crime to society. It measures only the direct losses suffered by the victims of crime. It does not include the multimillions of dollars worth of annual transactions within the "criminal economy," including the drug trade and prostitution. On any measure, crime is big business.

Why People Commit Crimes

Individuals commit crimes for many different reasons, ranging from poverty to ideology, from ignorance to pure malice, from casual indifference to uncontrollable passion. From an economic point of view, however, criminal activity, like other behavior, can generally be explained in terms of the marginal costs and benefits. As Gary Becker explained, "Some persons become 'criminals' . . . not because their basic motivation differs from that of other persons, but because their benefits and costs differ."[12] The presumption is that the satisfaction of criminal preferences—whatever the sources of those preferences—depends on the costs and benefits of criminal activities, relative to alternative occupations.

This marginal cost and benefit explanation of criminal conduct seems consistent with the theory that the crime rate varies with economic conditions, rising when the economy deteriorates and declining as economic conditions improve. Although this theory is intuitively sensible, the empirical evidence does not wholly support it. During some periods, such as the 1990s, a strong economy coincided with a decline in the crime rate. In other periods, such as the mid–1950s through the early 1970s, the crime rate rose despite a (mostly) strong economy.[13] The reported crime rate actually fell in the mid–1930s, during the Great Depression. Other factors help to explain changes in the crime rate, including relative levels of private spending on crime prevention (alarm installations, fences, security guards) and public spending on law enforcement (police on the streets and prison construction). It remains likely, however, that the rate of crime is significantly related to the perception that the expected benefits of criminal conduct exceed the expected costs (for the criminal), including the risk of detection, arrest, and conviction, plus opportunity costs. Surely no rational individuals would, say, rob a bank if they expected that (1) the bank had little money, (2) the probability of apprehension approached 100 percent, and (3) the likely punishment for attempted bank robbery was death by hanging. It would be even less likely if they could obtain more money, with less risk, by getting a job at the bank.

THE ECONOMICS OF CRIME PREVENTION, CRIMINAL PROSECUTION, AND PUNISHMENT

Data on Law Enforcement, Arrests, Convictions, and Punishments

A primary purpose of the criminal justice system is to limit the social costs of crime. Society invests a great deal of money, time, and effort into preventing, policing, detecting, investigating, prosecuting, and punishing criminal behavior. In 2000, federal, state, local, and tribal law enforcement agencies employed nearly 800,000 full time officers. In 1999, they spent more than $146 billion, not including private spending, on crime avoidance.

Authorities made 13.9 million arrests in 2000, leading to criminal prosecutions for either misdemeanors or felonies. A misdemeanor is a less serious crime, usually punished by just a fine, community service, and similar requirements. For some misdemeanors, the sentence may include a relatively short prison term (usually one year or less), but no one goes to jail just for jaywalking or littering. Such offenses comprise the majority of arrests in a given year. A felony is a more serious offense, which can result in far longer terms of imprisonment and, in some cases, capital punishment (i.e., the death penalty).

In 1998, state and federal courts convicted a total of 980,000 adults for committing felonies. Sixty-eight percent of those convicted in state courts were sentenced to some term of imprisonment in either a state prison or a local jail; 32 percent were given probation. The average sentence for those incarcerated in state prisons was 5 years, but the average convict served only 47 percent of a sentence before release. At current rates of imprisonment, it is estimated that 5.1 percent of the total U.S. population will spend some time in prison during their lifetimes.

Those newly incarcerated in 1998 added to already burgeoning prison populations. As of 2002, federal and state prisons and local jails housed more than 2 million inmates. About half of those inmates had been convicted of violent offenses; drug offenders and those convicted of property crimes (such as burglary) each comprised another 20 percent, respectively, of the prison populations. As prison populations have expanded, states and the federal government have had to build more new prisons. Between 1985 and 2000, a period when the national crime rate fell, a majority of states doubled or tripled their prison budgets. On average, state spending on prison construction rose by 166 percent. By contrast, during that same period, the growth in state spending on higher education was just 24 percent.[14]

The demographics of prison populations are strikingly different from the demographics of the U.S. population at large. In 1996, 63 percent of all inmates belonged to racial or ethnic minorities.[15] African-Americans and Hispanics were notoriously overrepresented. In 1997, of the nearly 5.7 million convicts in prison, in jail, or on parole or probation in the United States, fully 38 percent were African-American. Meanwhile, African-Americans comprise just 12.9 percent of the general population (according to the 2000 U.S. Census). The Bureau of Justice Statistics of the U.S. Department of Justice estimates that 28 percent of all black males will enter state or federal prison during their lives, compared to 16 percent of Hispanic males and just 4.4 percent of white males. Women comprised only 6 to 7 percent of federal and state prison populations in 2001.

Selecting the Levels of Crime Prevention and Law Enforcement

Not every crime is detected, prosecuted, and punished. It may be that society does not spend enough on police, prosecutors, and prisons. Even if spending is insufficient, however, it certainly is *not* the case that the optimal level of crime in society is zero. The optimal level is that at which the next dollar spent on prevention or enforcement would yield less than $1 worth of reduced crime. It is doubtful that U.S. society is anywhere near—or even knows how to get to—the optimal level of criminal law enforcement. As already noted, criminal activity in the United States cost society more than $13 billion in the year 2000. This amount is in addition to the $146 billion spent during the previous year on crime prevention and law enforcement, not including private investments in alarm systems, security guards, and so on. Thus, the joint costs of crime and public spending on crime prevention and criminal law enforcement are in the neighborhood of $160 billion per year or about 1.6 percent of the U.S. gross domestic product.

Is that figure too high, too low, or just right? How much *should* crime and law enforcement cost? Again, the economic goal is to minimize the sum of the costs of crime, crime prevention, and criminal law enforcement.[16] If it costs more for society either to prevent a crime or to enforce the law against the criminal, then it would be more efficient to allow the crime. For that reason, the optimal level of crime is extremely unlikely to be anything close to zero. This reasoning is difficult to square with ethical prohibitions of murder, for example. From an ethical point of view, the only socially acceptable level of murder is zero. From an economic point of view, the optimal level is unlikely to be zero, even for the crime of murder.

So, does society spend enough on crime prevention and law enforcement? It depends on whom you ask. Law enforcement policy always is a contentious issue, and the proper level of spending always is debatable. Politicians always can claim that society is spending too little on police, prosecutors, and prisons; and anyone who dares to disagree is liable to be labeled, "soft on crime."

The Economics of Criminal Punishment

The end of the criminal justice system is to *punish* those convicted of crimes in order to *deter* them, and others, from committing crimes in the future. This goal assumes, of course, some connection between punishment and deterrence. Such an assumption is both intuitive and substantially supported by empirical evidence. Surveys of criminals and studies of their behavior suggest that they make decisions about both types and levels of criminal activity based on information they possess about the likelihood of arrest and conviction and the severity of punishment.[17] Evidence indicates that the significant fall in the rate of violent crime during the 1990s was not exclusively—and maybe not even primarily—due to fortuitous economic conditions.

As the murder rate fell by 30 percent between 1993 and 1998, the probability of imprisonment for committing a murder increased by 53 percent. The incidence of rape fell 14 percent, while the likelihood of imprisonment for committing rape increased by 12 percent. At the same time, the average length of incarceration increased substantially. Between 1980 and 1996, the expected punishment for murder nearly doubled; for rape, it nearly tripled.[18] Rational criminals could reasonably be expected to respond to the increasing likelihood and severity of punishment by reducing their activity levels.[19]

Which has a greater deterrent effect on criminal behavior: increasing the likelihood of punishment or increasing the severity of punishment? The empirical evidence does not offer a clear-cut answer. In 1993, a panel of the National Academy of Sciences reported that a 50 percent increase in the likelihood of imprisonment prevents about twice as much violent crime as a 50 percent increase in the length of prison sentences.[20] By contrast, a 1980 study found that the severity of prior punishment for violent crimes had a stronger deterrent effect on subsequent criminal behavior than the likelihood of future arrest and conviction.[21] It is fair to conclude that both the likelihood and the severity of punishment are important factors. Increasing either can add to the deterrent effect; increasing both can add even more.

Criminal behavior is, however, a complex phenomenon with important biological and environmental components, not all of which are susceptible to explicit or implicit price signals. For example, criminal activity seems to be strongly correlated with elevated levels of lead in the blood. In one study, researchers in Edinburgh, Scotland, found that lead poisoning was the strongest predictor of disciplinary problems in school, which in turn were the strongest predictor of arrests among 7- to 22-year-olds.[22] Such biological and environmental factors can compromise the rationality assumption of traditional economic theory, and create uncertainty about whether any given change in the rate or severity of punishment would have a particular effect on the rate of crime.

Even in cases where the rationality assumption holds, increasing the severity of punishment might not increase deterrence of crime *if* the marginal increase in severity is insufficient to alter criminals' opportunity cost calculations. Crime may still be perceived, especially in areas of chronically high unemployment and short life expectancy, as the "best" of a bad set of opportunities, even if it is punished severely.

SELECTED ISSUES IN CRIME AND PUNISHMENT

The "War on Drugs"

President Richard M. Nixon, in 1973, first invoked the metaphor of warfare to describe his antidrug policies. Since then, the federal government has waged an ever-escalating "war on drugs," which for the past several years has been led by a presidentially appointed "drug czar." *War* and *czar* are grandiose and arguably inapt metaphors for what is, in essence, a long-standing, and so far only marginally successful, federal effort to eradicate both the supply of and the demand for illegal drugs, such as marijuana, cocaine, and heroin. In fiscal year 2002, the federal government spent more than $18 billion fighting the war on drugs.[23] Was this money well spent?

Illegal Drug Use in America

The worldwide illicit drug industry is worth $400 billion a year, and the United States is that industry's largest market. Between 5 and 6 million Americans are hard-core users, spending $100 to $500 per week on drugs.[24] Together with an even larger group of casual or recreational users, American drug consumers spend nearly $60 billion per year.[25] This money goes into the pockets of not only drug sellers but farmers, processors, and transporters around the world. Entire regions of Mexico, Colombia, and other South American countries have grown economically dependent on the drug trade with the United States. The profit margins for drug suppliers are huge, and production costs are relatively small.

Two reasons explain the high profit margins in the illicit drug trade. First, drug prices are high because (1) the drug trade is illegal, and therefore a high risk occupation, which will not be undertaken unless rewards are sufficiently large; and (2) much of the drug trade is a cartel operated by organized crime groups. Second, the demand curve, for hard-core drug users at least, is inelastic, which means that when prices rise, the percentage increase in price is significantly greater than the percentage decrease in the quantity demanded.

Why Certain Drugs (But Not Others) Are Illegal

Drug use is criminalized ostensibly because drugs are perceived to be dangerous for the users and society. To the extent drugs are dangerous for the users themselves, criminalization is, in essence, paternalistic; the drug laws aim to protect drug users from themselves. To the extent drugs create risks for individuals other than the users, criminalization has the goal of internalizing the social costs of drug use.

The war on drugs is not, however, a war on *all* drugs. No federal policy prohibits the sale and use of aspirin, prescription antidepressants, or alcohol for that matter. This situation raises a question about how the government distinguishes drugs that are socially acceptable from those that are not. One obvious basis for distinction would be between substances that create a high risk of harm to the users or others and those that do not. Government policy is not premised on any such distinction. Alcohol and tobacco are not illicit, but they certainly can cause great harm to users and others. Even aspirin can cause death if used improperly. Of course, aspirin use has medicinal benefits that may, in most cases, outweigh its risks. The same can hardly be said of tobacco.

Legal distinctions between various drugs may best be explained not by chemical properties, behavioral effects, or even benefit-cost analyses, but by politics and the theory of public choice. It was the politics of Prohibition that led to the adoption in 1919 of the Eighteenth Amendment to the U.S. Constitution, which criminalized the manufacture, sale, and consumption of alcoholic beverages, including beer and wine. It was economics, however, that led, 14 years later, to the Twenty-first Amendment, which ended Prohibition.

Does the History of Prohibition Suggest That the War on Drugs Is Futile?

Prohibition lasted from 1920 to 1933. Its proponents called it a "noble experiment," but the experiment failed. At the beginning of Prohibition, alcohol use declined (in fact, it was already in decline before the Eighteenth Amendment was ratified). Then, in 1921, alcohol use began to rise again. Americans' demand for alcohol seemed to prevail over their respect for the Constitution. By the end of the 1920s, annual per capita consumption of alcohol surpassed pre-Prohibition levels. Making alcohol illegal did *not* stem demand. However, it did significantly increase the cost of alcohol production and consumption. Economist Mark Thornton has written:

> Alcohol became more dangerous to consume; crime increased and became "organized"; the court and prison systems were stretched to the breaking point; and corruption of public officials was rampant. No measurable gains were made in productivity or reduced absenteeism. Prohibition removed a significant source of tax revenue and greatly increased government spending. It led many drinkers to switch to opium, marijuana, patent medicines, cocaine, and other dangerous substances that they would have been unlikely to encounter in the absence of Prohibition. Those results were documented from a variety of sources, most of which, ironically, are the work of supporters of Prohibition—most economists and social scientists supported it. Their findings make the case against Prohibition that much stronger.[26]

Social scientists detect several similarities between this history of Prohibition and the war on drugs, including increased rates of drug-related crime and imprisonment. They argue that the war on drugs is doomed to fail for many of the same reasons that Prohibition failed in the 1920s.

One of the biggest reasons for the failure of Prohibition was the relative inelasticity of demand for alcohol. The Eighteenth Amendment greatly increased the price of alcohol. Normally, in a competitive market we would expect a price increase to reduce the quantity demanded of whatever product. Recall the discussion of *demand elasticity* in Chapter 1. In some markets—such as the market for the AIDS drug AZT, among those infected with HIV—the demand curve is nearly vertical, and reflects the fact that the quantity demanded remains little changed regardless of changes in the price of the good. In the case of alcohol during Prohibition, the demand curve was relatively inelastic (although not vertical). So there was a small initial decline in quantity demanded but only because price rose dramatically. Over time, as demand itself grew, a greater quantity was demanded despite the higher price.

The question becomes whether demand for drugs, during the war on drugs, has been as inelastic as was the demand for alcohol during Prohibition. We might presume that changes in price affect demand among casual or recreational drug users more than hard-core users. In fact, the rate of casual drug use has declined by an estimated 50 percent over the past two decades, that is, during the war on drugs. Although, whether this falloff in recreational drug use is due to higher prices or to changing preferences in response to social policies aimed at discouraging drug use is unclear. Among hard-core users, however, changes in the price of drugs seem to have had little effect on demand. Since the early 1980s, as the rate of recreational drug use has fallen, hard-core drug use has remained basically unchanged.[27]

When drugs become more expensive for hard-core users, they seem to respond not by reducing their consumption but by spending more of their disposable income on drugs. Of course, many hard-core drug users do not have surplus disposable income; their drug habits may prevent them from holding down legitimate jobs. Increasing the price of drugs through criminalization may, as a consequence, create an incentive for them to engage in higher levels of criminal activity—particularly property crimes—to gain the resources needed to support their increasingly expensive habits. If so, the war on drugs may raise, rather than lower, the social costs associated with drug use.

The Death Penalty

If increasing the severity of punishment increases the law's deterrent effect on criminal behavior, by raising the cost, does maximizing the severity of punishment by imposing the death penalty create maximum deterrence? Those who support the death penalty on utilitarian (as opposed to moral-absolutist, e.g., "an eye for an eye") grounds argue or assume that the answer to this question is yes. As long ago as 1764, however, the Marquis of Beccaria argued that life imprisonment is more costly than death to any rational person, and therefore possesses a *greater* deterrent effect.[28] Moreover, as Richard Posner explained:

> Capital punishment is . . . supported by considerations of marginal deterrence, which require as big a spread as possible between the punishments for the least and most serious crimes. If the maximum punishment for murder is life imprisonment, we may not want to make armed robbery also punishable by life imprisonment, for then armed robbers would have no additional incentive not to murder their victims.[29]

The Death Penalty in American History

The death penalty has a long and colorful history in the United States.[30] It was ubiquitous throughout the states during the colonial and republican eras. In 1779 Thomas Jefferson proposed eliminating the death penalty in Virginia for all offenses except murder and treason. The State did not immediately heed Jefferson's advice, but in 1796 Virginia limited the death penalty to cases of murder and certain offenses committed by slaves.[31] For the most part, however, the death penalty remained the ultimate punishment throughout most of the United States well into the twentieth century. Two states, Michigan and Wisconsin, abolished the death penalty before the end of the nineteenth century, but they remained alone until the mid-1900s.

In the 1950s, sentiment toward the death penalty, as reflected in public opinion polls, began to fall. By the mid–1960s, more Americans opposed than supported it. Meanwhile, execution rates fell off sharply. In 1935, a peak year for executions, 199 men and women were put to death in the United States. In 1968, only one convicted criminal was executed.[32] Then, in 1972, the United States Supreme Court, in one fell swoop, overturned all existing death penalty statutes.

In *Furman v. Georgia*,[33] a deeply divided court held that all existing death penalty laws violated the U.S. Constitution. Importantly, however, the court did *not* hold that the death penalty *per se* constituted "cruel and unusual" punishment, which would have meant the death penalty was inevitably unconstitutional. Only two of the justices voting with the majority favored such an interpretation.[34] The other justices in the majority found that the existing death penalty statutes violated the "cruel and unusual" punishments clause because they were arbitrary or discriminatory in design or application; but they held open the possibility that states might enact and apply death penalty statutes that were nonarbitrary and nondiscriminatory. In fact, just four years after deciding *Furman*, the Supreme Court upheld Georgia's new death penalty law in *Gregg v. Georgia*.[35] Other states quickly enacted similar measures, including procedural safeguards designed to pass constitutional muster. Public attitudes, meanwhile, began to shift again, this time in favor of the death penalty. By the mid–1980s, more than 70 percent of Americans favored capital punishment.[36] Having met constitutional requirements, and with public opinion on their side, the states picked up the pace in seeking the death penalty and executing convicts. During the 1990s, more than 400 convicted criminals were put to death in the United States. In 2002, 71 individuals were executed, nearly half of them in the State of Texas. As with other crime and punishment statistics, African-Americans are disproportionately represented on death row and among the executed. Of the more than 3,500 prisoners on death row at the end of 2001, 43 percent were African-American.[37]

Does the Death Penalty Increase Marginal Deterrence?

Not every state has reinstated the death penalty since *Gregg v. Georgia*. A dozen, including Massachusetts, Michigan, Minnesota, and Wisconsin, have bucked the trend, thereby creating the conditions for a useful natural experiment. Because some states have the death penalty while others do not, it is possible to compare rates of murder and other capital crimes to test the deterrent effect of the death penalty. The eminent legal historian Lawrence Friedman has done just that:

> The murder rate is very high in some states that use the death penalty (Texas), some that do not (Michigan); very low in some states (Maine) that lack it entirely. Does the death penalty make a difference to the crime rate? The evidence is conflicting; on the whole, the no's seem to have the better of the argument. But why should this be the case? Common sense tells us that criminals, like everybody else, are afraid to die, and prefer not to die. . . .
>
> But matters are not that simple. The real question is not whether death deters, but whether it deters more than, say, life imprisonment. After all, nobody suggests, as an alternative to the death penalty, a gold medal, a pension, or a slap on the wrist; the alternative is a lifetime locked up like an animal behind bars, often life without possibility of parole; in any event, long, tough, dreary years in prison. Very few murders would be worth the penalty, on a raw cost-benefit basis, even without the death penalty. Would killing a store clerk ever be worth twenty years in prison, if you thought about it? Nobody seriously denies that the threat of severe punishment

might act as a deterrent; or even that it actually deters some people. Besides, most people are already deterred: by conscience, by fear of prison, and the like. The question then is, does capital punishment add anything extra to the strong deterrents already in place. And it is not at all clear that it does.[38]

Friedman's analysis is consistent with the weight of the empirical evidence. "By the end of the twentieth century," another legal historian, Stuart Banner, observes, "there was an abundant literature in journals of academic law and economics. A few studies found a deterrent effect, but most did not."[39] Two of the most recent empirical studies came to starkly contrasting conclusions. In one, Naci H. Mocan and R. Kaj Gittings examined relations between homicide rates and execution rates from 1977 and 1997. They found that each execution deterred five to six homicides; and just as importantly, each commutation of a death sentence led to between 1 and 1.5 additional homicides.[40] In the other, Lawrence Katz, Steven Levitt, and Ellen Shustorovich examined crime rates relative to execution rates and prison conditions from 1950 to 1990. They found that prison conditions were far more likely to deter crimes, including homicide, than executions. In fact, the effect of execution rates on crime rates was so small as to be statistically insignificant.[41]

This finding does not necessarily conflict with the economic theory of criminal punishment, according to which raising the price for committing homicides should reduce the quantity of homicides. According to Gary Becker, the Nobel laureate who first studied systematically the economics of crime and punishment,

> The disincentive or deterrent effects through the death penalty will be higher if prisons are made more comfortable . . . because that means death [would be] a much worse alternative to imprisonment. On the other hand, it's hard to believe that death penalty [deterrence] can be very high under present conditions, when few get it, it's often very delayed and its imposition is highly uncertain.[42]

Becker suggests that the death penalty's deterrent effect might be increased either by making prison conditions more comfortable or by making executions more swift and certain. But, in the final analysis, the extent to which the death penalty actually deters homicides and other violent crimes remains an unsettled question.

Gun Control

Few issues in crime and punishment are as contentious as gun control. On one side, an uneasy coalition of law enforcement agencies and political "Liberals" contend that "getting guns off the street" is crucial to reducing the number of gun-related crimes and deaths. On the other side, the National Rifle Association (NRA) and associated libertarian and "Conservative" organizations contend that the Second Amendment to the U.S. Constitution, which guarantees the right to bear arms, prohibits virtually any limits on private ownership and possession of weapons. Moreover, they worry about the potential consequences for property and other civil liberties, if the police and other government officials are the only individuals legally entitled to own and carry firearms. From an economic point of view, however, the chief issue in gun control debates is whether laws limiting handguns and other weapons actually reduce the cost of crime in society.

Does Gun Control Lead to Less or More Crime?

For many years, it was widely assumed that the increasing homicide rate following World War II was tied closely to the increasing availability of handguns. Guns made it easier to kill (relative to knives and other substitute weapons) and to commit other crimes, such as robbery. Some empirical evidence correlated rates of homicide and other violent crimes with the proliferation of handguns.

State and local governments devised numerous strategies to deal with the increasing rate of handgun-related crime. Among the least controversial were laws increasing the severity and certainty of punishments for criminals who used guns in committing crimes. These laws did not upset the gun lobby or civil libertarians because they focused not on gun ownership or possession but on criminal conduct; they were consistent with the NRA's slogan that "guns don't kill people; people do." More controversial law enforcement strategies included an outright ban on all (except police) handguns in the jurisdiction of Morton Grove, Illinois (a suburb of Chicago). Less extreme, but still controversial, were compulsory permitting laws, which required that all handguns be registered, and laws that prohibited the carrying of concealed weapons. But did these laws work to reduce the rate of gun-related crime and violence?

In 1997, an economist named John Lott published an empirical study in the *Journal of Legal Studies* that challenged all of the conventional wisdom about guns, crime, and gun control. Lott and coauthor David Mustard conducted a quantitative analysis comparing rates of violent crimes and accidental deaths, between 1977 and 1992, in states with laws authorizing citizens to carry concealed firearms and states without such laws. They found that laws allowing citizens to carry concealed firearms deterred violent crime, without increasing accidental deaths. It stood to reason: a criminal would think twice about robbing or attacking someone who might be carrying a concealed firearm. Had other states allowed citizens to carry concealed weapons, Lott and Mustard estimated, it would have meant 1,500 fewer murders, 4,000 fewer rapes, 11,000 fewer robberies, and 60,000 fewer assaults each year.[43] Lott subsequently published a book, the title of which bluntly stated his thesis: *More Guns, Less Crime*.[44]

According to Lott's theory and evidence, gun control laws were misguided. Instead of restricting the legal availability of guns, which for obvious reasons would be unlikely to affect gun possession by criminals, state and local governments should be making it easier for potential crime *victims* to carry guns. Even further, the authorities might consider requiring citizens to own guns.[45]

The reception of Lott's work has been predictable: as public choice theory would predict, opponents of gun control embraced it and advanced policy arguments based on Lott's findings; advocates of gun control, by contrast, attacked Lott's methodology, evidence, and conclusions.

Politics aside, Lott's arguments are supported by some impressive empirical evidence. A growing body of evidence also points in the other direction, however. An empirical study by John Donohue and Ian Ayres, for example, undercuts some of

Lott's more important specific findings and casts doubt on his general conclusion that more guns lead to less crime. Utilizing what they characterized as a "more complete" data set, Donohue and Ayres found no credible statistical evidence that the right-to-carry laws reduce the crime rate. Moreover, the "best data" (however imperfect) suggest that right-to-carry laws actually increase the total cost of crime by approximately $1 billion per year due.[46] Similarly, Tomislav V. Kovandzic and Thomas Marvell, using panel data for 58 Florida counties from 1980 to 2000, examined how the number of right-to-carry permits affected violent crime in that state, and found "no credible statistical evidence that permit rate growth (and presumably more lawful gun carrying) leads to substantial reductions in violent crime, especially homicide."[47] Whether the Kovandzic and Marvell study constitutes "the final bullet in the body of the more guns, less crime hypothesis," as John Donahue suggests,[48] remains to be seen. The debates over statistical methodologies, data, analyses, interpretations, and conclusions are likely to continue.[49]

CHAPTER SUMMARY

This chapter introduced the economic theory of criminal laws and punishments, including an explanation of why the legal system labels some wrongs as crimes and others as mere *torts*. These labels mark an important difference in the way the legal system treats different classes of wrongs because crimes, but not torts, may be punishable by imprisonment. We also examined relations between criminal punishments and criminal behavior. And we explored three important issues in the law and economics of crime and punishment, including gun control, the death penalty, and the war on drugs.

QUESTIONS AND PROBLEMS

1. Gary Becker suggests that the deterrent effect of the death penalty would be enhanced by (a) making prison more comfortable, and (b) making the death penalty more swift and certain. Does his suggestion make sense as a matter of economic theory? If so, does it automatically make it good policy?

2. A famous Polish dissident (under Communism), Jacek Kuron, remarked the irony that police states generally have lower rates of murder, other violent offenses, and property crimes than democratic societies. Are citizens of police states consequently better off than citizens of democratic states? If not, then how do we know when we have enough crime prevention?

3. Sections of this chapter on gun control and the death penalty relied heavily on quantitative empirical studies of their relations with crime rates. None of the empirical studies seemed to settle any issues, however. Data, analyses, and interpretations were all contested. Does this controversy suggest that quantitative empirical studies are inherently flawed, and not really worthwhile?[50]

4. Why might economists expect antidrug laws to have less effect on addicts than on casual users?

5. Does the empirical evidence of the differential deterrent effects of antidrug laws on casual users and hard-core users suggest that society should institute different policies for dealing with those two groups? If so, what might those different policies look like?

6. Does economic theory support the legalization (or, at least, decriminalization) of drugs?

7. It is well known that drivers often exceed the posted speed limit. Why do they? Would driver behavior change if penalties were made more severe? Would they slow down, for example, if they knew that their license would be suspended automatically for one year for a single speed limit violation? If so, why don't we have more severe penalties for such an endemic law violation as speeding?

8. Can you think of any plausible socioeconomic explanations for the demographic differences in at-large and prison populations?

9. What, if anything, do the case studies of gun control, the death penalty, and the war on drugs suggest about how economic analysis affects political decision making?

NOTES

1. Richard A. Posner, "An Economic Theory of Criminal Law," 85 COLUMBIA LAW REVIEW 1193, 1204–5 (1985).

2. Lawrence M. Friedman, *Crime and Punishment in American History* (New York: Basic Books, 1993), p. 107.

3. 28 Ala. App. 147, 180 So. 592, 594 (1938).

4. 66 Cal. App. 2d 894, 153 P. 2d 464, 467 (1944), quoting 4 AMERICAN JURIST 130, § 6.

5. *See* Lawrence M. Friedman, *Crime and Punishment in American History* (New York: Basic Books, 1993), p. 287.

6. In some cases, firms may also be placed on probation, allowing government officials to interfere in their day-to-day operations to ensure compliance.

7. For a brief survey of the economic literature on corporate criminal liability, *see* John R. Lott, Jr., "Corporate Criminal Liability," in B. Bouckaert and G. DeGeest (eds.), *V Encyclopedia of Law and Economics* (2000), p. 492.

8. U.S. Department of Justice, Office of Justice Programs, Bureau of Justice Statistics, *Criminal Victimization in the United States, 2000 Statistical Tables* (August 2002), Table 82.

9. Crime rate statistics are from Federal Bureau of Investigation, *Crime in the United States 2000: Uniform Crime Reports* (2001).

10. Federal Bureau of Investigation, *Crime in the United States 2000: Uniform Crime Reports* (2001), p. 14; *and* U.S. Department of Justice, Office of Justice Programs, Bureau of Justice Statistics, *Criminal Victimization in the United States, 2000 Statistical Tables* (August 2002), Tables 59 and 82.

11. U.S. Department of Justice, Office of Justice Programs, Bureau of Justice Statistics, *Criminal Victimization in the United States, 2000 Statistical Tables* (August 2002), Table 82. This figure underestimates the actual costs: nearly 10 percent of all the reported crimes involving economic losses did not specify the extent of those losses.

12. Gary S. Becker, "Crime and Punishment: An Economic Approach," 76 JOURNAL OF POLITICAL ECONOMICS 169, 176 (1968).

13. Other factors that might explain the increase in the crime rate between 1950 and 1970 include an increase in the return on criminal activity, for example significantly higher profits in drug trafficking, combined with more lenient criminal punishments and/or a lower probability of being caught and convicted.

14. Justice Policy Institute, "Cellblocks or Classrooms: The Funding of Higher Education and Corrections and Its Impact on African American Men" (2002).

15. All of the statistics cited in this paragraph are from the Bureau of Justice Statistic's Web site, available at http://www.ojp.usdoj.gov/bjs/welcome.html.

16. Notice that the economic goal of crime prevention and criminal law enforcement mirrors the economic goal of the tort system, as discussed in Chapter 10 (p. 214), which is to

minimize the sum of accident avoidance, accidents, and the costs of administering the tort system.

17. *See* Richard T. Wright and Scott H. Decker, *Burglars on the Job* (Boston: Northeastern University Press, 1994); Derek B. Cornish and Ronald V. Clarke (eds.), *The Reasoning Criminal: Rational Choice Perspectives on Offending* (New York: Springer Verlag1986); Jack P. Gibbs, *Crime, Punishment, and Deterrence* (Westport, CT: Greenwood Publishing Group, 1975).

18. All of the statistics in this paragraph come from National Center for Policy Analysis, "Crime and Punishment in America: 1998," NCPA Policy Report No. 219 (September 1998).

19. *See* Gary S. Becker, "Crime and Punishment: An Economic Approach," 76 JOURNAL OF POLITICAL ECONOMICS 176 (1968). Becker estimates the cost of imprisonment to the convicted criminal as "the discounted sum of the earnings foregone and the value placed on the restrictions in consumption and freedom." (p. 179).

20. Albert J. Reiss, Jr. and Jeffrey A. Roth (eds.), *Understanding and Preventing Violence* (Washington, DC: National Academy Press, 1993).

21. A. Witte, "Estimating the Economic Model of Crime with Individual Data," 94 QUANTITATIVE JOURNAL OF ECONOMICS 57 (1980). *See also* Donald E. Lewis, "The General Deterrent Effect of Longer Sentences," 26 BRITISH JOURNAL OF CRIME 47 (1986).

22. "Toxic Criminals: Test May Offer Clues about Lead's Effects," 1(3) CRIME TIMES 4 (1995).

23. National Drug Control Strategy, FY 2003 Budget Summary 6 (February 2002), Table 2.

24. National Drug Control Strategy, 2000 Annual Report (2001), Table 3.

25. National Drug Control Strategy, 2000 Annual Report (2001), p. 114.

26. Mark Thornton, "Alcohol Prohibition Was a Failure," Cato Policy Analysis No. 157 (July 17, 1991).

27. National Drug Control Strategy, 2000 Annual Report (2001), Table 3.

28. Cesare Beccaria, *An Essay on Crimes and Punishments* [1764] (Brookline, MA: Branden Publishing Co., 1992).

29. Richard A. Posner, "An Economic Theory of Criminal Law," 85 COLUMBIA LAW REVIEW 1193, 1210–1 (1985).

30. *See* Stuart Banner, *The Death Penalty: An American History* (Cambridge: Harvard University Press, 2002).

31. Lawrence M. Friedman, *Crime and Punishment in American History* (New York: Basic Books, 1993), p. 73. These limits meant that someone convicted for the third time of stealing a pig could no longer be put to death (p. 42).

32. Lawrence M. Friedman, *American Law in the 20th Century* (New Haven, CT: Yale University Press, 2002), pp. 217–19.

33. 408 U.S. 238 (1972).

34. Such an interpretation is difficult to maintain because the death penalty existed throughout the states when the Eighth Amendment was adopted . No evidence indicates that the Founding Fathers considered it per se "cruel" or "unusual" punishment. It is possible, however, to argue that the death penalty is unconstitutional because it is not possible to apply it in a consistent, nonarbitrary, and nondiscriminatory manner. This argument is the basis, for example, of Justice Blackmun's belated conclusion that, "despite the effort of the States and courts to devise legal formulas and procedural rules to meet this daunting challenge, the death penalty remains fraught with arbitrariness, discrimination, caprice, mistake. . . . Experience has taught us that the constitutional goal of eliminating arbitrariness and discrimination from the administration of death . . . can never be achieved without compromising an equally essential component of fundamental fairness— individualized sentencing. . . ." *Collins v. Collins*, 540 U.S. 1141, 1144 (1994) (Blackmun, J., dissenting).

35. 428 U.S. 153 (1976).

36. *See* Lawrence M. Friedman, *American Law in the 20th Century* (New Haven, CT: Yale University Press, 2002), p. 219.

37. Bureau of Justice Statistics, *Capital Punishment Statistics* (2003).

38. Lawrence M. Friedman, *American Law in the 20th Century* (New Haven, CT: Yale University Press, 2002), p. 222.

39. Stuart Banner, *The Death Penalty: An American History* (Cambridge: Harvard University Press, 2002), p. 281.

40. Naci H. Mocan and R. Kaj Gittings, "Pardons, Executions, and Homicides," NBER Working Paper No. w8639 (December 2001).

41. Lawrence Katz, Steven Levitt, and Ellen Shustorovich, "Prison Conditions, Capital Punishment, and Deterrence," 5 *AMERICAN LAW & ECONOMICS REVIEW* 318 (2003).

42. *Quoted in* Douglas Clement, "A Punishing Debate: Does the Death Penalty Deter Homicide? New Economic Studies Seek the Answer to an Age-Old Question," 16(2) *THE REGION* 12 (June 2002).

43. John R. Lott and David B. Mustard, "Crime, Deterrence, and Right-to-Carry Concealed Weapons," 26 *JOURNAL OF LEGAL STUDIES* 1 (1997).

44. John R. Lott, *More Guns, Less Crime: Understanding Crime and Gun-Control Laws* (Chicago: University of Chicago Press, 1998).

45. In 1980, the town of Kenesaw Mountain, Georgia, in response to the Village of Morton Grove's ban on gun possession, passed an ordinance requiring the head of every household in the town of 5,000 to own a gun and ammunition. The rate of violent crime subsequently plummeted, and has reportedly remained quite low ever since.

46. Ian Ayres and John J. Donohue III, "Shooting Down the More Guns, Less Crime Hypothesis," 55 *STANFORD LAW REVIEW* 1193, 1193, 1202 (2003).

Ayres and Donohue are unable to offer a "compelling theoretical justification" for this result, which they admit casts doubt on the "predictive validity" of their model.

47. Tomislav V. Kovandzic and Thomas B. Marvell, "Right-to-Carry Concealed Handguns and Violent Crime: Crime Control Through Gun Decontrol?" 2 *CRIMINOLOGY & PUBLIC POLICY* 363, 387 (2003).

48. John J. Donohue III, "The Final Bullet in the Body of the More Guns, Less Crime Hypothesis," 2 *CRIMINOLOGY & PUBLIC POLICY* 397 (2003).

49. *See, for example,* Florenz Plassmann and John Whitley, "Confirming More Guns, Less Crime," 55 *STANFORD LAW REVIEW* 1313 (2003); Ian Ayres and John J. Donohue III, "The Latest Misfire in Support of the 'More Guns, Less Crime' Hypothesis," *STANFORD LAW REVIEW* 1371 (2003).

50. *See* Donald Braman and Dan M. Kahan, "More Statistics, Less Persuasion: A Cultural Theory of Gun-Risk Perceptions," Yale Law School, Public Research Paper No. 05 (2002), which suggests that econometric studies of relations between the availability of guns and crime rates have generated more heat than light.

Chapter 14

Antitrust and Regulated Industries

INTRODUCTION

Preceding chapters focused on laws that regulate the nature of exchange and production. This chapter examines legal rules established to regulate the internal structure and behavior of firms and industries.

If a business or a group of businesses for one reason or another is thought to have too much power in the marketplace, the U.S. government, and the governments of most industrialized nations, enact laws to mitigate or eliminate anticompetitive behavior. Indeed, governments have empowered themselves to divide companies into smaller companies, and to end standard industry practices. Moreover, firms and industries determined by the courts to be anticompetitive may even be subject to criminal prosecution under what are known in the United States as antitrust statutes.

The rationale for these rules has a solid economic foundation. Market power, especially monopoly power, tends to be inefficient. It can result in wasted social resources. Industries that are dominated by a single firm or by a cartel of several firms may operate like a monopoly, charging prices that are in some sense too high, and possibly preventing a more efficient entrant from gaining a foothold in their markets. Monopolies, by definition, eliminate competition and, with it, the benefits for efficiency that competitive markets produce.

Two distinct sets of legal rules deal with monopolies and monopolistic practices. The first, antitrust law, is intended to prevent industry concentration and anticompetitive practices. These rules allow the government to prosecute firms that behave in ways that restrain trade or give them excessive market power. The second is regulated industries or public utilities law, which is premised on the assumption that some industries—especially those providing essential services—should be monopolies; indeed they sometimes are called *natural monopolies*. As such, they need to be regulated so that they do not abuse their monopoly power, charging excessive prices or otherwise taking undue advantage of suppliers and customers. This chapter presents two case studies to illustrate the rules of antitrust law and regulated industries law: the Microsoft case and the troubled attempt at electric utility deregulation in California.

THE PROBLEM OF MONOPOLY

A monopoly—an industry of only one firm—has the potential to abuse would-be rivals and consumers. A firm that controls an entire market likely will have power to set prices and determine the level of output. That alone might warrant government intervention. Moreover, a monopoly is also likely to be inefficient. The economic argument against monopoly is that it leads to social waste.

To understand why monopolies are inefficient, it is useful to compare a monopoly market with a competitive market. Figure 14-1 describes a competitive market. Chapter 1 described the equilibrium point in a competitive market as an efficient allocation of resources because all producers will supply the product or service to all consumers at the equilibrium price, leaving no unsatisfied demand and no surplus supply. Recall also that the supply curve is, in fact, a representation of firm cost. These costs tend to rise as output increases because it is more costly to produce an additional unit of a good or service. In economic terms, marginal costs increase as output rises.

By contrast, Figure 14-2 shows how price and quantity decisions are made in a market devoid of competition, controlled by a single supplier—a monopoly market. Note that this figure shows a demand curve, but not a curve labeled "supply." The reason is that a monopolist does not supply goods based on cost relative to price. Rather, it chooses an output level based on its costs relative to its revenues. Its chosen output level, then, sets the market price. In other words, by virtue of being the lone supplier, the monopolist can simply choose how much it wants to produce; in theory, it can produce at any level of production it wants. Economists assume, however, that the monopolist will choose a level of output that it expects will maximize profits, defined as revenues minus production costs. So, instead of a supply curve, the figure

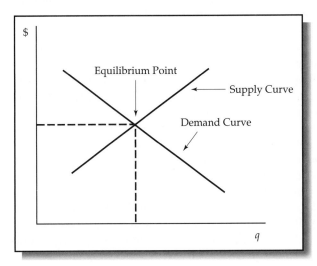

Figure 14-1
Equilibrium in a
Competitive Market

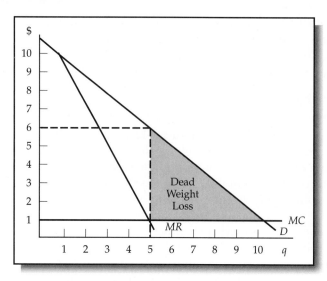

Figure 14-2
A Monopoly Market

includes marginal cost (MC) and marginal revenue (MR) curves, which show, respectively, the costs and revenues for each additional unit of output. For simplicity, we assume that marginal costs of production are constant over the range of demand. That is, for each increment of output, the cost to the monopoly producer is the same. However, the monopolist still uses the same formula to determine its level of output and market price, even if its marginal costs of production are rising.

The marginal revenue curve lies below the demand curve at all levels of output greater than one. This relationship is always the case in monopoly markets. Suppose a monopolist—the sole car wash in a small town—knows the demand curve it faces. It can sell one car wash per day at $10. The additional revenue gained (the marginal revenue) is identical to the price and, so, at a point where demand equals one, marginal revenue and price are the same; and price and MR both intersect the demand curve at one unit. But consider what happens if the monopolist wants to sell two car washes. Going down the demand curve to two units, we see that the monopolist must lower the price, say to $9, and it must charge the same price for both washes. At that price, total revenue would be $18, but the marginal revenue (the additional amount from the next unit) would be only $8, and so the MR curve at two car washes is $1 below the price paid by consumers (depicted on the demand curve in Figure 14-2). The rational monopolist will choose that level of production where its marginal revenue equals the marginal cost. That is, the amount of output where the additional revenue gain is matched by the cost of production. By producing up to (but not beyond) that point, the monopolist maximizes profits. In the preceding case, let's say it costs the monopolist a constant $1 for every car wash. Then producing one wash yields $9 profit; two yields $16 (2 × $9 − $2); three, $21 (3 × $8 − $3); four $24. Five, $25, but six, just $24 (6 × $5 = $30 − $1 × 6 = $24). These results illustrate *the basic rule of monopoly pricing*: choose the price and output where MR = MC. In this case, MR = $1 = MC at 5 units. Observe that at the profit-maximizing point the monopolist will produce five car washes, and the price it charges consumers will be $6 per wash.

The figure describing the monopoly market also shows the consequences of monopoly pricing for social welfare. In a competitive market, price is driven down toward marginal cost.[1] Profitable markets that are open for entry and competition can be expected to attract new suppliers, who will increase supply relative to demand and thereby drive prices down toward the marginal costs of production. In the example, if the price were in fact equal to MC ($1) then more consumers could have purchased the product. But because the industry is a monopoly—the market is not open and competitive—they don't get the chance. The graph shows a triangle labeled "Dead Weight Loss." It represents a loss to social welfare of output that could have been, but was not, produced profitably.[2] Resources that, in the absence of monopoly, would have been invested in this production went elsewhere; demand that could have been satisfied was not. Thus, monopoly generates market failures. Though the goods are sold in the market, the market does not efficiently allocate resources so as to achieve and maintain the proper level of production. Too little is produced, and it is sold at too high a price. Moreover, a monopolistic market of this kind is in equilibrium. It will not be made efficient by changes in demand. For a monopoly market to change, many would argue, some legal force must be exerted on it. Most developed countries have laws concerning monopolistic practices sometimes referred to as competition laws. In the United States, we call them *antitrust laws*.

Although a monopoly market is by definition inefficient, it is not always the case that industries dominated by a single firm can actually exercise monopoly power. As with all profitable industries, a monopolized industry will attract new suppliers, who, if allowed to enter, will destroy the monopoly. To prevent losing a monopoly, the monopolist must either erect robust barriers to entry or behave as though the market were already competitive, that is by marginal cost pricing. By setting prices at or close to its marginal costs of production, the monopolist would reduce the incentives of new suppliers to enter the market; it would become more difficult for new entrants to undercut the incumbent's prices and gain market share. At the same time, consumers would benefit from prices at or near competitive market levels. Of course, if the new entrant has significantly lower costs of production (for technological or other reasons) than the incumbent supplier, the monopoly will end.[3] Even where such a scenario is possible, however, the mere existence of single-firm dominance in an industry is often considered reason enough to raise government concern about market failure.

At the same time, substantial market power may be exercised by an industry of more than one firm. That is, a multifirm industry may be able to act like monopolists. The obvious case is that of a *cartel*, such as OPEC (Organization of the Petroleum Exporting Countries), where firms (or countries in the case of cartels of nationalized industries) deliberately attempt (not always successfully) to coordinate output and pricing decisions, so as to gain monopoly profits. These are forms of horizontal control of an industry. Firms may also gain market power by vertical integration. For example, a producer that also owns sources of raw materials or retail outlets may make it very difficult for entrants to compete at any given stage of the process. In 1955, the U.S. government sought to block a proposed merger between the Brown Shoe Company and the Kinney Shoe Company. Kinney had a large chain of retail outlets, and the government feared that Brown, one of the largest manufacturers of shoes, would dominate the shelf space at Kinney outlets to the detriment of other shoemakers, especially new market entrants.[4] The government feared that the practical consequence of the merger would have been the same kind of market inefficiency produced by pure monopolies.

When confronted with actual or perceived monopolies, governments may make at least three possible responses:

1. Do nothing.
2. Break up the monopoly in an effort to convert an uncompetitive market into a competitive market.
3. Allow the monopoly to persist, but attempt to ameliorate its detrimental effects on social welfare through regulation.

In the United States, since the late nineteenth century, the federal government almost always has opted for either alternative 2 or 3.

ANTITRUST LAW

The Sherman Act

During the second half of the nineteenth century, American business enterprises grew to unprecedented size and wealth. In many cases, however, these firms faced vigorous competition that benefited consumers. The large companies began to regard such competition as "ruinous," especially during economic recessions. They responded to this competition in one of two ways.[5] In some cases, they sought to combine in a trust, so as to create a monopolistic entity that could set prices and determine industry output. One example was the Northern Securities Trust, a railway cartel that eventually was prosecuted under antitrust laws.

Alternatively, firms attempted to form cartels that allocated market shares and set prices. These efforts were often unsuccessful, and even where successful, they usually did not last long. Individual members of cartels often could not resist the lure of fast profits by defecting from cartel agreements and lowering their prices. All it took was one defector to wreck the cartel and reintroduce competition. In the relatively rare cases where cartels were successful over a substantial period of time, they effectively transformed competitive markets into something resembling single-firm monopolies. One example of such a successful cartel was the railroad express cartel, which controlled much of the parcel post transport in the United States during the second half of the nineteenth century.[6]

As trusts and cartels proliferated, their growing market power threatened small businessmen and farmers, who sought government protection. In 1890, Congress responded with the first major antimonopoly law, the Sherman Act. The Sherman Act made illegal business "combination in the form of trust or otherwise, or conspiracy in restraint of trade or commerce," and it outlawed monopolization of trade (in fact "any part of trade") as well.[7] The law made even the *attempt* to create a cartel or monopoly a criminal act, punishable potentially by jail sentences for the conspirators.[8] The government or private individuals harmed by a business combination could also file civil suits.

Although the Sherman Act clearly was aimed at the large trusts and cartels of the era, the language of the act was quite vague. It did not specify exactly what constitutes a *restraint of trade* or a *conspiracy*. Would it be a conspiracy, under the act, if two firms in an industry shared information? In the case of a proposed merger, what size market share would be considered a restraint of trade or monopolization? If the market is small, must it accommodate multiple firms? If two firms raised prices together, would that necessarily constitute collusion in restraint of trade? Meanwhile, as Richard Posner has noted,[9] the Sherman Act "was ineffectual in dealing with collusive pricing that does not generate detectable acts of agreement." Moreover, the act created substantial measurement problems (high transaction costs) that the courts were expected to resolve; but they were poorly equipped to do so.

The following case shows the value of the Sherman Act in limiting market power, but it also illustrates some of the problems generated by the law's ambiguous guidelines. The case, *Northern Securities Co. v. the United States,* is considered of major historical importance in government efforts to constrain the size and power of firms. Two large railroads operating from the Midwest to the West Coast, the Northern Pacific and the Great Northern, were effectively merged by selling their stock to a single New Jersey-based holding company, the Northern Securities Company. The U.S. government led by trust-busting President Theodore Roosevelt sought the dissolution of the merger under the Sherman Act. The companies fought the suit on a number of grounds: (a) their legality, as state-created corporations, was a state, not a federal, issue; (b) they had not actually been shown to have restrained commerce; and (c) the individual railroads had not merged but rather had contracted with the Northern Securities Companies, and under the Constitution Congress could not infringe on the "liberty of contract."

As the following excerpt illustrates, a majority of the Supreme Court rejected these arguments. But Justice Oliver Wendell Holmes, in a vigorous dissent, argued that mergers were not by definition restraints of trade. It should be noted that although the Sherman Act prohibits combinations that act to monopolize markets, it does not specify at what point mergers or combinations constitute illegal restraints on trade. As Justice Holmes's dissent illustrates, the issues were far from clear-cut.

Northern Securities Co. v. United States

193 U.S. 197 (1904)

Justice Harlan, for the Majority.

This combination is, within the meaning of the act, a "trust;" but if not, it is a *combination in restraint of interstate and international commerce;* and that is enough to bring it under the condemnation of the act. The mere existence of such a combination and the power acquired by the holding company as its trustee, constitute a menace to, and a restraint upon, that freedom of commerce which Congress intended to recognize and protect, and which the public is entitled to have protected. If such combination be not destroyed, all the advantages that would naturally come to the public under the operation of the general laws of competition, as between the Great Northern and Northern Pacific Railway companies, will be lost, and the entire commerce of the immense territory in the northern part of the United States between the Great Lakes and the Pacific at Puget Sound will be at the mercy of a single holding corporation, organized in a State distant from the people of that territory.

**

We will not incumber this opinion by extended extracts from the former opinions of this court. It is sufficient to say that from the decisions in the above cases propositions are plainly deducible and embrace the present case. Those propositions are:

That although the act of Congress known as the Anti-Trust Act has no reference to the mere manufacture or production of articles or commodities within the limits of the several States, it does embrace and declare to be illegal every contract, combination or conspiracy, in whatever form, of whatever nature, and whoever may be parties to it, which directly or necessarily operates *in restraint* of trade or commerce *among the several States or with foreign nations;*

That the act is not limited to restraints of interstate and international trade or commerce that are unreasonable in their nature, but embraces all *direct restraints* imposed by any combination, conspiracy or monopoly upon such trade or commerce;

That railroad carriers engaged in interstate or international trade or commerce are embraced by the act;

That combinations even among *private* manufacturers or dealers whereby *interstate* or *international commerce* is restrained are equally embraced by the act;

That Congress has the power to establish *rules* by which *interstate and international* commerce shall be governed, and, by the Anti-Trust Act, has prescribed the rule of free competition among those engaged in such commerce;

That *every* combination or conspiracy which would extinguish competition between otherwise competing railroads engaged in *interstate trade or commerce,* and which would *in that way* restrain *such* trade or commerce, is made illegal by the act;

That the natural effect of competition is to increase commerce, and an agreement whose direct effect is to prevent this play of competition restrains instead of promotes trade and commerce;

That to vitiate a combination, such as the act of Congress condemns, it need not be shown that the combination, in fact, results or will result in a total suppression of trade or in a complete monopoly, but it is only essential to show that by its necessary operation it tends to restrain interstate or international trade or commerce or tends to create a monopoly in such trade or commerce and to deprive the public of the advantages that flow from free competition;

That the constitutional guarantee of liberty of contract does not prevent Congress from prescribing the rule of free competition for those engaged in *interstate and international* commerce; and

That under its power to regulate commerce among the several States and with foreign nations, Congress had authority to enact the statute in question.

**

The judgment of the court is that the [lower court ruling against Northern Securities] be and hereby is affirmed, with liberty to the Circuit Court to proceed in the execution of its decree as the circumstances may require.

**

Justice Holmes, Dissenting.

Great cases like hard cases make bad law. For great cases are called great, not by reason of their real importance in shaping the law of the future, but because of some accident of immediate overwhelming interest which appeals to the feelings and distorts the judgment.

**

The question to be decided is whether, under the [Sherman Act], it is unlawful, at any stage of the process, if several men unite to form a corporation for the purpose of buying more than half the stock of each of two competing interstate railroad companies, if they form the corporation, and the corporation buys the stock. I will suppose further that every step is taken, from the beginning, with the single intent of ending competition between the companies. I make this addition not because it may not be and is not disputed but because, as I shall try to show, it is totally unimportant under any part of the statute with which we have to deal.

Again the statute is of a very sweeping and general character. It hits "every" contract or combination of the prohibited sort, great or small, and "every" person who shall monopolize or attempt to monopolize, in the sense of the act, "any part" of the trade or commerce among the several States. There is a natural inclination to assume that it was directed against certain great combinations and to read it in that light. It does not say so. On the contrary, it says "every," and "any part." Still less was it directed specially against railroads. There even was a reasonable doubt whether it included railroads until the point was decided by this court.

***

A partnership is not a contract or combination in restraint of trade between the partners unless the well-known words are to be given a new meaning invented for the purposes of this act. . . . The law says nothing about competition, and only prevents its suppression by contracts or combinations in restraint of trade, and such contracts or combinations derive their character as restraining trade from other features than the suppression of competition alone. To see whether I am wrong, the illustrations put in the argument are of use. If I am, then a partnership between two stage drivers who had been competitors in driving across a state line, or two merchants once engaged in rival commerce among the State whether made after or before the act, if now continued, is a crime. For, again I repeat, if the restraint on the freedom of the members of a combination caused by their entering into partnership is a restraint of trade, every such combination, as well the small as the great, is within the act. ■

***

Holmes argued that mergers do not per se restrain trade, but the majority opinion suggested that any merger between competitors is at least potentially bad because it reduces competition. Justice Harlan's majority opinion is replete with references to "every" and "any" combination that is perceived to restrain trade. While conceding that the majority probably was correct that the Northern Securities holding company attempted to restrain trade, Judge Richard Posner argues that the majority's reasoning was flawed in that it viewed all mergers as, in effect, cartels.[10] He notes that two small firms might well merge in order to gain from economies of scale, but that would not give them the market power of a monopoly. Arguably, the Sherman Act sought to prevent monopoly power, not all mergers. Posner's argument is in essence the same one Holmes advanced in his dissent. Holmes's fear seems to have been that the majority's interpretation of the Sherman Act could be used capriciously to attack any merger regardless of its ability to restrain trade.

Of course, mergers occur all of the time today. Many are subject to Justice Department review, but few are ultimately challenged by the government. In cases since *Northern Securities Co.*, the courts have not assumed that mergers are by definition anticompetitive or otherwise in restraint of trade. Courts have tried to apply the "rule of reason" to merger cases, asking whether, in a particular case, the merger actually harms consumers. Still, the Sherman Act provided a great deal of room for judicial interpretation. Justice Harlan offered one interpretation: that "every" combination constitutes an illicit effort to create monopoly. Justice Holmes offered another: that not all mergers constitute illicit monopolies.

Expansion of Antitrust Law

With so many shortcomings in the Sherman Act, it was only a matter of time before Congress undertook an effort to better define the kind of behavior that would constitute restraint of trade. The Clayton Act of 1914[11] and the Federal Trade Commission (FTC) Act[12] of the same year were intended to provide the corrective. The Clayton Act specifically identified types of monopolistic behavior including price discrimination, exclusive-dealing arrangements, and mergers between competitors. Many sections of the Clayton Act were intended to prevent exclusionary practices, that is, practices designed to exclude entrants from a market. But the Clayton Act, too, generated ambiguity because it declared practices illegal only if they substantially lessened competition or tended to create a monopoly. The principal focus of the FTC Act was the creation of a body specifically to investigate and prosecute antitrust violations. Still, the language of the FTC Act left a lot of room for interpretation. The act declared that "[u]nfair methods of competition in or affecting commerce, and unfair or deceptive acts or practices in and affecting commerce, are . . . unlawful." The measurement problem clearly was not solved and much discretion remained with the courts. Further expansion of antitrust statutes has not ameliorated this basic problem.

Courts have wrestled with antitrust issues for more than 100 years now. In one landmark case, the U.S. government attempted to break up the Aluminum Company of America (Alcoa). This case addressed the important issue of whether a firm should be broken up simply because it controlled a large percentage of a market, even though it did not appear to be acting like an inefficient monopolist. Indeed, an alternative to Alcoa was likely to reduce, not enhance, economic efficiency.

Alcoa did control a large share of the production and sale of what was called "virgin" aluminum ingot. Virgin ingot was aluminum that was smelted from bauxite ore, and was distinguished from secondary ingot which was smelted from aluminum scrap, what we would call recycled aluminum today. Secondary ingots were a substitute, albeit an imperfect substitute, for virgin ingots, but some industries used only the latter. The competitive market for secondary ingots no doubt put limits on Alcoa's pricing power. Still, in the virgin ingot market Alcoa controlled about 90 percent of domestic U.S. sales during the 1930s when the case was brought. The remaining 10 percent of the sales came primarily from imports.

Alcoa was not only the largest producer of virgin ingots, but it also held many patents for the processes. Over the years, it had continued to perfect its processes and to expand capacity in order to meet expected increases in demand. Alcoa, though far less dominant in other parts of the aluminum business, was nonetheless prominent in fabricated products. Did these factors mean that they were in restraint of trade? The following opinion, by the famed jurist Learned Hand, suggests that question was not the key issue.

United States v. Aluminum Co. of America, et al.

148 F. 2d 416 (2d Cir. 1945)[13]

Opinion: L. Hand

***

[I]t would be hard to say that 'Alcoa' had made exorbitant profits on ingot, if it is proper to allocate the profit upon the whole business proportionately among all its products—ingot, and fabrications from ingot. A profit of ten per cent in such an industry, dependent, in part at any rate, upon continued tariff protection, and subject to the vicissitudes of new demands, to the obsolescence of plant and process—which can never be accurately gauged in advance—to the chance that substitutes may at any moment be discovered which will reduce the demand, and to the other hazards which attend all industry; a profit of ten per cent, so conditioned, could hardly be considered extortionate.

There are however, two answers to any such excuse; and the first is that the profit on ingot was not necessarily the same as the profit of the business as a whole, and that we have no means of allocating its proper share to ingot. It is true that the mill cost appears; but obviously it would be unfair to 'Alcoa' to take, as the measure of its profit on ingot, the difference between selling price and mill cost; and yet we have nothing else. It may be retorted that it was for the plaintiff to prove what was the profit upon ingot in accordance with the general burden of proof. We think not. Having proved that 'Alcoa' had a monopoly of the domestic ingot market, the plaintiff had gone far enough; if it was an excuse, that 'Alcoa' had not abused its power, it lay upon 'Alcoa' to prove that it had not. But the whole issue is irrelevant anyway, for it is no excuse for 'monopolizing' a market that the monopoly has not been used to extract from the consumer more than a 'fair' profit. The [Sherman] Act has wider purposes. Indeed, even though we disregard all but economic considerations, it would by no means follow that such concentration of producing power is to be desired, when it has not been used extortionately. Many people believe that possession of unchallenged economic power deadens initiative, discourages thrift and depresses energy; that immunity from competition is a narcotic, and rivalry is a stimulant, to industrial progress; that the spur of constant stress is necessary to counteract an inevitable disposition to let well enough alone. Such people believe that competitors, versed in the craft as no consumer can be, will be quick to detect opportunities for saving and new shifts in production, and be eager to profit by them. In any event the mere fact that a producer, having command of the domestic market, has not been able to make more than a 'fair' profit, is no evidence that a 'fair' profit could not have been made at lower prices. [citation omitted] True, it might have been thought adequate to condemn only those monopolies which could not show that they had exercised the highest possible ingenuity, had adopted every possible economy, had anticipated every conceivable improvement, stimulated every possible demand. No doubt, that would be one way of dealing with the matter, although it would imply constant scrutiny and constant supervision, such as courts are unable to provide. Be that as it may, that was not the way that Congress chose; it did not condone 'good trusts' and condemn 'bad' ones; it forbad all. Moreover, in so doing it was not necessarily actuated by economic motives alone. It is possible, because of its indirect social or moral effect, to prefer a system of small producers, each dependent for his success upon his own skill and character, to one in which the great mass of those engaged must accept the direction of a few. These considerations, which we have suggested only as possible purposes of the Act, we think the decisions prove to have been in fact its purposes. ■

***

To some extent, this ruling seemed to bear out the fears expressed by Justice Holmes in the *Northern Securities Co.* case. Alcoa was convicted not because it restrained trade, not because it disadvantaged consumers by charging exorbitant prices, but merely because it was too big. In fact, the court makes an important point in arguing that Congress had a social goal in mind that overrode any efficiency argument. That is, a competitive industry of small producers would have a positive, though indirect, effect on society. It was more "moral." It was better in principle to have competitive markets because they make for a better society

Alcoa was not actually split into smaller pieces; rather, the government sold aluminum production facilities that it had created during World War II to two companies that became Alcoa's competitors. It is doubtful that this move improved efficiency or social welfare more generally. Prices do not appear to have fallen, although again, that was not Judge Hand's goal. Regardless, the implication of the *Alcoa* ruling was clear: Bigness was problematic per se. In fairness, the court also held that Alcoa had engaged in "exclusionary" practices, but such charges were often ambiguous and, in some instances, not strictly illegal. Still, a dominant firm that tried to protect its monopoly position was considered a likely candidate for antitrust action.

The *Alcoa* ruling guided court opinion for most of the next 25 years. In recent decades, however, the courts have not always adopted the perspective that market domination is bad per se. Cases against Kodak and IBM , for example, were dismissed even though both of those giant companies acted to protect what were largely monopolized markets.[14] Still, the question of monopoly and bigness persists, as the government's recent antitrust action against Microsoft illustrates.

The Microsoft Case

In the early 1980s, IBM Corporation chose Microsoft Corporation's DOS software to be the standard operating system on its personal computers (PCs). IBM placed no restrictions on other computer vendors using the same basic hardware, configured around a microprocessor made by the Intel Corporation. Consequently, IBM-type hardware and the DOS operating system became the general standards for PCs worldwide. Later, Microsoft developed a new, object-based operating system called Windows, which replaced DOS in all Intel-based PCs. The pairing of Windows operating software and Intel microprocessors gave rise to the abbreviation WINTEL to describe the generations of personal computers developed since the original IBM-DOS PC.

Because its system became *the* standard, Microsoft became the dominant player, with something like a monopoly in the market for PC operating systems, and the company grew increasingly wealthy through the 1980s and 1990s. The value of Microsoft stock soared to almost $500 billion, and its chairman, Bill Gates, was renowned as the world's richest person, with personal wealth at one point estimated at close to $100 billion.[15] This financial success was tempered by increasingly unfavorable public perceptions of both Microsoft and its founder. They were seen as arrogant, and in fairness often seemed to behave in ways that suggested they thought themselves above the law. More than a few people felt that a company so rich and so contemptuous of competitors and the government had to be doing something wrong. As with Alcoa, the sheer size, market dominance, and financial success of Microsoft brought antitrust scrutiny to bear.

The Federal Trade Commission (FTC) first began investigating Microsoft's practices in 1991. That investigation lasted two years. In the end, although some of the commissioners urged that antitrust charges be brought against the company, the FTC did not proceed with any formal complaints. In the meantime, however, the Department of Justice had begun its own investigation into the business practices of this high-profile company. At issue was whether Microsoft acted illegally by packaging application software (such as the word processor, Microsoft Word) with its operating system (Windows). This investigation led to a settlement in 1994, pursuant to which the company agreed not to require PC makers to accept its application software along with Windows.

Computer technology was changing rapidly. In 1994, when Microsoft settled with the Justice Department, PCs were being used mainly for word processing and spreadsheets. Just a few years later, one of the most important uses of the PC had become access to the Internet and e-mail. By 1997, the Justice Department was back in court charging that Microsoft had violated its earlier agreement because it was now bundling its Internet browser, Explorer, with its Windows operating system. U.S. District Judge Thomas Penfield Jackson issued an injunction against Microsoft, requiring the company to offer Windows without Explorer, if that is what PC makers preferred.[16]

The key antitrust issue in the new case against Microsoft was not monopolization, but rather what is called *tying*. Tying is essentially "an agreement by a party to sell one product but only on the condition that the buyer also purchases a different (or tied) product, or at least agrees that he will not purchase that product from any other supplier."[17] This practice is specifically prohibited in the Clayton Act, and its impropriety is at least implied in the Sherman Act. Thus, if Microsoft sold Windows only on condition that PC makers adopt other Microsoft software, it would presumably be a case of tying.

Cases of alleged tying create line-drawing problems for the courts. As legal scholar and former judge Robert Bork has noted, almost any product can be broken down into components that could conceivably be sold separately.[19] It is tying of a sort, when a PC maker includes a keyboard, a case, a mouse, and a sound card with the basic microprocessor. But we accept that sort of tying. Indeed, consumers benefit by having a complete package, which can be evaluated against other complete packages. This kind of tying lowers transaction costs for buyers.[18] Therefore, eliminating it could well be socially inefficient

The question then was: What sort of tying was the browser? It does appear that Microsoft bundled Explorer with Windows at least in part to lock out (or disadvantage) Netscape, whose Navigator software competed directly with Explorer. At the same time, most observers agreed that bundling Explorer with Windows was convenient for consumers and probably functionally useful. Because Explorer was designed by the same company that made the operating system, it was certain to be compatible in all respects with the basic software of the computer. Also, and perhaps more important from an antitrust standpoint, no one claimed that bundling was costly to consumers. Windows did not cost more because of Explorer. Explorer was essentially offered to consumers free of charge. Most analysts agreed that, overall, consumers got a sound product at a reasonable price.

Microsoft protested that it was not engaging in anticompetitive behavior, but in January 1998, it offered PC makers the option of removing or hiding Explorer. This offer did not satisfy the Justice Department or the attorneys general of 20 states, however. They filed antitrust charges against Microsoft in U.S. District Court, the case to be heard, once again, by Judge Jackson. Microsoft was charged with tying, entering into exclusionary contracts with Internet providers, and, ironically, attempting to collude with Netscape to divide the browser market. A little less than two years later, Judge Jackson issued his ruling.

The thrust of the ruling was that Microsoft had frozen out the competition, not only acting as the default browser of choice for most PC users, but creating a system that made it difficult for other vendors to write Internet and network applications programs such as "instant messaging" (so-called *middleware*). This difficulty would hurt two competitors in particular, Netscape and Sun Microsystems, whose Java programming language was widely used by net programmers. But in Judge Jackson's view, it would ultimately hurt consumers, too.

United States v. Microsoft Corp.
84 F. Supp. 2d 9 (D.D.C. 1999)

Thomas Penfield Jackson, Judge.

The debut of Internet Explorer and its rapid improvement gave Netscape an incentive to improve Navigator's quality at a competitive rate. The inclusion of Internet Explorer with Windows at no separate charge increased general familiarity with the Internet and reduced the cost to the public of gaining access to it, at least in part because it compelled Netscape to stop charging for Navigator. These actions thus contributed to improving the quality of Web browsing software, lowering its cost, and increasing its availability, thereby benefitting consumers.

To the detriment of consumers, however, Microsoft has done much more than develop innovative browsing software of commendable quality and offer it bundled with Windows at no additional charge. As has been shown, Microsoft also engaged in a concerted series of actions designed to protect the application's barrier to entry, and hence its monopoly power, from a variety of middleware threats, including Netscape's Web browser and Sun's implementation of Java. Many of these actions have harmed consumers in ways that are immediate and easily discernible. They have also caused less direct, but nevertheless serious and far-reaching, consumer harm by distorting competition.

***

Most harmful of all is the message that Microsoft's actions have conveyed to every enterprise with the potential to innovate in the computer industry. Through its conduct toward Netscape, IBM, Compaq, Intel, and others, Microsoft has demonstrated that it will use its prodigious market power and immense profits to harm any firm that insists on pursuing initiatives that could intensify competition against one of Microsoft's core products. Microsoft's past success in hurting such companies and stifling innovation deters investment in technologies and businesses that exhibit the potential to threaten Microsoft. The ultimate result is that some innovations that would truly benefit consumers never occur for the sole reason that they do not coincide with Microsoft's self-interest. ■

Judge Jackson argued that consumers were harmed, but his argument was largely theoretical. Apparently, other software *might* have been written that *might* well have been beneficial. However, Judge Jackson failed to consider whether the social benefits of increased and lower-cost public access to the Internet, resulting from Microsoft's tying of its Web browser with Windows, outweighed the costs of that theoretical harm.

As a remedy, Judge Jackson in a later ruling ordered Microsoft broken up into two separate companies: an applications company to sell products such as Word and Explorer, and an operating system company that focused on Windows and its variants. Unsurprisingly, Microsoft appealed and in June 2001, the U.S. Court of Appeals upheld some of Judge Jackson's ruling but overturned more of it. Yes, Microsoft had broken antitrust laws by maintaining its operating system monopoly. The appeals court also generally accepted the argument that Microsoft had undertaken anticompetitive actions with respect to middleware. But the court did not agree either that the tying charge had been proven, or that Microsoft had acted to monopolize the browser market. Most importantly, the court of appeals declared Jackson's remedy to be wholly inappropriate. In a unanimous opinion, an unusual seven-judge panel[19] held as follows:

> We vacate the District Court's remedies decree for the additional
> reason that the court has failed to provide an adequate explanation
> for the relief it ordered. The Supreme Court has explained that a
> remedies decree in an antitrust case must seek to "unfetter a market
> from anticompetitive conduct," to "terminate the illegal monopoly, deny to
> the defendant the fruits of its statutory violation, and ensure that there
> remain no practices likely to result in monopolization in the future." The
> District Court has not explained how its remedies decree would accomplish
> those objectives. Indeed, the court devoted a mere four paragraphs of its
> order to explaining its reasons for the remedy. They are: (1) Microsoft "does
> not yet concede that any of its business practices violated the Sherman Act";
> (2) Microsoft "continues to do business as it has in the past"; (3) Microsoft
> "has proved untrustworthy in the past"; and (4) the Government, whose
> officials "are by reason of office obliged and expected to consider—
> and to act in—the public interest," won the case, "and for that reason
> alone have some entitlement to a remedy of their choice." Nowhere
> did the District Court discuss the objectives the Supreme Court deems
> relevant.[20]

The appeals court also directly criticized Judge Jackson's conduct in the trial, which the appellate judges felt showed a lack of decorum. Judge Jackson was in fact removed from further consideration of the case.

In November 2002, the case came to an end. Microsoft was required to provide middleware interfaces and codes to application writers, so that Windows could be more fully utilized as a platform for a variety of vendors. Microsoft also could no longer have arrangements with Internet access providers, requiring them to utilize Microsoft products only. Further, for five years Microsoft could offer only uniform licensing agreements with leading computer manufacturers so as to prevent the kind of side agreements that would violate the general thrust of the settlement. District Court Judge Colleen Kollar-Kotelly also dismissed appeals by eight states that had continued to argue for stricter rules against Microsoft.[21]

In the aftermath, many scholars opined on the efficiency and the equity of the ruling. Much ink was spilled in dozens of law review articles, books, and editorials evaluating the merits of the original case as well as the final outcome. As critics recognized, one of the main problems with the case from the outset was the nature of the industry itself. Software technology (and computer technology generally) moves far more quickly and unpredictably than do the wheels of justice. While the courts were taking months of testimony and depositions over Microsoft's treatment of Netscape, the latter merged with AOL, the largest Internet access company. While the courts were struggling with the questions of codes and software protocols and the nature of middleware, a programmer in Europe wrote an alternative operating system called Linux, which began to take market share from Microsoft for network applications. Undoubtedly, government has an economic role to play in curbing excessive market power, but it is unclear whether the legal institutions created for the late nineteenth century are wholly (or even largely) applicable to high-technology industries in the twenty-first century. Perhaps it is time to rethink antitrust law with respect to new industries in the years ahead.

REGULATED INDUSTRIES

Despite the federal government's strong commitment to antitrust law, it does not attempt to prevent or break up every monopoly. In fact, it has sometimes expressly authorized or, as in the case of the U.S. Postal Service, *created* monopolies. In such cases, instead of attempting to convert a monopoly market into a competitive market, the government allows the monopoly market to persist, but attempts to regulate it in the interest of consumers.

Since at least the seventeenth century, legal scholars have argued that certain industries are, in the words of one British jurist, "affected with the publick interest,"[22] and therefore require some kind of public (i.e., government) oversight. In the seventeenth century, seaports, bridges, and other kinds of public facilities were singled out for government regulation. By the nineteenth century, the list of industries and facilities had been expanded to include public services (e.g., postal services) and utilities such as gas pipelines, telephones, and electric power systems. In many countries, these industries were operated and owned by government agencies, supposedly to ensure that they would be managed in the public interest. In the United States, vigorous debate surrounded not only about the allocation of ownership—public or private—but also the proper structure of these vital industries.

Some economists argued that such services were inherently monopolies. As such, they would inevitably embody the problems of monopoly that antitrust laws were enacted to combat. It was thought that antitrust was not the best way to deal with the monopoly problem for these industries because they were inherently or "naturally" monopolies. A natural monopoly was defined as an industry in which one firm could supply consumers more efficiently than two or more firms. So, for example, electric power production was said to be a natural monopoly because it required huge up-front investment costs, including the costs of running wires from the production facilities to electricity consumers, but declining marginal costs of electricity production. It was said to be cheaper overall to have one large supplier of electricity for a community than several smaller suppliers, each competing for customers. Thus, for natural monopolies, competition would be economically inefficient. Consequently, it would be inefficient for government to break up natural monopolies under antitrust laws.

Instead, the government maintained natural monopolies as monopolies, but sought either to own them or to regulate privately owned natural monopolies, so as to ameliorate their tendencies to underproduce and overprice. In the United States, since the early the twentieth century, electric utilities have been either publicly owned or privately owned, but government regulated monopolies.

In the landmark 1876 case of *Munn v. Illinois*,[23] the Supreme Court made it clear that such government regulation of businesses in the public interest was entirely legal.[24] Eleven years later, Congress created the first regulatory agency, the Interstate Commerce Commission, to oversee the railroads. Since then, industries such as telecommunications, airlines, natural gas pipelines, water companies, and electric power have been government regulated. Many of them still face a significant amount of government supervision today.

In recent years, however, most of these industries have at least to a degree become less regulated. Has this shift been a good idea? Was the original theory of natural monopoly wrong? Is there still good reason to regulate certain industries? What, indeed, is the future for government regulation?

The Theory of Natural Monopoly

Pick up an economic principles textbook and go to the index. Look up "Natural Monopoly" (it may be under "Monopoly–natural") and turn to that page. You will find a definition that reads something like this: "A monopoly that arises because a single firm can supply a good or service to an entire market at a smaller cost than could two or more firms."[25] The text will typically include a graph, such as Figure 14-3, to accompany this definition.

Here, as with Figure 14-2, we have a graph of a market with a demand curve but no supply curve. Instead, we introduce a new curve representing the average cost of production, defined as the total cost of production divided by total output. In this case, the curve slopes downward throughout the entire range of demand. Thus, the more that is produced and sold to consumers, the lower the average cost of producing that output. Basically, costs will fall in this manner because of economies of scale. Scale economies occur when a firm can increase the amount of inputs and derive from them a proportionally greater amount of output. For example, doubling the diameter of a gas pipeline increases its carrying capacity by more than double; an electric generator of 100 megawatts does not require twice as many coal inputs as a generator that produces 50 megawatts.[26]

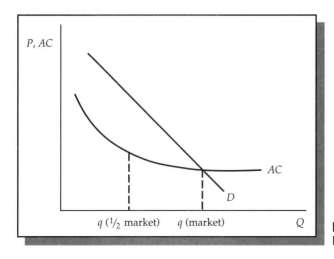

Figure 14-3
Natural Monopoly

The consequences of pervasive economies of scale are great. Because a producer must recoup the average cost with each sale, a producer that can meet the entire amount of market demand must necessarily be able to sell at a price below that of any producer that can meet less than the entire range of demand. Suppose that in a market that looks like Figure 14-2, someone wanted to sell to half the market. At that point, the average cost of production is much greater than it is to the single producer who could supply the whole market. A firm that can meet all demand will set a price below that of anyone who sells to only a portion of the market. The market must, apparently, become a monopoly—a natural monopoly.

We say "apparently" because whether the graph of a natural monopoly represents any real industry is open to question. Though the existence of natural monopolies was taken as fact by many economists, business leaders, and politicians in the first half of the twentieth century, the model is far too simple to be a realistic representation of actual business concerns. For example, few companies produce only one product. Electric power companies typically supply two products: (1) they produce electricity, and (2) they distribute electricity, which are separate functions. In addition, electric utilities typically provide technical service, information, and so on. Each of those functions entails its own costs, and its own economies or diseconomies of scale. Indeed, different kinds of costs are incurred; while some may be falling with increasing size, others, like bureaucratic costs, are likely to be rising (reflecting diseconomies of scale). Some economists find little reason to believe that any natural monopoly firm has ever existed.[27]

Be that as it may, Figure 14-3 leads to a logical conclusion. If such an industry is unregulated, the monopolist will (in theory) draw marginal revenue and marginal cost curves, find the intersection and produce the quantity at that point, and price it at the point where that quantity intersects the demand curve. As we saw earlier, this situation will not be socially efficient. It necessarily entails a waste of social resources, or deadweight losses. Too little will be produced, and it will be sold at too high a price.

The goal of the regulators then is to see that this outcome does not occur. Therefore, the government needs to control prices so as to induce the monopolists to produce the socially optimal quantity. This goal requires a delicate balancing act. The government does not want to restrict prices so much that companies cannot earn profits, causing them to go out of business. The regulators' objective is to ensure that the companies earn no more *and* not less than "reasonable" profits. This point assumes, of course, that they know what rate of profit *is* reasonable. Companies, consumers, and government regulators might well offer very different assessments of "reasonable profit." At the very least, it requires that regulators possess a good deal of information about the cost structures of individual firms and the regulated industry as a whole.

As a general rule, governments in the United States—local, state, and federal—arrived at this basic approach to industries thought to be natural monopolies. In most instances the states took the lead in establishing public utility commissions to regulate utilities. In addition, the federal government in accord with its constitutional authority over interstate commerce, created agencies (e.g., the Federal Power Commission, the Federal Communications Commission, the Civil Aviation Board) to regulate many industries whose economic impacts crossed state lines. Typically, the result was that firms would be given a monopoly franchise, locally, regionally, or nationally depending on the industry. In return for monopoly, these firms guaranteed service to all who could pay for it. Government, meanwhile, would regulate rates, capital expansion, and other aspects of these businesses in order to (it was hoped) arrive at a socially beneficial outcome that would combine something close to the prices that would exist in a competitive market with the scale economies of monopoly production.

In general, large players in natural monopoly industries favored this approach. In electricity, for example, leading companies sought regulated monopolies as an alternative to competition or government ownership.[28] Still, companies did on occasion challenge various parts of the regulatory process, especially during the 1930s when the federal government assumed greater oversight roles previously managed by the states. For example, when the Federal Power Commission lowered one company's prices for natural gas, the action was fought to the Supreme Court. But the court sided with the government:[29]

> The argument that the provisions of the statute applied in this case are unconstitutional on their face is without merit. The sale of natural gas originating in one State and its transportation and delivery to distributors in any other State constitutes interstate commerce, which is subject to regulation by Congress. It is no objection to the exercise of the power of Congress that it is attended by the same incidents which attend the exercise of the police power of a State. The authority of Congress to regulate the prices of commodities in interstate commerce is at least as great under the Fifth Amendment as is that of the States under the Fourteenth to regulate the prices of commodities in intrastate commerce.

Any effort to set rates (i.e., prices) through regulation is, of course, subject to a fundamental problem. In a market economy, prices are set by the dynamics of supply and demand, which reflect the costs of producers and the preferences of consumers. Government price setting, which is what this process entails, can never match the market, either in accuracy or speed, and always must come down to a judgment of less than perfectly informed individual commissioners, who may be influenced by a variety of factors besides the cost of production and the apparent demands of consumers. Many economists have suggested ways to systematize rate setting, but more often than not regulatory agencies have set rates unsystematically, in an attempt to assure consumers a "fair" price, while providing producers and their stockholders a "reasonable" return on their investments.

The Deregulation Movement

From the late 1800s until the middle of the twentieth century, government regulation of business increased. By 1960, agencies with important regulatory oversight authority included not only the classic natural monopoly industries such as water, telephone, and electricity, but also industries such as banking, shipping, trucking, and the airlines.

Beginning in the early 1970s, however, when the Federal Communications Commission relaxed various regulations with respect to satellite and common carrier access, the federal government initiated what has been called a "wave of deregulation."[30] Major legislative efforts substantially deregulated industries including airlines, railroads, cable television, natural gas, and shipping. Court action, including the breakup of the American Telegraph & Telephone Company (AT&T), brought competition to many parts of the telecommunications industry. Ironically, AT&T had been charged by the Justice Department with antitrust violations, even though it was essentially through government regulation that AT&T's telephone monopoly had been created in the first place.[31] In the 1990s, efforts at both the state and federal levels sought to reduce the regulatory strictures and to create competitive markets in electric power as well.

This move toward deregulation occurred for several reasons. First, ideology played a role. Free market advocates, especially during the administration of President Ronald Reagan, believed that markets allocated resources more efficiently than government. Second, technical changes meant that industries seen as necessarily monopolistic no longer had to be. Where once all phone conversations had to pass completely through a set of wires, for example, now they could be beamed to satellites or from one microwave tower to another. This technology made it unnecessary for one company to own an entire network. Indeed, one company tended to inhibit innovation in these new technologies. Competition, by contrast, encourages innovation as well as increased choice for consumers. Third, it was becoming clear that some of the economies of scale that were supposed to necessitate monopoly never really existed in the first place. For example, some economies of scale were obvious with respect to electric power production, but as electric generators grew ever larger those scale economies disappeared. In some instances, smaller generators were actually cheaper to build and operate than larger ones. And finally, in a new analysis of the premises of natural monopoly theory, the economist Harold Demsetz showed that even in the event that a firm bore many of the characteristics of a natural monopoly, it would not necessarily be able to charge monopolistic prices. Notably, a firm may be prevented from setting prices if even the potential for other firms to enter the market is present, which may well be the case in most instances.[32] Indeed, many monopoly industries, at closer look, had the potential to be competitive. Airline markets, for example, were plainly contestable; that is, they could be entered and contested by multiple firms. Consumers would gain the benefits of deregulation not only in the form of more choices but in lower prices.

It was one thing to recognize the potential benefits from deregulation, but another to realize them. Even though consumers have generally benefited from the deregulation wave, transition costs were inevitable as industries adapted to a new set of rules. Moreover, although regulators sometimes encouraged competition, they often did so by imposing rules that were more constraining and problematic than the former regulations had been. This tendency led in one case, electric power, to a widely publicized disaster, which halted in their tracks most efforts to deregulate that industry.

California's Power Crisis[33]

In 1996, the California state legislature passed Assembly Bill 1890, which was intended to restructure the electric power industry in the state so as to permit competition. Initially, however, competition would be reserved for the wholesale power market. In other words, any independent producers of power could sell electricity to power distribution companies through a state-run market. This market was expected to reduce the price of power because sales would go to producers with the lowest prices.

Although this legislation introduced a measure of competition to the industry, it did not by any means deregulate electric power. In fact, it was closer to re-regulation than deregulation. The State of California simply replaced one set of regulatory rules with another set that doomed the restructuring experiment to failure. To a real extent the market was even more constrained by government rules after the passage of Assembly Bill 1890 than it had been under the natural monopoly system. Here were some of the problems:

- Despite the existence of a competitive wholesale market, the retail market (i.e., the sale of electricity to homes and businesses) still had fixed prices. Consequently, if the cost of wholesale power rose above the retail price, the distributing companies would be given a Hobson's choice between selling at a loss or simply not buying any power to sell. In fact, they had no choice. Under state law, they had to sell to consumers at the fixed price.
- Not only was the retail price fixed; it was mandated to *fall*. This mandate was based on the assumption that costs would continue falling for power producers. As it happen, production costs rose. But retail suppliers were forced, by law, to lower their prices anyway. The result, of course, was that they suffered huge losses.
- Those losses might have been mitigated if the distribution company could have entered into long-term contracts with power suppliers. Purchasing all power through long-term contracts would mean that the risk of rising costs would be transferred from the distributor to the generating company. Of course the contract price would likely have been higher than the current market price (can you see why?), but then the distributor could have lowered costs by buying some power daily in the market and some through long-term contracts. In that case, the risk would have been spread. Generally speaking, in a market economy such contracts are written routinely. They could not be written in California, however, because Assembly Bill 1890 prohibited long-term contracting for wholesale electricity purchases.
- If distributors owned power production facilities as well as the distribution network, they could have guaranteed themselves some power in times of need. But the California law required that the distribution companies sell off most of their generating capacity. This requirement was supposed to make for a more competitive environment because the distributors were also large generators. But because all sales had to go through a state-run clearing center, the distributors probably could not have used their size anticompetitively. In any case, the distributors were subject entirely to a market in which they participated only as buyers not as sellers.

In the years following the enactment of Assembly Bill 1890, California faced rising demand from a booming economy and an influx of new residents. In 2000, supplies of natural gas—the main fuel for most of the local generating facilities— became tight, causing wholesale prices to rise. Soon the distribution companies were paying more on average for electricity than they could recoup from customers because of the state's retail price caps. Consumers benefited by paying less than the going market price for electricity, but as a consequence they received no signals about tightening demand or rising costs. Thus, they did not possess the information that would have been provided by market prices, which might have led them to conserve electricity or otherwise curtail their demand. Moreover, some generators made matters worse by engaging in schemes to confuse the state authorities as to the amount of power in the system. They indicated there was too much power, and so were paid to remove it. In fact, too little electricity was flowing through the system, and distributors were having an increasingly difficult time meeting demand.

Before long the distribution companies were near bankruptcy. They were having trouble buying power because many generators realistically feared they would never be paid. So high demand and tight supplies led to rolling blackouts and, by late 2000, a statewide crisis. Early in 2001, the state began to undo the new regulatory system that had been created in 1996. Wholesale prices were capped, and retail prices increased. Plans for retail competition were dropped and the state entered into long-term power contracts. However, these agreements were signed at the height of the crisis and left the state saddled with prices well above the long-term cost of electricity, which state officials later sought to renegotiate. Overall, the experiment with restructuring in California was clearly at an end.

The California misadventure was described, albeit incorrectly, as a failed effort at deregulation. It is more appropriately seen as a failure of a different kind of regulation—regulation so full of contradictions that it was doomed to failure. Still, the perception that deregulation had produced the disaster chilled efforts throughout the country at deregulation of electric power. Time will tell whether this setback was temporary or a watershed whereby the old regulatory system was reinstated with respect to this one industry for the long term.

CHAPTER SUMMARY

Government regulation of business through antitrust and regulated industries law has been aimed at solving market failures and improving the efficiency and equity of the economic system. A large body of law and an extensive network of agencies and commissions evolved to oversee these efforts. In some cases real abuses have been corrected, and probably many others forestalled. However, the regulatory process is, as noted in this chapter, an inexact one. Measurement costs and information problems always leave the results of regulation less than optimal. In some instances, it seems clear that deregulation—a transition to market forces—is a more efficient alternative. In Coase's terms, the social costs of market failures due to unregulated economic activities may be lower than the social costs of government failures from regulating economic activities. This conclusion is not to deny any legitimate role for government regulation of business but merely to identify the importance of comparative institutional analysis. The reality is that governments and markets both fail. From the perspective of efficiency, government should regulate business activity only when the costs of the unregulated market failure exceed the expected costs of any likely government regulatory failure.

QUESTIONS AND PROBLEMS

1. If monopolies are so bad, why does government sometimes create them, for example via the system of intellectual property rights (as discussed in Chapter 5)?
2. From a Coasean perspective, how might we analyze the measurement problems of antitrust acts?
3. Under what circumstances would combinations of firms benefit the economy? In these cases, should antitrust laws prevent such combinations?
4. How might antitrust laws be changed to deal with a rapidly changing technology?
5. What would public choice theory predict about state efforts to deregulate electric utilities and other regulated monopolies?
6. What, if anything, limits the prices a monopolist will charge?
7. Why might economies of scale lead to a monopoly?
8. Microsoft has most of the market for personal computer operating systems. Is this market position a monopoly? Does it have monopoly pricing power?
9. Was the ruling in the *Northern Securities* case efficient? Why or why not?

NOTES

1. Marginal costs include the opportunity cost of using the money for some other purpose, say, for a bank deposit. Therefore, to say price equals marginal cost means that the producer recoups the cost of inputs plus the benefit (profit) it would have received from the next best use of the money. In other words, marginal cost pricing includes some profit, sometimes referred to as normal profit.
2. In other words, they could have been produced at a price at or above marginal cost. However, much of those benefits would accrue to the consumer. The monopoly firm earns its highest profits at the monopoly price and quantity.
3. *See* William J. Baumol, John C. Panzar, and Robert D. Willig, *Contestable Markets and the Theory of Industry Structure* (Stamford, CT: International Thomson Publishing, 1989).
4. *See Brown Shoe Company v. United States*, 370 U.S. 294 (1962).
5. They also sought a third alternative: protection from competition as a legal monopoly, which would not be subject to the antitrust laws.
6. The U.S. Post Office did not offer parcel service until 1913. *See* Peter Z. Grossman, "The Dynamics of a Stable Cartel: The Railroad Express 1851–1913," 34 ECONOMIC INQUIRY 220 (1996).
7. 26 Stat. 209 (1890).
8. The original limits were imprisonment of up to one year and fines up to $5,000. Note that in the period 1890 to 1914—while the Sherman Act was the primary basis for antitrust prosecution—no jail sentences were ever imposed.
9. Richard A. Posner, *Antitrust Law: An Economic Perspective* (Chicago: University of Chicago Press, 1978).
10. Richard A. Posner, *Antitrust Law: An Economic Perspective* (Chicago: University of Chicago Press, 1978), p. 28. Mergers are treated in the Clayton Act, discussed in the next section.
11. 38 Stat. 730 (1914).
12. 38 Stat. 717 (1914).
13. This case was decided by the U.S. Circuit Court of Appeals, Second Circuit rather than the U.S. Supreme Court because four Supreme Court justices had previously been involved in aspects of the case, and they felt they could not rule on it. Having only five justices available, the Supreme Court lacked a quorum and ceded authority to the next highest court, the Court of Appeals.
14. *Berkley Photo, Inc. v. Eastman Kodak (1979); Telex Corp. v. International Business Machines Corp. (1975).*

15. Most of his wealth was just the paper value of his Microsoft stock, which he could not have sold en masse without diminishing its value considerably, and indeed the value fell by about 50 percent in the early 2000s. Still, by any standards Bill Gates had become a hugely wealthy individual.

16. 980 F. Supp. 537 (D.D.C. 1997).

17. *Northern Pacific Railroad Co., et al. v. United States*, 356 U.S. 1, 5–6 (1958).

18. *See* C. Ahlborn, D. S. Evand, and A. J. Padilla, "The Antitrust Economics of Tying: A Farewell to Per Se Illegality," AEI-Brookings Joint Center for Regulatory Studies Related Publication 03–3 (2003).

19. Robert Bork, *The Antitrust Paradox* (New York: The Free Press, 1978). Most federal court of appeals cases are heard and decided by three-judge panels.

20. *United States v. Microsoft Corp.*, 253 F. 3d 34 (D.C. Cir. 2001).

21. 231 F. Supp. 2d 144; Civil Action No. 98–1232 (CKK).

22. Lord Chief Justice Mathew Hale, *De Portibus Maris* (c. 1670).

23. 94 U.S. 113 (1876).

24. Although this ruling was interpreted by many to apply mainly to utilities and other essential facilities, a 1934 Supreme Court decision in *Nebbia v. New York* gave states the right to regulate basic commodity prices as well—notably the price of milk.

25. N. Gregory Mankiw, *Principles of Microeconomics*, 2nd ed. (Cincinnati, OH: South-Western College Publishing, 2001), p. 318.

26. For a discussion of natural monopoly, see William W. Sharkey, *The Theory of Natural Monopoly* (Cambridge: Cambridge University Press, 1982).

27. This argument is especially true with respect to electric power. *See* Peter Z. Grossman, "Is Anything Naturally a Monopoly?" in Peter Z. Grossman & Daniel H. Cole (eds.), *The End of a Natural Monopoly: Deregulation and Competition in the Electric Power Industry* (New York: Elsevier Science, 2003), p. 11.

28. *See* Robert L. Bradley, Jr., "The Origins and Development of Electric Power Regulation," in Peter Z. Grossman & Daniel H. Cole (eds.), *The End of a Natural Monopoly: Deregulation and Competition in the Electric Power Industry* (New York: Elsevier Science, 2003), p. 43.

29. *Federal Power Commission v. Natural Gas Pipeline Co.*, 315 U.S. 575 (1942).

30. W. Kip Viscusi, John M. Vernon, and Joseph E. Harrington, *Economics of Regulation and Antitrust* (Boston: MIT Press, 1995), p. 302.

31. Antitrust actions against AT&T can be found throughout the twentieth century. The suit that finally led to the breakup was filed by the government in 1974 against AT&T and its subsidiaries (Civil Action No. 74–1698). AT&T was charged with monopolization of telecommunications services and equipment in violation of section 2 of the Sherman Act. AT&T agreed to the breakup of the company eight years later in part so that it could enter the computer business. The terms of the settlement are detailed in *United States v. AT&T*, 552 F. Supp. 131 (D.D.C. 1982).

32. Harold Demsetz, "Why Regulate Utilities?" 11 *Journal of Law & Economics* 55 (1968).

33. This section is adapted from Peter Z. Grossman, "Does the End of a Natural Monopoly Mean Deregulation?" in Peter Z. Grossman & Daniel H. Cole (eds.), *The End of a Natural Monopoly: Deregulation and Competition in the Electric Power Industry* (New York: Elsevier Press, 2003), p. 215.

Chapter 15

Environmental Protection

WHAT IS POLLUTION?

Like the concept of economic cost, the term *pollution* describes a negative human value judgment about something. Simple reflection on how the word is used and not used makes the concept easier to understand.

We use the word *pollution* to describe sulfur dioxide emissions from a power plant smokestack, but not to describe sulfur dioxide emissions from a volcano. We use the term to describe wastes left by human visitors to national parks, but not wastes produced by the parks' animal inhabitants. So, it would seem, pollution is necessarily a by-product (not necessarily artificial or inorganic) of human activities.

Not *all* human wastes appear to constitute pollution, however. The extent of emissions seems to matter. Each of us, for example, emits a small amount of carbon dioxide when we exhale, but we do not generally consider breathing to be a polluting activity. Moreover, plants require a certain amount of carbon dioxide to grow. So the complete eradication of carbon dioxide would precipitate an ecological disaster. At the other extreme, a sizeable majority of atmospheric scientists believe that vast amounts of carbon dioxide in the atmosphere can cause potentially significant changes in the climate, such as global warming. Computer models suggest that those changes could have disastrous ecological consequences. Obviously, carbon dioxide concentrations in the atmosphere can range widely between too little to support plant life and too much to maintain stable climatic conditions. The question becomes: At what point do human-source carbon dioxide emissions become pollution?

It is not just the amount of the stuff that counts, but also where it is put. Location matters. Human emissions of chlorine gases, which are considered to be pollution, have depleted the ozone layer high above the earth in the stratosphere. That ozone layer protects the earth and its inhabitants from the sun's harmful ultraviolet rays, which can cause cancer. So, we have an environmental problem of *too little ozone* in the stratosphere. At a lower level of the atmosphere, closer to the earth's surface, we have an environmental problem of *too much ozone*. Molecules of ozone, in the lower atmosphere, interact with other constituent atmospheric elements to form smog,

313

exacerbating respiratory diseases such as asthma, and causing aesthetic blight. If only we could find an efficient way to transport some of that low-level ozone to the stratosphere.

In sum, pollution is (1) too much of something that (2) humans (a) produce, (b) negatively value, and (c) dispose of improperly or in an inappropriate location.

POLLUTION AS AN ECONOMIC PROBLEM

Almost every introductory economics textbook illustrates the problem of market failure with a pollution example, perhaps because pollution problems illustrate so well several of the reasons why markets fail. These reasons include high transaction costs, externalities, and public goods. Any one of these reasons alone could cause a market failure. Pollution typically combines them all in various degrees.

Pollution as a Negative Externality

Pollution constitutes a negative externality (as defined in Chapter 1) by definition. An activity that bears all its own costs is not considered a polluting activity. To cause pollution, it must generate social, not just private, costs; and to generate social costs, someone besides the actor must be harmed.

Like other externalities, pollution problems are signals of market failure; that is, they reflect the failure of the market to attain optimal allocative efficiency. Here is a common illustration: A factory produces widgets, which it sells at a certain price. The price is based on several factors: fixed costs, including plant and machinery; variable production costs, including labor, capital, and resource inputs; plus some profit margin. In the process of production, suppose the factory emits a ton of dust for every 100 widgets it produces. That dust constitutes a cost of production. It is a cost because dust is a constituent element of smog, which causes aesthetic blight and exacerbates respiratory problems, such as asthma and emphysema. In addition, when the dust eventually settles back to earth, it can damage agricultural crops. Some of the damages are easy enough to quantify as costs; others, such as aesthetic blight, are not. All would cost money to rectify or avert. These costs are not borne by the widget factory owner/operator, however. Instead, they are sent up the smokestack and out, away from the factory, along with the pollution emissions. They are literally externalized. The air pollution becomes an *externalized* cost of widget manufacture.

This externalization of pollution costs leads to allocative inefficiency in the market. Specifically, the widget factory's externalized pollution costs result in improper price signals that skew the quantity of widgets supplied and demanded. Because the pollution costs are externalized, the widget manufacturer does not have to pay for them. Consequently, the price of widgets to consumers will not reflect them. This externalized cost is a good thing for consumers of widgets, who, like consumers in other markets, rationally prefer lower prices to higher prices. But the effect of the externality is overall inefficiency and a waste of social resources. To understand why, it is worthwhile to review a figure first drawn in Chapter 1.

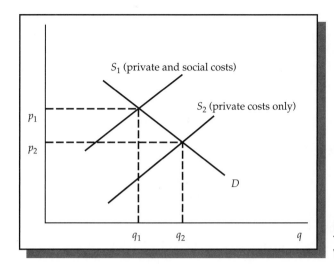

Figure 15-1
The Market for
Widgets

Figure 15-1 contains two supply curves (S_1 and S_2). Supply curves are determined by several factors but principally by the cost of production. Thus, if a firm can externalize some of its costs, it has the same effect as if the cost were reduced due to a gain in productivity. However, in this case the cost is not eliminated; rather, it is paid by others outside of the market. Thus, the supply curve S_1 reflects the marginal costs of production including pollution costs. The supply curve S_2, by contrast, reflects the case in which the costs of production do not include pollution costs—those costs are externalized. As a consequence, the market equilibrium point (where supply and demand curves intersect) is at a lower price and higher quantity for S_2 than for S_1. In other words, because the market for widgets does not include the (externalized) pollution costs associated with widget production, too many widgets are sold at too low a price. A fairness issue arises with respect to externalities when the costs fall, without consent, on those who may not benefit in any way from the widget market. But even on strictly efficiency grounds, negative externalities are a drain on social welfare.

If the widget maker had to internalize the pollution costs associated with widget production, it would produce along S_1 rather than S_2. Prices would rise and the quantity demanded would consequently fall. It would also mean that the amount of air pollution associated with widget manufacture would fall. In the absence of some mechanism for internalizing pollution costs, however, the market will continue to overproduce and underprice widgets in comparison to other goods and services.

It should be remembered, however, that not all externalities are bad (or negative). If Ben plants a beautiful garden in his front yard, so that all of his neighbors can enjoy the flowers without having to contribute financially or physically towards the garden's creation or upkeep, Ben has generated positive externalities (or external benefits). Likewise, when a company opens a new plant in a community, the jobs it creates may increase the overall level of productivity and prosperity; and the property taxes it pays will enhance local schools. These benefits stem from economic activity that is not captured by the actor in profits or rents. However, the word *pollution* always refers to a negative externality.

Moreover, not all negative externalities should be internalized. Allocative efficiency is maximized not by the *complete* internalization of costs but by the *efficient* internalization of costs. Where the cost of internalizing some externality exceeds the benefits to be gained, then it would be economically inefficient to require internalization.

Environmental Amenities as Public Goods

For the same reason that pollution is a negative externality or a "public bad," environmental amenities, such as clean air and water, can be thought of as public goods (as defined in Chapter 1). These goods are likely to be underprovided by markets because private producers cannot capture enough of the benefits to cover the costs of providing them. Imagine a socially conscious entrepreneur who sought to deal with air pollution problems privately by building a plant that would supply clean air. The plant might be nothing more than a giant pollution filter, taking in dirty air and emitting clean air. It would, of course, cost something—presumably a good deal of money—to build and operate the plant. Those costs might be worth bearing because the plant would be producing something of substantial economic value, namely clear air. The problem is, however, that the entrepreneur might not be able to capture enough of that economic value to compensate for the costs of providing the product. Every person within the locale of the entrepreneur's plant would benefit from having clean air to breathe. Ironically, the greatest part of the *economic* benefits might accrue to other plants that produce pollution. To the extent the pollution they produce is offset by the clean air from the socially conscious entrepreneur's plant, they may come under less political or legal pressure to reduce their own emissions. The entrepreneur will not able to capture (i.e., internalize) those benefits of the clean air plant, and will not be able to charge everyone who uses the clean air the plant produces for the marginal value of their uses. First of all, the entrepreneur could not possibly identify everyone who benefits in a significant way from the air-filtering activity. Even if that were possible, the entrepreneur would not be able to exclude anyone who refused to pay from using the clean air the plant produces.[1] This problem is a technical one: Once the clean air leaves the plant, the entrepreneur has no means of controlling who gets to use it, and thus, no way of internalizing the external benefits of this socially desirable activity. Knowing these factors, a rational entrepreneur would not build the clean air plant in the first place. For this reason, the production and protection of environmental amenities has largely been viewed throughout history as a function of governments rather than private markets.[2]

Transaction Costs and Pollution

Optimal Environmental Protection Would Be Achieved Automatically in the Mythical World of the Coase Theorem

Pollution is, at bottom, a problem of transaction costs. This assertion may not appear obvious at first blush, but it becomes intuitive with a simple thought experiment. Imagine environmental protection in the counterfactual world of the Coase theorem. In that world of neoclassical economic theory, markets function perfectly; the social welfare function is known and completely specified; cost and benefit functions are fully known; property rights are completely specified; and, of course, transaction costs, including the costs of information, are zero. Consequently, social costs and benefits would necessarily equal private costs and benefits.

By virtue of the assumptions that constitute the world of the Coase theorem, the optimal level of environmental protection is attained automatically. Polluters and those harmed by pollution would costlessly transact their way to efficient pollution levels. If Plant created pollution that caused $500 worth of harm to Farmer, and Farmer held the entitlement to be free of pollution, Plant would compensate Farmer for the harm. If it could not afford to pay compensation, Plant would stop production, which would be an efficient outcome. If, however, Plant held the entitlement to pollute, then Farmer would either purchase the entitlement from Plant at a price below $500, or suffer the harm. The distribution of pollution costs differs depending on who holds the entitlement, but the total social costs and benefits remain the same.

Even if the initial entitlement—the allocation of property rights—is uncertain, in the world of the Coase theorem Plant and Farmer would costlessly negotiate a contract allocating the risks/costs of pollution and pollution control. By virtue of the assumption of perfect markets and low information costs, no inefficient externalities, positive (public goods) or negative (pollution), would result.

Why then wouldn't the level of pollution be zero in the world of the Coase theorem? The efficient level would be zero only if the benefits of pollution control exceeded the costs (including the opportunity costs) for the first marginal unit of pollution, which is an inconceivable scenario. Try to imagine a world with virtually zero production of goods and services. It is doubtful that we would consider ourselves better off in such a world simply because it would be almost (but never completely) devoid of pollution. If society's goal is to maximize some social function, be it wealth, happiness, utility, or welfare, the optimal level of pollution must be above zero. Although, it is likely to be lower than it is now in many places.

The optimal level of pollution is that at which society would be less well off with any more or any less pollution. Where the optimally efficient level of pollution (and pollution control) has been attained, the social cost of reducing the next unit of pollution emissions (marginal cost) would exceed the social benefit (marginal benefit), so that society would be made worse off. By the same token, any additional pollution would reduce net social welfare by creating more costs than benefits. This optimal level of pollution would be attained automatically in the world of the Coase theorem, by virtue of the assumptions that constitute that world. Environmental protection, as a consequence, would simply not be a problem.

Transaction Costs and Pollution in the Real World

Environmental protection *is* an economic problem in the real world, where none of the assumptions of the Coase theorem obtains. In the real world, the social welfare function, if it exists at all, cannot be known;[3] property rights are only imperfectly specified; cost and benefit functions may not be known; markets do not function perfectly; and, of course, transaction costs are always positive and often quite high.

Among those transaction costs is endemic uncertainty about the costs and benefits of different levels of pollution and pollution control. Because of that uncertainty, it might not even make sense to talk about "optimal" levels of pollution or expect to actually attain them, let alone attain them *automatically*.

Part of the uncertainty stems from the fact that not all attributes of pollution or its effects are priced in markets. In 1989, the oil tanker *Exxon Valdez* ran aground in Prince William Sound in Alaska, spilling 11 million gallons of oil in a previously pristine bay. The cost of the lost oil was well understood. Less well understood, and far more difficult to quantify, were the costs associated with environmental harm, including an estimated 250,000 dead sea birds, 2,800 dead sea otters, 300 dead harbor seals, 250 dead bald eagles, and as many as 22 dead killer whales.[4] No (legal) secondary markets exist in which bald eagles or killer whales are priced. Calculating the value of such environmental costs, in the absence of market prices, is among the great challenges of environmental protection.

If all the birds and animals killed or injured by the *Exxon Valdez* oil spill had been privately owned and tradeable, a secondary market would have provided calculations of the costs of the environmental damages, and the owners of harmed animals would have been able to claim compensation, through lawsuits if necessary. The prospect of jury awards or settlement payouts presumably would have increased the incentives for the owners/operators of the *Exxon Valdez* to take additional precautions to reduce the likelihood and possibly the magnitude of potential accidents. However, transaction costs also obstruct the extension of private ownership to all the birds in the sky and fish in the oceans. For such wide-ranging animals, private property rights would be costly, almost certainly too costly, to establish and enforce.

Because many of the environmental costs of economic activities are difficult to quantify, so too are the *benefits* of regulatory measures designed to reduce environmental harm. It is relatively straightforward to calculate the costs of environmental regulations; for the most part, those costs are borne by industry and are reflected in reduced production and higher costs of goods and services. The value of benefits of environmental regulations, however, tends to be far more nebulous. We will return to this point later in this chapter, when addressing the role of cost-benefit analysis in environmental policy making.

POLLUTION AND THE COMMON LAW

Environmental law—the legal regulation of polluting activities—is commonly thought to be a relatively new area of law, invented in the twentieth century to resolve pollution problems that arose in the wake of the nineteenth century's Industrial Revolution. In reality, environmental law has a long history, stretching back at least to the beginning of the fourteenth century, when the City of London enacted a ban on the burning of "sea coal" to reduce local air pollution. In medieval Europe, Italian cities enacted waste disposal laws to reduce noxious odors and protect water supplies, while French cities forced environmentally harmful activities to move beyond city limits.

Environmental Nuisances

Not all early pollution control efforts took the form of ordinances or regulations, however. Common law causes of action, most notably nuisance and trespass,[5] early on developed into useful mechanisms for controlling environmentally harmful activities. As early as 1498, the English courts enjoined water polluting activities as nuisances. In the *Prior of Southwark's Case*,[6] Chief Justice Brian awarded an injunction against a glovemaker who located a lime-pit for treating calf skins so close to a stream that it "corrupt[ed]" the water. The glovemaker's pollution harmed neighboring residents, all tenants of the Prior of Southwark, who relied on the stream for various domestic purposes, including watering their animals, cooking and cleaning, and dyeing their clothes.

Somewhat later, the common law courts extended nuisance coverage to air polluting activities. In 1610, William Aldred successfully sued his neighbor, whose pigsty polluted the air about Aldred's home.[7] "Ever since Aldred's case," according to the U.S. Supreme Court,

> it has been the settled law, both of this country and of England, that a man
> has no right to maintain a structure upon his own land, which, by reason
> of disgusting smells, loud or unusual noises, thick smoke, noxious vapors,
> the jarring of machinery or the unwarrantable collection of flies, renders the
> occupancy of adjoining property dangerous, intolerable or even uncomfort-
> able to its tenants. No person maintaining such a nuisance can shelter him-
> self behind the sanctity of private property.[8]

Courts in the United States and the United Kingdom have consistently denied that any right to pollute exists; to the contrary, landowners possess enforceable rights to be free from substantial environmental harm. Not every act of pollution amounts to a violation of the common law, though, for reasons articulated by Lord Justice Westbury in the 1865 case of *St. Helens Smelting Co. v. Tipping*:

> [I]f a man lives in a town, it is necessary that he should subject himself
> to the consequences of those operations of trade which may be carried
> on in his immediate locality, which are actually necessary for trade and
> commerce, and also for the enjoyment of the property, and for the benefit
> of the inhabitants of the town and the public at large.[9]

Nuisance plaintiffs cannot prevail simply by proving that they have suffered some slight inconvenience because of noises, odors, or other ubiquitous features of the modern, industrialized world. They must prove that the defendant acted *unreasonably* under the circumstances, and pollution is not per se unreasonable. An economically productive activity that produces a slight odor, which a few individuals might find offensive, ordinarily will not be branded a nuisance. But an activity that produces significant environmental harm will create nuisance liability.

Thus, the common law courts do not seek to internalize *all* pollution externalities; in accordance with economic principles, the goal of the common law is not zero pollution. Rather, the courts seek to strike a balance. Polluters have no legal right to pollute, but the court only offers a remedy to those who suffer unreasonable harm from their pollution.

The Limits of Common Law Remedies for Pollution Problems

Few law and economics scholars believe that common law remedies alone are sufficient to achieve an economically efficient level of environmental protection. One reason is historical: prior to the emergence of the "regulatory state" in the twentieth century, the common law was (with the exception of local ordinances and a few state statutes) *the* primary vehicle for pollution control in the United States and the United Kingdom. Still, it hardly made a dent in the massive pollution increases that accompanied the Industrial Revolution. Ronald Coase, as usual, articulated a clear, concise, and cogent explanation for why the common law failed to provide sufficient environmental protection:

> [I]f many people are harmed and there are several sources of pollution, it is more difficult to reach a satisfactory solution through the market. When the transfer of rights has to come about as a result of market transactions carried out between large numbers of people or organizations acting jointly, the process of negotiation may be so difficult and time-consuming as to make such transfers a practical impossibility. *Even the enforcement of rights through the courts may not be easy. It may be costly to discover who it is that is causing the trouble. And, when it is not in the interest of any single person or organization to bring suit, the problems involved in arranging joint actions represent a further obstacle.* As a practical matter, the market may become too costly to operate.
>
> In these circumstances it may be preferable to impose special regulations (whether embodied in a statute or brought about as a result of the rulings of an administrative agency).[10]

The causation-proof problems Coase recognizes are especially important. Many pollutants travel long distances, and pollution-related diseases can have long latency periods. To prevail in court, plaintiffs must be able to trace their harm to a particular pollution source that might be located hundreds of miles away, and that their harm was proximately caused by exposure to a certain pollutant that may have occurred several decades ago. This evidentiary burden is often unbearable, and always expensive. Moreover, common law courts have traditionally restricted nuisance remedies to cases involving *visible* air pollution, such as smoke and dust; bad odors were usually not enough state a claim.[11] Of course, many harmful pollutants, including some of the most toxic, are invisible.

In addition to the problems of identifying defendants and proving causation that Coase articulated, the common law is insufficient for the task of pollution control for a number of reasons, including the following:

1. Common law remedies typically operate only after the fact of harm. If it costs more to remediate or compensate for pollution than to prevent it in the first place, then common law remedies are likely to be less efficient than proactive regulation. In a few cases, where substantial harm is highly probable, the common law may preempt a nuisance. In practice, however, plaintiffs invoke this doctrine only rarely, and they do so successfully even more rarely. This criticism of the common law is sometimes overstated, however. Common law remedies create precedents for future cases, and thus create incentives for pollution prevention. The real question is whether those remedies create *sufficient* incentives for *efficient* precaution.
2. Nuisance and trespass protect only plaintiffs who have property rights in the environmental amenities that are harmed by the defendants' pollution. If you do not

own property, you cannot sue to stop or reduce pollution unless you personally suffer bodily harm. Nor do the common law remedies remediate environmental harm to unowned or common-property resources.

3. In environmental joint cost situations involving complex fact patterns and large numbers of parties, the transaction costs of utilizing the court system may be high compared even to a presumptively expensive regulatory system. Recall the case of *Boomer v. Atlantic Cement Co.* in Chapter 6. In deciding not to enjoin the cement plant's dust emissions, the court expressed concern about the institutional limitations of the courts and the common law for dealing with complex and large-scale environmental problems. ■

Boomer et al. v. Atlantic Cement Company, Inc.

26 N.Y.2d 219; 257 N.E.2d 870 (1970)

Bergan, J.

The public concern with air pollution arising from many sources in industry and in transportation is currently accorded ever wider recognition accompanied by a growing sense of responsibility in State and Federal Governments to control it. Cement plants are obvious sources of air pollution in the neighborhoods where they operate.

But there is now before the court private litigation in which individual property owners have sought specific relief from a single plant operation. The threshold question raised by the division of view on this appeal is whether the court should resolve the litigation between the parties now before it as equitably as seems possible; or whether, seeking promotion of the general public welfare, it should channel private litigation into broad public objectives.

A court performs its essential function when it decides the rights of parties before it. Its decision of private controversies may sometimes greatly affect public issues. Large questions of law are often resolved by the manner in which private litigation is decided. But this is normally an incident to the court's main function to settle controversy. It is a rare exercise of judicial power to use a decision in private litigation as a purposeful mechanism to achieve direct public objectives greatly beyond the rights and interests before the court.

Effective control of air pollution is a problem presently far from solution even with the full public and financial powers of government. In large measure adequate technical procedures are yet to be developed and some that appear possible may be economically impracticable.

It seems apparent that the amelioration of air pollution will depend on technical research in great depth; on a carefully balanced consideration of the economic impact of close regulation; and of the actual effect on public health. It is likely to require massive public expenditure and to demand more than any local community can accomplish and to depend on regional and interstate controls.

A court should not try to do this on its own as a by-product of private litigation and it seems manifest that the judicial establishment is neither equipped in the limited nature of any judgment it can pronounce nor prepared to lay down and implement an effective policy for the elimination of air pollution. This is an area beyond the circumference of one private lawsuit. It is a direct responsibility for government and should not thus be undertaken as an incident to solving a dispute between property owners and a single cement plant—one of many—in the Hudson River valley. ■

***

4. In addition to the constraints recognized by the court in Boomer, courts are limited to dealing with the facts presented by the cases before them. They cannot undertake independent research or hold public hearings to gain information and a broader overview of pollution problems and solutions. Environmental protection via the courts is inevitably ad hoc, rather than systematic, and it is likely to differ significantly from one jurisdiction to another to the detriment of interstate commerce. It may seem ironic, but it is understandable that interstate industries, including trucking companies, strongly supported enactment of the 1970 Clean Air Act.[12] They rationally preferred a uniform system of federal regulations to the prospect of having to meet potentially 50 different sets of legal standards in 50 different states.

5. Finally, as Neil Komesar has pointed out, the activity level of courts is limited by the number of available courthouses, courtrooms, and judges.[13] Judges can hear only so many cases. If the number of environmental disputes demanding judicial resolution outstrips the supply of courts and judges, then pollution will likely be underdeterred, no matter what the legal rules.[14]

For all these reasons, the common law is highly unlikely, by itself, to create sufficient incentives for efficient levels of pollution control. In some cases at least, regulatory approaches are likely to be both more effective and more efficient at controlling pollution.

THE COSTS AND BENEFITS OF ENVIRONMENTAL REGULATION

As mentioned at the start of the last section, environmental regulation is not new. European cities have been enacting regulations to deal with waste disposal and air and water pollution problems since at least the fourteenth century. However, it was only in the twentieth century that pollution control regulations became ubiquitous at all levels of government, for a number of reasons. First, the types and quantity of pollution increased dramatically in the wake of the Industrial Revolution. Second, the common law, for reasons already discussed, proved incapable of dealing with technically complex environmental disputes involving large numbers of parties. Third, the growth in environmental regulation reflected the rise and expansion of the welfare/regulatory state during the progressive and New Deal eras.

For much of the twentieth century, however, environmental regulation was predominantly a state and local matter. The federal government did not become seriously involved until the 1970s, when Congress enacted (among other environmental statutes) the following:

- The 1969 National Environmental Policy Act (which took effect on January 1, 1970)
- The 1970 Clean Air Act
- The 1972 Clean Water Act
- The 1974 Safe Drinking Water Act
- The 1976 Toxic Substances Control Act

- The 1976 Resource Conservation and Recovery Act
- The 1980 Comprehensive Environmental Response, Compensation, and Liability Act (Superfund Law)

Today, the pollution control statutes of the federal government of the United States consume more than a thousand pages in the U.S. Code (the official compendium of federal laws). The Clean Air Act alone runs to more than 350 pages. Regulations promulgated by the federal Environmental Protection Agency (EPA) to fill in the gaps and implement Congress's statutes take up thousands of pages in the Code of Federal Regulations (the official compendium of federal agency regulations). Agency "guidance documents," which instruct regulated industries on how to comply with those regulations, add thousands more pages to the federal regulatory system. Throw in the environmental statutes, regulations, and ordinances enacted by state and local governments, and you begin to get some idea of the sheer mass of the public regulatory system of pollution control.

A massive regulatory system requires an equally massive organization to run it. Not surprisingly, the federal EPA is one of the largest administrative organizations in the United States. In addition to its headquarters in Washington, D.C., the agency has 10 regional offices and 17 laboratories located around the country. The EPA's staff numbers more than 18,000, including several hundred attorneys and more than 100 economists. Because the states are responsible for implementing and enforcing many of the federal environmental laws as well as their own supplementary regulatory systems, each state has its own mini-version of the EPA.

Some argue that the problem is too much regulation and, as a consequence, too much bureaucracy, resulting in job losses, competitive disadvantage for U.S. industries in international markets, and dampened economic growth. Others argue, to the contrary, that too little environmental regulation results in too much socially costly pollution. Questions of over- or underregulation aside, it is difficult to dispute that the regulatory system for pollution control is immensely expensive. As of 1990, environmental protection measures in the United States were estimated to cost about $150 billion per year in direct expenditures (not including effects on production or productivity), or about 2 percent of gross domestic product. Each year the promulgation of new regulations adds to those costs. In 1990, the Clean Air Act alone produced estimated annual compliance costs (not including administrative costs or effects on the national product or consumption) of up to $25.3 billion.[15] According to a 2002 report by the President's Office of Management and Budget, major new EPA regulations promulgated between 1999 and 2001 entailed total gross costs to society of $11.3 billion to $12.8 billion.[16]

Cost estimates do not, by themselves, tell us anything about the overall social utility (or disutility) of environmental regulation. We also need to know the benefits side of the equation in order to determine whether they outweigh the costs. However, estimating the benefits of environmental regulations is, generally speaking, a trickier task than estimating the costs. Most of the costs, after all, are borne by economic actors, and so are priced in markets. Economists can aggregate those costs fairly easily. Some of the benefits of environmental regulations, such as decreased medical expenditures and productivity increases, are similarly priced in markets. Yet, as noted earlier, some of the other consequences of pollution reductions, such as avoided harm to wildlife and scenic vistas, are not priced in markets and are therefore more difficult to quantify. Perhaps for this reason, no one has even attempted to estimate the overall social benefits of environmental regulation.

Some useful partial estimates of regulatory benefits have been made. For example, the EPA recently calculated the benefits of the Clean Air Act, using only easily quantified benefits such as reduced health expenses and increased worker productivity. The mean estimate of annual benefits in 1990 amounted to $1.25 trillion.[17] On this estimate, the Clean Air Act produces far more benefits than costs for society. In fact, the EPA estimates that the Clean Air Act produced "net, direct, monetized benefits" of between $5.1 trillion and $48.9 trillion, with a central estimate of $21.7 trillion, between 1970 and 1990.[18] As for the new environmental regulations promulgated between 1999 and 2001, which the President's Office of Management and Budget estimated would cost between $11.3 billion and $12.8 billion, they are expected to produce social benefits that are two to five times higher—between $23.3 billion and $56.1 billion.[19]

The accuracy and reliability of such cost and benefit estimates are inherently contestable. Nevertheless, the most extensive independent study to date agrees that environmental regulations, overall, produce more benefits than costs for society.[20] The question of their value persists because regulatory cost and benefit estimates presume a calculable social utility function and involve subjective, even if nonarbitrary, determinations such as the valuation of nonpriced goods and the choice of a discount rate.

What is the value of a human life saved? Of an asthma attack avoided? Of a scenic vista unclouded by smog? Of seabirds and ocean mammals unharmed by oil slicks? Of biodiversity? As with all other valuations, no objectively right—and, therefore, no objectively wrong—answers are available. More importantly, these goods have no commonly accepted market-based valuations, or prices. Price, as represented by what one person (the buyer) is willing to pay and another (the seller) is willing to accept for some good or service, is an accurate measure of the relative values those two people place on the good or service. In the absence of market prices, accurately assessing economic value becomes highly problematic. Nevertheless, environmental economists have been experimenting with various substitute methods, none of which has so far provided anything close to a generally acceptable substitute for market prices. These methods include the following:

- *Contingent valuation.* Researchers survey individuals to find out how much they would be willing to pay to preserve some environmental amenity or, alternatively, how much they would be willing to accept to allow that amenity to be reduced or destroyed. The problem is that, if people are not forced to put their money where their stated preferences are, they are likely to exaggerate either how much they would be willing to pay (as buyers) to conserve some environmental good or how much money it would take to gain their permission (as sellers) to reduce or destroy that good. Consequently, contingent valuation tends to systematically overestimate the value of environmental goods.[21] However, advocates of contingent valuation claim that the methodology is steadily improving, and that it already supplies at least some useful information for cost-benefit analyses.

- *The travel-cost method.* Researchers examine how much people actually spend to reach certain environmental amenities, such as national parks. The problem is that this approach systematically underestimates the value of environmental goods. The amounts people spend to get to environmental amenities almost never reflect their total valuations of those amenities. Moreover, it ignores the valuations of those who are too poor to travel to certain socially valued amenities.[22] It also ignores survey data that show that people want certain environmentally pristine locales preserved even though they may never have occasion to visit them. Calculations can, however, be roughly adjusted to account for these problems.
- *Hedonic pricing.* Researchers estimate the value of environmental amenities, such as open space, based on the measurable effects of those amenities on market-valued goods such as housing. Because people are often willing to pay more for housing located close to environmental amenities such as parks and open space, it is possible to gauge the value of those amenities by examining the differentials between housing close to those amenities and comparable housing located at some distance from those amenities. One problem with this approach is that it only applies to a relatively few environmental amenities that relate in some perceptible way to housing values. Another is that the differences in housing values may be attributable to various factors, which complicate the process of parsing the precise effects of environmental amenities on those differences.

In addition to resource valuation problems, the problem of choosing a *discount rate* by which future costs and benefits are quantified in present-day dollars also arises. A given environmental regulation will have effects—both costs and benefits—that extend into the future. In order to properly evaluate those costs and benefits, they must be expressed in present-day dollars. Because of inflation and real economic growth, a dollar in hand today is highly unlikely to have identical buying power of a dollar 5, 10, or 50 years from now. Over time, inflation will likely devalue that dollar so that it will have only a fraction of today's value. Alternatively, we might invest that dollar today at some positive rate of interest, and obtain more than a dollar over time. For example, one dollar invested today at an interest rate of 8 percent will be worth precisely two dollars nine years from today. The discount rate is simply an interest rate operating in reverse. So, for example, at a discount rate of 8 percent, one dollar of cost or benefit that we will receive in nine years is worth half as much (50 cents) today. Discounting in this way gives policy makers a more accurate present-day view of future cost and benefit streams. At a high discount rate, future costs and benefits are worth less in present-day dollars than at a lower discount rate.[23]

No discount rate is objectively right or wrong. Discount rates are inherently subjective (though nonarbitrary). We all use them, whether consciously or not. Consider the decision of whether to buy a special long-life, energy-saving lightbulb or a normal, incandescent lightbulb. The retail price of the normal bulb is about $1.00; the "special" bulb is priced at $7.00. Two customers, both of whom are rational economic actors, are standing in the lightbulb aisle of the hardware store, deciding which bulb to purchase. Both are aware that the special bulb is expected to last 20 times longer than the normal bulb, and will consume less electricity over its lifetime. Over two or three years, the special bulb will "pay for itself" and, as a consequence, be less expensive than the normal bulb. It will also be responsible for less pollution because it uses less electricity than the normal bulb to produce the same amount of light. Neither of the customers has any reason to believe that the bulbs differ in quality. They have identical budget constraints, preference orderings, and neither has a cash flow problem. One of the customers decides to buy the special bulb; the other buys the normal bulb. This discrepancy in buying behavior is explained by a differential in the two customers' discount rates. The customer who buys the normal bulb has a higher discount rate than the customer who purchases the special bulb. Neither is right or wrong.

The same is true with respect to the so-called "social rate of discount," which is the rate at which the government discounts the future costs and benefits of actual or proposed public policies. As Paul Portney and John Weyant recently explained, "Those looking for guidance on the choice of a discount rate could find justification [in the literature] for a rate at or near zero, as high as 20%, and any and all values in between."[24] The difference between a zero and a 20% discount rate is vast, especially for long-term policies/investments. Yet, even a small difference in the discount rate can dramatically alter the outcome of a cost-benefit analysis. For example, a policy/investment that would produce $10 million in net benefits 100 years from now has a present value of just under $30,000 at a discount rate of 6%. Changing the discount rate from 6% to 4% would increase the present value of policy/investment benefits to almost $200,000. At a 3% discount rate, the present value of the future benefits rises to more than half a million dollars. Thus, changing the discount rate can fundamentally alter the outcome of a cost-benefit analysis. Again, neither the 6% nor the 3% rate is objectively "correct" or uniquely appropriate for use in a cost-benefit analysis.[25]

Because even small changes in the discount rate can dramatically affect cost-benefit analyses, especially those concerning long-term projects/investments, the choice of a social discount rate to use in environmental policy has become a political contest. Proponents of environmental regulation prefer the application of lower discount rates in cost-benefit analyses of environmental regulations because lower discount rates tend to justify more pollution control and resource conservation.[26] Opponents of environmental regulations prefer higher discount rates because they tend to justify less regulation.[27]

Those who write about the methodology of cost-benefit analysis recommend that because discount rates are subjective, policy makers should never premise their estimations of future costs and benefits on a single discount rate; rather their analyses should include alternative cost and benefit estimates based on several discount rates. For example, in its estimates of the costs and benefits of the Clean Air Act between 1970 and 1990, the Environmental Protection Agency incorporated alternative discount rates of 3%, 5%, and 7%. In addition, many economists now recommend that the choice of discount rate should vary depending on the time horizon of the policy under analysis.[28] The longer the life span of a policy—the period over which costs and benefits accrue—the lower should be the discount rate.

Martin Weitzman recently surveyed 2000 of his fellow economists for their "professionally considered gut feeling" about the appropriate discount rates for measures to minimize or mitigate global warming.[29] Their responses led Weitzman to design the following schedule of discount rates, which declines as the time horizon grows larger.

Time from Present	Discount Rate (%)
1–5 years	4
6–25 years	3
26–75 years	2
76–300 years	1
More than 300 years	0

Note the similarity between Weitzman's schedule and the following U.K. Treasury's recommended schedule of declining long-term discount rates.[30]

Period of Years	Discount Rate (%)
0–30	3.5
31–75	3
76–125	2.5
126–200	2
201–300	1.5
301+	1

The fact that the U.K. Treasury's schedule of declining long-term discount rates does not precisely track Weitzman's schedule confirms the lack of consensus on what discount rate should be used, even among those who agree that discount rates should decline as costs and benefits extend further into the future.

Because discount rates and valuations of nonpriced environmental goods are inherently subjective and disputable, analyses of environmental regulations are inevitably subject to uncertainty and are always contestable. Few law and economics scholars believe that these limitations negate the utility and desirability of cost-benefit analysis for environmental regulation. But some environmentalists argue that environmental values are "incommensurable" with economic values; that is, they cannot be valued in dollars and cents, and so such valuation should not be attempted.[31] Even if this incommensurability were true, excluding environmental values from cost-benefit analyses would, as a practical matter, be potentially ruinous for the environment. All too often in the past, difficulties in estimating the economic value of environmental goods led to their being assigned, explicitly or implicitly (i.e., by exclusion), a price of $0 in cost-benefit calculations. For reasons discussed earlier in this chapter, it would be equally harmful to society to assign environmental goods infinite value. But if environmental goods are to be assigned some economic value between zero and infinity, then cost-benefit analysis becomes not only desirable but inevitable. The key is to recognize that, like the Kaldor-Hicks efficiency criteria upon which it is based, the process of cost-benefit analysis does not yield unambiguous conclusions about social welfare. It cannot take the politics out of policy making.

One question remains about cost-benefit analyses of environmental regulations: Should they be *required* as part of the regulatory process? In many cases, they are. However, some statutes limit the extent to which economic analysis can inform the environmental regulatory process. For example, §109(b)(1) of the Clean Air Act calls for the EPA to set National Ambient Air Quality Standards—the maximum allowable concentrations of certain pollutants in the atmosphere, measured either in parts per million or micrograms per cubic meter—so as "to protect public health" with "an adequate margin of safety."[32] Since 1970, the EPA has interpreted this language to prohibit the use of cost-benefit analysis in setting air quality standards. The agency claims that the language and legislative history of §109(b)(1) allows it to consider only scientific and public health information in setting the standards. In 1980, the U.S. Court of Appeals for the District of Columbia Circuit endorsed the EPA's interpretation of §109(b)(1).[33] Subsequently, when Congress amended the Clean Air Act in 1990, it tacitly acquiesced in EPA's interpretation by leaving §109(b)(1) unchanged. Congress certainly could have amended that section if it had wanted the EPA to consider costs in setting national ambient air quality standards. Then, in 1999, the American Trucking Association (and other plaintiffs) asked the D.C. Circuit to reverse its earlier ruling (upholding EPA interpretation of §109(b)(1)). The D.C. Circuit declined,[34] and the Supreme Court upheld that decision,[35] despite the following *amici curæ* (friend of the court) brief filed by several prominent economists, including four Nobel laureates, in favor of cost-benefit analysis.

American Trucking Associations, Inc., v. Browner

No. 99–1426

1999 U.S. Briefs 1426

July 21, 2000

On Writ of Certiorari to the United States Court of Appeals for the District of Columbia Circuit.

Brief Amici Curiae of AEI-Brookings Joint Center for Regulatory Studies, Kenneth J. Arrow, Elizabeth E. Bailey, William J. Baumol, Jagdish Bhagwati, Michael J. Boskin, David F. Bradford, Robert W. Crandall, Maureen L. Cropper, Chistopher C. Demuth, George C. Eads, Milton Friedman, John D. Graham, Wendy L. Gramm, Robert W. Hahn, Paul L. Joskow, Alfred E. Kahn, Paul R. Krugman, Lester B. Lave, Robert E. Litan, Randall W. Lutter, Paul W. MacAvoy, Paul W. McCracken, James C. Miller III, William A. Niskanen, William D. Nordhaus, Wallace E. Oates, Peter Passell, Sam Peltzman, Paul R. Portney, Alice M. Rivlin, Milton Russell, Richard L. Schmalensee, Charles L. Schultze, V. Kerry Smith, Robert M. Solow, Robert N. Stavins, Joseph E. Stiglitz, Laura D' Andrea Tyson, W. Kip Viscusi, Murray L. Weidenbaum, Janet L. Yellen, and Richard J. Zeckhauser in Support of Cross-Petitioners

***

This brief is being submitted on behalf of a group of economists. The purpose of the brief is not to attempt to guide the Court on legal issues but to inform it on economic ones. To put ourselves in the best possible position to offer the Court our expertise, we have tried to understand, in light of the legal task confronting the Court, where our own economic expertise might have a useful role to play.

To that end, we understand that the lawyers who brought this case framed the following question for the Court's consideration: "Whether the Clean Air Act requires that the Environmental

Protection Agency ignore all factors 'other than health effects relating to pollutants in the air'" when setting National Ambient Air Quality Standards (NAAQS). We also understand that this question has arisen in part because the United States Court of Appeals in Washington, D.C., whose responsibility it is to review air quality standards issued by the Environmental Protection Agency (EPA), has interpreted the Clean Air Act as barring the EPA from even considering the potential costs of its air quality regulations.

The merits of this legal debate between the D.C. Circuit and the counsel who have contested the D.C. Circuit's views are beyond the scope of our economic expertise and hence of this brief. Nonetheless, we respectfully offer the following observations with hopes that they may ultimately prove useful.

The importance of this issue cannot be overstated. Both the direct benefits and costs of environmental, health, and safety regulations are substantial—estimated to be several hundred billion dollars annually. If these resources were better allocated with the objective of reducing human health risk, scholars have predicted that tens of thousands more lives could be saved each year. All presidents since Nixon—both Democratic and Republican—have attempted to make environmental, health, and safety regulations more efficient by requiring some form of oversight attempting to balance benefits and costs. . . .

***

The concern of the . . . signatories is how analytical methods, such as cost-benefit analysis, should be used in regulatory decisionmaking. These methods can help promote the design of better regulations by providing a sensible framework for comparing the alternatives involved in any regulatory choice. Such analysis improves the chances that regulations will be designed to achieve a particular social goal specified by legislators at a lower cost. In addition, they can make the regulatory process more transparent by providing an analytical basis for a decision. Greater transparency in the process, in turn, will help hold regulators and lawmakers more accountable for their decisions.

These analytical methods are neither anti- nor pro-regulation; they can suggest reasons why it would be desirable to have tighter or more lenient standards depending on the results of an analysis. For example, the cost-benefit analyses in the RIA [Regulatory Impact Analyses] on particulate matter and ozone could be interpreted as suggesting that the ozone standard should not be lowered while a new PM standard for fine particles should be introduced to protect public health.

Nothing in the following statutory text of section 109(b) of the Clean Air Act precludes consideration of costs:

> National primary ambient air quality standards . . . shall be ambient air quality standards the attainment and maintenance of which in the judgment of the Administrator, based on such criteria and allowing a margin of safety, are requisite to protect the public health. *42 U.S.C. §7409*(b)(1).

Indeed, the plain aim of this provision is protecting the "public health," and that aim is unlikely to be achieved without, at least, an implicit balancing of benefits and costs.

Cost-benefit analysis is simply a tool that can aid in making decisions. Most people do a kind of informal cost-benefit analysis when considering the personal pros and cons of their actions in everyday life—more for big decisions, like choosing a college or job or house, than for little ones, like driving to the grocery store. Where decisions, such as federal environmental regulations, are by their nature public rather than private, the government, as a faithful agent of its citizens, should do something similar.

Carefully considering the social benefits and social costs of a course of action makes good sense. Economists and other students of government policy have developed ways of making those comparisons systematic. Those techniques fall under the label cost-benefit analysis. Cost-benefit analysis does not provide the policy answer, but rather defines a useful framework for debate, either by a legislature or, where the legislature has delegated to a specialized agency the responsibility of pursuing a general good, by that agency.

Economists, other policy experts, and the regulatory agencies themselves have produced a large literature on the methods and applications of cost-benefit analysis. There are, and always will be, many uncertainties and disagreements about those methods and their application in particular cases. Nevertheless, a wide consensus exists on certain fundamental matters. In 1996, a group of distinguished economists, including Nobel laureate Kenneth Arrow, were assembled to develop principles for cost-benefit analysis in environmental, health, and safety regulation. Here, we summarize and paraphrase for the Court a number of principles that we think could be helpful in this case, which involves the review of the EPA's NAAQS standard-setting decisions.

A cost-benefit analysis is a useful way of organizing a comparison of the favorable and unfavorable effects of proposed policies. Cost-benefit analysis can help the decisionmaker better understand the implications of a decision. It should be used to inform decisionmakers. Cost-benefit analysis can provide useful estimates of the overall benefits and costs of proposed policies. It can also assess the impacts of proposed policies on consumers, workers, and owners of firms and can identify potential winners and losers.

In many cases, cost-benefit analysis cannot be used to prove that the economic benefits of a decision will exceed or fall short of the costs. Yet cost-benefit analysis should play an important role in informing the decisionmaking process, even when the information on benefits, costs, or both is highly uncertain, as is often the case with regulations involving the environment, health, and safety.

Economic analysis can be useful in designing regulatory strategies that achieve a desired goal at the lowest possible cost. Too frequently, environmental, health, and safety regulation has used a one-size-fits-all or command-and-control approach. Economic analysis can highlight the extent to which cost savings can be achieved by using alternative, more flexible approaches that reward performance.

Cost-benefit analysis should be required for all major regulatory decisions. The scale of a cost-benefit analysis should depend on both the stakes involved and the likelihood that the resulting information will affect the ultimate decision.

Agencies should not be bound by a strict cost-benefit test, but should be required to consider available cost-benefit analyses. There may be factors other than economic benefits and costs that agencies will want to weigh in decisions, such as equity within and across generations.

Not all impacts of a decision can be quantified or expressed in dollar terms. Care should be taken to ensure that quantitative factors do not dominate important qualitative factors in decisionmaking. A common critique of cost-benefit analysis is that it does not emphasize factors that are not easily quantified or monetized. That critique has merit. There are two principal ways to address it: first, quantify as many factors as are reasonable and quantify or characterize the relevant uncertainties; and second, give due consideration to factors that defy quantification but are thought to be important.

***

We believe all of the available information should be considered in making any important decision. If costs or other types of data are deliberately left out, the quality of decisionmaking is likely to suffer. In particular, we make one recommendation . . . : The Court should allow the EPA to consider costs in setting NAAQS, so that these costs can then be assessed along with benefits and any other important information.

We believe that it would be imprudent for the EPA to ignore costs totally, particularly given their magnitude in this case. Together, the EPA estimates that those standards could cost on the order of $50 billion annually. Not considering costs makes it difficult to set a defensible standard, especially when there is no threshold level below which health risks disappear. The EPA acknowledges that exposure to ozone presents a "continuum" of risk, as opposed to a threshold below which adverse health effects cease to occur. If the EPA is required to set a standard "to protect the public health" with an "adequate margin of safety," then ignoring costs could lead to a decision to set the standard at zero pollution. That alternative, however, would be self-defeating—it would harm public health by threatening the very economic prosperity on which public health primarily depends. ∎

***

These economists' arguments evidently failed to convince the Supreme Court in *American Trucking*. But it is important to understand that the Supreme Court does not rule on the basis of whether the government's policies are good or bad; it restricts itself to adjudging the *legality* of government actions. Not everything that is legal is good policy, or vice versa. Even if the EPA's interpretation of the CAA is bad policy, it is legal. In the *American Trucking* case, the Court found the EPA's interpretation of §109(b)(1) consistent with the language of the statute and with other evidence of congressional intent. If Congress dislikes that conclusion, it could amend §109(b)(1) to require explicit cost-benefit analysis.

ENVIRONMENTAL INSTRUMENT CHOICE

Even if environmental regulations improve social welfare, which is itself a contested point, that does not mean they are as efficient as they might be. No one believes that the current regulatory system produces the biggest bang for the buck—the greatest social benefits per dollar spent. Certain legal policy approaches to environmental protection are more efficient than others. And critics complain about the use of inefficient policies, where alternative policies exist that would be more efficient.

Types of Regulatory Approaches

A government might use several different regulatory means to achieve a certain pollution control or reduction goal. They all fall into one of two broad categories of regulatory approaches: direct regulation and economic (or market-based) instruments.

Methods of Direct Regulation
- *Ambient environmental (air or water) quality standards* are maximum allowable concentrations of pollutants in the ambient air (or water), measured in parts per million or micrograms per cubic meter (or micrograms per cubic liter for water). Usually, these standards are not imposed on discrete pollution sources; rather, they are the responsibility of state and federal government agencies to achieve via the imposition of emissions limitations on individual pollution sources. The previous section of this chapter dealt with one such ambient environmental quality standard under §109(b)(1) of the Clean Air Act.
- *Design or technology-based standards* specify how a certain plant, or equipment within the plant, should be designed to reduce pollution emissions. Most often, this type of standard will take the form of a numerical emissions limitation, based on the EPA's determination that pollution sources will have to install a certain type of pollution control device, such as a scrubber or filter on a smokestack, or process to achieve that standard. In some cases, when emissions standards are based on technology that is not yet available, they are known as technology-forcing standards. Design or technology-based standards are sometimes referred to as command-and-control, because the government specifies not only how much polluters need to reduce their emissions

but specify (more or less) how they must do so. An example of this type of regulation is motor-vehicle emissions standards under the Clean Air Act.

- *Performance standards* specify how much polluters must reduce their emissions without specifying how they must do so. In other words, these standards are not based on some underlying technology that would have to be installed to achieve them. Performance standards include emissions limitations on hazardous (i.e., carcinogenic) air pollutants under §112 of the Clean Air Act.

- *Product bans* simply prohibit the use of pollution-causing substances. Such bans can be immediate and complete, as with the 1972 ban on the use of the pesticide DDT; or, they may be phased in over a period of time, as with the bans on lead in gasoline and on the use of chlorofluorocarbons (CFCs) in refrigeration systems.

Economic (or Market-Based) Instruments

- *Emission taxes* allow the government to set a price per unit of emissions for a certain pollutant. Each pollution source is authorized to emit any amount of that substance, but they have to pay the tax for each unit they emit. As a consequence, a pollution source can be expected to emit up to that point where the cost of the tax payment exceeds the benefits provided by the next unit of production and its attendant emissions. Emission taxes are little used in the United States, but are widely used in many European countries.

- *Tradeable permits* take the form of limited entitlements whereby the government allocates to pollution sources permission to emit a certain pollutant. First, the government determines current emissions levels. Then, it subtracts from that amount emission reductions necessary to achieve the desired level of total emissions. The remainder is then unitized in the form of emissions rights, permits, or allowances, which are allocated among the pollution sources. The number of allowances determines each pollution source's quota limit. Each source is authorized to emit up to its quota limit, and no more. However, emissions allowances are tradeable, which means that pollution sources can buy and sell them to one another. Because emissions are tradeable, the costs of achieving necessary emissions reduction should be reduced. Sources that can reduce emissions at relatively low cost may reduce emissions below quota limits, which will leave them with excess (unused) emission allowances to sell to those sources with higher control costs. Thus, the sources with the lowest costs of control will bear most of the emissions reduction burden. The extent to which each source reduces emissions or purchases additional allowances to remain within its quota limit will be determined by the difference between its cost of emissions control and the price of available allowances on the emissions market. The best known example of a tradeable permit program is the acid rain program of the U.S. Clean Air Act, which will be discussed in some detail later in this chapter.

- *Environmental contracting* occurs when the government signs an actual agreement with an individual pollution source concerning that source's pollution control responsibilities. Polluters have an incentive to enter into such agreements because these "environmental contracts" operate in the shadow of possible regulation. They are, in effect, individualized substitutes for regulations that might otherwise be imposed. Pollution sources rationally would prefer to contract with the government, when they perceive that their contract obligations would be less onerous than alternative regulatory burdens. Environmental contracts have been used extensively in some European countries, such as Denmark. To date, they have been used only sparingly in the United States.

- *Information-based regulations* include reporting and record-keeping requirements, as found in most of the federal pollution control laws of the United States, and product labeling requirements. A typical reporting requirement will require pollution sources to disclose to the EPA how much of a certain pollutant they emit each year. This requirement that makes polluters gather and disclose evidence against themselves eases environmental law enforcement. Other information-based regulations take advantage of so-called *green consumerism*—the increasing tendency of consumers to base buying decisions on environmental considerations. For example, publicly traded firms now must regularly disclose information about their environmental performance to the Securities and Exchange Commission (SEC). This requirement brings market pressure to bear on firms not only to comply with environmental laws and regulations but to go beyond compliance, lest their share prices drop as a result of negative publicity.

- *Subsidies* are really not a form of regulation; they are the antithesis of regulation. Instead of using regulatory or taxation "sticks" to attain pollution reductions, the government can employ subsidy "carrots," paying polluters to reduce emissions. For example, in the first couple of decades following enactment of the Clean Water Act in 1972, the federal government heavily subsidized the construction of municipal waste-water treatment plants.

This list of four prevalent forms of direct regulation and five types of economic instruments raises an important question: What makes one regulatory approach an economic instrument and another a direct regulation? Realistically, *all* regulatory approaches are economic instruments in that they seek to create incentives for polluters to reduce emissions using explicit or implicit prices, including the threat of penalties (including both civil and criminal penalties) for noncompliance. A product ban creates an implicit price on the use of that product in the form of expected civil or criminal penalties for noncompliance.

Compliance Cost Advantages of Economic Instruments

Those who distinguish between direct regulations and economic instruments observe that the former, in practice, ignore the differential costs of compliance among regulated polluters. A design standard, for example, forces all polluters to accomplish the same emissions reduction goal in the same way, even though it might cost one polluter 10 times (or 100 times) more than another to do so. It would be more economically efficient, critics of direct regulation argue, to impose the greatest share of the pollution control burden on those industries and individual plants with the ability to reduce emissions at the least cost.

Here is a stylized example to illustrate how direct regulations can produce excess compliance costs.[36] In the State of Industria, current total emissions of "pollutox" are 150 tons per day. Various scientific and epidemiological studies have determined that these emissions are harmful to public health. To avoid these negative health consequences, total emissions of pollutox would have to be reduced by 30 percent, or 45 tons per day. No significant negative health consequences result from pollutox emissions at or below 105 tons per day. All pollutox emissions in Industria come from just two sources: a widget plant that produces 100 tons per day and a gadget plant that produces 50 tons per day. The state must now decide how much of the necessary emissions reduction should come from the widget and gadget plants, respectively.

Various options are available. Assume for all options that the emissions from the two plants have uniform effects, so that emission reductions from either plant would contribute in equal measure to achieving Industria's goal. In other words, a 1 ton reduction in emissions from the widget plant equals a 1 ton reduction in emissions from the gadget plant. However, because of individual plant design features and production processes, the two plants have different cost structures for emissions reductions. It would cost the widget plant a lot more than it would cost the gadget plan to reduce emissions.

The widget plant could install a filter on its smokestack at a cost of $80,000 per day. This filter would reduce pollutox emissions by 30 percent, or 30 tons per day. The widget plant could further reduce emissions by 30 percent (from original levels) by installing a new production process at an additional cost of $450,000. The gadget plant, by contrast, could reduce its pollutox emissions up to 70 percent (35 tons per day) by installing a filter at a cost of $40,000 per day. It could reduce emissions by another 20 percent (from original levels) by installing a new production process at a further cost of $30,000. Table 15.1 summarizes the regulatory options, emissions reductions, and costs.

The lowest compliance cost means of achieving Industria's pollutox reduction goal would be to require the gadget plant to install a filter and introduce process changes, but require no emission reductions from the widget plant. The total cost of compliance would be $70,000, which is less than any other option for reducing pollutox emissions to healthful levels. This option will *not* be the outcome under any likely form of direct regulation. It is improbable that the State of Industria would promulgate a regulation that directly imposed the entire emission reduction burden on just the gadget plant. That approach would appear unfair, especially considering that the widget plant produces two-thirds of all pollutox emissions in the State. In all probability, the State's regulation would be designed to require emission reductions according to some ostensibly neutral formula that would not obviously favor one source over another.

Table 15.1

		EMISSIONS REDUCTION		
PLANT	CONTROL TECHNOLOGY	TONS/DAY	%	COST/DAY
Widget	Filter	30	30	$ 80,000
Widget	Process change	30	30	450,000
Gadget	Filter	35	70	40,000
Gadget	Process change	10	20	30,000

Imagine a regulation based on the following, blunt *design standard*: "All emitters of pollutox must install filters." This apparently neutral rule would ensure that Industria's pollutox reduction goal of 45 tons per day will be achieved. Both the widget and gadget plants will install filters, resulting in total emission reductions of 65 tons per day. But the total cost of compliance will be $120,000, which is $50,000 (or 42 percent) higher than the least-cost approach of imposing the entire emission reduction burden on the gadget plant.

Next, imagine an alternative *performance standard*: "Each source of pollutox must reduce emissions by 30 percent from existing levels." This rule is also facially neutral. It is a performance standard rather than a design standard because it imposes emissions limitations that are based on its pollution reduction goal, rather than on some particular technology. The outcome will be just the same as under the design standard: both plants will install filters, reducing total emissions of pollutox by 65 tons per day, at a total compliance cost of $120,000. The total compliance cost, again, is $50,000 (42 percent) higher than the lowest compliance cost solution.

Now, notice how economic instruments can reduce compliance costs, compared to direct regulations. The State of Industria requires a 30 percent (45 ton per day) reduction in total pollutox emissions. So, it imposes on each emitter of pollutox a quota limit 30 percent below current emissions levels. The widget factory thus has an emissions quota of 70 tons per day or 70 daily "allowances," each of which equals a 1-ton emission of pollutox; the gadget factory has a quota of 35 tons per day or 35 daily allowances. This allocation (assuming enforcement) ensures achievement of the State's pollution reduction goal. So far, it is just a performance standard. Here is the crucial difference: The regulated parties are permitted to buy and sell their allowances. Allowances can be redistributed by private contracting in the market, from those who value emission allowances less to those who value them more highly. In this case it is extremely likely that the widget plant would value the allowances more highly than the gadget factory because it has higher costs of compliance; that is, it costs the widget plant more than it costs the gadget plant to reduce its emissions to its quota limit. It is this difference in compliance costs that could well lead to *emissions allowance trading* between the two plants.

Consider the cost to the gadget plant of attaining its initial quota limit of 35 tons per day: $40,000 per day, the price of installing a filter. (Note that installing the filter will reduce the gadget plant's emissions by 35 tons per day, down to 25 tons per day, substantially below the required level.) At the same time, it would cost the widget plant $80,000 per day to attain its initial quota limit of 70 tons per day. Instead of making those particular changes, the widget plant could save money by offering to purchase emission allowances from the gadget plant at some price below $80,000. Purchased allowances would raise the widget plant's quota limit, perhaps as high as 100 tons per day, its preexisting emission rate. The gadget plant, meanwhile, would profit from the deal. As noted earlier, the gadget plant could, by itself, achieve the State's pollutox reduction goal by installing both a filter and process changes at a total cost of $70,000. Suppose the widget plant offered to buy 30 emissions allowances from the gadget plant at a price of $1,500 per allowance or a total of $45,000. If the gadget plant accepted this offer, that transaction would defray the gadget plant's total cost of compliance with state imposed pollution reduction requirements by more than half: from $70,000 to $25,000. The widget plant, at the same time, would benefit from the transaction. Instead of having to pay $80,000 to reduce its emissions by 30 tons per day to attain its initial quota level, it would only have to pay $45,000 to increase its quota limit from 70 to 100 tons per day, which would obviate the need for any emission reductions. The State's pollutox emissions reduction target would still be achieved between them; the widget and gadget plant would have reduced their combined emissions by 30 percent, or 45 tons per day. Yet the total compliance cost would be only $70,000, rather than the $120,000 price tag for compliance with direct regulations. Thus, economic instruments can save on regulatory compliance costs.

Monitoring and Enforcement Costs of Environmental Regulation

Because economic instruments are associated with lower compliance costs, it is often mistakenly assumed that those instruments must be more efficient overall than direct regulations. That assumption ignores the existence of other potential cost differentials, including monitoring (i.e., information) and enforcement costs, which can differ significantly between regulatory approaches. In order to conclude that economic instruments, such as tradeable pollution allowances, are more efficient than direct regulations, such as nontradeable quotas, based on either performance or design standards, we must compare the sums of compliance, monitoring, and enforcement costs under the two regimes. When administrative and enforcement cost differentials are either insignificant or favor economic instruments, the compliance cost advantages of economic instruments are highly likely to make them more efficient overall than direct regulations.

In some cases, however, the administrative and enforcement costs associated with economic instruments are likely to be higher than those associated with direct regulations, particularly design standards. These cases arise due to either technological or institutional constraints on monitoring or enforcement.

TECHNOLOGICAL CONSTRAINTS ON EMISSIONS MONITORING

Imagine a situation in which no technology exists for measuring emissions of pollutox from gadget or widget plant smokestacks. Plant managers, neighbors, and government officials can all see some kind of smoke coming out of the stacks, but they cannot tell how much pollutox is in that smoke. They know, however, there must be a substantial amount of pollutox in the smoke because inhabitants of the State of Industria are experiencing health problems associated with pollutox, and the widget and gadget plants are the only two potential sources in or around the State.

In this circumstance, any attempt by the State to use an economic instrument is going to run into insuperable difficulties. Suppose, for example, the State attempted to impose an emissions tax of $100 per ton on pollutox emissions. In the absence of cost-effective emissions monitoring technology, the State could not accurately assess the tax. It could only guess how much pollutox is coming out of the widget and gadget plants' respective smokestacks. As a consequence, the assessed tax is likely to be either too high or too low. If it is too low, the tax might be insufficient to alter the polluters' analyses of the benefits and costs of emissions reduction. So, the plants would continue emitting at or near pretax levels, in which case the State's pollution control goal would not be achieved. If the assessed taxes are too high, they can create incentives for the plants to invest too much in pollution control. If so, they could lose their compliance cost advantages over direct regulations.

An alternative tradeable permit scheme would run into similar problems. In the absence of effective and efficient emissions monitoring, the State could not know that the widget and gadget plants are in compliance, at any given time, with their emissions quotas. This lack of knowledge would make the quotas unenforceable. The widget and gadget plants would have no incentive (other than a possible ideological commitment to obeying the law) to comply with them. In the absence of an incentive to comply, tradeable permits become ineffective and inefficient, even as compared with direct regulations.

The absence of emissions monitoring technology would *not*, however, create similar problems for the enforcement of direct regulations. Consider, once again, the previously discussed design standard, which simply requires all emitters of pollutox to install filters. The State does not know current emissions levels; so it cannot know precisely how much those emissions will be reduced by the filters. But it does know that the filters are designed to reduce pollutox emissions by some uncertain amount. Installation of the filters may or may not achieve the State's pollutox reduction goal, but filters will achieve some emissions reduction. In this case, the installation of the filters itself becomes the enforceable standard of compliance. The State need not measure emissions, which it could not do anyway at finite cost. It only has to ensure that the filtering technology has been installed, and is operating, which can be done at some finite cost.[37] Given the assumption that emissions monitoring equipment does not exist, direct regulation through design standards may well be more efficient overall than economic instruments such as taxes or tradeable permits, despite the fact that it entails higher costs of compliance.

This greater efficiency is not just hypothetical. It is quite likely, for example, that the U.S. Clean Air Act's early reliance on technology-based emissions standards was efficient compared to any conceivable market-based alternative.[38] In 1970, when the Clean Air Act became law, many felt that air pollution levels nationwide were too high, but actual ambient concentration levels and emissions rates were hardly known. Emissions monitoring was then in its infancy and was woefully deficient. For the most part, the government relied on industry self-monitoring and self-reporting for information about emissions levels. Some industries simply refused to provide emissions information, knowing that the information they provided might be used to regulate them. What information the government did receive was of questionable accuracy because of both technological limitations and the economic incentives of those who gathered it. The government or any other organization simply had no way to precisely measure emissions in order to accurately assess emissions taxes or to ensure compliance with emissions quotas, whether tradeable or not. In these circumstances, it made sense for the government to rely on design standards, which required air polluters to install various kinds of technological devices on their smokestacks. As economists Michael T. Maloney and Bruce Yandle observed,

Congress's technology-based approach to air pollution control may have been "the best possible approach" in 1970 because of the "number of practical problems associated with" monitoring actual emissions. The advantage of technology-based design standards was that the installation of the technology itself became the basis for determining compliance. "If approved technology was in place, and its working order documented, emission control was being accomplished." By contrast, Maloney and Yandle noted that "more direct measurement of emissions might be required" to ensure compliance with an emissions tax or trading program.[39]

With the development of more advanced, more accurate, and affordable emissions monitoring systems, the administrative feasibility of economic instruments improved. This improvement is particularly evident in the close relation between the development of continuous emissions monitoring systems (CEMS) for sulfur dioxide (SO_2) and the institutionalization of an emissions trading program for SO_2 under the Clean Air Act's acid rain program.

By 1990, when Congress enacted its most recent set of major Clean Air Act amendments, CEMS had become widely available and affordable. These systems made it possible for the federal EPA to accurately monitor real-time emissions of SO_2 at major sources (particularly fossil-fuel fired power plants) 24 hours a day, 7 days a week, at relatively low cost. This capability reversed the administrative cost advantage of direct regulations, and Congress responded by introducing an emissions trading program for SO_2 as an experiment, to see whether the theoretical compliance cost advantages of that system could be realized in practice. They were. The result was a greater than expected (and required) reduction in SO_2 emissions, resulting in a 10 to 25 percent reduction in acid precipitation in the northeastern United States, and sizeable cost savings. Just four utilities estimated their aggregate savings, in the first half-decade of the allowance trading "experiment," at more than $700 million.[40]

Congress itself recognized, however, that it was the technological development of CEMS that made this success story possible. Congressional reports included in the legislative history that accompanied the 1990 Clean Air Act amendments noted, "The requirements for CEMS is [sic] the linchpin for this title for without good emissions data, a problem that has hampered enforcement of the Act to date, no allowance or emissions trading scheme can affectively [sic] operate." The legislative history further included an explicit warning that several analysts have subsequently ignored: "Unlike other control requirements of the Clean Air Act, utility emissions of sulfur dioxide . . . are capable of verification in a cost-effective manner through the use of continuous emissions monitors."[41] To this day, for some combinations of pollutants and sources, CEMS or other advanced cost-effective monitoring systems are *not* available. Those combinations of sources and pollutants lack feasible alternatives (e.g., emissions trading programs or taxation) to direct regulations.[42]

Institutional Constraints on Enforcement

The costs of administering and monitoring environmental regulations are determined not only by technological circumstances. Institutions matter too. Imagine a country that tried to employ market mechanisms for pollution control in an economic system where prices did not matter for economic survival. Poland, for example, tried this method in the 1970s when its communist government instituted an elaborate, but wholly ineffective, system of environmental taxes. The problem was that taxes and other market mechanisms for environmental protection require functioning markets to be effective (let alone efficient).

Environmental taxes function by creating price signals that alter polluters' cost-benefit analyses of pollution and pollution control. Suppose it costs a plant zero to pollute (denoting the absence of both regulation and the threat of private litigation), but to reduce emissions would cost it $50 per ton for the first 50 tons, and $150 per ton for any emissions reductions in excess of 50 tons. Obviously, in this case the plant will maximize its emissions; it will not control its pollution at all. Now suppose the state imposes a flat emissions tax of $100 per ton. This alters the plant's cost-benefit analysis of pollution control. Assuming accurate monitoring and tax assessment, the plant will reduce its emissions by 50 tons because the cost of those reductions would only be $2,500 ($50 per ton) as opposed to $5,000 ($100 per ton), which it would have to pay in taxes if it chose not to eliminate those emissions. The plant would not reduce emissions beyond the first 50 tons because the cost of emissions reductions beyond 50 tons rises to $150 per ton, which exceeds the $100 per ton tax. For those emissions, the plant would rather pay the tax than eliminate the emissions. Environmental taxes thus create incentives for marginal reductions in pollution by internalizing at least some of the costs of the pollution to the polluter, making those costs part of the polluter's normal business analysis.

For taxes to have this effect, however, the polluter's behavior must be subject to price signals, which is not always the case. In Poland, the government introduced pollution taxes in a socialist economic system where price signals were largely ignored because profit was unnecessary for economic survival. In that system, all polluters were state-owned enterprises. As such, they were subject to what the economist János Kornai has called "soft budget constraints."[43] Firm survival depended not on earning profits in the market but on political criteria—most commonly sheer quantity of output—established by central planners. As long as producers met planned production targets, they survived, even if the cost of their production exceeded its value. Note how such institutional factors would negate the effectiveness of environmental taxes as instruments of environmental protection: the basic incentive of socialist enterprises was not to ensure that revenues exceeded costs but merely to meet administratively set, quantitative production quotas. Prices, as such, meant nothing to them. It simply did not matter if environmental taxes increased their costs of production because production costs themselves were irrelevant to survival. Even if prices had mattered, soft budget constraints would in many (if not most) cases have negated the effects. As long as enterprises met their annual production plans, they were fully compensated by the government, including for any environmental fees or fines they owed. Environmental taxes would be taken out of one pocket and put back in another, in the form of increased budgets.

In communist Poland, almost all *real* pollution control (of which there was not a great deal before the fall of communism in 1989) resulted not from the primary system of environmental taxes—an economic instrument—but from direct regulations, most notably plant closings.[44] Those direct regulations might not have been efficient compared to some theoretical market-based alternatives, but a completely ineffective economic instrument cannot be said to be more efficient than even a highly inefficient direct regulation (assuming inefficient levels of pollution).[45]

This analysis might be supposed to have limited relevance in a world that has generally repudiated socialism as an alternative to capitalism. However, proponents of economic instruments for environmental protection, of which there are many (including the authors of this textbook), sometimes act as if those economic instruments are always and everywhere economically superior to direct regulations. However, in plenty of places in the world, especially developing countries, market institutions are virtually nonexistent or only weakly established. In those places, advocates of market-based approaches to environmental protection should be cautious, whatever the theoretical efficiency advantages of effluent taxes and tradeable emissions permits. Again, institutions matter in environmental policy choice.

CHAPTER SUMMARY

This chapter examined environmental problems as combined problems of law and economics. To the extent environmental problems stem from inefficient, negative externalities, the solution is efficient internalization, defined as internalization to that point where the next unit of internalization would cost more than the benefits to be gained from additional pollution reduction. No single approach to dealing with pollution problems has proven sufficient, however. Consequently, every society relies on a variety of approaches, including common law remedies, such as nuisance and trespass, and various types of government regulation, from command-and-control regulation to environmental taxes and tradeable permits. Assessing the costs and benefits of pollution problems and alternative solutions remains problematic and controversial, largely because of valuation and time-preference issues inherent to the process of cost-benefit analysis.

QUESTIONS AND PROBLEMS

1. Would pollution exist in the world of the Coase theorem?
2. A rule of international law, known as the Polluter Pays Principle, holds that polluters should bear *all* pollution costs. Does this rule reflect a Coasean or a Pigovian approach to externalities?
3. What parts, if any, of cost-benefit analysis are inherently subjective and, consequently, always disputable?
4. The Morgan family owns a restaurant in Guilford County, North Carolina. Right next door, the High Penn Oil Company locates an oil refinery. The refinery produces noxious fumes and odors which cause substantial harm to the plaintiffs, and significantly reduces the market value of their land. Assume no other properties are implicated in this conflict. Should the refinery be liable for the harm? If so, what remedy should the court award the plaintiffs?[46]
5. Nitrogen oxides (NOx) are emitted into the atmosphere by coal-fired power plants and internal combustion engines. It is a pervasive pollutant known to harm human health and the environment. Virtually every county in the State of California has several sources of NOx. Plants that emit NOx, in order to be good neighbors, build tall smokestacks to place their emissions high into the prevailing winds, which carry them far away from the source. This practice avoids creating local air pollution problems. The winds carry the NOx emissions

hundreds of miles away. It is difficult and, therefore, expensive to determine where the NOx emissions originate. But they cause health and environmental problems where they fall. Automobiles are another major source of NOx emissions. Every single car emits a small amount of NOx—too little by itself to cause any significant harm. But tens of thousands of cars within a 30-mile or so radius can cumulatively produce enough NOx to create a local public health threat. One day, several residents of Reno, Nevada, were working in their gardens, when they began to suffer acute respiratory problems and were hospitalized—some for a few hours, others for several days. The doctors determined the cause of their respiratory problems was an unusually high concentration NOx in the atmosphere. Few major sources of NOx are located in the Reno, Nevada, area, and too few cars to produce such a high concentration level. Will common law remedies adequately compensate the victims for their injuries? Why or why not?

6. Virtually all scientists now agree that increasing anthropogenic (i.e., human source) emissions of greenhouse gases, including carbon dioxide and methane, are contributing to a "greenhouse effect" that is slowly causing global warming. Experts disagree, however, about the probabilities and magnitude of the risks associated with this phenomenon. The major sources of greenhouse gas emissions are located in industrialized countries, located largely in the Northern Hemisphere. According to some models, however, much of the anticipated harm from global warming is likely to occur in the equatorial zone, in less-developed countries that have contributed little to the problem. Which environmental instrument(s) might you choose to deal with this problem, and why?[47]

7. Should the extent of environmental protection be determined by cost-benefit analyses?

NOTES

1. This situation is an instantiation of the free-rider problem introduced in Chapter 1.
2. As explained in Chapter 1, governments do not actually have to supply public goods. In some cases, private entrepreneurs supply public goods, such as lighthouses, subsidized by government funding.
3. See the discussion of Arrow's theorem in Chapter 3.
4. This information comes from The *Exxon Valdez* Oil Spill Trustee Council Web site, available at http://www.oilspill.state.ak.us/.
5. These causes of action were introduced in Chapter 6.
6. (1498) YB Trin. 13 Hen. 7, f. 26, pl. 4, *reprinted in* C. H. S. Fifoot, *History and Sources of the Common Law: Tort and Contract* (1949), p. 87.
7. (1610) 9 Coke, 59, 77 Eng. Rep. 816.
8. *Camfield v. United States*, 167 U.S. 518, 522–3 (1897).
9. (1865) 11 HL Cas. 642.
10. Ronald H. Coase, "The Federal Communications Commission," 2 JOURNAL OF LAW & ECONOMICS 1, 29 (1959) (emphasis added).
11. *See generally* Noga Morag-Levine, *Chasing the Wind: Regulating Air Pollution in the Common Law State* (Princeton, NJ: Princeton University Press, 2003).
12. The fact that the Clean Air Act was strongly supported by both interstate industries and environmental groups largely explains why the law was enacted unanimously by the House and Senate, a rare occurrence in recent American legislative history.
13. *See generally* Neil Komesar, *Law's Limits: Rule of Law and the Supply and Demand of Rights* (Cambridge: Cambridge University Press, 2001).
14. Of course, the same would be true for a regulatory regime if the number of environmental disputes demanding resolution outstripped the available supply of regulatory enforcers. Suffice it to say, however, that it is easier (i.e., cheaper) to increase the number of environmental enforcement officers who do not require elaborate legal training, than to increase the number of judges who do.

15. Council on Environmental Quality, Executive Office of the President, "Environmental Quality: The Twentieth Annual Report of the Council on Environmental Quality Together with the President's Message to Congress" (1990), pp. 470–72, tables 42 and 43.

16. Office of Management and Budget, "Stimulating Smarter Regulation: 2002 Report to Congress on the Costs and Benefits of Regulations and Unfunded Mandates on States, Local and Tribal Entities" (2002), p. 38, Table 7.

17. Office of Air & Radiation, U.S. Environmental Protection Agency, "The Benefits and Costs of the Clean Air Act, 1970–1990" (1997), p. 54, fig. 19.

18. Office of Air & Radiation, U.S. Environmental Protection Agency, "The Benefits and Costs of the Clean Air Act, 1970–1990" (1997), p. ES-9. The vast range of estimates suggests that the amount is subject to large errors in calculation. But even at the bottom of the range, benefits significantly exceeded costs. Moreover, the broad range in the estimates was due not only to EPA's inclusion of alternative valuations but also alternative discount rates. The mean estimate was based on a 5% (net of inflation) discount rate; alternative rates of 3% and 7% were also utilized.

19. Office of Management and Budget, "Stimulating Smarter Regulation: 2002 Report to Congress on the Costs and Benefits of Regulations and Unfunded Mandates on States, Local and Tribal Entities" (2002), p. 38, table 7.

20. *See* J. Clarence Davies and Jan Mazurek, *Pollution Control in the United States: Evaluating the System* (Resources for the Futures, 1998).

21. If, however, the rate of overestimation is consistent, analysts should be able to correct for it.

22. It is worth noting that market valuations similarly exclude the valuations of those too poor to be demanders.

23. In formal terms, present value = future value/$(1 + discount rate)^{number of periods}$; or PV = FV/$(1 + r)^t$. Thus, the PV of \$10.00 received in 9 years discounted at 8% per year is PV = $10/(1 +.08)^9$ = \$5.00.

24. Paul R. Portney and John R. Weyant, "Introduction," in P. Portney and J. Weyant (eds.), *Discounting and Intergenerational Equity* (Resources for the Future, 1999), p. 4.

25. It is also worth noting that reducing the time horizon could radically alter the consequences of choosing between one discount rate and another. So, for example, if our policy/investment is expected to return \$10 million in 30 years, rather than 100 years, the present value would be \$4.1 million with a 3% discount rate and about \$1.75 million with a 6% discount rate.

26. The economist Partha Dasgupta recommends applying a *negative* discount rate in cost-benefit analyses of long-term environmental protection initiatives, including policies to combat global warming. Partha Dasgupta, *Human Well-Being and the Natural Environment* (Oxford: Oxford Press, 2002).

27. In a 1986 article purporting to expose the high costs of government health and safety regulations, John Morrall III of the President's Office of Management and Budget employed a discount rate of 10%. *See* John F. Morrall III, "A Review of the Record," REGULATION (November–December 1986), p. 25.

28. *See, for example*, C. M. Harvey, "The Reasonableness of Non-Constant Discounting," 53 JOURNAL OF PUBLIC ECONOMICS 31–51 (1994).

29. Martin Weitzman, "Gamma Discounting," 91:1 AMERICAN ECONOMIC REVIEW 261 (March 2001).

30. *See* HM Treasury, "Greenbook, Appraisal and Evaluation in Central Government" (2003), Annex 6, Table 6.1, available at http:// greenbook.treasury, gov.uk/annex06.htm.

31. *See, for example*, Frank Ackerman and Lisa Heinzerling, *Priceless: On Knowing the Price of Everything and the Value of Nothing* (New York: The New Press, 2004).

32. 42 U.S.C. § 109(b)(1).

33. *Lead Industries Association v. Environmental Protection Agency*, 647 F. 2d 1130 (D.C. Cir. 1980), *cert. denied* 449 U.S. 1042 (1980).

34. *American Trucking Assns., Inc. v. EPA*, 175 F. 3d 1027 (1999), *reversed on other grounds*; *Whitman v. American Trucking Assns., Inc.* 531 U.S. 457 (2001).

35. *Whitman v. American Trucking Assns.*, 531 U.S. 457 (2001).

36. This problem is adapted, with permission of Aspen Publishers, from a similar problem in Peter S. Menell and Richard B. Stewart, *Environmental Law and Policy* (New York: Aspen Publishers, 1994), pp. 240–41.

37. In the early 1970s, for example, the Los Angeles County Air Pollution Control District

physically inspected every stationary source in the county once a month. *See* Daniel H. Willick and Timothy J. Windle, "Rule Enforcement by the Los Angeles County Air Pollution Control District," 3 ECOLOGY LAW QUARTERLY 507 (1973).

38. *See* Daniel H. Cole and Peter Z. Grossman, "When Is Command-and-Control Efficient? Institutions, Technology, and the Comparative Efficiency of Alternative Regulatory Regimes for Environmental Protection," 1999 WISCONSIN LAW REVIEW 887.

39. Michael T. Maloney and Bruce Yandle, "Estimation of the Cost of Air Pollution Control Regulation," 11 J. ENVIRONMENTAL ECONOMICS AND MANAGEMENT 244, 246–7 (1984).

40. U.S. General Accounting Office, "Air Pollution: Allowance Trading Offers an Opportunity to Reduce Emissions at Less Cost" (1994), pp. 33–34.

41. Environment and Natural Resources Policy Div., Library of Congress, 103d Congress, 1st Sess., "A Legislative History of the Clean Air Act of 1990," (1993), p. 1040.

42. *See* Daniel H. Cole and Peter Z. Grossman, "Toward a Total-Cost Approach to Environmental Instrument Choice," in T. Swanson (ed.), *An Introduction to the Law and Economics of Environmental Policy: Issues in Institutional Design* (New York: Elsevier Science, 2002).

43. *See* János Kornai, "The Soft Budget Constraint," 39 KYKLOS 3 (1986).

44. For a more detailed institutional analysis of environmental protection in Poland before, during, and after communism, *see* Daniel H. Cole, *Instituting Environmental Protection: From Red to Green in Poland* (New York: Palgrave Macmillan, 1998).

45. Note that this argument does not favor direct environmental regulation over environmental taxes. More fundamentally, it becomes an argument for institutional change—specifically, the privatization of economic actors and the creation of competitive markets to harden budget constraints.

46. *See Morgan v. High Penn Oil Co.*, 238 N.C. 185, 77 S.E. 2d 682 (1953).

47. For differing economic views on this issue, *see, for example*, William D. Nordhaus, "After Kyoto: Alternative Measures to Control Global Warming," presentation prepared for a joint session of the American Economic Association and the Association of Environmental and Resource Economists (January 4, 2001) recommending a global carbon tax approach to reducing greenhouse gas emissions; Joseph E. Aldy, Scott Barrett, and Robert N. Stavins, "13 + 1: A Comparison of Global Climate Policy Architectures," Resources for the Future Discussion Paper No. 03–26 (August 2003), recommending a global emissions trading system, incorporating developing as well as advanced industrial countries; Thomas C. Schelling, "The Costs of Combating Global Warming: Facing the 'Tradeoffs,'" 76(6) FOREIGN AFFAIRS 8-14 (1997), recommending that developed countries introduce cost-effective measures to reduce their greenhouse gas emissions and provide foreign aid to developing countries, which are expected to bear the brunt of the costs from global warming, until their per capita income reaches a level where they can afford to invest in environmental protection; and Daniel H. Cole and Peter Z. Grossman, "Toward a Total-Cost Approach to Environmental Instrument Choice," in T. Swanson (ed.), *An Introduction to the Law and Economics of Environmental Policy: Issues in Institutional Design* (New York: Elsevier Science, 2002), suggesting that if emissions monitoring is very costly, which is likely to be the case for many countries, direct regulation in the form of technology-based standards could be as, or more, efficient than taxes or tradeable permits.

Index

design or technology-based standards, 331–332

performance standards, 332

product bans, 332

economic (market-based) instruments

emission taxes, 332

environmental contracting, 332–333

information-based regulations, 333

subsidies, 333

tradeable permits, 332

monitoring and enforcement costs of environmental regulation, 336

Environmental law, 32

Environmental protection. *See* Emissions monitoring; Environmental instrument choice; Environmental regulation; Pollution

Environmental Protection Agency (EPA), 32, 323, 326

Environmental regulation

American Trucking Associations, Inc. v. Browner (1999), 328–331

cost-benefit analysis, 322–331

costs of, 323

discount rate for future costs and benefits, 325–328

history of, 318–319, 322–323

social utility of, 323–324

statutes, 322–323

substitute pricing methods, 324–325

Environmental taxes, 338–340, 343n. 43

Epstein, Richard, 58, 241

Equilibrium price, 8–9

Escola v. Coca-Cola Bottling Co., 231

Evolutionary economics, 63

Exclusion, in market entry, 297–298

Exclusionary zoning, 144

Exclusion (property right), resource conservation and, 97

Exclusive-dealing arrangements, 297

Exogenous preferences, 3

Expectation damages, 195–197, 199

Expectations (contracts), 167–170, 183

Explicit costs, 3

External effects, contracts and, 165

Externalities

bilateral, 73–74

Coase theorem and, 72–87

defined, 14

internalization of

deterrence through (torts), 212–213

in strict liability, 233–234

joint cost aspect of, 82

multilateral, 74

negative, 14–15

pollution as, 314–316

in perfect contracts, 162, 163

positive, 15

property rights and, 101

Externalization, 14–15

Extraordinary remedy, 186

Exxon Valdez oil spill, 318

F

Factors of production, 96

Fair use, 114n. 11

False imprisonment, 209

Fault-based torts, 208–209

Federal Communications Commission, 307–308

Federal courts. *See* Court systems

Federal government, legislative and regulatory bodies and processes, 39–42

Federal Rules of Civil Procedure, 38

Federal tort reforms, 259

Federal Trade Commission (FTC) Act (1914), 297–298

Felony, 277

Fifth Amendment

eminent domain, 144–145

grand jury, 39

just compensation, 150

Firm(s)

crimes by, 275

failures of, 19

market failure and, 18–19

theory of (Coase), 56–57

First-best (optimal) solutions, 20

"First in time, first in right," 110–111

First possession, 110–111

First reading (of a bill), 41

Fischel, William, 153

Impossibility theorem (Arrow), 61
Inalienability rules, 132–134
Inalienable entitlements, 122–124
Incapacity, of contract parties, 170–171
Incarceration statistics, 277
Incentives
  to abate a nuisance, 128
  to innovate, 102–105
  negligence and, 217–218, 222
  strict liability and, 239
Incompetency
  of contract parties, 170–171
  legal, 163
Incomplete information, 163, 164
Indifference curves, compensation and,
      210–212
Individual rationality, in perfect
      contracts, 162
Industrial Revolution, 30–31, 238
Inelasticity of demand, 6
  for alcohol, during Prohibition, 281
  for illegal drugs, 280
Inelasticity of supply, 7
Information
  about risks, negligence and, 226n. 23
  asymmetric, 14, 164
  complete, 74–79, 181n. 14
  full, in perfect contracts, 162, 163
  imperfect, 14
  incomplete, in contracts, 163, 164
  perfect, 181n. 14
Information-based regulations
      (pollution), 333
Injunctive relief, 127, 141
  property, 120
  property rules and, 125–126
  public nuisance and, 142
Innovation, incentives for, 102–105
In personam, 113n. 3
In rem, 113n. 3
Institutional law and economics, 62
  evolutionary economics, 63
  *Institutions and Economic Theory: The
      Contribution of the New Institutional
      Economics* (excerpt; Furubotn and
      Richter), 64–65
  new institutional economics, 63–65

Instrumental influence, 29
Insurance
  medical malpractice, 253
  negligence law and, 223–225
  no-fault alternative, 261–266, 269n. 69
Intellectual property, 102–105
Intent, criminal, 274–275
Intentional torts, 209, 270n. 76
Internalization, 14–15
  externalities and, 73–74
    deterrence through (torts), 212–213
    in strict liability, 233–234
International Country Risk Guide
      (ICRG), 27
Internet, cyber law and, 31
Interstate Commerce Commission, 305
Investment, property and, 101–102

J

Jackson, Thomas Penfield, 301–303
Jefferson, Thomas, 282
Joint and several liability, tort reform and, 249,
      254–255, 259, 260
Joint cost(s)
  externality problems and, 82
  property allocation and, 111
  social costs and, 74
Joint supply, public goods and, 16
Judges
  common law and, 29–30
  decision-making, influences on, 29–30
  economic understanding of, 48–51
Judicial hindsight, 223–225
Jury, 35
Jury awards
  capped, 254
  for medical and products liability,
      268n. 26
  punitive damages, 249, 251–252, 268n. 29,
      269n. 46
  size of, public perceptions, 251–252
Jury instructions, 35
Just compensation, 145
  Fifth Amendment, 150
  legal process theory and, 153
Just deserts, 111–112

R

Racial covenants, 140
Rationality, 59
  bounded, 65–66, 164
  in corrective justice, 212
  criminal behavior, biological and environ-
    mental components, 279
  individual, in perfect contracts, 162
  monopolists and, 292
  transitivity and, 66
Rational preference-maximizers, 59
Reagan, Ronald, 308
"Reasonable," defining (negligence), 215
Reasonable person (torts), 206–207
Reciprocal nature of nuisance, 137–139
Reconciliation process (in legislative
    process), 41
Recurring litigation, 127–128
Redgrave v. Boston Symphony (1985), 195
Reform. *See* Tort reform
Regulated industries
  California's power crisis, 308–310
  created monopolies, 304
  deregulation movement, 307–308
  economies of scale, 305–306
  Interstate Commerce Commission, 305
  natural monopolies, 305–307
  public interest, 304–305
Regulations, 32
Regulatory bodies and processes, 39–42
Regulatory takings law, 145
  law and economics literature
    comparative institutional analysis,
      153–154
    efficiency, productivity, and
      demoralization costs, 151–153
    legal process theory and the economics
      of just compensation, 153
    public choice, 150–151
  Lucas v. South Carolina Coastal Council (1992),
    148–150
  Pennsylvania Coal Co. v. Mahon (1922),
    146–148, 150–151
Regulatory Takings: Law, Economics, and Politics
    (Fischel), 153
Relative price, 6

Relative scarcity, 2
Relativity of title, 91–93
Reliance damages, 197–200
Reliance, efficient, 193
Remaindermen, 48, 51, 69n. 3
Remand to the trial court, 36
Remedies
  in criminal law, 273
  defined, 28
  injunctive relief, 142
  See also Contract(s); Damages; Property;
    Tort remedy
Rent control, law and economics of, 47–48
Rent(s), 14
Rent seeking
  defined, 60
  institutionalists' view of, 62
  public choice theory and, 60–61
Replacement lenders, 46
Res communes, 94–95
Res ipsa loquitor, 253
Res nullius, 94, 95
Resource conservation
  Prisoners' Dilemma model, 97–98
  "Toward a Theory of Property Rights"
    (Demsetz), 99–101
  "Tragedy of the Commons"
    (Hardin), 96–99
Resource Conservation and Recovery Act
    (1976), 323
Resource(s), allocating entitlements to, 4–5
Resource scarcity, 1–2
  allocation of, 4–5
Res privatae, 94
Res publicae, 94
Restitution, 200–202
Restraint of trade, 295, 297
Reversal of a trial court's decision, 36
Rexite Casting Co. v. Midwest Mower Corp.
    (1954), 163
Richman v. Charter Arms Corp. (1983), 233
Richter, Rudolf, 64–65
Ricketts v. Scothorn (1898), 178
Rick v. West (1962), 140–141
Rights, 137
  to an attorney (criminal procedure), 35
  bundle of, 90–91